From 1968 to 1988 Geoffrey Blainey was successively professor of economic history and then history at Melbourne University. In 1982-83 he was at Harvard University as professor of Australian studies. His other books include *Tyranny of Distance*, *Triumph of the Nomads* and *Our Side of the Country*.

A LAND
HALF WON

REVISED EDITION
GEOFFREY BLAINEY

SUN
AUSTRALIA

First published 1983 by Sun Books
This edition published by Pan Macmillan Publishers Australia
a division of Pan Macmillan Australia Pty Limited
63-71 Balfour Street, Chippendale, Sydney

Reprinted 1987, 1989, 1992

National Library of Australia
cataloguing-in-publication data:

Blainey, Geoffrey, 1930-
A land half won.

Rev. ed.
This ed. first published: South Melbourne, Vic. Macmillan, 1982.
Includes index
ISBN 0 7251 0411 2
1. Australia – Social conditions – 1788-1900. I. Title.

944

Printed in Hong Kong

Contents

PART ONE
TO THE GRASSLANDS

1   The Europeans Come

On the north-west coast of Australia, four centuries ago, Aboriginals paddling a raft or gathering shellfish must have occasionally seen the puzzling sails of a ship far out to sea.

The first ships to be seen were probably Portuguese, sailing to their colony on the island of Timor. There Portugal had run a fortified trading post since about 1516, and it would be strange if such inquisitive navigators and merchants always kept to the sea routes between Goa and Timor or between Lisbon and Timor. Even if the Portuguese captains had lacked one ounce of curiosity, the capricious winds and the inevitable errors of reckoning would have diverted some ships from the intended route. The nearest point of Australian coast is only 300 miles from Timor, and for about three months of the year the north-west monsoon blows so regularly that a ship leaving Timor could reach Australia within two or three days. How much of the north-western coastline of Australia was discovered or mapped by Portuguese mariners will not be known. In Lisbon the great map library, Casa da India, was destroyed in the earthquake of 1755.

2

The Dutch were latecomers in the East Indies, and their first merchant fleet did not arrive until 1596. Ships sailing from Holland directly to the spice ports in the Indonesian archipelago sailed to the South Atlantic, passed to the south of South Africa and, taking advantage of the prevailing westerlies, sailed towards Australia. Near the Western

Australian coast they changed course and sailed northwards to the tropical seas. Mariners then had no certain
method of determining their longitude at sea: they had no
way of knowing exactly their position on an east to west line.
Accordingly, in the Southern Indian Ocean, they sometimes sailed too far east when the winds and currents were
strong. In 1627 a Dutch ship bound for the East Indies
sailed to within 500 miles of the site of Adelaide; and to this
day several high-cliff islands in the Great Australian Bight
carry Dutch names.

With the strong westerlies, many Dutch ships made quick
passages from South Africa to Australia. Several captains
made faster passages than they realized and, thinking
themselves to be still far from land, ran their ships onto the
Western Australian coast. In 1622 the British ship *Tryal*
struck an offshore reef and sank. Seven years later, the
Dutch ship *Batavia*, carrying 316 passengers and crew, ran
into the Abrolhos Islands near the modern Geraldton.
About 125 of the shipwrecked people were murdered – not
by Aboriginals but by their fellow Dutchmen. When a
Dutch rescue-party from Java eventually reached the
wreck, two of the murderers were sent into exile on the
Australian coast. They were the forerunners of an army of
European criminals who would be exiled in Australia.

More ships were wrecked along the coast. The surf
pounded the hulls and pulled apart the timbers until the
cargoes came to rest on the strewn timbers or the sea bed.
There lay eating plates and clay jugs, gold and silver coins,
coal and building stones, anchors and nails and implements
and utensils of iron and copper, and the pewter and the
blue Delftware. The first of the unfortunate ships, the
Tryal, had chanced to sink in deep water, and the wreck was
not pummelled by the waves. Discovered by divers three
and a half centuries later, just when that despised coastline
was beginning to export huge cargoes of mineral wealth,
the wooden ship seemed surprisingly well preserved – an
underwater museum of the time of Shakespeare and
Raleigh. Soon after the discovery of the wreck in 1969,
treasure-seekers secretly visited it, placed explosive charges

along the hull and in the mouths of the ancient cannons, and blew up the ship with such recklessness that part of the adjacent cliff slid down.

For several hundred years before the arrival of Captain Cook, the Dutch and Portuguese sat almost on the doorstep of north-western Australia and traded cargoes from the island of Timor. A hilly island, it was ruled by the Dutch at the one end and the Portuguese at the other. Its main export was sandalwood, and that white wood was prized in China as fine timber and as an incense to be burned in the temples. The sandalwood entered China through the Portuguese colony of Macao, and merchant houses in Macao also seem to have imported Timorese women as servants and prostitutes. Timor also produced precious beeswax. Melted and poured into bars about three feet in length, the beeswax was valued in Europe as the raw material for cosmetics and fine candles. Timor was thus a shipper of scented goods, a minor emporium for luxuries.

There was still no reason why the Dutch or Portuguese or British should set up a colony on the coast of Australia. The Dutch had seen the Gulf of Carpentaria; they had seen the long coastline of Western Australia and the high cliffs of the Great Australian Bight. Their bold seaman Abel Tasman had, during the course of an eight months' voyage in 1642 and 1643, discovered Tasmania, both the wild west coast and the sheltered east coast. He had also discovered the richer New Zealand. The Portuguese, too, saw stretches of Australia's northern and western coast. The famous Dieppe Map of 1536, based on information which must have been filched from the Portuguese, suggests a knowledge of the north-west coast of Australia which is more detailed and accurate than the contemporary maps of North America.

But all this geographical knowledge, widely known in Lisbon and Amsterdam, offered no inducement to settle any harbour in Australia or New Zealand. For what could those lands provide?

We belong to the age when the whole world can be seen in one coloured map. We are mesmerized by great spaces. We find it inconceivable that large lands could be dismissed as

5

valueless by sane rulers and sea-captains. We now know that desert lands can be irrigated and enriched by fertilizer; we know that dry lands can pasture huge flocks and herds with the aid of artesian waters, railways and road trains, and that refrigerated ships can carry the meat across the world. We know that a bay surrounded by rocky soil can have profound strategic value – can be an Aden, a Diego Garcia – even though all of its essential supplies are imported from afar. Above all, we know that stony plains can conceal minerals and oil of immense value, and that railways and pipelines can carry that wealth from places so isolated that, two centuries ago, they would have been worthless. But rulers in the year 1600 did not have that knowledge. They knew the limitations of their world, and they were sensible to ignore Australia. It seemed to offer no rich minerals near the coast; it did not offer energetic docile labour which could be sold into slavery; it seemed to offer no new timbers and spices or vegetables and fibres. It did not even offer a suitable port of call on the trade routes between Europe and more valuable lands. Only the western coast could provide a port of call and refreshment; but such a port was not required by the few ships travelling each year from western Europe to the Dutch East Indies and Portuguese Timor. By the time they had reached Western Australia they had almost completed their long voyage.

So Australia, by the standards of the age, was valueless. Even if the Dutchmen had known about the rich gold of Kalgoorlie, the huge bulbs of iron ore in the Pilbara, the copper of Mt Lyell, the bauxite of the Gulf of Carpentaria, the uranium of Arnhem Land – and those mineral deposits lay not far from stretches of coast which Dutchmen had navigated – they would have still shunned Australia. The continent was asleep. It could be awakened only by the industrial revolution. It could be well used only by sharper technology. Meanwhile the south-west coast remained an impediment to navigation, a graveyard for tall-masted ships from western Europe.

3

At least a century before the British first settled near Sydney, a straggling fleet of Indonesian ships arrived annually on the low-lying northern coast. Their home port was Macassar in the Celebes, and the vessels sailed with the aid of the north-west monsoon each November or December. In the steamy heat they approached Australia from the Timor Sea or the Arafura Sea – ungainly little vessels which, from some angles, resembled hen coops. Most of these ships sailed without the aid of compass or map, but with luck they covered more than one thousand miles in the space of a fortnight. As many as sixty vessels came annually and in a boom year their crews totalled two thousand: we know that in the year 1829 the ships which sailed into one bay in Arnhem Land, Raffles Bay, carried 1056 Macassarmen. Along a vast stretch of the northern coast, all the way from the Kimberleys to the western edge of the Gulf of Carpentaria, the men fished for the trepang or sea slug at the bottom of the sea. The slugs were shaped like a cucumber and came in many colours – white, black, grey, red and blue. Gutted by hand, boiled on the shore in iron cauldrons which were a yard in diameter, cured in bamboo smoke houses, perhaps six million of these shrivelled slugs were carried back to Macassar in March and April after the winds had swung around to the south east. Eventually these cargoes found their way to China – there to be fried, braised with vegetables, eaten in soup or taken as a mild aphrodisiac.

The Indonesians who worked on the sandy beaches of northern Australia – cutting the mangroves for their fuel, stoking the fires beneath the cooking cauldrons, or diving for the sea slugs visible beneath the tepid sea – were invaders. Most carried daggers, some possessed muskets, and their leading ships mounted a brass cannon in the bow. The Indonesians preferred to fish in peace rather than to fight the Aboriginals and in peace they usually lived. Indeed a few Aboriginal men willingly sailed away to Macassar with the departing fleet, and spent eight or nine months in that strange port ruled by Indonesian rituals,

Dutch law and Arabian religion. In 1876, it is said, seventeen Aboriginal men, mostly from Port Essington, were living in Macassar. In scattered coastal regions of north Australia the influence of Macassar could be seen in the long, flute-like pipes smoked by many Aboriginals, in the 'van dyke' beards seen on a few black faces, in their occasional iron knives and axes, their dug-out canoes, and the Aboriginal spear-points of sharp glass which once formed a bottle of Dutch gin or rum. The age of glass and iron had arrived quietly on the tropical Australian coast long before it reached the eastern coast. Even the songs, the ceremonies and the art of coastal Aboriginals were touched by Indonesian culture during annual contacts which extended from, perhaps, the year 1675 to 1907, when the last trepang vessel left the coast. These visits ruffle our mental picture of an Aboriginal Australia which – we wrongly imagine – lay in utter isolation until the coming of the British.

The Macassarmen brought religion as well as commerce, but only the commerce tinted the life of coastal Aboriginals. There is no sign that the Peace of Allah descended on those Aboriginals who paddled dug-out canoes or gathered shellfish on the beach. Islam was the property of the annual visitors and it sailed home with them in the wake of the south-east monsoon or was buried with those Indonesians who died in Australia. Excavations on several Australian sites have uncovered their graves. The skeletons lie on the right side and faithfully face Mecca.

For thousands of years, with rare interludes, Australia had been a long ribbon of beach on which the waves from the outside world had lapped gently, the water slipping back into the glassy sea. But now the waves rose high and would batter the shores.

4

In Europe in 1761 the day of the transit of Venus aroused enthusiasm amongst scientists. While the passage of the planet Venus across the face of the sun that day was observed only in the northern hemisphere – in places as remote as Bengal and Sweden – there were hopes that the next transit could be measured accurately from a variety of positions. If an accurate observation could be made of the time taken for Venus to move, like a black disc, across the face of the sun, then the distance of earth from sun might be accurately computed. Such a computation, it was believed, might revolutionize knowledge of distances in the solar system and even assist mariners to ascertain their longitude while far from land. The next transit of Venus was to occur on 3 June 1769, and that was one of only three days on which the transit would occur before the 21st century. If passing clouds or clinging mists were to prevent an accurate observation on that day in 1769, another opportunity would not arrive for 105 years. Accordingly, small parties set out to places as far apart as Murmansk in northern Russia and the coast of Spanish California in the hope of observing the transit. In the history of the exploration of outer space this was probably the most ambitious venture so far attempted.

A British expedition under the command of Lieutenant James Cook set out for the new-found island of Tahiti to observe the transit. His ship, a converted collier renamed the *Endeavour*, was so small she could have been dry-docked in a space the size of a suburban tennis court. She carried more than eighty sailors and marines, provisions for a very long voyage, and a scientific party led by Joseph Banks, a young botanist and scientist-at-large. Banks made the quarters even more cramped by leading aboard two artists, a Swedish secretary, two Negro and two English servants, and two dogs. From Plymouth the ship sailed to the south Atlantic, passed Cape Horn and reached Tahiti weeks before the day of the transit. On that long-awaited day, from 9.20 in the morning to three in the afternoon, Cook observed the transit as accurately as his instruments and the haze around the edge of the sun would allow. A slight haze also marked the observation in Banks' journal for that day: '3 handsome girls came off in a tent to see us.'

From Tahiti the *Endeavour* sailed to New Zealand which the courageous Dutchman, Abel Tasman, had found more than a century earlier. Cook went ashore at eight places and marvelled at the fertility of the land and the qualities of the Maoris – physically strong, artistic, brave and war-like without seeming to be treacherous. The two botanists, Banks and Solander the Swede, came away equally pleased, with more than 400 plants which were new to Europe. In the autumn of 1770 the *Endeavour* sighted the eastern coast of Australia, close to the present border of Victoria and New South Wales, and sailed north with the wooded coast in view almost the entire way. On 28 April she entered a wide bay – now encroached upon by the long runway of Sydney's airport – and anchored near the southern shore. In shallow water her crew caught and ate the large diamond-shaped fishes known as stingrays. At first the bay was called Stingrays Bay but soon the plants on the shores so supplanted the bay as the source of wonder that the name was changed to Botany Bay. For perhaps half a century this was to be the common name for Australia in the conversation of Britons.

Men from the *Endeavour* landed at only two harbours along the two thousand miles of eastern coastline. After spending eight days at Botany Bay they spent another seven weeks on the Cook River, the site of the present Cooktown, where they repaired the damaged ship and waited for a wind to take them out to sea again. If James Cook and Joseph Banks had been invited to sum up their impressions of eastern Australia in two words, they might have selected 'barren' and 'fascinating', or their 18th-century equivalents. At the same time the land was not irredeemable. They believed that pockets of soil near the coast could support small colonies of Europeans – so long as the colonists imported their seeds, plants and livestock. While the best valleys were not very productive for the nomadic Aboriginals they might produce much under European methods of agriculture.

Even this sweet and sour assessment of the land they had seen was clever guesswork and proved far too optimistic. The *Endeavour* had chanced to visit Botany Bay during a favourable week. April and May were the months of high rainfall at Botany Bay, and we know that the autumn of their visit must have been wet, because grass was growing on rich black soil like an English meadow and one creek was flowing so swiftly that Banks assumed that it was like an ever-flowing English stream and could even supply permanent power for the water-wheels of flour-mills. Banks had no way of knowing that the typical Australian stream was a chain of waterholes for part of the year.

On 1 May, Cook and Banks and a party of armed men walked inland until their feet were tired, and everywhere they saw the light sandy soil growing 'vast quantities of grass'. Largely on the strength of this day spent in the long grass Cook later remarked that in every season of the year long stretches of eastern Australia would produce more fodder than large herds of imported cattle could possibly eat. On 3 May, while Banks busied himself ashore with the drying of his marvellous collection of plants on a spreading sailcloth, Cook led a small party in another direction and, to his delight, came across deep black soil capable of growing any species of wheat or grain. Slowly his eyes feasted on a meadow which, in his view, was as fine 'as ever was seen'. When, eighteen years later, the First Fleet of settlers arrived from England at the height of summer no trace of the glorious meadow was to be found.

Cook and Banks could not possibly assess the soil and climate during such a brief visit. Here was a new land, lying on the opposite side of the equator and growing exotic plants; a land occupied by people whose way of life offered few clues about the land itself. Likewise the land was crossed by weather-bearing winds about which Europeans had the scantest knowledge. Did the east coast of Australia, all the way from the mouth of the Snowy to the tip of Cape York, have roughly the same climate? Even that question was unanswerable on such a brief visit. By the time Banks had reached north Queensland he had come to the conclusion that one climate probably ruled that long coast and that it consisted of a wet season and a dry season. Seeing places where the Aboriginals had dug up edible yams, but unable to see the leaves of the plant, he jotted in his journal that the dry season was probably at its height 'when we were there' and that the hot sun must have burned the leaves. Accordingly, he half-expected that in the wet season both Botany Bay and north Queensland would explode in a kind of tropical fertility. On that misconception the British were to plant their first settlement in Australia. Indeed they probably would have rejected the continent if the *Endeavour* had chanced to call at Botany Bay at the height of a dry summer rather than in a wet autumn.

Cook sailed his ship through Torres Strait and so entered that sphere of the Dutch and the Portuguese which for two and a half centuries had touched the edge of Australia. In September 1770 the *Endeavour* hugged the coast of Timor, and was probably seen by Europeans from the Dutch fort at Kupang. At this settlement lived Dutch officials, almost certainly a clergyman of the Reformed Church, Dutch soldiers and naval officers; but they would not have welcomed an English intruder in the heart of their trading territory. So Cook sailed away to the west, eventually calling at the Dutch island of Savu where he bought livestock for the cooking pots and sufficient palm-wine 'for futurity', wrote Banks. There they met the first European they had probably seen since – twenty-one months ago – they called at the port of Rio de Janeiro.

The time had now come for Cook to impound all the journals and log books kept in the ship and to warn everyone that, when they reached the Dutch-owned port of Djakarta, they must divulge nothing about where they had been. They were simply in an English ship bound for England. That they had spent a long time in strange seas might have been obvious to the master of a ship of the English East India Company who met the *Endeavour* in the open roadstead near Djakarta. He knew the date was Thursday 11 October 1770. In the *Endeavour*, however, it was still Wednesday.

When Cook returned to England from his voyage of exploration he did not say, privately or officially, that he had found valuable lands. Even Australia was not valuable. A gargantuan curiosity, it offered nothing which could yet reward England commercially. Admittedly, it did offer a mass of dryish land but we forget that an unexplored land mass was not seen as valuable by European powers until that phase of imperialism, late in the 19th century, when the globe's supply of lands was running out.

5

The revolt of the North American colonies began in April 1775 when Cook was in the great bay of Cape Town, near the end of his second voyage of exploration. Slowly, as the American colonies slid from England's grasp, eastern Australia rode into prominence in the minds of a few English ministers, scientists, ship-owners, and naval officers. In 1779 Joseph Banks was one who suggested to the English government that the British convicts, whose entry to the United States was now banned, might perhaps be sent to Botany Bay. His suggestion was premature. England was still looking for a land to which convicts could be shipped at virtually no expense to the Crown. As Virginia and the Carolinas had willingly paid for the labour of English convicts, the English government had been able, until 1775, to run its system of transportation at a small cost. Botany Bay, far away, offered no such economies.

In English courts the judges, throughout the eight years of the American War of Independence, continued to sentence many criminals to transportation across the seas. As no other colonies were willing to buy the services of these convicts, most of the criminals were placed in British prisons which were already crowded with debtors, petty criminals, and men and women awaiting execution. Increasingly these prisoners were placed in hulks – old English men o' war, captured French frigates, or unseaworthy Indiamen. In these floating prisons, moored in the busy rivers or harbours of southern England, the convicts could be sent out daily to build breakwaters and fortifications or dredge the shipping channels. Inadequately fed, dispirited, and usually impeded by a ring and chain

13

around one leg or two, they did not work as well as free labour; but at least they gave some return to the Crown. Several convict hulks, however, could provide no work. At Plymouth in 1788 the saintly visitor of prisons, John Howard, inspected the hulk *Dunkirk* and learned that, out of her list of 366 convicts, all but half a dozen were in 'total idleness'. He found that those who had tried to end the boredom by escaping were, as punishment, lying almost naked on a thin bed of straw in the dark bottom of the ship. Several hulks were really maritime morgues. In less than two years one hulk anchored on the Thames at Woolwich had received 632 prisoners, of whom more than one in four died while aboard. Plague was the main killer, and London feared less the men who escaped from the hulks than the contagious diseases which might escape. No batch of convicts shipped to Australia was to suffer such a death rate through disease as those who lived in the worst hulks.

London sought new outlets where convicts could do work for the enrichment of English commerce but at no expense to the government. About 200 convicts were sent to the Gold Coast to defend trading posts against the Dutch. A London merchant bought convicts, shipped them across to Central America and tried to sell them to British settlers in the Honduras. In 1785 the surplus of convicts offered a cheap way of manning a proposed British port of call on the coast of south-west Africa, between the Portuguese colony of Angola and the little Dutch colony at Cape Town. Free settlers would be landed at this proposed port at Das Voltas Bay where, it was hoped, they would employ the convicts to cut firewood, grow crops, tend cattle and so cater for visiting ships on the route to India. This scheme was the last serious attempt to revive the North American practice whereby the Crown paid virtually none of the expenses of guarding and caring for the convicts. The ship sent to survey Das Voltas Bay returned with sobering news. The land around the bay was sandy and parched.

The east coast of Australia slipped into favour as a likely place of exile for the multiplying inhabitants of British gaols and hulks. As a penal colony in Australia would attract few free settlers in its first few years, a new system of transportation was necessary if Australia were chosen. The English government would have to pay the expenses of shipping out the convicts, and guarding and employing them. This was a far more expensive method of using the labour of criminals. Such an expense called for compensating advantages, naval or commercial.

Those English ministers and officials who decided to place a settlement on Botany Bay were probably influenced by the desire to increase England's sea-power in the Indian and Pacific Oceans. In that vast expanse between South Africa and Cape Horn, England's main rivals were the Dutch, the French and the Spanish; and the competition for commerce depended partly on naval strength. In the last half century England had fought three wars against the French and the fighting had extended to the sea lanes between the Cape of Good Hope and India. England's main overseas empire, by the 1780s, lay in India rather than in North America, but in wartime her merchant ships were vulnerable on that long route from the English Channel to the coasts of India. Their only friendly port of call or refuge – in nine thousand miles of ocean – was the tiny island of St Helena in the south Atlantic. In contrast, the Dutch owned the Cape of Good Hope, with its superior harbours of Table Bay and Simon's Bay, while the French had the islands of Reunion and Mauritius, almost astride the sea route from the Cape to India.

In the peaceful years 1785 and 1786, both France and England seemed eager to strenghten their bases in the east. The French set up a new base in the south-east of Madagascar. The English thought of setting up a base at Das Voltas Bay. In the tropical waters of the Indian Ocean, the English also turned with the same secrecy to a small coral atoll, shaped like a horseshoe and lying in a remarkably strategic position half way between Mauritius and Ceylon. Sensing that here was a valuable place for naval vessels to shelter and refit when the next Anglo-French war occurred, the English sent four small vessels from Bombay to occupy the island in March 1786. The commander of the

15

expeditionwas instructed that if he found the French firmly holding the island he was to send a fast vessel to Cape Town with a secret despatch which would then be forwarded to London by a fast English vessel. The name of the island which the British occupied was Diego Garcia. There, almost two centuries later, American-Russian rivalry having replaced English-French rivalry in the Indian Ocean, the United States is creating its own naval base.

Further east the British trade with southern China was booming. Whereas most French people drank coffee from the West Indies, the English were the great drinkers of tea in Europe. Each year a growing fleet of English ships carried the Canton tea through the narrow straits of the Dutch East Indies and past South Africa in a booming trade which had increased one hundredfold in the previous hundred years. While many English tea-ships sailed from India to China – sometimes calling at Penang which, significantly, was founded in 1786 – more ships sailed directly from English ports to China and cut through the Indonesian archipelago to the west of Java (the Sunda Strait) or to the east of the Celebes (the *Pitt* passage). By the 1780s there was serious talk of sailing from England to China by harnessing the westerlies across the Southern Indian Ocean, rounding Tasmania and then sailing past Norfolk Island and the east of Papua and New Britain. This seems, at first sight, a strange way of sailing from the Thames to Canton. In time of war, however, it had advantages, for it avoided the narrow Indonesian straits where French or Dutch frigates could lie in wait. During the Napoleonic Wars at least one massive English fleet was to use this roundabout route to Canton.

By the mid-1780s an English settlement planted at Botany Bay could offer long-term advantages to the expanding English commerce. English ships might call there on their way to China for tea, and on their voyage to north-west America where Captain Cook had shown the potential of trade in the fur of seals. Ships might call at Botany Bay during whaling expeditions in waters which would ultimately attract some of those whaling ships which were now busy in the south Atlantic, or on trading expeditions to the eastern end of the Dutch East Indies where, since the Treaty of Paris in 1783, English ships had been freely permitted by the Dutch. In short, here was a new Diego Garcia of the future, providing the English with a headlong start when the Pacific was opened by those profit-chasing sea-captains and ship-owners of Europe.

Another vital reward of a settlement on or near the eastern coast of Australia was a supply of two strategic materials: timber for ships' masts and flax for the making of ships' sails and ropes. Captain Cook, in discovering lonely Norfolk Island in 1774, had discovered the stately Norfolk Island pine and an expanse of the New Zealand flax plant; and these raw materials were seen as a prize for a global naval power. Britain's defeat in the war against France and the American colonies – a defeat caused partly by a shortage of sound masts for Britain's navy – increased the value of the forest on Norfolk Island. As Britain depended on the Baltic for her supply of flax and as the Baltic could easily be blocked or blockaded, the new species of flax from Norfolk Island was especially attractive. Moreover tests at naval dockyards in England suggested that the tough, long fibres of the Norfolk Island flax were superior to the Baltic flax as the raw material for sails and ropes. As Admiral Sir George Young explained in January 1785 in a private letter to Lord Sydney, the new flax was a 'very remarkable plant' and could serve a wider variety of needs 'than any vegetable hitherto known' and would prove to be of profound strategic value to Britain should Russia 'at some future period think it her interest' to place an embargo on the export of her own Baltic flax. The French government was itself alert to the value of the new species of flax, and in 1785 instructed the explorer La Pérouse to investigate the plant and to bring home living specimens. The British government was even more alert and resolved to occupy Norfolk Island, keeping its plan so secret that Sir George Young did not know, for in May 1788 he sought permission to make a private settlement on Norfolk Island in order to supply cordage and masts to the British ships-of-war in India. Even before he wrote, Norfolk Island had been settled.*

---

*In the book *The Tyranny of Distance*, published first in 1966, I argued that eastern Australia was settled to provide Britain with vital naval raw materials and a useful place of exile for criminals. To these two main reasons could possibly be added a third: Britain's need for a port of call on the new trade routes in the Pacific and Indian Ocean. Since 1966 the evidence for the third reason has so accumulated that it must be regarded as beyond dispute. Delusions of climate, I believe, must now be regarded as a fourth vital cause of the settlement.

2 A Little Squadron Sails

The First Fleet prepared to sail from Portsmouth in 1787. Commanded by the governor of the new colony, Captain Arthur Phillip, the 'little squadron' consisted of the frigate *Sirius* of 20 guns, the small runabout *Supply*, six transport ships and three storeships. The convicts drawn from the hulks between Plymouth and the Thames numbered 759, and some 200 uniformed marines were to guard them and protect the colony. Many marines and a few convicts were accompanied by wife and children, so that the entire expedition, including sailors, amounted to more than 1400 people.

2

On the morning of 13 May 1787 the fleet slowly sailed away, passing the Isle of Wight and approaching the English Channel. It was Sunday, and those on deck could feel the east wind in their hair and probably hear the church bells ringing across the water, but the convicts who were locked below heard only their own chains clinking and felt only the strange rocking of the ship. Most people in those eleven ships would not see Europe again. Amongst the convicts, twenty men and three women did not even live to see Australia; amongst the free people six of the children and two adults were also to die between England and Australia. Such a low death rate surprised physicians who knew the hazards of long voyages, the dangers of scurvy, and the high mortality rates of the prison hulks in English ports.

The fleet of eleven ships called at the Spanish colony of

Tenerife in the Canaries for fresh water and vegetables and called at the Portuguese harbour of Rio de Janeiro where officials showed their optimism about the climate of Botany Bay by buying such tropical plants as they mistakenly thought would flourish there. They carried aboard the plants of coffee, cotton and indigo, none of which to this day has flourished in the vicinity of Sydney. Then the ships crossed the south Atlantic to the Dutch port of Cape Town where the decks of several of the ships were crammed like an ark with livestock and poultry for the new continent.

Cape Town was on the edge of the familiar world. Far to the east lay thousands of miles of ocean where no other European ship sailed, and the long coast where no European lived. Officers in the fleet imagined the wilderness that lay ahead of them, imagined the long term of isolation to which they were condemned, and hoped – during their month in Cape Town – that a fast ship might arrive with news from home. On free days many of the officers and marines went ashore and strolled in the neat Dutch gardens and orchards, knowing that for years they might see no full-grown European shrubs and fruit trees. Into the sweeping harbour sailed ships carrying English, American, Danish, Portuguese and Dutch flags, ships fresh from Europe or from India or China, and the sight of those ships of many nations all riding the bay beneath the great table-top mountain excited those who knew that they were sailing away to a bay where they might not see one foreign ship in the course of a year. As the Australian fleet sailed into the open ocean, David Collins, aged 31 and the secretary to the governor, recorded that he might never again see family, friends or the society of civilized people. His sense of impending isolation, he said, was made more poignant when in the last light of that day his ship passed within hailing distance of a ship fresh from London.

Nine weeks later, on the coast of eastern Australia, Aboriginals fishing in small canoes or walking near the hot sands saw the white sails of the straggling fleet and did not realize that the arrival of these tall masts marked, far more for Aboriginals than for the British convicts, the dropping

20

of a curtain on their history. Near the entrance to Botany Bay, a few Aboriginals stood on the shore and shouted at the men lining the deck of several of the ships and held spears and smaller weapons aloft and seemed to shake them at the ship. When the officials and parties of marines were rowed ashore the naked Aboriginals came close to them, seeming shy to some observers and bold to others. As a sergeant of marines noted in his private journal on 21 January 1788, the first meetings were a blend of goodwill and suspicion:

> the Natives here is Very Affable. & Will Except of Aney thing, that You Will Give them, (& Even take Aney thing that the Can Lay Hold of) –

The Aboriginals must have noticed that many Europeans also took anything that they could lay hold of.

The fleet, after less than a week at anchor in Botany Bay, sailed north to the safer Sydney Harbour, where the convicts went ashore after eight months of close confinement. Tents were pitched, scrub was cleared, trees were chopped down, and defensive ditches were dug. A tiny area over which Aboriginals had hunted or gathered food intermittently for countless generations was no longer their ground. The occupied area was soon widened, spreading inland and out into the fishing grounds. Aboriginals seemed to resent less the occupation of part of their tribal land than the nets of the English fishermen. Sometimes Aboriginals simply took many of the fish they saw lying in the English nets or on the bottom of the returning fishing boats.

The governor, Captain Phillip, believed that the convict colony would flourish. He himself seemed capable of coping with obstacles, human or geographical. Aged 49, a Londoner whose father was German and mother was English, he had served with the Royal Navy and the Portuguese navy and had commanded a 64-gun ship in Indian seas. He also had had the vital experience, for a colonist, of farming near Lyndhurst on the edge of the New Forest. His unusual experience of quarter-deck and

21

farmyard suggested that he could make the most of his poor labourers and poor soil.

Less than three weeks after the flag had been hoisted on the edge of Sydney Harbour, the governor carried out his orders to occupy Norfolk Island, 900 sea-miles to the north east. This, curiously, was the only specific place in the south seas which he was ordered to occupy. He could withdraw his settlement from Sydney or Botany Bay or any part of the Australian coast; but under no condition was he to abandon Norfolk Island and its valuable forests of pine. So the small party of twenty-four – consisting of two officers, a surgeon's mate and his assistant, two marines, two seamen, a flax weaver, and fifteen convicts – sailed from Sydney. In the following few years more marines and convicts were sent to the island, and its population almost equalled the town of Sydney. The climate was healthy, fish were plentiful, and the rainfall was usually reliable. The convicts could not escape, and no natives lived on the isolated island. Fertile soil – a black mould or a red earth – seemed to stretch from the coastal cliffs to the highest mountain and was gushingly acclaimed by Lieutenant P. G. King, the commander of the island, to be at least forty feet deep and to be 'the richest and deepest soil in the world'.

Norfolk Island eventually was more a market garden than a strategic prize. Many of the stately pine trees, growing more than 200 feet in height, were found to be rotten near the base; and the timber could no longer be trusted as masts in deep-sea ships. The tough flax leaves were harvested and manufactured, but they continued to defy simple treatment. In 1796 only twenty-two people were engaged in preparing and manufacturing the flax into a canvas, and more equipment and more flax weavers were wanted. Sails were made from the flax; convict clothes were made from the flax. Many tests were made in English dockyards in which the strength of rope and canvas made from New Zealand flax was compared – usually favourably – with the strength of the Russian naval stores; and as late as 1831 the government ordered 800 tons of the flax from New Zealand so that the navy could again test its merits.

Forty years after Norfolk Island was settled, three members of the Navy Board wrote confidentially their view that naval stores made from New Zealand flax 'are equal in quality to the same articles imported from Russia'; but the Antipodes were far away, and were a redundant source of naval stores during the long naval peace which was settling on Europe.

Everywhere in the new colony the original plans of 1788 were thwarted. Nothing was more embarrassing than the failure of the colony to produce enough food. The official instructions to Phillip were emphatic that his difficulty would not so much be to wring hard work out of his convicts as to find sufficient work for them to do. With spades and hoes and a few hours' work each day, they would surely grow more than enough food in that climatic paradise: the remaining time they were to spend in cultivating and treating the flax plant. In fact, Joseph Banks in 1770 had seen Botany Bay and the surrounding country at its most flourishing but had imagined he was seeing it at its worst. Phillip paid the price for Banks' opinion. He could not find the rich soil and the lush meadows. The soil was sandy and poor, the clearing of the tree-stumps and roots was heavy work, and the tools and implements were meagre: the colony lacked even a plough until 1796. Even if the labour force had been motivated and muscular, and even if there had been oxen and ploughs, the colony might still have struggled to grow enough food. A new kind of agriculture had to be learned. The ideal season for planting had to be ascertained by trial and error. The soft-grained wheat grown in England proved to be less suited for New South Wales: in contrast, the early European settlements in North America had the great advantage of growing a native plant, the prolific maize or Indian corn.

Fish were expected to be a vital food. The settlement, however, lacked suitable timber with which to build fishing boats. Moreover the English fishing techniques at first were not successful. So the Aboriginals and the English competed with each other for fish in the same calm harbour. Meat could have been eaten instead of fish, but the imported livestock had to be conserved until the small population of cattle, sheep and other animals had multiplied.

The economic hopes crumbled side by side with the social. The government in London had hoped that somewhere in New South Wales or in the South West Pacific, native women would be recruited as wives for the convict men. Phillip half expected that the Aboriginal men might allow some of their women to marry convicts, but no black brides came forward. Phillip had also been instructed to recruit native women when his naval vessels called at islands in the South Seas; Tonga and the Friendly Islands seemed an ideal recruiting ground. Unfortunately the two naval ships – all other vessels having sailed away – could not be spared to recruit wives for the convicts. Moreover the scarcity of food made it foolish to import more mouths. So men continued to outnumber women by a large margin, and the brief vision of a multi-racial society was slowly forgotten, to be revived nearly two centuries later.

Phillip was alarmed at the prospect of so many men living together and sleeping side by side. Before sailing from England he had noted that in the new colony only two crimes would merit death – murder and sodomy. He resolved that he would not hang a man found guilty of those crimes but instead imprison him until a ship, ready to sail to New Zealand, could deliver him to the Maoris – '. . . and let them eat him'. The scarcity of shipping ended that plan. The governor had to accept the scarcity of women and tolerate its consequences.

His view that hanging was pointless, and would deter nobody from crime, was soon challenged. His storehouses of flour, rice and barrels of salted meat were guarded day and night, but a colony of thieves did not lack people who were willing to try their luck. Phillip decided that men should henceforth be hanged for stealing food. Free men as well as convicts were sentenced to death; and one morning in March 1789 six guilty privates in His Majesty's Marines were led to the gallows which had been erected close to the food stores where they had committed their robbery. The other marines were ceremonially assembled to witness the execution; and Private Easty confided in his journal that most of the officers and men, as they watched their comrades hanged, had tears in their eyes. Martial law now ruled Sydney. The expectations fixed on climate and soil had been too high.

The Aboriginals who roamed near the settlement at Sydney Cove were also the unintended victims. Phillip had been instructed to live 'in amity and kindness' with the Aboriginals. He himself was sympathetic to the Aboriginals but convicts who escaped were not necessarily so. On the edge of the settlement, Aboriginals were shot and marines and convicts were speared.

The blacks were puzzled at the way of life which was spreading into their territory. The English gardens made no sense; the slow-moving domesticated livestock puzzled Aboriginals; and when they speared a bullock they saw no reason for the angry outcry of the white officials. Likewise whatever the Aboriginals did was mystifying or seen as a sign of their ignorance. Why were they naked? Why did they take no thought for the morrow? Why did they engage in no gardening and build no permanent houses? Why did they show faint interest in divine service, when, by all the signs, they were quick to learn the English language?

Portions of the land of the Aboriginals near Sydney were allotted in neat squares to selected men whose sentence of transportation had expired. A bachelor could receive a grant of thirty acres; a married man supporting five children could receive 100 acres. They were given the normal rations of food for one year as well as farming tools and, occasionally, animals and poultry. Land which is now suburban and worth millions was thus assigned to criminals who in their home country had not owned even an honest handkerchief. In contrast, the military, naval and civilian officials were not permitted to receive land during the first five years of the settlement, though many became land-owners thereafter.

When Governor Phillip, after serving almost five years in Sydney, prepared to sail for England, the colony was surviving rather than flourishing. He possessed a vision of how the colony might develop; but most of the colony's obstacles had not yet been tackled, let alone mastered. The food remained scarce, relations with Aboriginals were fickle, and the colony suffered acutely in its isolation from European ports. The hopes of supplying India with tall masts of pine and of supplying superior linen or sailcloth for Sydney and remote naval-bases were not fulfilled. As a port for English ships entering the new Pacific trades or sailing to China, its value lay in the uncertain future. And as a gaol it was too costly: the 4300 convicts who arrived between 1788 and 1792 were costing the government a higher sum than had been envisaged when Botany Bay was chosen.

Phillip boarded the *Atlantic*, and in the early light of 11 December 1792 the ship sailed through the high headlands into the wide Pacific and set course for the cold waters of Cape Horn, and home. With him travelled two Aboriginals; they were curiosities and friends. The ship also carried four fine kangaroos, several dingoes, and various birds and plants. The *Atlantic* was an ark. One achievement of the colony was its effectiveness as an observatory of a new world of people, animals, fish and plants, nearly all of which were unfamiliar to scientists in Europe. It was therefore appropriate that the *Atlantic* carried to England another rare species – convicts whose sentence had expired and who had sufficiently redeemed themselves to justify a homewards passage in the same vessel as the governor.

3

In years ahead perhaps the most controversial issue in early Australian history will no longer be the question why did the British decide to place a settlement in eastern Australia – but the question of why they did not abandon it or deliberately prevent it from growing. In almost every sense it had failed. Nowhere was the failure so marked as in the colony's inability to feed and to clothe itself, thus imposing heavy costs on a government which believed that transportation was a cheap solution to the crowded hulks and prisons. Why then did the costly settlement survive? Presumably Phillip, returning to London, gave optimistic assurances that the colony would succeed: how exactly it would succeed he did not make quite clear in his writings which have been preserved. The continuance of the colony was also aided by Lord Sydney's resignation as home secretary. He knew how much hope had been placed on the settlement. His successor, Lord Grenville, not knowing the specific aims, had less knowledge of the depth of the failure, though he did suggest that in retrospect the colony should have been placed on Norfolk Island and that no settlement should have been made on the Australian continent. If a different or more pessimistic man had been first governor of New South Wales, the settlement might well have been abandoned, and the convicts moved to another part of Australia, to New Zealand, to an isolated part of Canada or southern Africa, or even to England.

The settlement at Sydney was also reprieved by official inertia. It was there. A positive initiative would be required to close it. Moreover the expense of closing it, once five thousand people lived there, was high. It called for the hiring of such a large fleet to bring the people back to England – a fleet four times the size of the First Fleet – that the cost of withdrawal would be far larger than the annual loss in operating the colony. To remove the convicts to New Zealand would be cheaper, but New Zealand required – it was believed – a larger defensive force, because the Maoris were highly organized and skilled in warfare.

The outbreak of the French Revolutionary Wars possibly helped to cement the settlement. Phillip first heard of this war when his home-bound ship *Atlantic* sailed into Rio de Janeiro in February 1793, and he promptly mounted more guns in the ship as a precaution against the French privateers which he expected to meet when approaching the English Channel. During the subsequent two decades of war, England often had difficulty in sending convicts and supplies to Australia, but likewise it could not easily conceive of removing the settlement. To remove it would require a fleet, and a spare fleet was not easily found in time of war. Moreover Sydney at last was possessed of that strategic advantage which its founders had probably envisaged. As the seas near the Dutch port of Cape Town and as the narrow straits in the Dutch East Indies were now dangerous for English ships – the Dutch being allies of the French – the long route to China by way of Tasmania became attractive. During wartime that roundabout route was more than a chart-gazer's dream. Late in 1804 an English man o'war of 64 guns escorted a convoy of nine London merchant ships through Bass Strait and so past Norfolk Island and the east of New Guinea to the tea-port of Canton.

Sydney was also saved by the growth of Pacific commerce. In the early 1800s her merchants and shipbuilders and part-time traders sent ships to Tahiti for pork, and to India and Cape Town for flour and rum. They slew seals and sea elephants on the islands of Bass Strait and shipped the skins and the barrels of oil to China or other distant ports. Sydney ships sailed to the Fiji Islands to cut sandalwood, sought cargoes of timber and the tantalizing flax in New Zealand, and went on whaling voyages to nameless bays and estuaries in Australia and New Zealand. And Sydney Harbour was increasingly a base or port for English and American whaling ships which were turning from the South Atlantic to the new whaling grounds in the vast ocean stretching from the Cape of Good Hope to cold Cape Horn far to the east.

By 1803 any prospect that Sydney might be abandoned had passed. One sign of the new confidence was the British decision to settle three crucial points in Bass Strait: Port Phillip Bay on the north shore, the mouth of the Tamar River on the south shore, and King Island to the west. Bass Strait was the short cut from the Indian Ocean to the Pacific Ocean and, together with the southern capes of Tasmania, was the most vulnerable part of the long sea route from London to Sydney. That the strait must on no account fall into French hands was an affirmation of the importance of Sydney and the rising sea trades in the western Pacific. The new settlements on Bass Strait did not last long and gave way to permanent settlements at Hobart in 1803 and Launceston in 1806. The most southerly British outposts in the world, they were soon struggling to survive, for all the ground was tilled slowly with the hoe, the seed sown was said to be little better than chaff, and the most common meat was chunks of fresh or dried kangaroo.

4

Arthur Phillip was now a retired admiral living in comfort with his wife in the west of England. The last eight years of his life he spent at Bath, a town as artificial as Sydney: whereas the one was devoted to punishment, the other was devoted to enjoyment. Receiving an annual pension for his 'meritorious service' to New South Wales, and devouring eagerly the snippets of slow news which arrived from Sydney, Phillip lived in one of those elegant terrace houses standing near the Assembly Rooms, a sandstone house which could almost have been built of the yellow Sydney sandstone. He died in August 1814, in his seventy-sixth year, and his body was carried along the steep green valley to the village church of Bathampton.

Today, within the old church, stands a small Australian chapel with a floor of white Wombeyan marble and wooden furnishings of Australian black-bean. On one side of the stone wall of the churchyard runs an old barge canal, and on the other side the trunk railway, so that soon after his death his grave was hemmed in by those new forms of transport which were industrializing Europe and helping to shrink the world. As the world continued to shrink, and as Britain's appetite for raw materials grew large, Phillip's colony became valuable.

Just six weeks before he died, a gang of forty or fifty Australian convicts began to clear the scrub and build an unmetalled road across the Blue Mountains towards the Bathurst Plains. They were making a highway that would link the inland grasslands to the woollen mills of north England. The first maritime era of Australia was coming to a close, and the pastures would soon open a new era.

29

3 Colonizing with Thieves

Many convicts were bewildered by the first days of the voyage to Australia. Most of them probably had never seen the open sea until they boarded the convict ship, and few had travelled in a ship. Most had not visualized themselves making any journey of even 200 miles so long as they lived. And now, by sentence of the courts, they were about to begin one of the longest voyages any traveller could make. The normal time for the voyage to Australia in convict ships was four or five months. Only a voyage from England to China or the west coast of North America was longer.

2

The first stage in the long journey was the trip to the floating hulks near London, Portsmouth, Plymouth, and the Irish ports of Dublin and Cork. There the convicts might live for months, even years, before they were transferred to a sea-going convict ship. In the first days or weeks at sea their legs were in irons; their fastened ankles were linked by a short chain. The convicts could then shuffle or slowly walk but not run. Nimble convicts, however, could dance or jig in their chains and produce recognizable tunes. The jingling of the chains was heard all day until, the ship being far out to sea, the leg irons and the linking chain of most prisoners were removed.

Normally the convicts slept in long dormitories between the decks. Along the side were arranged two rows of sleeping bunks, one above the other. In the more spacious ships each bunk or berth was six feet long and six feet wide and held four men, so that when the prisoners went to bed at night, each with his own pillow and blanket, only an inch or two of space separated each sleeping man. At night the prisoners were locked below. The ladder leading down to their deck was removed, the outer doorways were heavily padlocked, and there the armed guards remained on duty. Near the equator the dormitories must have been stinking and stifling. On calm days the convicts were allowed to walk the main deck while their dormitory below was scrubbed and cleaned.

Convicts in most ships formed their own eating messes – six men or women to each group – and the leader of each mess collected the food rations and took them to his iron pot where the meat, soup and gruel were cooked. As most convicts were skilled thieves, food rations had to be watched with care. The simplest trick was to divide the cooked meal and the allowance of ship biscuits into six unequal portions: as a precaution the six men in each mess usually drew lots, and the winners had first choice. Food was also the main prize in cards and dice and other gambling games which were played, even when officially banned. Convicts were usually given a small weekly dose of lime juice in the hope that it would prevent an outbreak of scurvy; occasionally Spanish wine and rum were served. A voyage was usually regulated by a long list of rules covering food, cleanliness, good order, punishments, religious services and even the occasional afternoon dances where men danced with men, for the female convicts were normally separated or sent in a separate ship.

The voyage in a convict ship was cramped and monotonous. If the ship called at the Canary Islands or Rio de Janeiro or Cape Town for fresh water and fresh food, no convicts were allowed ashore. If the weather in the Southern Ocean was wild and the seas were high, the convicts were locked below day after day in half-darkness while the ship creaked and lurched. In crowded conditions the dysentery and fever spread with ease; and when the ration of food was skimped, the scurvy could devastate both

31

convicts and sailors. In an average voyage, over the whole period of transportation, two of every hundred convicts died; but the casualties were higher in the first years. In the deadly period from 1795 to 1801, one in every ten of the convicts who left the British Isles died before reaching Australia.

Of every twenty convicts who reached eastern Australia, thirteen came from England and six from Ireland. In contrast, Scotland provided only about one in twenty of the convicts sent to eastern Australia during the entire history of transportation. This was a low quota but then Scottish courts sent surprisingly few people to prison: indeed John Howard, visiting the two main prisons in the city of Edinburgh in 1782, found only forty prisoners, and sixteen of those were debtors and so not liable to be transported. In Australia today the people of Irish ancestry are more likely than those of English or Scottish ancestry to be the descendants of convicts.

Most of those who came ashore from the convict ships were thieves. New South Wales was often called 'the thieves' colony'; and amusement was raised at polite dinner-tables in England by speculations on how any property could be secure in a colony where so many people were convicted thieves. Eight of every ten convicts sent to Australia had been sentenced for larceny, and most held previous convictions for theft and robbery. Some had been highway robbers, some had been burglars, and some committed their crimes while armed. Many stole horses; to a poor man of Yorkshire the horse probably represented a more valuable prize than a car today. Many stole cattle and sheep – to steal a sheep was an offence punishable by death – and several sheep-stealers might well have ended their days on Australian grasslands, owning more sheep than any Englishman had ever possessed in his own home county. The first convict ship to reach Port Phillip Bay carried twenty-six sheep-stealers, and they set foot in 1803 on the fringe of grasslands which, a generation later, nourished so many million sheep that the theft of a single sheep was rarely detectable. The ships also carried to Australia hundreds of pocket-watch thieves, hundreds of jewellery thieves, thousands who stole clothes and textiles, and thousands who stole food from shops and houses.

Most of the women who came out as convicts – and one woman came for every seven men – were thieves. Nearly all had been domestic servants and so were well placed to steal: they stole for themselves or, less frequently, for the sake of their destitute families. As perhaps one in five of these women had also been prostitutes in the British Isles, they brought out professional qualifications which were to be useful in a land where men far outnumbered women. The typical convict came without husband or wife but – if the authorities consented – a convict with some money could bring out his wife and family in the same ship, or send for them once he was able to support them.

Citizens of Sydney occasionally saw small boys assembled on the waterfront with the new convicts. John Halfpenny, 12 years old and only 4' 2" in height, was a bootmaker's boy in Staffordshire when he was convicted of stealing money and sentenced to transportation. Sylvester Carthy, an Irish errand boy, was aged 10 when he was transported for stealing money. Two young convicts who arrived in 1803 had been nine years of age when sentenced. The child convict was not rare, and at least a thousand boys of fourteen years or younger were shipped to New South Wales, sometimes in company with criminals old enough to be their grandfather. Child convicts, in the long term, probably did not suffer more than the army of small girls and boys who, working in English coal-mines and textile mills, endured longer hours and more physical strain than the average convict in Australia endured.

When the convicts heard the judge sentence them to transportation, they could not be certain that they would reach Australia. Many convicts, though sentenced to transportation across the seas, spent their full term in a hulk or gaol in the British Isles. Others, during the French Revolutionary Wars, were sent to fight the French. Thus in January 1799 a party of 318 convicted Irishmen was transported, not on the long passage to Australia, but on the short journey to the German port of Emden, whence they marched inland as conscripts for the Prussian Army.

3

New South Wales, for several decades, was regulated minutely. A precursor of the police state, its secret files covered a higher proportion of the people than did the secret files of any nation in Europe; it must have been the only nation or colony where the description and whereabouts of nearly everyone, free or bond, was recorded on the official files. To ensure the maximum security the port after dark was like a makeshift chicken coop. The danger of escape being high, any 'idler' found loitering near the wharves before sunset was given hard labour and those loitering there after sunset were imprisoned. On the Hawkesbury River the small boats were numbered and registered, were chained up at night, and could not be rowed during hours of darkness. Small sail-boats and rowing boats floating in Farm Cove in Sydney Harbour after sunset were confiscated. In merchant vessels in port, guards were posted to prevent unauthorized colonists from coming aboard. Settlers wishing to leave the jurisdiction of the colony had to give one week's notice to the authorities and receive a special certificate entitling them to sail. Even the small ships which sailed regularly through Sydney Heads and hugged the northern coast to the mouth of the Hawkesbury or Hunter Rivers had to give two or three days' notice before they sailed. The magistrates in each main town periodically held roll-calls which every colonist in the neighbourhood was compelled to attend. At these Sunday musters, however, a few names were usually absent.

While the seaward gates of the gaol could be guarded effectively, the outer walls of the gaol were simply the perimeter of bush and the Blue Mountains, and they could not be guarded easily. For years the story circulated amongst the convicts that if they left Sydney and kept on walking they would one day reach China. The story was not altogether a delusion, because every convict knew that many of the ships which had carried them to Australia then set sail for China. The Irish convicts were particularly eager to reach China, and dozens must have set out on that lonely journey. In 1798 the bones of about fifty escapees were found in the bush – milestones on the imagined road to the Orient.

Free settlers reaching Sydney soon became familiar with the mesh of regulations and security procedures. Each evening a drum or trumpet sounded the tattoo, after which the strollers had to justify their presence in the streets. After the sounding of the trumpet only the recognized house-holders and officers of vessels were allowed to walk the streets unchallenged, and even they had to carry a lantern – their visible passport. Lightly or rigidly enforced, depending on the circumstances, these were only a fraction of the rules governing the coming and going of people and ships, the buying and selling of goods, and the conduct of freemen and convicts in the year 1806.

The government in Sydney tried to regulate nearly all economic activities in the first two decades. The government was the main buyer of meat and grain from the local farms, and a heavy buyer of foodstuffs and hardware from visiting ships. It fixed the prices charged by butchers, bakers, publicans and money-lenders. Every baker was instructed how much bran he should mix in his dough and how much he should charge for his bread; if a customer insisted on paying for her loaf of bread in wheat rather than coins, the price could be no more than 2½ pounds of wheat for the standard large loaf. As for the pound sterling the government decreed that it was worth twenty-one – not twenty – shillings.

As the government had imported most of the early sheep, cattle and oxen in New South Wales, it drew up rules for livestock. It sold or gave breeding animals to settlers, and tried to control the sale of the offspring. It hired out oxen to farmers who owned a plough or cart but insisted that the hired oxen or bullocks be used only in agriculture. It carefully watched over the butchers of Sydney, demanding a weekly account of where they bought their livestock and to whom they sold the meat. One rule prohibited the butchering of female animals. Whereas we now protect certain native species of animals and birds because of their rarity, the government then protected the imported species because of their rarity.

As the government originally laid claim to all the land, it regulated the granting of land to new settlers, the resale of that land, and even the sale of any European timber grown on private land. As for the 'woods' which stretched away from the edge of settlement, they too were controlled by the government. At first the gatherers of firewood could collect only fallen timber, and could carry it to town only in specified types of vehicles.

Understandably the governor did not employ sufficient soldiers, constables and minor officials to enforce all these orders in a settlement which steadily straggled outwards. Accordingly rewards were offered to informers and pimps: rewards large enough to sharpen the eyesight and loosen the tongue of the most unobservant convict. If, for example, a ship was detected illegally landing casks of spirits, and an informer gave evidence which led to a successful prosecution, the informer's reward could theoretically equal half the value of the confiscated ship and spirits. Wily merchants, however, soon learned how to steer their craft through the minefield of regulations.

4

At first nearly all convicts worked directly for the government, but increasingly convicts were assigned to independent employers – a mixture of government officers and officials, free migrants, and convicts who had fully served their time. The employers had to provide the same food rations*, clothes, and shelter as the government provided for convicts which it employed. In return, the

---

*The food ration varied from year to year. After 14 January 1802, for instance, each convict received a weekly ration of 8 lbs of flour or meal, 7 lbs of beef or 4 lbs pork, and 3 lbs of peas. Some prisoners sold part of their weekly rations to other inmates, but the practice was illegal.

convict worked for the free settler, in a farm or garden, house or workshop, for the prescribed working hours without payment. When the assigned convicts had worked the set daily hours, however, they could charge for their services, and work either for their own master or for a neighbouring settler. The essence of the assignment system was that the convicts should impose no expense on the Crown.

The assigned servants were to be most numerous in the 1830s, and they could be found working as shepherds, building huts and houses, working on the decks of small ships that sailed the coast, serving in warehouses and shops, weeding gardens and ploughing paddocks. They did a lot of the colony's work but much of their work was slovenly. The shrewd convicts worked an inch inside the boundary of the regulations, obsequiously or silently obeying orders, rarely guilty of wilful neglect, offering no cheek or defiance, but going along at their own slow pace.

Some convicts were less shrewd. In the Sydney police court on the last Friday of 1831 three convicts were charged, on the complaint of their master, with rank disobedience. When he ordered them to plant vine cuttings in his vineyard, they had planted them upside down, and when he instructed them to build all the walls of his new house to the same height, they had deliberately made one wall higher than the other. Found guilty the ringleader received 50 lashes, and his two mates received 25. Probably they soon found new ways – less defiant but not less effective – of thwarting their employer. They could accidentally break implements, cunningly allow cattle or horses to stray and secretly set fire to a haystack. The master did not invariably hold the whip hand over such a raggle-taggle workforce. The colony was unable to tap adequately its rich reservoir of natural resources, partly because of the inadequacies of labourers whose working tempo had been set when they worked in convict gangs.

The main work of women convicts was in domestic service, and the complaints against them were voluminous. The Very Reverend Dr Ullathorne claimed in 1838 that females who were assigned to private settlers in the towns were lazy servants from the start. They then graduated to pilfering and to drunkenness and – the final step for many – licentiousness. They thus followed in the footsteps of many of their masters. As convict women were far outnumbered by men, they had a superior bargaining position in one sense and greater vulnerability in another.

The female convicts were seen as so depraved that in the first decades their colonial-born children were anxiously scanned for defects of physique and character. Would they be as wild as their parents? To the surprise of newcomers the colonial-born children even by 1810 tended to be taller, slenderer, fairer, with smaller features and a different complexion: a 'reddish sallow' complexion, said one surgeon. Plentiful food and sunlight no doubt helped their physique. They were widely said to lack respect for the magistrates, the clergymen and anybody in authority. In other words, their sense of independence stood out in a servile society. They were said to be less given to drunkenness and idleness; they showed more stamina in their work. Naturally their crime rate was far below that of their parents. In many ways they were a generation to themselves, conscious that being free they were unlike their convict parents, and conscious that being Australians they were unlike the free immigrants. There was no disparity in the sexes amongst the colonial-born, and they tended to marry, and to marry within their group. Here was another fifth-column within the convict system – the growing number of free, native-born children and adults.

5

Money ruled part of the workforce; physical punishment ruled part. In most decades the average flogging was less than 50 lashes, but some convicts were punished with a severity that could only be called ferocious. In October 1800 five men were sentenced each to receive 1000 lashes, a punishment that could only be inflicted in doses. To suffer 200 lashes in the one session was not uncommon. While many convicts, it was alleged, were flogged with insufficient severity and solemnity, scarring, blood-spattering floggings were frequent.

Van Diemen's Land, the official name for Tasmania until 1855, became a synonym for harsh punishments. At first it was essentially a place for convicts who had misbehaved in New South Wales, but later it received convicts direct from England. It held two notorious places of punishment: Macquarie Harbour on the rainy, windswept, west coast and its successor, Port Arthur, on the milder east coast. More than one in seven of all convicts sent to the island spent terms at these prisons. Of all the convicts who came to Van Diemen's Land one in every hundred was convicted of a capital offence and hanged. Four of every ten prisoners who reached the island before 1841 received at least one flogging. Many convicts in Australia were physically maltreated in a way which was rare in the English prisons and the hulks of the time. The early governors of New South Wales and of Tasmania were naval or military officers who had used the lash as a common means of discipline on their decks and parade grounds. They knew that a flogging had many advantages over alternative methods of punishment. As the colony in its early years was often short of food, the full workforce was as necessary as in a sailing ship. Therefore any punishment which deprived the colony of the physical strength of one man was self-defeating. To place a sullen convict in solitary confinement meant that he consumed more food than he produced. To place him in a chain gang meant that, fettered, he worked less efficiently. In contrast, a flogging – so long as it did not lead to death – removed a culprit from the workforce for only a day or two. The first two decades in New South Wales were a desperate struggle by ill-fitted labour, unskilled overseers and poor equipment to till the hungry soil, and the desperation was sometimes visible in the punishments. The punishments were so selected that they placed the least strain on the production of food. If the soil had been more productive, the punishments would probably have been lighter.

Fear that the convicts might rebel was another inducement to use intimidating methods. The convict colonies were so isolated that if a serious rebellion occurred, no useful help could be expected from across the seas. In years of tension the officers and the magistrates ruled with iron gloves. As the forces of law were easily outnumbered by convicts or former convicts, they also recruited help from the ranks of convicts. Many constables, overseers of chain gangs, and those who administered punishment were convicts, and they carried on the brutal methods to which they had been subjected. Unfortunately there was no neutral group which could protest in the name of humanity. The colony lacked independent, educated citizens and it lacked strong philanthropic societies. The clergymen could hardly be expected to protest, for the salaries of many clergymen came from the government, and some clergymen employed convicts in their farms and kitchens. The voices of protest came more from England than from Australia.

Physical brutality and extreme pain, of course, were common in the first half of the 19th century in England and western Europe. They were common in the armed forces in peacetime and conspicuous in war, especially as the only anaesthetics during surgery were alcohol or opium. Brutality was common, too, in the treatment of children and animals, but the brutality towards convicts in Australia seemed at times to surpass the standards of a callous age.

6

Half of the criminals who were sentenced to transportation in Australia had to serve a term of seven years; and some of them had almost served that term when eventually they reached Sydney. For other convicts the term of transportation was longer, ranging from ten years to life. A variety of remissions and incentives enabled well-behaved or influential convicts to receive most of their civil liberties long before their term of transportation was over. The governor frequently issued 'tickets of leave', a precious passport which enabled a convict to be his own employer.

Thereafter he had to support himself in food and lodgings, had to attend periodical musters or roll-calls, and could not leave the district. A quiet convict might receive the ticket of leave after two or four years in the colony. Wealthy convicts were known to receive the ticket as soon as they had landed: in the old legal phrase, they had 'visible means of support'. Another passport was the 'conditional pardon' which conferred full freedom within the Australian colonies, though it did not permit the holder to return to England until his seven or fourteen years had expired. In contrast, the jubilant convict who received an 'absolute pardon' could return to England even though he had formally been transported for life.

The convicts who received no pardon or ticket had to work as a government servant or assigned servant until their sentence of transportation had expired. The likelihood of them returning to the British Isles was small. The ships were few, and the fare was expensive. Moreover they probably had lost all touch with relatives. And yet a small minority of convicts – perhaps numbering several thousand – did sail for England and set eyes on those green shores which they had not expected to see again. Some of those who went home also, in the fullness of time, set eyes on the Australian shores they never expected to see again, for in England they had again fallen into thieving, and were again sentenced to transportation. The jet-setters of their era, they crossed the world three times – twice at His Majesty's expense.

Transportation to New South Wales was a lottery with loneliness, pain and death at one wide extreme and astonishing riches at the narrow extreme. One convict who became richer than any free immigrant was Samuel Terry. Charged in the Lancashire cotton town of Salford with the theft of 400 pairs of stockings and some oddments, the court ordered in January 1800 that he 'be sent and transported to some part beyond the Seas for the space of seven years'. After months in the hulk he was taken, with irons on both legs, to the convict ship *Earl Cornwallis*, and issued with clothing for the long voyage through cold and

41

hot climates. He received his blue jacket and waistcoat, his Russian duck trousers, his two checked shirts, his pair of shoes, his woollen cap and – a meagre wardrobe for a man who recently had 400 pairs of stockings – a mere two pairs of stockings. Nearly one in every six convicts died on that voyage, but Terry and his mistress – a female convict – landed in sound health. Working first as a stonemason, Terry served out his time, became innkeeper and storekeeper and farmer, amassed money with speed, and married a widowed freewoman about the time that Governor Macquarie called on convicts to marry their women instead of following 'that pernicious custom so generally and shamelessly adopted' in the colony. His portrait suggests a pale, moon-faced man with the straight mouth of the martinet but he had a touch of sensitivity and generosity. When he discarded his old mistress he gave her a house, a horse and chaise cart, and a cow and heifer.

Terry speculated with such shrewdness that, in the years 1817 to 1820, he held one fifth of the total value of all the mortgages which were officially registered in New South Wales. He held more money in such mortgages than even the new Bank of New South Wales: and in that bank he was also one of the main shareholders, though for long he was not permitted, as an emancipated convict, to sit on its board. This money wizard acquired farms, pastoral lands, flour-mills, breweries, and city property, including much of the property enclosing the Sydney street, Martin Place. At one time he held as much land as all other former convicts added together. He also tried to commandeer the civil law, and in the Supreme Court he had brought at least twenty-eight actions by 1821.

If Samuel Terry had decided – as an act of remembrance – to give one pair of stockings to everyone who worked on one of his properties, he would have required more than 400 pairs. His fingers seemed to be in every large mercantile venture on land and water, so that for the last quarter century of his life, colonists must have kept on whispering to each other, 'what's he worth'. Now in 1838, on his death, they knew. His personal estate was valued at

42

£250,000, making him a millionaire by American measurement. He had made all that money but social recognition eluded him. Money could not buy the right to sit in the positions of civic honour but the band of the 50th Regiment played at his funeral. And his children could not be deprived of their rights. One of his daughters became, in 1842, the first mayoress of the City of Sydney.

James Underwood was another criminal whose journey to Australia was a lucky windfall. Sentenced to seven years' transportation, he arrived possibly as a teenager about 1791. In biblical accounting, his seven lean years were followed by seven fat years, and then by seven more. He became a merchant and shipbuilder, and ships he built or refitted were carriers of coal from Newcastle, seal skins and whale oil from Tasmanian waters, and sandalwood from the Pacific Islands. In the sealing trade Underwood was a giant, and with his partners he perhaps sold as many as 200,000 seal skins in London between 1803 and 1810. One ship in which he was part-owner, *Sydney Cove*, was actually chartered by the government to transport convicts to Australia. Nobody could have imagined, back in the 1780s, that the day would come when a wealthy ex-convict would provide a large ship in which to transport more convicts to Australia, and that in Sydney he would be living in a mansion which was larger than the governor's. Underwood died in February 1844 at Tulse Hill near London, to which he had retired to live in style. Had he redeemed himself by his life in Australia? Some observers said that he remained a rogue and, rather than repaying his debt to society, had increased his debt. On the other hand his enterprise helped to build an economy which gave thousands of free immigrants a chance to live a more prosperous life than Britain could offer.

Rarely in the history of the world can there have been a scheme of punishment which handed out such rewards. The large prizes in the casino of transportation worried many politicians in Britain. One aim of sending convicts to a remote land was to deter others from crime, but many London commentators thought the prospect of the voyage to New South Wales was as much an incentive as a deterrent. A surgeon who had made four voyages to Australia in convict ships concluded that most men imprisoned in the hulks on English rivers and harbours – men already sentenced to transportation – wanted to be sent to Australia: he had spoken to many such men and he concluded that the voyage across the equator, while not a joy ride, was rarely envisaged as a journey into hell. But for many it was such a journey, he said.

The idea even arose that people were actually committing crimes in order that they could say farewell to England and start life afresh in Sydney. This idea – possibly true for the stray simpleton – is mostly a myth. A thief's first hope was to steal something valuable and not be caught. He committed a crime in the hope of winning. If he succeeded in stealing a gold watch that prize was infinitely more attractive than the prospect of capture, the subsequent slow shuffling through prison and court and – if it so eventuated – the voyage to a new life in Sydney or Hobart. Moreover a conviction for crime did not lead inevitably to a convict ship. It could lead to the gallows or it could lead to a smaller sentence in the British Isles if the crime were deemed less serious.

7

Several thousand who came out in convict ships could perhaps be called political prisoners. Australia thus served as a Siberia for many who, in one form or other, made political and social protests against the British government. Most of these protesters came from Ireland. At least 300 who took part in the Irish Rebellions of 1798 and 1803 were eventually transported to Sydney. The last of the Irish political prisoners, sixty Fenians, were sent to Western Australia as late as 1867; so that several of them possibly lived long enough to become citizens of the new Irish Free State after the First World War.

Among those sent here for political crimes committed in England, three had attempted to kill or wound the Sovereign. One had thrown a stone at King William the Fourth at an English racecourse; one had fired a pistol at the young Queen Victoria in St James' Park, and a lieutenant of the Hussars was transported for striking her with a stick – the Queen was not amused.

While three men had attacked the monarch, hundreds attacked the new monarch, machinery. In an era when machines seemed to be taking away the traditional jobs of craftsmen and rural labourers, scores of Englishmen retaliated by destroying industrial machines or the harvests and haystacks of farmers who used agricultural machines. Sixty machine-breakers of 1812 – the Luddites – were transported to Australia. Some of the most pathetic groups of convicts were transported in the early 1830s after a futile protest against the steam-driven threshing-machines which were invading the barnyards of southern England. They had smashed many of the new threshing-machines, had set haystacks alight, and had made threats to land-owners because these machines were throwing them out of work in a changing social order in which the squire no longer felt an obligation towards those who had served him. Most of these rural men wished simply to return to the old days when a crowd of hard-working farmhands used wooden flails to separate the grain from the straw.

Nearly two thousand of these protesters were tried in English courts in 1830 and 1831. Three men who had set fire to a farmer's crop at Kenn, in Somerset, were sentenced to death, and as a deterrent to others were marched 42 miles from the place of sentence at Ilchester to the fields where they had committed their crime; and there they mounted the gallows, and were hanged. In all, twenty-two men were hanged, more than 1400 were imprisoned in England, and 481 were transported. Half of those who boarded the convict ships came from Wiltshire and Hampshire. The machine-breakers in the ship *Eleanor* reached Sydney on 26 June 1830, spent a fortnight waiting in the harbour before they were rowed ashore, fitted out with clothes and hats and boots, and assigned to the service of upcountry settlers. Fine healthy men, experienced in rural work, they were applauded by the *Sydney Herald* as an acquisition to the colony. 'They innocently expressed a

45

hope', noted the newspaper, 'that they would not be placed along with the housebreakers, pickpockets' and the common run of thieves. Many of these rural protesters were deeply ashamed that they had fallen amongst thieves.

Most of the wreckers of the steam threshing-machines were exiled to Tasmania. They possessed, by convict standards, not only a fine physique but also a good reputation. Less than one in three had previously been in prison, and many of those former prisoners were merely poachers. Most were ploughmen, and a ploughman also worked with his flail on the threshing floor after the harvest was carted in. Many of the other machine-breakers were blacksmiths, thatchers, slaters and rural tradesmen, and were eagerly snapped up by Tasmanian employers. There is perhaps the sniff of corruption in the fact that ten men convicted of machine-breaking in the Gloucester Quarter Sessions were sent to the windy estates of the Van Diemen's Land Company. Joseph Cripps MP, the chairman of the sessions in Gloucester, was an English director of that company, and he had passed word to the company that the protesters convicted in his court were 'all excellent workmen, strong and useful men'. He was thus indirectly a beneficiary of the sentence he imposed.

We know something about the life of most of these 300 rural protesters who reached Tasmania. Half were married men and some later brought out their wife and young children, and a few probably married bigamously – as the practice was – in Tasmania. Some who had set fire to haystacks in England now set fire to the throat of their Tasmanian customers because, their sentence served, they became sellers of spirituous liquors. A few committed serious crimes in Tasmania and at least seven were sent to the place of punishment at Port Arthur. At least twenty crossed to Victoria and were swallowed in a free society. A few of those rural convicts of the early 1830s, still pining for England, must have returned to villages which were now almost deserted by the impact of new rural machines. Most of those rural rioters remained in Tasmania and some became what they could never become in England – owners

46

of farmland. And so one wonders what that former convict Isaac Isles, living in his ninety-sixth year on his own Tasmanian farm at Brandy Bottom near Colebrook, thought of his years in Tasmania. He had been a ploughman near Andover when he was sentenced to transportation; but now in his last year, 1897, he was living on farmlands which, by the strenuous application of that new technology which he had once resented, were producing wheat and meat, apples and butter. In old age he was even sending some of these products in the steamships' to England, and one likes to think that his apples were even sold in the shops of Andover.

Nothing is more characteristic of Australian life in the 19th century than the eagerness with which labour-saving ideas were applied to rural life, and no fact does more to explain why Isaac Isles and his generation eventually enjoyed here a standard of living which made their cottage life in old England seem deprived. They were thus the beneficiaries, in one sense, of the process against which they had forcefully protested.

While the machine-breakers of 1830 had looked back to a golden age when the harvesting followed old ways, there were other prisoners whose views on politics belonged to the future. Their names are little known, but Australia was to become celebrated for practising their views. In March 1834 six agricultural labourers from the village of Tolpuddle, in a Dorset valley, were sentenced to transportation for – in effect – forming a trade union. Their leader, a ploughman and Wesleyan preacher named George Loveless, was shipped to southern Tasmania where he watched government flocks and herds on the fringes of Hobart and then worked for a farmer within sound of the present Hobart airport.

In the same months as Loveless had been sentenced to transportation for forming a trade union, a group of tailors in Hobart went on strike for higher wages. Their strike failed but they were not prosecuted. Here the frequent shortages of labour were to encourage union activity, and the same shortages were to encourage the application of technology to daily work; and the fruits of technology in turn helped the country to finance the higher wages and shorter hours which the trade unions demanded.

In Australia the first dramatic upheaval created by new productive equipment was not the threshing machine but a more insidious, more plentiful arrival. The new machine was usually white, it was halfway in size between a large dog and a calf, and was self-propelled. This productive machine could store its own output for a year or even longer. It required no lubricant, rarely required repairs, could stand unprotected in rain and sun, and required the oversight of few foremen. It produced a commodity which was increasingly demanded in Europe. Its name was the sheep.

4 The Quick March of the Sheep

In the year 1820 only a tiny part of eastern Australia was actually occupied by British settlers and convicts. The settlement lying furthest in the interior was Bathurst, west of the Blue Mountains, and nobody had yet travelled far enough to find the main rivers, the Murray and Darling. The British, one generation after their first settlement, occupied a segment of the continent which was roughly equal to one minute marked on the edge of a great clock.

As Australia was primarily a prison, an open prison, civil order could not be enforced if the convicts were too scattered. They could not be managed without the help of soldiers, constables, overseers, magistrates and the local flogger. Property in houses, stables, shops and ships could not be guarded adequately against thieves even when the main settlement was concentrated around Sydney. It was therefore hazardous to settle districts where the bush itself protected bushrangers and horse thieves. New South Wales at times employed one soldier for every nine convicts and free settlers. The cost of running a convict settlement would have been even higher if the people had been dispersed widely.

2

Sheep and cattle were already pushing down the prison walls. The First Fleet had taken sheep aboard at Cape Town in 1788, sheep with hair rather than wool. The tails of these Cape Town sheep were so long that travellers' stories describing them were sometimes disbelieved. According to

David Collins these sheep travelled well but the tail – weighing as much as seventeen pounds at the Cape – shrank during the voyage. Many of the sheep were safely landed in Sydney but did not multiply. Another 68 arrived in the ship *Gorgon* in 1791. A tiny flock of small, hairy Bengal sheep arrived in the following year. A few sheep, penned in ships which called at Sydney, were taken ashore and sold to citizens or to the great flock-owner, the government. In 1797 the first Spanish merino sheep arrived, having been bought from a farm owned by the wife of the Dutch commandant at Cape Town. Bengal sheep, South African sheep, Silesian sheep – all were to arrive in their cramped pens, but the Spanish merino was eventually to be the favourite and its fine wool was to delight the English wool manufacturers. Today three of every four sheep in Australia are merinos.

As late as the 1820s the sheep were valued more for their mutton than for the wool. The colony had to learn how to feed itself before it could learn how to clothe half of Europe. A few families were alert to the idea that ultimately the fortunes might be won from the export of wool. Captain John Macarthur was the son of a mercer and draper in the English port of Plymouth, an emigrant Scot who no doubt sold woollen goods made from English and continental wool. John at the age of 15 joined the army, served briefly in the British garrison at Gibraltar, and then sailed as a lieutenant in the second fleet. Aged 22 when he stepped ashore at Sydney, he was aggressive, energetic, and so eager to confront visible enemies and imagined enemies that later he was known as 'the perturbator'. In the Parramatta district he was quick to clear and plough his own grant of land. He was one of the first to acquire a few of the colony's precious Spanish merino sheep and he and his wife Elizabeth became alert breeders of sheep. After fighting in a duel in 1801 he was sent home to face a court martial; and in England – his name more or less cleared – he studied the market for wool and eventually sailed for Sydney with a prize cargo of seven merino rams and two ewes – normally prohibited exports. Curiously he lived in Australia for only four years between 1801 and 1817, and for the remainder of that time his wife Elizabeth skilfully tended the increasing flocks and their rising output of fine wool. By 1819 the Macarthurs employed a small regiment of convict labourers, owned some of the juiciest grassland near Sydney, and ran 6000 sheep. Such a large flock was marvelled at in those days. It was not yet conceivable that the time would come when one man alone would own one million sheep.

The noise of geese is said to have warned Rome against the quiet approach of invaders. On the grasslands across the Blue Mountains the bleating of sheep warned the governor how fragile were the walls of his compact prison-colony. As the sheep multiplied, the owners wanted more lands. By the year 1825 one third of the colony's sheep was grazing west of the mountains. Vast plains lay ahead of these expanding flocks. Here were grass and water for more sheep than any country owned. Successive governors faced the dilemma: should they foster the wool industry or should they prevent the sheep and their shepherds from venturing far across the great plains and thereby endangering the security of the prison? In the end the sheep were victorious.

No other country possessed such an expanse of grassland on which sheep could live in the open throughout the year. The early flock-owners near Sydney, it is true, had been nervous about the hot sun and cold nights. Thus the shepherd of Captain H. Waterhouse, watching a pioneer flock of fewer than a hundred Spanish merino sheep near Sydney, was careful to keep them in the shady bush on the hot days and careful not to drive them from the sheepyard into the grasslands until the morning dew had dried on the grass. To keep the sheep under a roof at night was the normal practice near Sydney. 'We always housed our sheep,' Governor Hunter recalled. 'Captain Macarthur', he added, 'made an experiment of keeping his sheep out, but he lost a good many by it.' But the time soon came when the sheep stood under the stars every night. One of the great discoveries in the early history of Australia was that here sheep and cattle could flourish without being pampered. If Australia's sheep had had to be housed in barns on winter nights, and if vast paddocks of hay had been reaped with the slow scythe each summer in order to hand-feed sheep in winter, wool would not have become the country's main export. And yet by the early 1830s wool had passed the busy whaling industry in export income, and by 1840 it dominated economic life.

The sheep multiplied so fast – a flock of 500 could become 900 in a year – that the demand for land was voracious. Many settlers, eager to take up the grasslands, bought sheep from existing flocks and set out for the virgin land with a bullock dray, a few riding horses and a couple of shepherds. They squatted three or five miles beyond the most distant squatter and began to graze their sheep and build their primitive hut of timber, bark or sods. There were no officers of the law to stipulate where newcomers should settle. In the Port Phillip District, an unwritten rule told the newcomer not to settle with his sheep within three miles of the home of the nearest squatter. The rule could easily be broken by latecomers; quarrels and scuffles were common; and pioneer squatters might spend much of their subsequent time moving their flocks – like chessmen – to that part of their sheep-run which was encroached upon by latecomers.

Some squatters were soon hemmed in by surrounding flocks. Some who went out to the dryer country far inland held virtually as much of the plains as they could see from the back of a horse. In Victoria in the late 1840s when the boundaries had become firmer, the great sheep-runs such as Charlotte Plains – east of the present Maryborough – spread over nearly 300 square miles while Dunrobin near Casterton and Mary Vale in the southern Wimmera occupied about 230 square miles. No cities in the world covered so much land. At the other extreme were the tiny sheep-runs like Ballan which, lying forty miles west of Melbourne, was so vulnerable – and so fertile – that it held less than eight square miles of grass.

A handful of squatters saw no merit in camping within

sight of the nearest neighbour. They wanted to be explorers. The Hentys crossed from Launceston to Portland Bay in 1834, and their tiny schooner was so hammered by winds and sea that they lost two of their six working bullocks, their two cows and two calves, and twelve of their twenty-five heifers. Before they shipped the first merinos to Victoria, they walked over the country with their fourteen dogs, and gaped at the pastures just waiting for their sheep. Edward Henty vowed that once the cattle and sheep ate the grass, their sides would 'shake with fat'. A thousand miles to the north, the 24-year-old Scot, Patrick Leslie, was to lead his 2100 sheep and his twenty-two convicts to the Darling Downs where he marvelled that so much grass should be simply waiting there. Many of these bold land-finders, happening to enter their paradise in a lush season, had the feeling that here were farmlands which had been planted with trees and grasses and then mysteriously abandoned. The landscape seemed cultivated and almost European.

Three of our ten largest cities were opened as sheep-ports or sheep-runs. In the 1820s the skinny sheep reached Canberra, a lonely pastoral valley; and the present government house (Yarralumla) and the present military college (Duntroon) were once the homesteads of squatters. Melbourne and Geelong were opened as sheep pens, and to those ports came small vessels crammed with Tasmanian sheep to stock the western country, and annually thereafter arrived the lumbering drays of wool, much of which had been grown by northern flocks that had originally come overland from Yass, Gundagai and Albury. The site of Melbourne in January 1835 had been like a park, with the falls and rockbar where Queens Bridge now crosses, with platypuses in the creeks and bellbirds in the wattles and the Yarra Yarra twisting its way towards the bay beneath arches of trees at the narrower banks. Not a sheep, not a ship was to be seen. Fifteen years later Melbourne was one of the three busiest wool ports the world had known.

3

When the search for grasslands was most vigorous, hundreds of parties were travelling inland. Many squatters made their expeditions in secret and returned in secret. If they found fine grasslands, they wished to occupy them ahead of all competitors, and so they said nothing.

Others pioneered stock routes from pastoral districts to distant ports where they hoped to sell their surplus cattle and sheep to local butchers or stock-agents. From the Seymour district, north of Melbourne, Hawdon and Bonney set out in 1838 for the new town of Adelaide with 340 head of cattle and a flock of sheep. They had to pass slowly through the territory of Aboriginals who had perhaps not seen white men and they had to discover their own water-holes and lagoons in dry country.

It must have been a strange sight when the expedition set out. Four horsemen, each with a spare horse, drove the cattle and a shepherd walked with his sheep. To carry all supplies for a journey which might last several months, the heavy dray was drawn by eight bullocks, and a lighter dray was drawn by six. Two men drove the drays, and there was a cook to prepare the meals, and a personal servant to look after Hawdon. The big dray carried presents for passing Aboriginals – the tomahawk was the favoured gift – and if presents should prove unpersuasive each man carried a carbine, a pair of pistols and a bayonet. For Aboriginals the approaching expedition must have been unbelievable: the long-necked horses, the dust rising from the herd of cattle, the barking of Hawdon's kangaroo dogs, and the strange revolving wheels of the drays.

The short journal in which Joseph Hawdon described his nine-week journey breathed a sense of wonder. He was pleased that no European had seen the sights he now saw; he was excited by the prospect that even in such a drought-stricken year he might find the richest pastures in the continent. Soon he had the satisfaction of coping with hardship and conquering adversity – a satisfaction less valued now that comfort is so widespread a political and personal goal. On the shores of still water, the silence of the land filled him with astonishment. Sometimes he fired his gun and listened to the bounding echo. He liked to announce his presence in a wilderness by carving his name or initials on a tree. The restrained behaviour of the young vandal is mingled with the curiosity of the naturalist and the excitement of the hunter. Like most explorers he could probably be called gun-happy. It was almost as if the sound of the gun reminded him that his technology made him the master of a hostile land. The gun was also a retrieving dog, bringing to his feet the strange creatures which he wished to examine. Seeing a new species of owl he shot it, opened it with a knife, and found that the crop of this owl was full of beetles. On the shores of a lake which swarmed with birds he saw a parakeet with a green back, yellow belly, light blue wings and a halo of crimson on the head. He said simply that it was one of the most beautiful birds he had ever shot.

Hawdon saw the majesty of the great kangaroos and the tall emus. Seeing an emu near the Murray River, he and his servant Harry gave chase. For seven miles they rode their horses in hard pursuit, and their greyhound bitch went so close to the emu that she snapped feathers from its tail. Finally the emu outdistanced the dog but Hawdon respected the emu; and in one sandy stretch where its footprints were vivid, he dismounted to inspect the length of the running stride; it measured exactly nine and a half feet.

Many explorations were as much a search for fresh water as a search for fresh lands. Hawdon travelled close to the river on his journey to Adelaide but spent much time in search of water. For nearly three weeks the sky was 'one vault of deep blue', and the land was mostly brown and the cattle could find little to eat but the clumps of coarse reeds. If by chance they smelled water at a distance they broke into a stampede. One yoked bullock, 'devoured with thirst', drowned itself in a long-awaited waterhole. In the sandy country Hawdon was frightened that at night all the cattle and horses would wander far in search of water. For the first time all horses had to be tethered and his men lit a ring of fires around the cattle to prevent them from straying.

One delight of an explorer was the naming of landmarks: the hills, mountains, valleys, bluffs, dry watercourses, springs, lakes and lagoons, and that rarity – the flowing river. Most explorers seem to have conferred their favourite names on watering places rather than on prominent hills. When Hawdon, riding to the top of a high sandhill near the present Victorian-South Australian border, saw a great lake fringed with gum-trees and vast beds of scented flowers and herbs, he summoned his straggling men, handed out eleven glasses of brandy, called for loud 'huzzas' and predictably named the water Lake Victoria. It so happened that Queen Victoria had come to the throne just when the land explorers had traversed the well-watered parts of Australia and were beginning to push towards the unknown deserts and the dry heart. No European monarch was to leave her name on so many arid places.

4

In the late spring and summer, in the sheep lands of New South Wales and Tasmania, an annual procession of slow drays was pulled by bullocks towards the ports. Stacked high with heavy bales of wool, the drays came to the very side of the tall-masted ships which were to carry the wool past Cape Horn to England. In the north of England the woollen mills with their new mechanical processes were demanding more wool than ever before. The flocks in England and the continent could not meet the demand, because more and more grazing land there was now ploughed for crops. In contrast, wool was about the only commodity which the Australian interior could successfully grow for market. Each bale of wool was so valuable that it could afford the high cost of transport by dray to the port and by ship across the world, and still earn profits for the owners of the sheep. Australia was so far from Europe that it was forced to specialize in those high-priced export commodities which could afford the cost of crossing the world.

Shepherds had become the largest group of workers.

They guarded the country's most important asset. As fences were rare in the sheeplands – except in Tasmania – the flocks were entrusted to shepherds; and all day the shepherd dawdled along with his sheep, and near nightfall he drove them to a rough portable sheepfold usually made of boughs or brushwood or hand-made hurdles. The hutkeeper and a tethered dog looked after the crowded sheep during the night, the hutkeeper sleeping in a small watchbox little larger than a coffin while one or two shepherds slept in the hut nearby. Most of the shepherds and hutkeepers were convicts or former convicts. They worked in loneliness every day of the year: the sheep provided no holiday. As the skills of the shepherds and the confidence of the owners were increased, the flock entrusted to one man rose from some 200 or 300 sheep in the 1820s to 1000 on many squatting runs in the 1840s, and even to 1500 and 2000 sheep. Such a large flock was manageable on treeless plains, but in timbered hills even a small flock was not easily watched, was more vulnerable to attack from dingoes and less easily rounded up at nightfall.

Shepherds and hutkeepers lived in squalor. The ground near the nightly sheepfold was closely cropped by the sheep, was muddy in winter and dusty in a dry summer, strewn with bits of sheepskin and bones and meat, and pervaded the year round by the smell of sheep dung and wool-grease. In summer the bush-flies settled on the shirt and hat of the shepherds as they sat in the shade tree or as they walked along with their stout stick; and most shepherds eventually wore a light veil of cloth to ward off the flies and the dust raised by the thousands of moving hooves. Most shepherds were 'dirty and grey-bearded, their torn moleskin trousers full of ragged holes and incredibly greasy with wool-grease from the sheep, their plaited cabbage-tree hats broken and drooping'. Few contrasts could be sharper than that of the shepherds here and the shoppers who, on the other side of the world, bought clean skeins of wool and bright woollen clothes.

New South Wales alone employed about 13,500 shepherds and hutkeepers in March 1846; and if the stockmen and those who tended cattle and horses are added to the shepherds, perhaps two of every ten people in the workforce of New South Wales were pastoral workers. In the outer districts three of every four employees were watchers of sheep. Scattered, ragged men, many must have been incapable of counting their sheep.

The sheep were the basis of rich personal fortunes, but many of the pioneers lost heavily and many struggled for years before they succeeded. Early in the 1840s the sheep industry faced its most serious crisis. The price of wool and sheep fell. An anxious search began for savings. The land itself offered no savings, because the sheep-owners in the main pastoral districts paid no rent until 1839 and even then an owner of 7000 sheep paid no more than £40 a year for his squatting licence and the levy of a penny a sheep. Wages were the main expense, and so the average flock was enlarged and wages of shepherds and hutkeepers were lowered. The quality of the fleeces of the flocks could be improved, but so long as fences were rare and the mongrel flocks easily mixed with the few well-bred flocks any systematic breeding was difficult. New methods of washing the sheep before shearing saved money, for cleaner wool earned more. The screw-down press, by squeezing wool into less bulky bales, slightly cut transport costs on the long journey to the coast and to England. But these slow improvements could not rescue squatters who were deep in debt to banks which had financed their original purchase of sheep.

The long march of the sheep to remote inland plains was slowed down, and the demand for sheep declined. If surplus sheep could not be sold, they could be boiled in vats for the production of tallow. Russia was the great producer of tallow, shipping it to St Petersburg and so to England where it was the main ingredient of cheap soaps and candles. In 1843 Australia seriously entered the tallow trade. Henry O'Brien, a middle-aged squatter from County Mayo, was the first settler to pasture sheep on the Murrumbidgee and his out-station was at Jugiong, that steep-sided valley down which the heavy transports on the

Hume Highway now roar day and night. In Sydney in the winter of 1843 he publicized how sheep could be melted at a profit. The idea became the rage in his own district. Queanbeyan district soon had eight boiling-down plants. People on the outskirts of Melbourne and Sydney could smell their own new industry.

Surplus sheep, especially old and diseased sheep, were driven to the plants and penned. 'A ferocious-looking man enters, armed with an axe, and commences knocking down the sheep right and left. Others follow with knives to complete the work of death.' The flock was 'prostrated in agony in a few minutes, the life-blood deluging the fold and bespattering the men', reported The Religious Tract Society. The sheep were skinned and the skins sold. The hind legs were cut off and, if near a town, were sold to butchers and salted, or smoked into mutton hams or sold as fresh meat. The skinned carcases were then thrown into the vats and reduced by intense heat or steam. The tallow was skimmed off and packed into bags made from animal hides or into wooden casks for export. Possibly four million sheep and a quarter million cattle were melted down in Australia between 1843 and 1851. Millions of hands in the British Isles were now washed with the soap made from surplus Australian livestock.

5

By 1850 the sheep here numbered some 18 million, the descendants of a few thousand sheep which had crossed the sea. The main sheep lands stretched in a wide arc which followed the coast from the verge of the tropics to the saltbush country near Port Augusta in South Australia. That arc of sheep land was perhaps 1400 miles long and, at the broadest point, about 250 miles wide. It is doubtful whether any man made the journey around that arc, all the way from Bundaberg to Port Augusta, during the early pastoral period: there was no reason for making such a journey. If a horseman, however, had ridden through the centre of the sheep lands in 1850 he could have ridden virtually the entire distance without opening a gate. Near the homesteads one or two paddocks were fenced in order to keep in the horses or working bullocks or to protect a small crop of wheat or oaten hay; but those fences enclosed small patches of ground.

On the other side of Bass Strait was another expanse of sheep lands, settled earlier and now subdivided by fences or the neat hedges of hawthorn and boxthorn. People travelling from the Tamar estuary in the north to the Derwent in the south could halt almost anywhere along the road on a frosty morning and hear the sound of sheep across the stillness.

In the largest ports the smell of wool was unavoidable: and from Hobart to Brisbane the tall warehouses gave off the sweetish smell of wool long after the season's clip had been shipped away to the auction rooms in London. Some of that wool eventually returned in the shape of woollen overcoats, blankets, scarves, socks or as skeins of knitting wool, for Australia was still primarily a producer of raw materials and an importer of manufactured goods. Australia's wool had to circle the globe in order to move from the backs of its sheep to the backs of its people.

Far more people in England than in Australia earned their living from handling Australian wool. In the cold mill-towns of northern England tens of thousands of families lived by sorting, washing, dyeing, spinning and weaving Australian wool. It might well have been true in 1850 that the total wage-earners in all occupations in Australia were fewer than the English people whose living came solely from handling Australian wool. To produce the wool in Australia required little labour, and much of that labour was leisurely. To process that wool in Huddersfield, Bradford and other English mill-towns required intense labour. A shepherd dozing under a tree on an Australian plain and a weaver working in a noisy English woollen mill depended on each other. By 1850 more than half of the wool shipped into England came from Australia, and Melbourne and Sydney dwarfed the wool trade of such famous wool ports as Hamburg and Bremen in Germany and Odessa in the south of Russia. If Australia in 1850 was not already the largest producer of wool in the world, it was about to become so.

The rapid rise of the pastoral industry involved not only the shipment of wool across the world. The increase of sheep and cattle also enabled the average Australian to eat more meat each week than any people in Europe. There was still no profitable way of shipping meat to the markets of Europe. To ship fat cattle was too dear – they would have eaten their heads off in the long voyage. Preserved meat was not tasty when exported in tins or barrels from Sydney to London. The first ship did not carry refrigerated meat to Europe until 1880.

The sheep were skinny and light-fleeced compared to their descendants but they were changing the face of the country. The annual wool clip had become the main source of the country's prosperity. Wool was leading to the amassing of large fortunes in a few hands. The sheep were undermining the convict system. They were opening the interior and preparing the way for the discovery of gold just beneath the soil where they grazed. They were also the spearhead of the invasion of Aboriginal territories and of the increasing tension wherever the shepherds and Aboriginals met.

5   White Ghosts Ride By

Australia in 1820 was still the land of the Aboriginals. British and French names had been given to many capes, straits and bays on the Australian coast, but the Aboriginals knew nothing of such names and continued to use the traditional names. The new European names on the coast were scarcely more relevant than if the Australian Aboriginals had chanced to give their own names to English and French rivers. They were names on a map, not names on the tongue. Nearly everywhere Aboriginal life in 1820 went on as if nothing had happened at Botany Bay. More than nine of every ten Aboriginals had not seen a white man. They probably did not know that such a creature existed.

2

The Aboriginals had lived in the continent for at least forty thousand years. The long span of their history made remote events in English history – the Battle of Hastings or the Roman invasion – seem like the events of yesterday. The Aboriginals' ancestors had arrived when the level of the sea was lower, and Tasmania and Australia and New Guinea formed the one land mass; and they had lived through that slow rising of the seas which created Bass Strait and Torres Strait and cut Australia from the outside world. Perhaps 300,000 Aboriginals lived in Australia and perhaps 7000 lived in Tasmania on the eve of the British invasion. Their way of life was nomadic and they usually did not camp long on the one site; and so they had few possessions, no pottery and iron and bronze, no large houses and no tall monuments.

They lived on a wide variety of roots, greens, seeds, nuts, berries and other vegetables and fruits as well as meat and fish. Their diet in 1800 was probably more diverse than that of the London rich, but they hoarded virtually nothing for a hungry day. By skilfully moving in small groups from place to place and using their knowledge of botany and zoology they usually lived in relative plenty, so long as the population in each region remained low. Their medicines were mainly herbal and psychological; their food-finding tools and hunting and fishing implements were simple but were supplemented by physical dexterity, a minute knowledge of the seasonal ways of plants and animals, and the ability to observe with eyes, ears and nose. They could not read a book but they read nature superbly. They could not write but they were fluent linguists. Australia had perhaps six hundred different languages and dialects. The people on the north shore of Sydney Harbour spoke a different language from that spoken on the south shore: they still do.

The continent was divided into hundreds of tribal areas, and each tribe spoke its own language or dialect, tended to follow its own religious beliefs and ceremonies and customs, inhabited its own territory, and usually married within that territory. A very populous tribe might consist of two thousand people, but they would probably not all meet in the one place even once in the course of a century. Only a miracle could have provided so many people with three or four successive meals on the one site, for they had no granaries, no gardens and orchards, no hoards of smoked meat and fish, and no domesticated animals except the dingo. When the fleet from England was anchored in Sydney Harbour for a few months in 1788, and about 1400 white people were living close together in ships and the shore camps, that probably formed a far larger crowd of people than the local Aboriginals had ever seen. Perhaps the typical Australian tribe held about 500 people, who normally were scattered in small groups over the tribal territory. The group dominated their existence and commanded their loyalties.

In the deserts the tribal territories were huge, but in fertile lands they were often the size of our rural shires. If an Aboriginal had walked from the present site of Adelaide to Melbourne he might have passed through twelve different tribal lands, of which the largest lay in the Ninety-Mile Desert. He was unlikely, however, to make such a long journey: there was no reason for it and probably some danger in it. Understandably the long voyages made by the settlers to the other side of the world did not easily make sense to Aboriginals.

3

For tribes living by the sea the first sight of Europe was the ships which sailed by mysteriously with livestock or supplies for the new ports. In South Australia the Aboriginals near Rivoli Bay saw their first ship about fourteen years before any settler came overland with sheep and cattle. The small vessel mesmerized them; they had seen nothing like it. As they used no sails in their own bark canoes, the purpose of the tall masts was incomprehensible. Years later a Scottish woman, befriending them, recorded their memories of that first intruding deep-sea ship: 'Some of them thought it was a drifting island and all who saw it became alarmed and began to think of a hiding place.' Mothers carrying babies hid themselves away. Others stood in fear and watched that drifting island on which bare trees stood staight. Later they called sailing ships *oorincarto*, their word for a big house.

When Aboriginals first saw white people, the white skin often puzzled them. They were also puzzled by the clothing, because the British explorers who went into the bush were clothed heavily. The white bushman, we forget, wore hats and many wore veils to keep off flies and dust. The sleeves of their shirts were not usually rolled up to expose forearm and wrist. They always wore long trousers and many wore leggings or high boots. Accordingly the naked Aboriginals could see only the white face and the white hands of the

64

visitors. Perhaps at first they thought the visitors were black men who had completely painted their exposed flesh, in the Aboriginal style, with white pipeclay.

A young Englishman travelling in Sturt's expedition to central Australia records how, at a waterhole on a hot evening of February 1845, the Aboriginals were surprised to discover that the leg of his trousers covered a white ankle. He then allowed them to unlace his boot and to take off his sock. The white foot was fascinating and even perplexing. The first wish of some Aboriginals who saw white men for the first time was to blacken the white faces. When the French expedition visited the eastern coast of Tasmania in 1802, an Aboriginal woman produced a piece of charcoal from a woven rush-bag, crushed it in her hands, and painted the faces of two Frenchmen in a manner which suggested that black was beautiful.

Aboriginals tried to explain to each other the origins of these white-skinned intruders. Inevitably they looked to the past, because when they were puzzled they appealed to history perhaps as much as the Englishmen appealed to history. Whereas Englishmen tended to see the Aboriginals as relics of an early stage in the history of mankind, many Aboriginals who first saw white-skinned men were inclined to greet them as the returning spirits of their own dead relatives. In Victoria the Jajowurrong tribe of the Loddon Valley actually chose, to describe a white man, the same word which they had traditionally used to designate a spirit which had been released from the body by death. Since many of the white settlers had come across the sea from Tasmania, these Victorian Aboriginals quickly deduced that Tasmania must be the land to which the spirit of the Aboriginals flew after death.

In thinking that the white men were the reborn spirits of their own folk, Aboriginals were building on their knowledge that a white skin was appropriate for birth or rebirth. Nearly all their own babies had cream or white skin at birth. It was therefore logical that one of their resurrected ancestors should appear in a white skin.

The explorer George Grey was travelling north of Perth

in 1837 when to his astonishment an old black woman, ugly and filthy, fell upon him. With tears trickling down her cheeks, she hugged him and rested her head on his chest. Deliberately she kissed him on each cheek. 'Yes, yes, in truth it is him,' she said. She was convinced that Grey was the ghost of her son who had died from a spear wound. In turn the sister, brothers, and father of the dead Aboriginal embraced Grey with every sign of recognition, welcoming him back from the dead. Grey remarked in his journal that he lacked the heart to disillusion these people and to wipe away their joy. He also noticed that other members of his party were assumed to be dead Aboriginal warriors who, killed in battle, had returned to their ancestral land. He offered a persuasive reason why Aboriginals should have held this belief. He argued that Aboriginals could not conceive of themselves leaving their own tribal lands and therefore they could not comprehend that the English would leave their homeland in order to settle in Australia. So, 'when they see white people suddenly appear in their country, and settling themselves down in particular spots, they imagine that they must have formed an attachment for this land in some other state of existence'. There was possibly another reason for the Aboriginals' belief. The white people who arrived first were almost invariably men and they were usually of fighting age. Accordingly it was easy to imagine that they were the returning spirits of Aboriginals who had been killed while fighting.

As the first Englishmen to enter the tribal lands frequently brought valuable gifts to the Aboriginals, the idea that they were kinsmen seemed sensible. Who but a kinsman would leave such gifts? A few Aboriginals continued to cling to the idea that certain white people were their own blood-relatives long after relations between the two races had ceased to be idyllic. There are stories of Aboriginals, once a year or more, travelling long distances from the bush in order to greet and hug their white-faced relatives. Many tribes, however, had no belief that the white men were Aboriginals who had 'risen from the grave'.

The belief in reincarnation must have influenced many

of the first encounters, sometimes blunting the spears of the Aboriginals. Thus they neglected an opportunity to defend their lands at the very time when their knowledge of their own terrain and the opportunity to use surprise were their strongest defensive weapons. But the benefits of the faith in reincarnation did not all settle on the white men. If they were welcomed as the returning spirits of a certain tribe, and if the word – the fantastic word – spread to an enemy tribe, the white men would not have been welcomed in the territory of the tribal enemy. Some of the surprise attacks on English exploring expeditions possibly stemmed from a belief that the Englishmen were the spirits of warriors from hostile, not friendly, tribes.

In certain regions the white men ceased to be hailed as returning ghosts. Their arrival instead was interpreted as a portent of natural disasters. As many districts in south-eastern Australia were first settled by flocks and herds on the eve of the drought of the late 1830s, was the drought itself the result of the coming of white men? Lake Burrumbeet, a wide stretch of water by the present Melbourne-Adelaide highway, was virtually dry from 1839 to 1841, and such dryness was probably unprecedented in the memory of the local Aboriginals. The drought was blamed on the invaders: 'when the white people come the water goes away,' they said.

4

Many Aboriginals were dumbfounded when they first saw the animals which came with explorers. A man riding a horse was not at once comprehended, when seen from a distance. Was this a man mounted on a beast or was it a beast with two heads, one in the front and one on top? As no Aboriginals had heard of a riding animal they were tempted to conclude that the man and horse shared the same body. Joseph Hawdon, pioneering a westwards stock route to Adelaide in 1838, was riding near the lower stretches of the Goulburn River when he suddenly came into the view of two old Aboriginals who were netting for fish. The two people 'stood perfectly petrified', wrote

67

Hawdon, 'gazing on our horses in blank astonishment'. Again and again explorers, in places as far apart as the Darling River and the coast of north-western Australia, recorded the dread with which Aboriginals viewed horsemen for the first time.

The combination of horse and armed rider was to prove deadly in the intermittent warfare between white and black, especially on the open plains. A few inland Aboriginals had probably been warned what to expect by coastal tribes who told of the magical alliance of armed men and horse. The surprise or shock when a horseman came into sight stemmed perhaps as much from the mystique of the rider's firearms as from the hooves, mane and long legs of the horse or from the towering height of the rider. An armed horseman must have been, to many Aboriginals, as terrifying a symbol as it was to the Mexicans whom the Spanish horsemen conquered.

A herd of cattle or the meek straggling sheep aroused less concern. The puzzle, for Aboriginals, was the relationship between the animals and the Europeans. As Aboriginals kept no herds they wondered why the animals and the white men kept so close together and why they so often travelled together. Aboriginals in tropical Australia, seeing the livestock travelling with the explorer Leichhardt, thought the bullocks were the white men's women-folk. The horses were seen as large dogs. Joseph Hawdon, during his droving expedition down the Murray Valley, met groups of Aboriginals who greeted the cattle as if they were rational creatures possessing a close kinship to their owners. At one place he observed four or five Aboriginals waving green boughs – tokens of peace – at the moving cattle and even greeting the cattle with the same friendly phrase they addressed to the stockmen: 'Bo, Bo, Marwood.' At the junction of the Murray and Darling an old spear-carrying man came to Hawdon in some puzzlement and, pointing to the heifers, enquired whether they were the wives of the men. This enquiry was perhaps understandable: the first Englishmen who went inland were rarely accompanied by women. Hawdon and his friend laughed loudly at what they called the old man's 'ridiculous blunder'. Aboriginals, in their turn, must have laughed at the blunders of these strangers.

The wheels of the slow-moving drays were another puzzle. Aboriginals would crowd around a dray and crouch down to inspect a wheel, touching it, pushing it, chattering about it, for the wheel was unknown in Australia or the Americas until the Europeans arrived. England's technology, its gadgets and its useful objects, often entranced Aboriginals. They felt the texture of the blankets which overlanders carried into the outback; they were astonished at the tinderbox which quickly produced fire; they were enthralled by the sound of a flute or violin played at night in a bush camp. When one overlander showed about fifty Aboriginals his pocket watch and a few personal trinkets, 'they raised a loud shout of amazement', and the shout was swelled by many Aboriginals who could not see from the back of the crowd but caught the infectious air of wonderment. The regular ticking of the watch was, perhaps more than any other manufactured object, the symbol of the difference between the faraway world of the invaders and the land which they were infiltrating. The English way of life early in the 19th century was increasingly enchained by the clock and by the industrial and agricultural discipline of regular work. This 'monotonous' discipline was as puzzling to Aboriginals as their own seasonal wanderings were puzzling to English observers.

While most of the English possessions which Aboriginals saw were merely items of wonder or amusement, a few were grafted quickly on to tribal life in the few years of it which remained. Iron articles were prized the most. An iron knife, iron tomahawk, iron bolt, iron bar, a stirrup iron and even a metallic pin or button were so valued for their cutting edges that they were pilfered with skill from the night camps of bushmen. When a pistol or double-barrelled gun in a camp was stolen by a light-fingered Aboriginal, the iron fittings were valued more than the complete weapon. As the iron could shape wood and bone more quickly than the traditional stone instruments, many Aboriginals who were given an iron tomahawk or a discarded piece of iron would leap up in delight. Occasionally the second explorer to reach the remote interior would find, still used regularly, the pieces of iron which had been received from the first explorer in that region many years previously. In October 1844, west of the Darling River, Charles Sturt's party noticed to their surprise that several Aboriginals were carrying worn-down tomahawks – 'worn to the very eye' – which must have come from Major Mitchell's expedition years earlier. One Aboriginal carried, fastened to a wooden handle, an iron blade which he had patiently made from a small strip of iron that had been scavenged from the rim of a dray wheel. Its cutting edge, thanks to the skill of this primitive blacksmith, was sharper than the edge of the tomahawk. Major Mitchell, while exploring in central Victoria in 1836, had himself seen how quickly the iron could reach remote nomadic camps. North of Mount Macedon in what he called a wild region still remote 'from civilized man's dominion', one of his men found an iron cut-throat razor. On the blade Mitchell read the inscribed trademark, 'Old English'.

So the newcomers were both enemies and friends, the carriers of the wanted and the unwanted. They were the bringers of iron and thus the importers of that labour-saving technology which at first was welcomed by Aboriginals in the belief that it would ease their daily chores. They were also the bringers of firearms.

The Europeans' most powerful articles, the most inexplicable, were their muskets and pistols. In the eyes of Aboriginals these weapons must have appeared harmless when held in the hand; if they were throwing weapons, a kind of European spear or boomerang, they did not appear to be very dangerous. If, on the other hand, the firearms were really clubs and waddies then they were no more to be feared than the Aboriginals own wooden clubs. The Aboriginals did not know that a firearm was really a woomera, a launching instrument which propelled a weapon or bullet that wounded. Such an idea was not easily grasped because the lead bullets were invisible in flight and seemed too tiny to hurt. The noise of the firearm was its clearest characteristic, and that noise certainly imprinted itself in the minds of the Aboriginals who heard a musket discharged for the first time.

Dick Roughsey, one of the first Aboriginals to write a book about his people, could recount his own father's recollections of the coming of Europeans to a small island in the Gulf of Carpentaria. When the dark islanders saw the oncoming ship with its sails shaped like great sea shells, gliding along without even the splash of hand-held paddles, they ran to shelter themselves in the scrub on an overlooking hill. There 'all our poor naked people' hid in fright because they had heard from other tribes that white men could create a thunder which launched invisible spears. Increasingly, reports and rumours of the white people preceded their arrival.

There must have been thousands of such encounters in which groups of Englishmen and Aboriginals faced each other for the first time, but we possess only scattered clues and fragments with which to glue together the feelings of the Aboriginals. We have only broken glimpses of their jubilation and terror, their wonder and anger, at contacts which would mark the start of their surrender to an invasion that was directed not by a powerful military commander but more by the halfpenny fluctuations in the price of wool on the other side of the world, or by the results of the lambing season several hundred miles away.

6   War on the Grasslands

The British government, in sending the First Fleet to Australia, had intended to occupy only one or two points on the Pacific coast. They hoped that the marines and convicts would live side by side with Aboriginals in vague harmony. As the Aboriginals were a roaming people it was assumed that the British settlement would not interfere with their life. Moreover there seemed an eternity of space in which the two peoples could follow their own separate existence.

2

Once the wool industry boomed, and the inland pastures became a prize, race relations became infinitely more confused and hazardous. As the white settlers moved inland, and leap-frogged along the coast, the contacts with the Aboriginals were multiplied. The government could not police adequately the conduct of those settlers who moved with flocks and herds far beyond the beat of military sentries and constables.

On the open grasslands to the west of the Blue Mountains the conflict exploded in the mid-1820s. The sheep-owners and the Aboriginals were competing for the same grasslands, and neither was willing to retreat. Aboriginals – without wishing offence – killed sheep and cattle and set fire to the grass. British settlers – without wishing offence – killed kangaroos and possums, the meat supply of the Aboriginals. The livestock grazed especially in the fertile valleys where the Aboriginals for countless centuries had gathered plantfoods and fished. The shepherds sometimes chanced to build their hut or gather their flock at night on sacred Aboriginal sites and treated many Aboriginals who tried to visit those sites as intruders and sheep thieves. Nearly all the white invaders were men, and many took Aboriginal women, sometimes by friendly negotiation and barter and sometimes by force. The Aboriginals acquired a taste for flour and sugar, and broke into the isolated huts and homesteads of the sheep-owners and shepherds and stole food. These foods were delicious to tribes whose only sugar previously had come from the mean hives of native bees and whose only flour was a rough wholemeal speckled with grit and sand gathered during the stone-grinding of wild grains.

On the plains around Bathurst the bloodshed was averted for about eight years. Steadily the white settlers multiplied, and their livestock and fences interfered more with the Aboriginal food-gathering. Episodes of violence were reported. In May 1824, in the space of two days, seven whites were killed. More Aboriginals were shot. In August the government declared martial law in the district, and the law prevailed for four months. In one battle in the vicinity of Mudgee sixteen Aboriginal men were killed. The invaders and their flocks and herds slowly took control of the district. The warfare moved further out, following the sheep.

In Tasmania, as the sheep moved inland, the way of life of the crinkly-haired Tasmanian Aboriginals was disrupted. Today we often look on Aboriginals as gentle, passive and powerless people and in some ways this is so, but they were also capable of terrorizing settlers. In Tasmania in the 1820s they gained ascendancy in many valleys and waged guerilla warfare against isolated shepherds and stock-keepers. They lived off the land, travelled lightly and swiftly, and attacked suddenly. As most shepherds lived in lonely huts they were vulnerable to sudden attack. Moreover being convicts they were not usually provided with firearms. The Aboriginals often crept close to a hut at night and set fire to the thatched roof. The unarmed shepherd was a simple target for spears as he ran from the blaze. The Aboriginals were more wary of attacking the larger houses, for they knew that the occupiers were armed.

The uniformed British soldiers could do little. They could not be everywhere at once; and when they were conspicuously protecting one sheep station the Aboriginals filed quietly through the bush to an unprotected station. Private expeditions of revenge and attack were launched against the Aboriginals. Near the Norfolk Plains the stockmen mounted horses and chased Aboriginals and shot them down. A wild bushman named Douglas Ibbens conducted his own war against the eastern tribe and killed many, it was said, by creeping up and 'firing amongst them with his double-barrelled gun'. The double-barrel was then a luxury and would have cost as much as three years' savings for a frugal freeman shepherd.

The guerilla war went on. The wool industry in the outer districts was endangered by the attacks of the Tasmanians. In the spring of 1830 the government acted decisively. It planned the largest military operation to be seen in Australia in the 19th century. It marshalled one sixth of the men in the island in the hope of capturing all the surviving Aboriginals in eastern Tasmania and conveying them then to a secure place where they could be raised in 'the scale of civilization' and rescued at last from 'the miseries of perpetual warfare'. Gathering together about 3000 settlers, including 550 troops and 738 convicts, the governor posted them along a line running from Deloraine near the north coast to Campbelltown in the midlands and so to St Mary's near the east coast. To feed this army, mounds of provisions arrived in drays and packhorses. A quartermaster's store was set up at the town of Oatlands with a reserve of firearms, handcuffs and 30,000 cartridges. There were more handcuffs than Aboriginals at large!

The movements of the long line of men were planned with military precision, or as much precision as rugged bush would allow. And so the line stretching for 120 miles – every man in sight of another on both sides – began to walk slowly southwards, in the hope of driving all Aboriginals into an isolated peninsula in the south east. At night the advancing

The Aboriginals had a hundred uses for fire. Here, Darby Djambid-jimba, of Yuendumu in the Northern Territory, makes fire by rubbing softwood against his hardwood spear-thrower, thus setting alight the tinder of dry grass.   *Robert Edwards*

Aboriginals with hunting spears in central Australia.   *Australian News Information*

line was halted, bugles were blown, supplies were drawn from the haversacks, and cooking fires and sentry fires were lit. Throughout the night the sentries marched to and fro in the hope of preventing Aboriginals from slipping past the guarded line. Bonfires were lit in dark patches so that any escaping Aboriginal might be detected. Night after night the precautions were followed; day after day the line advanced southwards, across sheep-runs, through shallow streams, and over timbered ridges and mountains. After seven weeks a frayed human net was drawn tight to reveal only two captives – a grown man and a boy of 15. In the last stage of the operation another two had been shot. The remainder had escaped.

The Tasmanian remainder was now a sad remnant. In 1830 perhaps only 300 Tasmanian Aboriginals survived. Disease had killed most of them but warfare and private violence had also been devastating. This distinctive people had inhabited Tasmania for at least five hundred generations. Then in the space of barely one generation it had virtually been extinguished.

When the pastoralists swept across Victoria in the second half of the 1830s those who had come from Tasmania wondered whether they would see again the terrifying guerilla warfare. In Victoria, however, the Aboriginals in no district held the initiative for long. The balance of power had swung strongly to the invaders. The double-barrelled gun was now more common, and more of the invaders in Victoria were armed; as fewer Victorian shepherds and hutkeepers were convicts, they could carry a gun. Above all, in most parts of Victoria the lie of the land was less suited to that kind of guerilla war which the Aboriginals conducted skilfully. Victoria had vast areas of lightly timbered plains which gave an advantage to a horseman in pursuit, whereas in Tasmania so many of the outer sheep stations were on the edge of mountains or timbered tracts in which the Aboriginals could move or hide with ease. Victoria was forced to organize no long march against the Aboriginals.

Across the countryside Aboriginals were killed in isolated episodes, or were killed in small-scale battles. In Western

Australia in October 1834 the governor, Sir James Stirling, led a band of armed men in search of Aboriginals who had taken life and property. In the 'Battle of Pinjarra' that followed at least fourteen Aboriginals and perhaps even double that number were killed. At the cattle station of Myall Creek near Muswellbrook in New South Wales in June 1838 at least twenty-two Aboriginals were roped together and driven to an isolated place and executed. The episode became notorious less because of the Aboriginals murdered than because of the seven white murderers who where brought to trial and hanged. That sentence, and the shockwaves which it initiated, was not a deterrent to all pastoral people. Six years later, on Bolivia station in the New England District, a flock of wethers returned to their nightly fold without their shepherd. A search was made, and in a river was found the speared, tomahawked, naked corpse of the shepherd. Armed men set out in pursuit, found a tribe which they believed had thrown the spears, and shot some members and threw others over the precipice at Bluff Rock. On the rocks far below lay the dead and the crippled. 'None of that tribe', said one informant, 'was seen on that station after that.' So the ruthless lessons were taught.

On the coast of South Australia in the winter of 1840 the ship *Maria*, sailing from Adelaide towards Hobart, was wrecked and her crew of ten and her sixteen passengers reached the shore. For a time they were cared for by the Milmenrura Aboriginals. Then all the white people – except for a small girl – were murdered. A year later in South Australia more than thirty of the Rufus River tribe were murdered by a large avenging expedition commanded by the Protector of Aboriginals: an enquiry was held and the episode condoned. In 1840, several hundred miles to the south east, Aboriginals stole a small flock of sheep from squatters who had arrived at the Glenelg River, just outside the South Australian border. Seven white men set out on horseback and found the Aboriginals and sheep near a clump of scrub at a place which henceforth was known as the Fighting Hills. The fighting there was

76

one-sided. Of the fifty-two Aboriginals all but one were shot. And long after, confided a Scottish squatter of the district, 'the bones of the men and sheep lay mingled together bleaching in the sun at the Fighting Hills'. He added the Old Testament comment that those neighbours who maltreated the Aboriginals did not prosper: 'It seems strange none have done any good who were murderers of these poor creatures.' He offered no further details. 'I will here change the subject, for it is too painful to dwell on.'* Across the world many families living in the safety of a Bristol or Berlin house and sleeping each night beneath blankets of Australian wool did not know the bloodshed which had accompanied the raising of part of that wool.

Many murders were more the result of misunderstandings, of imaginary offences, of blind terror and error. The lack of a common language and common social customs increased the chance that acts of goodwill could be misinterpreted. We hear of shepherds who seem to have treated Aboriginals generously, but were suddenly speared or clubbed and their sheep driven away. There must also have been Aboriginals who brought gifts to Europeans, perhaps even the gift of a woman, and then were – inexplicably in the eyes of their friends – shot through the skull by an ex-convict shepherd or hutkeeper. Again and again innocents were slaughtered. It may well be that along the pastoral frontiers of south-eastern Australia three of every four victims were shot or speared or brained in seeming punishment or retaliation for earlier incidents in which they were innocent. This was the tragedy of the warfare which slowly rolled from the beaches to the sandy deserts. Like the fighting in northern Ireland in the mid-1970s many targets of violence were haphazard symbols of the enemy.

In some districts no fighting is known to have occurred;

*The Macassarmen who came annually from Indonesia to fish for trepang in northern Australia were also in violent incidents with Aboriginals. About 1850, it is reported, twenty Macassarmen and two Aboriginals were killed in one episode.

the wide Monaro district of southern New South Wales seems to have been occupied peacefully. In scores of large squatting stations the relations with Aboriginals were uneasily peaceful or even harmonious. The surviving knowledge of the Aboriginals' habits and beliefs and language in many places comes from sympathetic squatters who did everything to befriend and help the Aboriginals, feeding and caring for all who camped near the main homestead.

3

During the gold-rushes of the 1850s, the entry of the pastoralists into new territory virtually ceased. Through the scarcity of reliable labour, they could barely work the established sheep and cattle stations, let alone set up new ones. On this halted pastoral frontier the most northerly outposts were in central Queensland, and they were exposed to Aboriginals' attacks, for they lacked enough men to watch the sheep adequately, and the rugged timbered terrain was suited to guerilla warfare. Near the Fitzroy and Dawson Rivers, the scrub and broken land formed continuous belts along which Aboriginals could travel for days without being seen. When troopers entered the scrub in pursuit, they had little chance of surprising Aboriginals. Even at night the Aboriginals' camp-fires on the banks of the lagoons were hidden by surrounding scrub. 'You go into the scrub, the blacks are all around you, and you can see nothing of them,' said one settler.

In central Queensland the fighting was often more organized than in Victoria. Aboriginals came together in numbers such as were not seen in any Victorian raid: possibly the Queensland Aboriginals were less affected by sickness and disease, and possibly their tribal numbers were larger. Likewise the government of New South Wales, which still ruled Queensland, trained native troopers. Hundreds of Aboriginals in Queensland, it is likely, were killed by uniformed and mounted Aboriginals.

A camp for native police was set up at the Rannes pastoral

station, on a tributary of the Dawson River, about 50 miles
to the south of the present Rockhampton. Despite their
presence the troubles continued: Aboriginals were shot,
shepherds killed, sheep stolen, and the supply drays raided.
On 13 December 1854 Sub-Lieutenant Robert Walker,
accompanied by three native troopers and an Aboriginal
woman, was riding about 14 miles to the south west of
Rannes when he saw that the track was blocked by about 200
men with spears. The Aboriginals stood in the shape of a
semi-circle, the men two rows deep, and urged the troopers
to come forward and fight. As Walker's account alone
survives, we can't be sure which party launched the first
weapon, but two Aboriginals were killed and the others
retreated, leaving behind sufficient weapons to form a large
pile. That night the Aboriginals quietly tracked down
Walker and his troopers and in the darkness of 2 a.m.
attacked them with yells and spears. Walker's men replied
with their pistols and carbines. Later, rounding up their
horses, they pursued the Aboriginals and killed at least
seven. Only the tiredness of their horses and a scarcity of
cartridges made the troopers give up the pursuit.

At the police camp at Rannes on the night of 23
September 1855 the local Aboriginals launched an attack
which obviously had been planned with care. While the
native police slept, their carbines and pistols were quietly
taken away. Many Aboriginals, waiting in nearby scrub,
rushed on the police. Two troopers were speared to death, a
third died later from a spear-wound in the lungs, and the
other four troopers were wounded. The aim of the attack
was probably to drive the pastoral industry from the
district. Certainly it dislocated that industry.

Three months later, about 70 miles east of Rannes, the
sheep station at Mt Larcom was the target. There, three
white men and one white woman were attacked by perhaps
fifty Aboriginals, and killed with spears and nulla-nullas.
The body of the woman, it was alleged, was violated after
she had died. One Aboriginal employee of the station, Peter
Blackboy, was also killed. The attackers took away sheep,
flour, sugar, cloth and various oddments such as books,

handkerchiefs, tobacco, pipes and the marriage certificate of the murdered woman. We know details of the raid but lack details of the retaliation, except that at least eleven Aboriginals were killed while others hid safely, their hearts thumping, in the salt-water creeks near the Fitzroy River. The arithmetic of the fighting frontier was a life for a life, usually with compound interest.

In the pastoral settlements along the coast many white people and black people must have wondered in 1855 whether they would live to see the new year. At the tiny port of Maryborough, the attacks by Aboriginals were so consistent that some white men returned in the steamship to the safety of Sydney. In the township there were unfinished buildings, because the sawyers were frightened to enter the scrub to saw timber. At the end of 1855 the Commissioner of Crown Lands at Maryborough made a long list of murders and robberies which he believed Aboriginals had recently committed. The reported episodes of one fortnight ran thus:

November   25—flour stolen from a dray
            26—two bullocks speared
            27—man speared
               two men beaten, ill-used and robbed
            28—man beaten and robbed
December   2—dray robbed
            5—two men murdered and robbed
            6—man robbed and 'nearly murdered'
            7—store broken into and robbed
            8—robbery from house and garden

More attacks were to come. Early in 1856 Captain Knight was standing on the deck of his steamer *Waratah*, alongside the wharf in Maryborough, when a spear was thrown at him.

On the Upper Dawson River the head stations of Eurombah and Hornet Bank lay ten miles apart, on the very edge of European civilization. Here the Aboriginals were not yet defeated. In their eagerness to fight for their lost lands they were as courageous as the white people defending those new-won lands. At Eurombah, about

November 1856, a German-born shepherd named Andrew Volk died after his head was struck by a tomahawk. Eventually the native troopers learned of the killing, set off in pursuit, and killed or wounded eight Aboriginals. Killed or wounded? The distinction is wide, but a failure to distinguish between the living and dead is a characteristic of many of the hasty reports of this warfare. Fearing a counter-attack, the victors rarely waited around the battlefield in order to count the score.

Aboriginals renewed their attack on Eurombah. In the spring of 1857 they killed six whites. Just ten miles away, with nothing in between, the sheep station of Hornet Bank was equally vulnerable to the sudden raids of the dispossessed Aboriginals. On Hornet Bank, by a shaded billabong, lived Mrs Fraser, a widow aged 43, and her daughters and sons. The daughters ranged in age from Elizabeth, 19, to Charlotte, three. With the younger boys, they were given tuition by a private tutor who lived on the property. When Aboriginals in June 1857 made an attack on Hornet Bank station and failed, that should have been warning for the women at least to retreat south to a safer place. The mother, however, seemed determined to stay, hoping to keep the family together and realizing too that her sons were too inexperienced to be left on their own.

Hearsay evidence suggests that the older Fraser boys were in the habit of taking young women from the Aboriginals' camps nearby and that they also allowed their own Aboriginal employees to raid those camps, giving them tacit protection. It also seems that an overseer of the sheep station had shot an Aboriginal who, he believed erroneously, had stolen food. These grievances possibly increased the Aboriginals' determination to recapture those lands where their ancestors had roamed for generations. Perhaps a hundred Aboriginals prepared to attack, but this was no more massive than many others launched in central Queensland.

On the moonlight night of 26-27 October 1857 the Fraser household was asleep. In the space of a few minutes Mrs Fraser and seven of her children were killed: three of them,

81

it appears, were also sexually violated. Near the homestead three other white men – the tutor and a hutkeeper and shepherd – were murdered. While eleven in all were killed, two of the Fraser sons survived. The oldest, aged 23, was far away in Ipswich buying supplies for the station. Another son, dazed by the waddy blows on the head, crept under a bed and lay there until the slaughter was finished. When daylight broke he began to walk to the nearest source of help, arriving there exhausted at eleven in the evening.

Far to the south, in Sydney and Melbourne, these episodes on the Queensland frontier seemed to belong to another world. The fights and skirmishes between rifles and spears lacked the pageantry and continuity of formal war. These setbacks to the slow pastoral flow which for the first time was about to cross into tropical Australia, seemed less important than those military setbacks occurring to the British forces in India at the same time. Even in Australia, 1857 was remembered more as the year of the Indian mutiny. When the slow mail steamships reached Australia in 1857 with the first news of the massacre at Cawnpore, the sensation in the mind of the public made the news of the massacre at Hornet Bay seem puny.

At the end of the 1850s, the cavalcade of bullock drays and flocks began to move at snail's pace into new tribal lands, for the price of wool was still high in London, and the cost of hiring shepherds and carters was no longer so dear as the gold excitement waned. Horatio Spencer Wills was one experienced sheep-owner who moved into the new lands just across the Tropic of Capricorn. The son of an English convict transported for life for highway robbery, Horatio Wills at the age of 20 had become the editor, printer and publisher of the Sydney weekly journal, the *Currency Lad*. Its motto was 'Rise Australia', and Wills was one of those young Australians who quickly rose. In the summer of 1839-40 he travelled overland to Victoria with 5000 sheep and 500 cattle and settled west of Ararat, a squatter on the large scale, living in style and sending one of his sons to England to study at the Rugby School which under Dr Arnold had recently become celebrated. In the legislative assembly of Victoria in 1856, Wills was one of the few Australian-born members, and was proud to sit in that parliament which in the eyes of many of its members symbolized the fulfilment of that motto, 'Rise Australia'. In 1858 Wills made the long journey to Europe to place three of his sons in a school in Germany, and when he returned he set his heart on occupying a great estate in central Queensland. In January 1861, with his son Thomas, who had returned from Rugby School and was now one of Victoria's finest cricketers and footballers, he sailed from Geelong to Brisbane. Making the long trek north with bullock wagons and drays the Wills expedition acquired a nucleus of more than 10,000 sheep.

Wills set up his new sheep station on virgin land at Cullinlaringo, about 250 miles west of the port of Rockhampton. On the hot afternoon of 17 October 1861, during the siesta time at the new homestead and huts, the Aboriginals suddenly attacked the resting people. Horatio Spencer Wills was beaten to death and eighteen of his white employees were killed in one of the most devastating of all the Aboriginal victories. His son, Thomas, was saved, being two days along the track on the day of the massacre. He carried no grudge against the Aboriginals as a people and indeed was the main promoter of the fine team of Aboriginal cricketers which played at the Melbourne Cricket Ground on Boxing Day 1866 in a match billed as Australian Natives versus the World. Ten thousand spectators saw Wills play that day and significantly he played with the Natives.

4

On all the grasslands the Aboriginals had the advantage of numbers. They knew intimately their own terrain and they held the weapon of surprise. In most regions, however, their military assets were outweighed by weakness. At a time when Aboriginal alliances could have been a vital defence, the tribes rarely united. Tribal warfare went on during the invasion, and in some regions the white settlers were invited by Aboriginals to attack their tribal enemies or were applauded when they drove them away. In Australia, too, the white people were more united than on the newly settled lands of North America. There the rivalries between English and French increased the bargaining power of the American Indians, who were sought as allies and sometimes armed. But in Australia the Aboriginals were given firearms only when they were recruited as native police by the government.

In weapons the Aboriginals were usually inferior. Spears and nulla-nullas were no match for the firearms made in Birmingham and London. The superiority of firearms, however, was not overwhelming and at times might have been more psychological. At first the thunder of the muskets and the invisibility of their flying bullets were probably as decisive as their power to kill. Even in the year 1840 most firearms used in the outback were not accurate at a distance of fifty paces. After the shot was fired the firearm had to be reloaded, and that might have taken twenty or thirty seconds. During the slow ticking of the seconds in which the white man was reloading his gun, an Aboriginal could throw many spears at his still target and a few paddy-melon sticks as well. Gideon Lang, a squatter, recalled that even from seventy yards away the flying spears could be deadly. 'I have known one man to be pierced in the thigh by two spears successively, thrown at seventy yards off.' In surprise attacks the Aboriginals had the advantage, but in retreat they were vulnerable. The enemy alliance of horse and firearms was psychologically devastating, especially on the open plains. Those bush Aboriginals who, in a chase, managed to escape unwounded from the galloping thunder must have lain that night with the terrifying sounds still pounding in their mind.

If more Aboriginals had acquired firearms the pastoral expansion in Australia would have been much slower. Many Aboriginals quickly became accurate with a carbine, but few bush Aboriginals acquired guns. Unlike the American Indians, they had no furs or other valuable commodities which they could trade for firearms and ammunition. Occasionally they stole guns when they raided the huts and homesteads of the sheep-runs but they did not use them for long. Traditionally the Aboriginal men – even more than the women – travelled lightly, and a small bundle of spears was a lighter burden than a gun for men travelling through the bush. Aboriginals who chanced to obtain firearms did not care meticulously for them, did not clean them, and left them lying on sand and dirt. In the rains, moreover, they might forget to keep their gunpowder dry. Even those who had gained some experience with muskets were probably prone to accidents unless they were supervised with care. The native police in Queensland in the 1850s used only simple single-barrel carbines, and when the lock of the guns called for oiling or the guns called for close inspection, the white sergeants of police and not the Aboriginal troopers normally carried out the work.

Old Balyang, one of the few Aboriginals who remained on the plains between Geelong and Melbourne in the late 1840s, liked to hunt wild turkeys on the Werribee River, and on occasions he donated his catch to the police magistrate in Geelong. 'He was a particular friend of mine,' wrote the magistrate Foster Fyans. 'By some means he became possessed of an old musket, of which I on many occasions told him to be careful, or he would shoot himself.' When Fyans pointed out that he should use spears or boomerangs rather than the musket, Old Balyang simply laughed. One morning, leaving his mia-mia, his gun accidentally discharged, killing him.

5

Edged out of their own lands many Aboriginals attacked the invading sheep and cattle. Quickly they learned how to steal livestock in their hundreds. Even a riding horse on which they had first looked with awe was sometimes mounted and ridden without the aid of a lesson. In north-west Queensland a pastoralist was to lament in 1871 that 'they not only kill our cattle and destroy our stations with impunity, but they steal our horses to drive the cattle'. By then the Aboriginals had been mustering and droving – and slaughtering sheep and cattle by stealth – for a full generation in districts stretching for two thousand miles along the eastern plains and in countless humps and valleys of the Great Dividing Range. Squatters searching for lost sheep found them deliberately hidden in remote gullies and natural clearings in the bush, and even in yards built by Aboriginals from bush boughs. Near Wide Bay in Queensland in 1850 a settler searching for some four hundred stolen sheep tracked the flock over two mountains and through a strip of rain forest to the slopes of the next mountain where the Aboriginals were preparing to bridge a creek with logs. Some Aboriginals did not bother to drive away the settlers' animals. They simply speared them or broke their legs. One hundred sheep could be crippled in one raid. On cattle-runs the stockmen occasionally had to pull spears from the sides of cattle which were wounded but still walking. 'I recollect', wrote a Victorian squatter, 'a cow being brought into a stockyard stuck all over with spears, like a porcupine.'

By the 1840s, on pastoral stations as far apart as South Australia and southern Queensland, a few men were deliberately mixing poison with flour and handing the mixture as a gift to begging Aboriginals or leaving it temptingly for them to steal. Many sheep stations had begun to use strychnine – a new poison identified in Europe as recently as 1819 – to kill the dingoes which molested the sheep. 'I also wish you', wrote pastoralist Russell in 1848 to a Glasgow firm, 'to send me out about £20 worth of the poison called Strychnia: we have for some time past found it of great use in destroying the native dog.' A few found it even more useful in destroying the native people. In Queensland the best-known allegation of the poisoning of Aboriginals – at Kilcoy in 1842 – will always be associated with the name of the owner of the station. The owner was E. Mackenzie, and his name entered the tribal language as the word for strychnine.

Aboriginals died from a dose of Mackenzie. Others died from the tasteless white oxide of arsenic, which made a burning pain in the stomach and started convulsive tremors. Some Aboriginals, once they suspected that their food had been poisoned, made themselves vomit and perhaps recovered, but others died the death of a baited dingo. Poison however cannot have been used frequently, and on several stations the poison was probably stolen by Aboriginals, carried away in blankets or packets, and eaten in ignorance.

6

No negotiations brought the fighters permanently together. In many regions both the invaders and defenders would have gained from the kind of treaty signed in other lands. In North America, from time to time, governments signed treaties which reserved land for the American Indians; in New Zealand in 1840 the Maoris' rights to lands were set out in grave legal language in the Treaty of Waitangi; and when in the 1880s the British and Australians were to enter Papua they generally respected the traditional land rights. In contrast, in Australia, any agreements became frayed even where the governors and local Aboriginals had originally negotiated in a spirit of good will.*

So many Aboriginal groups and so many Aboriginal languages existed that negotiations were hampered even when good will was present on both sides. The Aboriginals had no all-powerful chieftain who could take the lead in negotiating a peace. As the neighbouring tribes could not easily be brought together, let alone live in agreement, any peace treaty would cover only one or two of the numerous lands which formed each region. Nor could the Aboriginals understand at first that the white men they met were the subjects of a remote government across the sea. Aboriginals

---

*The Australian attitude to peace treaties with Aboriginals is illustrated in the best-known treaty, John Batman's private treaty with Aboriginals in 1835. Batman had privately arranged with Aboriginals a few miles from Melbourne, to occupy 600,000 acres in return for £200 of trade goods annually. This contract has traditionally been looked on with amusement or cynicism, being interpreted as a confidence man's trick to deprive any other pastoralists of that attractive estate. In fact, in a small way it recognized Aboriginal rights to the land.

knew only personal, face-to-face government. If they killed or drove away the first Europeans who had settled on their tribal land, they did not realize that reinforcements would come from far away. Nor could the Europeans understand that the Aboriginals, though not gardeners and not inclined to remain long in the one place in their traditional life, could love their own ancestral land so intensely that they could not conceive of parting with it. How could they sell their grasslands to sheep-owners when their land, in their eyes, was inalienable, having been presented to them for all time by their great ancestors. The pastoralists and their far-away government could not grasp this complicated fact of Aboriginal life: that land was a spiritual as well as a material possession and virtually unsaleable, no matter how happily the Aboriginals might smile their assent at the ceremony at which they were understood to be surrendering forever their ancestral lands. Eventually we will realize how delicate, and perhaps how insoluble, was the initial collision of two peoples who were far apart in customs, social organization, and perceptions.

It is now a fashion to see the Aboriginals as traditionally living in harmony, each tribe keeping to that home territory which it had held since time immemorial. If this view is correct it virtually compounds the terror and the dislocation which the coming of the British created in the Aboriginal country, for a land of ancient peace quickly became a rolling battlefield. Now this view may be incorrect. One cannot describe traditional Aboriginal society with certainty, but the evidence of strong tribal enmities is widespread. There is even evidence of Aboriginal tribes pushing out traditional holders of territory. The Konejandi people in the far north west, possessing a larger territory than the modern African nation of Gambia, lost their open plains but not their ranges to the neighbouring Walmadjari. The Koreng people, occupying part of the present wheat belt in Western Australia – indeed occupying more land than the present Northern Ireland – moved west under pressure from Aboriginal neighbours. In central Australia, in an arid tribal territory as large as Ceylon, the

Pitjantjatjara were driven by drought to expand into the territory of a neighbour.

Several of these invasions might be partly explained by a domino theory: the coastal invasion of the whites initially pushing over one black domino which in turn pushed down outer dominoes. But it would be sensible to believe that dominoes were also rising and falling occasionally during the centuries of black history. We should be wary of whitewashing the white invasion. We should also be wary of the idea that Australia knew no black invasions.

Even when Aboriginal tribes clung to their traditional territory, fatal fighting within the same tribe or between members of hostile tribes was common. It is possible that many tribes suffered more deaths through warfare in the 18th century than they suffered through warfare with the British colonists in the 19th century. In the whole continent the 18th century could well have been as war-like as the 19th century. The highest estimate, so far offered, of Aboriginal deaths caused by warfare with white races during the 19th century is a grand total of 20,000 – an alarming number. To reach an equally long death roll in the 18th century, one in every 600 Aboriginals would have had to die during warfare in a typical year. Evidence I have gathered – of Aboriginal fighting in traditional times – suggests tentatively that such a death rate was not impossible. Even a death rate twice as heavy was possible.

Many Englishmen who thought kindly of the Aboriginals and felt shame at their countrymen's treatment of them genuinely believed that one blessing of the ultimate conquest would be the spreading of peace through a war-like continent. The main weakness in this belief was that in many tribal lands few Aboriginals survived to enjoy the new time of peace.

7

In isolated parts of the world the arrival of Europeans had exposed isolated races for the first time to raging infections. Each civilization, entering new territory, carried not only its culture and technology but also its viruses. The virus won the quickest victories. The arrival of smallpox and measles weakened the late Roman Empire. In the 14th century, along the caravan routes of the Mongol empire in central Asia, travelled the plague known as the Black Death; and in Europe there was no immunity, and perhaps one third of the population was killed. The people of the Americas in the 16th century had long lived in isolation from Europe and Asia, and they were vulnerable when the Spaniards arrived with smallpox and measles, typhus and influenza. Mexico was conquered more by disease than by arms. In half a century its population fell from thirty to three million, a more devastating and more sudden decline than even the Aboriginals were to suffer.

Here, diseases were the destroyers even more than firearms and poisons. Smallpox in Sydney in 1789 killed perhaps half of the local Aboriginals in one outbreak. Another epidemic of smallpox near Dungog in New South Wales killed perhaps two of every three Aboriginals in 1836. Influenza was capable of massacres. An epidemic of measles was said to have killed half of the Aboriginals in the York district of Western Australia in 1865. When these new diseases reached a district they sometimes swept with the speed of a grassfire. Venereal disease was one of these grassfires, and in districts as far apart as Port Phillip Bay and King Sound it was sometimes said to be the main cause of the death of the Aboriginals. At times its initial deadliness was exaggerated, the effect being more to reduce births than to increase deaths.

The rum bottle, the brandy bottle, gin and whisky, provided a jagged spearhead of the invasion of Australia. Traditionally the Aboriginals did not know how to make alcohol, and indeed alcohol is not likely to be found in nomadic societies which have no pottery and no beasts of burden. Unfortunately, Aboriginals first tasted alcohol in an era when it was mostly drunk in the form of spirits. In the shepherd huts and the outback grog shanties in early Australia, beer and wine and cider were virtually unknown. The cost of carrying casks and kegs by dray into the interior was so high that only those beverages high in alcohol and

On Melville Island the Aboriginals erected burial poles around the
graves. The 19th century, for Aboriginals in most parts of Australia,
was the century of mourning.   *Robert Edwards*

Aboriginals picking hops in east Gippsland in the mid-1870s.
                              University of Melbourne Archives

Long teams of bullocks carried the wool from the plains to the ports, where sailing ships loaded the wool. These bullocks were near Cloncurry and the ships were at Port Augusta.

PORT AUGUSTA.

low in water were carried: after all, who in his sober mind would pay a small fortune to carry casked water to the outback? Aboriginals thus were introduced to alcohol in its fieriest form, at a time when it was a common form of payment, the main form of entertainment, and the medicine prescribed for many ills. Many Aboriginals, like the white shepherds and draymen and shearers, found solace in alcohol. As the security of the old wandering life crumbled, they drowned their sadness with gulps of spirits. Few Aboriginals could afford to become drunk very often, and many became drunk once only, went to sleep in wet clothes or on damp ground and caught the pulmonary complaint of which so many died. Christian missionaries were the main protectors of Aboriginals from alcohol but few missions could gain a foothold in the interior. The Aboriginals were wanderers, and unless the missionaries wandered too they preached the gospel to congregations which slowly vanished.

The abandoning of the nomadic ways further impaired their health. So long as they wandered regularly from place to place the small Aboriginal groups left their excreta behind them: mobility gave them a sewerage system. But once they were encouraged to settle in more permanent camps, they were more vulnerable to infectious germs or the eggs of worms which lived in the excreta. Similarly the Aboriginals were encouraged to wear clothes, but the officials and philanthropists who gave them blankets and clothes did not realize that nomads had no tradition of washing clothes, that they often had no access to soap and to clean running water, and that they did not realize the danger of sleeping in a wet dress or damp blanket. In putting on clothes they were often putting on burial garments. In covering their skin they were cutting off that ultraviolet light which for thousands of years had helped to destroy bacteria on their naked flesh. Sadly the black people and white people did not have sufficient knowledge to realize the price that was charged for the fashion – intense in the Victorian era – of frowning on nakedness. Nor was it realized how much their diet suffered when they turned to flour, refined sugar, potatoes and the carbohydrates. In ceasing to gather the variety of native greens, nuts, fruits, seeds and tubers of their traditional diet and in spending fewer hours in hunting and fishing they became less healthy and were thus less able to resist the old and new kinds of illnesses. Deficiencies of food made more women sterile and killed many of their infants. A dearth of children was one of the marks of this shattered society.

Those Englishmen who lived amongst the Aboriginals and admired their virtues and respected them as individuals were stunned by the speed with which they died. They kept them from the spirits bottle; they gave medical help to the sick; they somehow kept epidemics at bay; and yet the outcome was the same. Simpson Newland ran an early sheep-run on the Darling River and most of his shepherds were black and he regarded them as if they were his own people.

> It is pathetic to be thrown among the aboriginals and note how they wither away when brought into contact with the people of our race. It seems to make little difference how kindly they are treated, how well clothed or fed, they tend to die out on the appearance of the white man. Among those that I have known, this has been brought about by no epidemic, nor the use of intoxicants, or cold, or hunger ... I can vouch for their being well fed and clothed, and for years spirits were almost entirely kept from them; yet they died off, the old and the young, the strong and the weakly alike, sometimes with startling suddenness, at others by a wasting sickness of a few days, weeks, or months.

It was almost as if the will to live had faded. In many parts of the land were lonely men and women who were the last survivors of their tribe. Sometimes the survivor was no more than 30 years old. In some places the last members of a tribe knew that death would soon come, even though they themselves seemed fit and well. They lived in brushwood shelters on the edge of a town or banks of a creek or corner of a fenced paddock, receiving rations from the government or from local well-wishers, serving as handymen or assistant nursemaid when they were healthy, receiving occasionally simple lessons in Christianity. Some were half-persuaded that when they died they would live with Christ in a happy land, but the happy land which they imagined was probably their own tribal land with its hills and gullies and plains, its rituals and gatherings and hunts, and its vanishing people.

8

The succession of fighting defeats for the Aboriginals had great consequences. They paved the way for the rise of strong rural and mining industries on which at first the economic growth of the new Australia was based. The first phase of the economic history of British Australia depended firstly on the conquest and occupation of the land. The old recipe for rabbit pie says, 'First, catch your rabbit'. The traditional recipe for economic progress is, first, control the land. By 1850 the most promising land in the temperate zone of Australia had been occupied. Ironically by selling that land, the government was now raising revenue with which to finance the fares of those British migrants who were coming increasingly to settle in Australia. And as migrants poured in, even the labour of the dispossessed Aboriginals was seen as superfluous.

For the Aboriginals the decisive defeats in warfare deprived them of their main rights. If they had fought more successfully, like the Maoris or many tribes of Red Indians in North America, they would have received the rights to tracts of lands and perhaps even a tentative place and a modicum of respect in the new nation that had supplanted them. Instead they became lost tribes in their own land.

Once conquered they suffered further, because they had no useful place in the new society. That was probably the saddest fate. Even a slave is valued for his labour and his health is safeguarded in order to protect his labour, but in most parts of Australia the work of Aboriginals was little needed. When white labour was scarce, many Aboriginal men were employed as shepherds, as sheep-washers, shearers, reapers, as gatherers of bark, as stockmen, sealers and whalers. In many months of the 1840s perhaps as many as a thousand were employed full-time by private employers in country districts – perhaps many more. A few remained with their employer for half a lifetime but most came and went on their own whim or were told by employers to go. As manual labourers they were less reliable and showed less stamina in hard tasks.

It was ironical that the qualities of the Aboriginals which were most appreciated were those which assisted the continued invasion of their lands. As many Aboriginals were fine trackers, linguists, explorers, finders of scarce water and lost horses, and as they thrived on the wandering life, they were hired by pastoralists, and later by the gold-seekers who went into new terrain. Most of the large exploring expeditions were aided by Aboriginal guides who had been recruited in the settled districts. Famous in their brief day their names were given to creeks and hills along the explorers' tracks, and their merits were sometimes praised in the travel books which were read in the English circulating libraries. When these guides died – mostly at an early age – a few were honoured with an obituary notice in a colonial newspaper and even an iron railing around their grave.

Yuranigh, with his glossy combed black hair, was one of these alert Aboriginal guides, venturing into lands which he could not have safely entered in old tribal days. He went north with Major Mitchell's party of twenty-eight white men to explore tropical Queensland in 1846. He was so versatile and intelligent that Mitchell recorded that, like a great dictionary of bushlore, 'he was ever at my elbow'. Four years later Yuranigh died near his native Molong, to the west of the Blue Mountains, and when Mitchell heard of the death he inscribed and erected a headstone:

TO NATIVE COURAGE HONESTY AND FIDELITY

Countless attempts were made to halt the wanderings of the Aboriginals in the hope that, once they settled down, they might slowly adapt to the new society. As early as 1814 Governor Macquarie built huts and laid out gardens for black people at George's Head near Sydney; and the experiment of turning them into gardeners and farmers was to be repeated with scant success. A few citizens adopted or educated Aboriginals. Children were willing learners, especially of the chanted lessons, for they were brilliant mimics; but an ability to read and count and write did not persuade them from wandering when they grew older. The towns and the farms seemed like gaols: they wished to be free. Missionaries tried to convert them, giving them clothes and food and light work. The Reverend L. E. Threlkeld, a Londoner who had been a Congregational missionary in the Pacific, was perhaps the first to learn carefully one of the many languages. Settling at Lake Macquarie from 1825 to 1841 he learned the Awaba language and – with the constant help of the gifted black linguist Eaglehawk – translated the gospels of St Luke and St Mark and parts of the Book of Common Prayer. He won no visible converts. Before his eyes the Awaba people virtually vanished from existence, leaving him as one of the few speakers of the language in the district.

9

Conscious that they were occupying extensive tribal lands, the governors, high officials, explorers and a few pastoralists began to discuss the morality of this creeping, unplanned invasion. Some were uneasy but many found strong moral and legal justification. They could not imagine that a later generation would challenge their logic, let alone their sincerity, just as it is inconceivable to various advanced guards of opinion today that their sincerity and logic may well be challenged in the 21st century.

Perhaps their main justification of the conquest was that Aboriginal society was only a flicker of light compared to the torch of Western civilization. Apologists were convinced that Aboriginals would gain by abandoning their beliefs.

They pointed out that British rule would give them peace in place of tribal warfare. British rule would control nakedness and immodesty, would prevent the killing of infants and the practice of bigamy, and would cultivate those qualities prized in England in the Victorian age. Western civilization would bring the benefits of reading, writing, and enable the tribes to acquire scientific and mechanical and medical knowledge.

The journals of many explorers breathe the confidence that they are instruments of God. Commander John Lort Stokes, surveying the coast of northern Australia in the *Beagle*, imagined the spires of many Christian villages soaring on the plains of the Queensland gulf country where the spire even today is virtually unknown. He rejoiced that the 'unspeakable blessings of Christian civilization' would displace the native sorcerers along the Swan River. Like many explorers Stokes saw himself as a communist cadre might see himself today, the carrier of a wonderful formula to the ends of the earth. In 1839, far up the Victoria River, Stokes placed an account of his explorations in a bottle as a memento of his visit, hoping that before 'the sand of my life-glass has run out' British cities would rise where now 'the prowling heathen' lights his fire. Man's happiest achievement, he said, was in subduing the wilderness and in taking Christian civilization to the ends of the earth.

Even explorers who sympathized with the Aboriginals and admired their skills were swept away by their faith in that all-conquering civilization of which Britain had become the most strenuous missionary. This was the era when great cities such as London and Manchester were fed from afar: a time of spreading literacy and popular education, an annual fanfare of technical innovations ranging from railways to gaslight, increasing peace and order, and a web of commerce which carried goods cheaply across the world. We forget that commerce then had the esteem possessed by planners in socialist nations today. The explorer George Grey was one of many who saw the London merchant operating in Australia as a sower of the seed of civilization. The merchant's purchases of Australian wool or his shipments of knick-knacks to remote ports were changing the world's wildernesses:

> With the wizard wand of commerce, he touches a lone and trackless forest, and at his bidding, cities arise, and the hum and dust of trade collect – away are swept ancient races; antique laws and customs moulder into oblivion. The strong-holds of murder and superstition are cleansed, and the Gospel is preached amongst ignorant and savage men. The ruder languages disappear successively, and the tongue of England alone is heard around.

The expanding flocks represented the 'wizard wand of commerce' in Australia. The flockmasters were taming the land for the arrival of civilization. Just as the large islands of the Pacific from Hawaii to New Zealand had become fields for Christian missions between 1797 and 1850, so the Aboriginals were assumed to be ripe for Christian conversion once their wanderings had ceased.

Learned judges justified the occupation of Aboriginal lands. In 1836 Mr Justice Burton ruled that the Aboriginals could not be held to have the land rights of 'free and independent tribes' because they were few in number and frail in political organization. Other lawyers explained that the land had not been effectively used by the tribes. The Aboriginals did not till the land; and the quiltwork of ploughed fields in the British Isles made the Australian grasslands, in contrast, seem waste lands. Indeed the phrase 'waste lands' was used again and again in those official documents which discussed those Australian lands still remaining with the Aboriginals.

As Aboriginals seemed to possess no individual property beyond their hunting equipment, and as they seemed merely to wander over the lands, the loss of their hunting grounds was not counted as a severe loss to them. Many learned Englishmen believed this, out of ignorance. As the explorer Edward Eyre pointed out in 1840, people who did not cultivate the soil still depended on the soil: 'Does it not supply grass for the sustenance of the wild animals upon which in a great measure they are dependent for their subsistence? – does it not afford roots and vegetables to appease their hunger, water to satisfy their thirst, and wood to make their fire?'

The beneficiaries of the new sheep industry in Australia were far more numerous than simply the sheep-owners, their financiers, and all those Australians whose jobs depended on wool. In the heart of winter, when half of Europe and North America might be covered with snow, millions were kept warm with Australian wool in the middle years of the 19th century. By the end of the century three million Australians and millions of people in other lands were being fed by a continent which, in its tribal heyday, had supported only a fraction of that number. In one sense the multiplying of the loaves and fishes was the most valid justification for the occupation of the Aboriginal lands. While this was an argument of convenience to some, it was an argument of principle to others. Even in the 18th century the respected writings of the Swiss jurist Vattel and the English jurist Blackstone cast doubts on the rights of nomadic peoples to occupy lands which they did not cultivate and did not adequately use.

Australia of the nomads was relatively rich in natural resources but peopled sparsely. The Aboriginals, even on the eve of the industrial revolution, were amongst the more prosperous peoples of the earth, but they could not exploit their rich resource-bowl adequately. Divided into hundreds of republics, and weak in armaments, they were also unable to defend their lands. This dilemma – of a small population occupying a wide and valuable land – was also to haunt the society which supplanted the Aboriginals.

7   West and South

In the first forty years every settlement had been launched with the aid of the labour of convicts. In 1829 the first free settlement was made, and quickly it showed the disadvantages of freedom.

2

British settlers sailed from England to the Swan River, in Western Australia, and came ashore in June 1829. Here, they believed, they could quickly establish a free colony like those which had long flourished in North America. The land seemed to be fertile, with a wide river flowing slowly to the sea. The land too was sensationally cheap, and anyone who invested £18 in the new settlement received a bonus of a square mile of land.

The propaganda floated in London by Captain James Stirling who had explored the Swan River was seductive, and all kinds of city folk sailed for the Swan. They arrived with capital to invest and therefore were entitled to take up so much land that an area equal to several large English counties was required to satisfy them. The pleasing land on the banks of the lower Swan River was all apportioned by September 1829: it was carved between a mere twenty-one settlers. The fertile banks of the Canning, which flowed into the Swan, accommodated another eleven settlers. Scores of settlers with entitlements to land still wanted their share, and all those who now owned land were looking for labourers to clear and plough and fence the land. There was no convict labour and not much free labour for this

handful of soft-handed employers and their large estates.
The cost of importing free labour from London or Glasgow
was almost prohibitive.

Most newcomers who clustered on the beach at Fremantle
or settled at the newly surveyed town of Perth were soon
disappointed. The first summer was hot and dry, beyond
their previous imagining. Bushfires, sandflies and mosquitoes pestered them. Many suffered from sore eyes – the
effects of glare, flying sand, and flies. Many died from
scurvy and dysentery. Meanwhile, energetic settlers went
inland and began to clear the ground and build houses and
barns. The more timid settlers – and some of the bolder –
sailed away to Tasmania, where the labour of convicts was
cheap and plentiful. Most people had left by the end of
1830.

The farmers faced an unusual obstacle. They were trying
to create, without yet realizing it, the first agricultural
settlement in the more arid zones of Australia. By the
standards of Sussex, the Swan River district was parched for
much of the year. Even by the standards of Bathurst and
Hobart the soil and climate were daunting. It so happened
that Captain Stirling, in exploring the Swan River, had seen
probably the longest strip of alluvial soil on the entire
coastal plain of Western Australia. He assumed that the soft
landscape of the Swan was typical of the land stretching
along the coast to Albany. He did not realize that sand
dunes, swamps and thin, gravelly soil were more typical.
Explorers are especially given to wishful thinking, to
exaggerating the value of their discoveries. Without
Stirling's exaggeration, Perth would not have been
founded.

The first settlers had to live with that exaggeration. Even
those who had taken up fertile soil were soon puzzled. The
soil, deficient in phosphate like so many Australian soils,
was half-exhausted after several crops had been reaped.
The river lands along the lower Swan seemed ideal but were
found to be salty. In selecting land the newcomers worked
by rule of thumb and sometimes the thumb misled them.
The tall, stately jarrah tree, with its grey, stringy bark and its

red-coloured wood, was so tall near Perth that many settlers imagined that the soil around its roots must be rich. Painfully they cut down the jarrah trees, or ringbarked them and eventually burned the skeletons. Much of the timber was so hard that axes and saws were quickly blunted; the cleared ground was also so hard that spades, hoes and ploughs were blunted or broken. Slowly some of the early settlers realized that the soil covered by jarrah trees and the banksias was poor, while the meaner-looking clay soils covered by wandoo and marri trees were superior.

In Western Australia so much had to be learned or unlearned. Wheat and potatoes could not be sown according to the English calendar. Wheat seed had to be soaked in strong brine so that it would germinate more rapidly and be free from smut. Sown ground had to be rolled to retain the moisture. Sheep had to be penned on a field about to be ploughed, so that manure could be provided. Scarecrows were erected in the hope of frightening the flocks of birds which fed on the ripening grain. As for the caterpillars, which in wet weather feasted on the crops near the Swan River, no scarecrow could frighten them. Settlers also imported difficulties. Weeds arrived with the imported seed; and some weeds multiplied in unbelievable ratios. Two species of Cape tulip, one of which was brought from South Africa to make the fields prettier, became a pest.

Settlers pushed inland with sheep and cattle and took up patches of ground for grazing. Labour was scarce and so herdsmen and shepherds were too expensive. In this land of barter people were often paid in goods, and some of the inland herdsmen received as wages one third of the herd's increase. There were no convicts to build roads, and the carting of supplies through the sand country was costly. In 1841 the carrying of supplies from Fremantle to the inland town of York was said to be at least eight times as dear as the cost of shipping them all the way from England to the port. Without the gangs of convict road-makers the steep slopes had to be tackled dangerously. On the road to Toodyay the descent of the hill at Jimperding was so precipitous that large logs were towed behind the bullock carts, the logs serving as rough brakes which prevented the carts from running away and crashing into the yoked bullocks below.

The predictions made by Captain Stirling in promoting the colony began to appear crazy or airy. He had spoken of shipbuilders setting up shipyards with the aid of the native timbers. He had predicted that Fremantle would be a busy port of call for ships sailing from Europe to places as far apart as Canton and Sydney and that Cockburn Sound might become a British naval base. He said that the healing climate would enable Perth to become a convalescent home for Englishmen laid low by the heat and disease of India. The failure of all these hopes would have mattered less if the new settlement had had a safe harbour. Stirling had announced that the bay at Gage Roads, near Fremantle, was safer than the famous Table Bay at Cape Town, but it proved to be dangerous for anchored ships during the north-westerly winds. The first settlers living on the beach were dismayed to see the newly arrived vessel *Marquis of Anglesea* blown on to rocks near the mouth of the Swan River and wrecked before their eyes.

After ten years the white population of Western Australia was only 2000. People left or wanted to leave but to whom could they sell their houses, drays, skinny sheep, stock-yards, paddocks, and all the 'improvements' made with aching limbs? It was the history of Sydney written again. Whereas in early Sydney most of the pioneers had to stay, in Perth they were free to leave; and they did.

3

It is puzzling that the fine land near the mouth of the Murray and on the eastern gulf of South Australia remained untouched as late as the mid-1830s. A few whalers and sealers camped near sheltered bays but no land was ploughed and no flocks were watched. Presumably the deep indentation of the coastline meant that the safest harbours of South Australia were too far from the known sea routes. South Australia had no appeal in an era when 'the seas – and the headlands and promontories that jutted out towards the trade routes – were seen as more valuable than Australian land. It was therefore not settled by soldiers and convicts, and remained one of the few attractive places for a free colony when the era of free migration gathered pace.

South Australia was founded on a blueprint. To its English founders the phrase 'systematic colonization' was as precious and as reassuring as is the phrase 'the four modernizations' in China in 1980. South Australia was to admit no convicts, was to penalize no religious sect, was to offer to Englishmen their traditional liberties, and was not to enthrone the governor and his bureaucracy. In one sense the colony was planned as firmly as a new Soviet province in Siberia, though its values were primarily those of individual enterprise. Settlers were not to straggle out to the frontier but were to remain in compact rural and urban settlements. Poor immigrants were to work hard for several years – a colonial apprenticeship – before they bought or rented their own small farm. South Australia's formula for rural planning was not edicts, travel permits and a labour bureau but rather the official control of the sale of land. All land in South Australia was to be expensive. The money raised from the sale of the land was to be spent on shipping poor but healthy migrants from England. The migrants were to live only in the compactly settled coastal districts.

The compactness of the new colony offered an ideological advantage. The services and amenities of civilization could be provided: the preachers, judges, school-teachers, booksellers, newspaper editors and all the carriers of that Christian civilization which had not yet flourished in the dispersed pastoral settlements of Australia.

The chairman of the colonization commissioners of South Australia was Colonel Robert Torrens, an Irishman in his fifties who had fought in Spain in the Napoleonic Wars and sat in the House of Commons as member for the Lancashire cotton town of Bolton. An economist, he believed that the new economic and social formula would make South Australia a paradise both for the middle class and for the labouring immigrants. For seven years Colonel

Torrens was almost a full-time chairman, lecturing and publicizing the new colony. He did not, however, visit Adelaide – he did not see that limp river which honours his name. The first secretary of the commissioners was a Birmingham Unitarian named Rowland Hill, who wrote pamphlets on cures for pauperism and crime; South Australia was to be one of his cures. Hill was also the inventor of the postage stamp and of the penny post. Few colonies had such a distinguished and public-spirited band of absentee founders. Few colonies, likewise, had such theory-bound founders. The men who set up South Australia believed that they possessed a magical pocket-calculator which – by fixing the price of an acre of South Australian land – could thereby provide a formula for social and economic progress. Offering a dear package embracing 80 acres of rural land and one acre of town land in South Australia for the sum of £81, they soon sold enough land to launch the colony and despatch the first ships.

4

Many of the pioneers of the new colony sat on the beach near Adelaide in 1836 and wondered what had happened to them. The landscape, the dazzle of the light at midday, the colour and feel of the bark of trees, and the sandiness of the coastal soils were quite unlike the place which they envisaged when they resolved to leave England. On the beach at Glenelg they slept in tents, and even in Adelaide many people pitched their tents and lived for months in a makeshift way which would have astonished their friends at home. 'Often', recalled Mary Thomas, the mother of young daughters, 'have I got out of bed during a high wind and held the tent pole with all my strength', all the time fearing that tent and pole would fall. When heavy rain pounded the tent and the water trickled inside, the Thomases lay in bed with umbrellas spread above them. At night they heard the howl of dingoes, and in stormy nights the lightning flashed so brilliantly that the tent for an instant seemed to be alight. For many newcomers nothing was so strange as their first Christmas in South Australia when they perspired in oven

104

heat and thought nostalgically of the icy winds and snow of home. Their main consolation was that they subscribed to a theory of colonization which insisted on a compact community. In their misery they were not alone.

By the end of 1838 about sixty ships had sailed from Europe to South Australia and they carried nearly six thousand people. The swift rise of this utopia delighted its founders, and especially Robert Gouger who came as colonial secretary: 'No colony of which I have heard or read, has been formed so rapidly, or with so complete an absence of suffering.'

The poorer migrants who came to Adelaide were hand-selected. In return for their free fare they signed the declaration embodying the ideology of the colony: 'I go to the colony as one willing and intending to work there for wages, until, by such means, I shall have saved sufficient to enable me, in the same manner, to employ others.' The commissioners for their part promised to provide work for each assisted migrant and so were careful to choose migrants with useful skills. They tried to select an equal number of men and women. They tried to select half of their colonists from those aged between 15 and 30. They gave preference to agricultural labourers, shepherds, sawyers, harness-makers, blacksmiths, wheelwrights, tanners, bootmakers, tailors, and other useful hands. These men had to present, before they could board the ship, letters from two 'respectable householders' affirming that they were honest, sober, industrious and of good character. Unmarried women were more likely to be granted a free fare if they were experienced as domestic servants, farm hands, dairy maids, seamstresses or straw-plaiters. And what, pray, would a straw-plaiter do in a new colony? She could make straw braid for the wide-brimmed hats which everyone would surely wear in the warm fields.

Little was forgotten in planning the colony. All emigrants had to be vaccinated; single women were, preferably, to be accompanied by a respectable chaperon. South Australia was to be the sanitarium of good health and morality; and by some definitions it was.

The original blueprint of colonization was increasingly neglected. Divided control between a governor in Adelaide and absentee commissioners in London proved clumsy, and the governor alone ruled. The pocket-calculator was not employed to assess the ideal price for land or the market for labour. When the land was too dear or the wages were too low, many people simply travelled on to Hobart, Port Phillip or Sydney. This was one weakness of the ingenious theory. It assumed that there was no other colony in the southern world except South Australia. This assumption, even today, is not unknown.

5

South Australia did what no other colony had succeeded in doing: it enticed thousands whose homeland was not the British Isles. In Prussia in the 1830s many Lutherans were resisting the government's attempts to unite them with the Calvinists, and the young pastor of one of these congregations, August Kavel, sought a place to which his people could emigrate. Visiting Hamburg, the port from which most emigration ships sailed to the United States, he heard of the possibility of emigrating instead to South Australia. That colony offered freedom of worship but, more enticing, it might somehow offer a loan for the fares of his congregation. Pastor Kavel crossed to England and met George Fife Angas, one of the colonization commissioners of South Australia. Angas was a Baptist, a sect which valued its independence from the state. He was sympathetic to the plight of Kavel's oppressed congregation and was optimistic that South Australia could offer religious toleration such as no other known British colony could offer. Angas also belonged to a wealthy family which owned ships in Newcastle-on-Tyne and traded in the West Indies and so was able to lend money to finance the fare of 200 members of Kavel's flock. Indeed Angas had a strong interest not only in toleration but also in his own South Australian estate, and anything he could do to provide hard-working migrants for Adelaide and potential tenants for his own land was doubly pleasing. Significantly, South Australia with its independent promoters was the only colony likely to help such congregations. If Kavel had gone to London and sought official help in emigrating to Sydney or Hobart, the British government would have told him that poverty in Britain and Ireland had a higher call on emigration funds than religious persecution in Germany.

The first five hundred Germans to land at Adelaide came from Klemzig in Prussian Silesia. With Kavel as their pastor they settled in 1838 at a new Klemzig, a village now swallowed by Adelaide, and grew corn and market vegetables on small rented farms. Later Kavel and some of his congregation moved inland to the Barossa Valley where they settled on Angas's land. Other groups of German Lutherans – led by Pastor Fritzche – settled in the Adelaide hills and built churches at Hahndorf, Lobethal and other villages. When Angas himself sold his assets in England and emigrated in 1851 to the colony which he had vigorously promoted, he heard that the energy with which the German families worked on the land was already a byword. The Germans in South Australia were to become almost as important as the Scots in Victoria or the Irish in New South Wales. Later, many German families and their drays and wagons were to travel east to farm the rolling countryside to the north of Albury, the wheatlands of the Wimmera, and the Victoria Mallee where they built slim-spired Lutheran churches and farmed dry wheatlands in the South Australia manner. Essentially people of the land they remained on their farms at a time when most migrants from the British Isles were huddling in the Australian cities.

With the opening of rich copper mines at Kapunda and Burra in the mid-1840s and the vigorous opening of the coastal wheatlands, South Australia became the boom colony, and its air of purpose and bounding energy appealed to many visitors. While Sydney was said by one observant sheep-owner to be light and gay and thoughtless, Adelaide seemed to possess 'a spirit of keen Yankeeism'. The time would come when Melbourne and Sydney would in turn be widely known as the Yankee city, for in Australia this phrase was migratory and attached itself to the capital city which seemed likely to pass all others. But now the pacemaker was Adelaide, and in the 1840s its population was multiplied by five, was about to pass Tasmania's, and – but for the discovery of gold – might have passed Victoria's.

6

It is sometimes said that the quality of the settlers in South Australia – especially that striving determined quality of which the Germans and the English nonconformists were exemplars – explains why South Australia was more successful than Western Australia. But the contrast between the two colonies was so stark that other causes must also have been working. South Australia had the disadvantage of the later start, but by 1840 it held about six times as many white people as Western Australia. By 1850 South Australia had eleven times as many people. Why then did Western Australia fall far behind the other free colony when they seem to have so much in common?

Western Australia now holds as many people as South Australia and its natural resources are conspicuously the more abundant and varied. And yet in the 1830s and 1840s South Australia had the more accessible resources. And in those decades, before steam revolutionized transport on land and hastened it on sea, accessibility was crucial. In South Australia the good wheatlands lay close to the sea and the rich mineral deposits were close not only to the sea but also to the wheatlands. In contrast, nothing did more to retard Western Australia than the fact that her main cereal lands – and they are now twice as productive as South Australia's – were far from the sea. Moreover her most attractive mineral deposits – to 19th-century eyes – were the gold deposits, and they lay in the dry lands far from the sea. The gold of Kalgoorlie, being remote, was not discovered until half a century after the first copper was found to the north of Adelaide. In essence Nature had placed her resources in the wrong places in the West and in the handiest position in South Australia. Nature could have apologized for this trick by giving the West a long, navigable river. Instead she gave South Australia the long river; not that the Murray River added many people or much wealth to South Australia before the 1860s. The early collapse of Western Australia's hopes largely reflected the slowness and the high expense of transport in the era when the bullock dray was the main vessel of the inland plains.

Nature played another game with Western Australia. Not only did it bury her assets perversely. It also placed her too far to the west. At least she was too far to the west, in the light of conditions of the time. Her people gained little of the expected trade with Asian and African countries fronting the Indian Ocean and were too far from the growing markets of Melbourne and Sydney and Hobart. Unfortunately there was no overland stock route from the eastern colonies, and the sea route was often impaired by strong westerlies.

In 1850 Western Australia celebrated her coming of age with a white population of a mere 5000 in a vast area which was six times as large as California. Here was one of the most dismal episodes in the history of European coloni-zation. The solution to the failure was as riveting as the failure. The free citizens invited the British government to send out convicts. In June 1850, when transportation to Sydney had already ceased, seventy-five convicts and their pensioner guards reached Western Australia to open the new era.

8 The Cities Rise: The Chains Break

The free immigrants were taking over the land. In the first quarter century, few citizens had come voluntarily to Australia to settle. More came in the 1820s, often men of money who were promised free land. In 1828, for the first time, the free immigrants to Australian ports exceeded 1000. In 1829, the first year of the Western Australian settlement, they exceeded 2000. In 1831 the British government began to subsidize the fares of poorer migrants, and soon the subsidized migrants to New South Wales annually exceeded those who paid their own fares. In Sydney and occasionally in Hobart could be seen the strange sight of a convict ship and an immigrant ship anchored close together in the bay and sending ashore their passengers to start their very different lives. The year 1841 was an early peak of free immigration to New South Wales, whether to Sydney or Melbourne, and more than 20,000 landed after a voyage made largely at the public's expense. In that year alone the subsidized migrants amounted to one quarter of all the convicts who had reached the colony since the arrival of the First Fleet.

Most settlers from the British Isles preferred to migrate to North America. They paid their own fare but the voyage was short and the prospect of returning home was reasonable if not high. In comparison, Australia was less attractive. A voyage of four months was expensive; moreover no income could be earned during the voyage. The subsidized fare was to become essential for most migrants to Australia in most years of the 19th century. The source of the subsidy was the revenue raised from the sale of Australian land.

The free migrants, whether they paid their own fare or came with help from the government, had profound effects on convict colonies. The free settlers on average were more independent, more radical in many of their political views, more attached to family. Whereas the convicts were overwhelmingly male, the free settlers included more women. In 1830 in New South Wales the white males had outnumbered white females by three to one, and amongst adults the predominance of men was even more marked, but by 1846 there were only two adult men for every adult woman. That discrepancy faded as free migrants arrived and as Australian births contributed more to the population.

2

The free settlers even more than the convicts were a challenge to law and order. They demanded liberties and privileges which a convict society could not easily concede. Slowly, however, the civil liberties of the free migrant and the emancipated convict were enlarged. Trial by jury in both Tasmania and New South Wales was introduced cautiously in 1823 in civil lawsuits and slowly extended to criminal cases. Convicts who had served their sentence and had become prosperous could sit on a jury from 1832. The old-time criminal court consisting of a judge and military or naval officers gave way entirely to trial by jury in 1839. Similarly the freedom of religion was now limited more by the scarcity of clergymen than by government decree; and in one sense the conscience was protected more in Sydney than in London and Dublin where a citizen had to pay taxes to support the established church even if he opposed that church.

The press gained its freedom after painful struggles.

In 1829 the editor of the *Monitor* was forced to write his editorials in the privacy of the Parramatta gaol, after publishing a seditious libel against Governor Darling and a criminal libel against a military commandant. To the same gaol came the editor of the *Australian*, after publishing the criminal libel that the governor was unfit to rule over any British colony. How much freedom the governor should grant the press in a convict colony was not a simple question. Darling was sometimes arrogant and cantankerous but perhaps he was entitled to suggest that the maintaining of order in a convict colony was difficult when strong attacks on him were read publicly by soldiers, or when some convicts were known to walk five miles after work to read, in the latest edition, claims that the governor was incompetent. Under Darling's successor, the liberal Sir Richard Bourke, the press in Sydney was treated perhaps more generously than were newspapers in England. In Sydney the newspapers were exempt from the heavy tax of fourpence which was imposed on every copy printed in England. Moreover, in June 1835, Bourke allowed the colonial newspapers to pass free through the post office so long as they were posted in open envelopes within seven days of publication. Henceforth they filled the mail bags which went upcountry in the weekly or bi-weekly mail coaches. Years before any elections were held for public office the newspapers had thus become His Majesty's Opposition.

The press could sting – and its sting was vital – in those years when an election for public office was unknown in Australia. All public appointments of importance were made in London. Even the members of the advisory legislative council in New South Wales and Tasmania were either chosen by the governor or sat by virtue of their office. Not even in local government was there an election in any Australian town before 1840. Indeed there was no municipal government in the normal sense, and small support for it. In a convict colony the central government readily used convict labour to build roads and bridges, and employed policemen to guard convicts and maintain order. Why then should each district elect a local council and pay rates in order to finance what the government was already financing? Local government is firstly a tax, and there were few volunteers to pay taxes.

Adelaide was given a short-lived town council in August 1840 and its members were elected, perhaps the first election for public office in Australia's history. Market commissions were authorized by the New South Wales government to provide markets on public land for the sale of fruit and vegetables, cattle, hay and corn, and other perishable goods and in 1841 market commissioners were elected by owners and occupiers of houses and land in Parramatta and Melbourne. The market poll was the first public election ever held in Victoria, and was contested by Johnny Fawkner who had virtually founded the city. Fawkner issued blue rosettes to his supporters, entertained them at the William Tell tavern in Collins Street, made sure that they voted for him at an election in which no secrecy was allowed, and presumably rewarded them again at the tavern when he became one of the eight victorious candidates. So democracy – the democracy of those who owned property or paid large rents for property – inched forward. And then, in 1842 and 1843, it leaped.

Sydney was created a city and Melbourne a town in 1842, and the first councillors were elected by the larger ratepayers. In 1843, for the first time, men of property were permitted to elect most of the members to the reformed legislative council of New South Wales, the jurisdiction of which stretched from Bass Strait to Torres Strait. The new legislative council elected its own speaker. It could ask embarrassing questions and seek information from the government. It could initiate legislation and vote on the governor's own proposals; and no laws could be introduced without the council's approval. The governor, however, was not answerable to the legislative council. It could pass a vote of no confidence in him day after day, but he could merely nod his acknowledgement and continue on his way. He, not the council, had the power to dismiss or discipline the heads of the departments of government. Any bill which was passed by the legislative council he could veto; if he wished to seek the advice of the government in London, he could reserve or defer the contentious bill. He indirectly controlled the main colonial source of revenue –

the Crown lands. He therefore excluded the legislative council from any influence on the crux of all colonial controversies – who should possess the land, and on what terms? This lonely man, however, was caught between the bite of the home government on the one side and the bark of the legislative council on the other. On many key issues the policy was made in London, and on many other key issues he could not create new policies without the council's consent.

Of the 36 seats in the new legislative council, 12 were filled by nominees of the governor and 24 were elected. William Charles Wentworth, a clever barrister and businessman who had found a way across the Blue Mountains three decades ago, topped the poll of the Sydney candidates and made it clear that this first concession to democracy was a trifling gesture in his opinion. He simply enquired why thirty-six citizens, 'clods of earth', should in their collective wisdom be thought inferior to the thirty-seventh clod, the governor Sir George Gipps? The first elected members took their seats in the council chamber in Sydney, just when the depression was deepening, and promptly passed laws to ease their own plight as businessmen and sheep-owners. In 1843 in a revolutionary step which stunned English bankers and politicians, the legislative council allowed financiers to lend money to squatters on the security of their sheep and cattle or the wool which lay unshorn on the sheep. The council also allowed squatters who were technically insolvent to continue to manage their own sheep-runs, free from the danger of foreclosure. In an even bolder step – so bold that Governor Gipps drew his breath and for a time postponed his approval – the council virtually abolished the imprisoning of those who could not pay their debts. So many citizens were in debt or on the brink of debt that they loudly applauded the new law.

In the late 1840s few could assess how quickly the British government would grant independence, but the forces favouring independence were now powerful. Once convicts ceased to come to New South Wales, the home government

114

no longer had the strongest incentive to control the colony. As the colony had its own rising sources of revenue, especially from the sale of land, it no longer had to depend heavily on the English Exchequer. Likewise many of the articulate exponents of a widening franchise for England could hardly ignore their countrymen in Australia. Events in Canada heightened these arguments. In 1837 and 1838 there were rebellions in Upper and Lower Canada, and England became increasingly anxious not to forget the lessons taught by the American colonists in the 1770s. By 1848 Canada and Nova Scotia had self-government.

In 1850 the British government decided to extend the New South Wales form of government to Tasmania, South Australia, and to Victoria, which would be a separate colony from the year 1851. Across eastern Australia elections were held in the first months of 1851 for seats in these new legislative councils, but the elections in many districts seemed of scant significance. For the seat of Loddon in Victoria the public election was held outside the police-man's simple hut at Carisbrook, a crossing place on a flooded creek. There was one candidate, the squatter William Campbell. There were only two voters and perhaps a couple of adult spectators. So Campbell became the elected spokesman for more than a million sheep.

3

The free institutions began to flourish, just as the needs of the convicts became less important. The last convict ships had sailed into Sydney Harbour in November 1840, but the fear that more convicts would come to the colony persisted amongst the average free labourers and artisans. Occasionally the fear was justified, and as late as 1849 transportation to New South Wales was revived briefly. Meanwhile Tasmania became the heart of the convict system, and in the 1840s it received from the British Isles more convicts than in any previous decade. When in Hobart in May 1853 the ship *St. Vincent* sent ashore the last consignment of convicts, Tasmania had received almost as many convicts as New South Wales during the long history of transportation.

Western Australia now remained the only convict colony and it received its last convict ship on 9 January 1868. For eighty years convicts had been shipped to Australia, and a total of 163,000 had set out on that voyage from which few returned. In the modern history of Europe there was not a planned deportation on a more ambitious scale until the era of Stalin and Hitler.

No Australian settlement had escaped the influence of convicts. Adelaide was proud that it had not been a convict colony, but in fact convicts arrived there privately in ones or twos rather than in occasional shiploads. Coming overland with mobs of cattle or around the coast in sailing ships they calmly entered the colony and stayed. No policeman questioned them at the port and no clerk recorded their life history. Early in 1840 a new sub-inspector of police in Adelaide was astonished to learn that most of the major crimes were committed by men who had once been convicts in the eastern colonies. In the gullies behind Adelaide, on dark nights, they would emerge, reported the police officer, 'and commit daring black-faced robberies and burglaries in the city'. The former convicts were also the kings of the cattle thieves.

Victorians of a later generation boasted that their colony had never been stained by convicts. Victorians in the 1840s made no such boast. Even small children knew, from the murder reports in the newspapers and from gossip in the home, that former convicts were plentiful. The census in March 1846 revealed that at least one in every three of the men working on the sheep stations had been convicts. In Melbourne the former convicts were less numerous but even in that town, six years after transportation to New South Wales had ceased, forty-seven men and three women still carried tickets-of-leave, their sentence having not expired. In the 1840s the Port Phillip District also received direct from London about 1700 former prisoners who carried conditional pardons: they were free men, so long as they did not leave the huge colony of New South Wales. When the gold-rushes began in 1851, Tasmanian convicts filed into Victoria – in cockleshells and mail ships – in such

116

large numbers that a law was passed in the vain hope of sending them home across the strait.

We like to write THE END beside every period of history but the sorting of the past into neat time-slots is sometimes deceptive. The convict era lived in thousands of lives long after the last convict ship had arrived. Tasmania could not easily escape that influence because in the 1850s transported people still formed so large a part of its population. In 1857, four years after the last convict ship arrived, half of the adults in the island were convicts or former convicts. Ten years later, seven of every ten serious crimes committed in the island were the work of those who had been transported though, presumably, a former convict was perhaps more likely to be arrested and even convicted in a small society where criminal records were public knowledge. In 1877 Port Arthur, the notorious place of detention, was still a prison for men transported at least quarter of a century ago. The convict era died slowly.

When the first federal parliament was opened beneath the dome of the Exhibition Building in Melbourne in May 1901, and a son of Queen Victoria watched the slow procession of newly elected members who had come from every corner of the nation, he did not know the history of one of the oldest of those parliamentarians who arranged themselves around the royal dais. The old man was William Henry Groom, the honourable member for Darling Downs, and the title of honourable must have gratified him.

As a baker's boy of 13 Groom had been convicted of theft in Plymouth, England, and sentenced to transportation for seven years. He reached Sydney in the convict ship *Hashemy* in June 1849, during the brief revival of transportation to New South Wales. After receiving his conditional pardon he settled on the new gold-fields around Bathurst and then moved to Toowoomba where he became storekeeper, publican, Queensland politician and the owner of a country newspaper which preached to small farmers the message that virtue and hard work would eventually be rewarded. At the first federal election in 1901 he won his seat in the house of representatives by a margin of nearly four to one.

His distant past was probably known to few of his electors: he was chosen as a man of the 20th century. He must have been a proud man when he was invited – more fittingly than anybody could have realized – to move the address in reply at the first session of the first parliament of a new nation.*

The convicts had dominated the first phase of the British era in Australia. They had given birth to most of the first generation of white Australian children. They had built the ports and towns, the roads and bridges; they had cleared the land, hoed and ploughed the soil, brought in the harvest, driven the bullock teams, and cared for the sheep. They had cooked meals and cleaned house and made dresses and chairs and baked bread. By the year 1850 Australia held 400,000 white people, but if the continent had depended solely on free settlers only one fifth of that population, at the very most, would have then lived in Australia. The convict era gave Australia a high English and Irish population and a predominance of men, a tendency to disdain authority and resent policemen, and probably a love of leisure and an indifference to religion. The convict era imposed on governments from the outset a high and detailed role in economic and social life. Some of these convict influences were fragile and were quickly erased or reversed by the waves of free immigration; some were reinforced by later events, so that they persist to this day.

4

One early effect of the convict era was the tendency of Australians to live in towns. Migrants reaching Australia were often surprised to find so many people living in the ports and so few in the countryside. By 1850 Sydney had more than 50,000 people, or about half as many as the port

---

*A frequent lament of the convict era was the biblical warning that the sins of the fathers would be visited on the children: in essence, a land settled with unrighteous stock would remain corrupted for many generations. It so happened that Groom died in August 1901 and his vacant seat was won by his son Littleton Groom, and he won eleven successive elections, finally losing in 1929 because, as Speaker of the House, he had defied his own party on what, to him, was an issue of principle.

of New Orleans. Melbourne and Hobart each held close to 25,000 and Melbourne then was only fifteen years old. The townsmen were proud of their new cities, the speed at which they had grown, the church spires and ornate banking chambers and mansions which reminded them of home. Many visitors were not so impressed. 'Melbourne', wrote a Scottish woman in 1849, 'is not a pretty town: it is full of dust in summer and mire in winter; the houses are built so irregularly that you would think there had been an earthquake.' Sydney and Hobart, being older, had straightened themselves.

While the cities were surprisingly fat, the countryside was thin. The migrants who left the main ports and walked along the lonely roads came across few towns with as many as fifty people. Some settled areas in the interior were as large as Scotland but contained fewer people than could be seen in one street of Glasgow on a Saturday night. In the census of 1848 almost half of the Tasmanians were found to be living in Hobart, Launceston and their immediate vicinity. The census held in eastern Australia in March 1851, on the eve of the gold-rushes, revealed that about 47% of the people in the huge colony of New South Wales lived in towns.* Even in South Australia the towns must have held more than half of the colony's people. Australia, much more than the United States, was a country of town-dwellers.

Perhaps only England, of all the nations, had a higher ratio of town-dwellers than Australia. It was easy to

---

*In 1851, on the eve of the gold-rushes, the main cities and towns in Australia could probably be ranked in this order:

1. Sydney 54,000	9. Parramatta 4100
2. Melbourne 29,000	10. Brisbane 2500
3. Hobart 24,000	11. Bathurst 2300
4. Adelaide 18,000	12. Perth 1550
5. Launceston 13,000	13. Goulburn 1500
6. Geelong 8000	14. Windsor 1400
7. Burra 5000	15. Newcastle 1300
8. East and West Maitland 4200	16. Portland 1000

The figures for towns in Western Australia, South Australia and Tasmania are estimates. Nine of the top ten towns were river-ports or sea-ports.

understand why England was a land of cities: it was the global workshop and foundry, making a variety of factory wares for customers in every continent. In contrast, Australia was the global shepherd, and that being one of the most rural activities it did not easily explain why such brimming towns existed in Australia. Indeed the owners of sheep were puzzled that they could not easily entice immigrants to leave the lamplit streets and kerbstone corners of the ports. So many Australians were puzzled that their towns were proportionately so big. Some were embarrassed by it, seeing it as a sign of softness; some were proud of it, seeing the towns as the proof that English civilization had crossed the equator.

The two early towns, Sydney and Hobart, grew partly because they were convict towns; a gaol is an urban industry. The harbours of Sydney and Hobart were also havens for whaling ships, and whaling fostered the businesses of these ports. Many whaling ships were built there, were repaired there, bought supplies there, and sold or transhipped their barrels of oil and catches of whalebone at the wharves and jetties. The sailors of the whaling fleet spent their pay in harbourside hotels and dens, and when they put out to sea their wives and families remained in port, thus augmenting the population. Whaling was thus one of the early spurs to the growth of the towns rather than the countryside.

Melbourne and Geelong, the wool-ports which possessed neither convicts nor a whaling fleet, must have been bolstered by strong forces hidden within the wool industry. How wool aided urbanization was probably not fully known to the mayors, merchants, and land auctioneers who rubbed their hands as their cities grew in the 1840s. Even now we cannot be certain that we know the full causes. Certainly, one of the reasons why the town-ports grew was the way in which a single man tended to find work on the sheep-runs in the outback while a married man – and his wife and children – preferred the towns. They preferred towns because the cost of living was much cheaper – and they had many mouths to feed – and because social amenities existed in the towns. Moreover women, whether single or married, could find positions as cooks, house-maids and pantrymaids in the towns; domestic service was overwhelmingly an occupation of the towns and indeed formed one eighth of the Victorian workforce in 1851.

In the country the sheep-owners usually preferred to employ single men, paying them with a combination of money and food supplies, such as meat, flour, sugar, rice, tea and tobacco. As the owners customarily fed everyone on the sheep-run – and as cartage of goods from the coast was dear – women and children who lived near the homestead and did no work were a burden. So in pastoral Australia a high proportion of the working men lived in the bush and an unusually high proportion of the women and children lived in the towns. The two Victorian ports of Melbourne and Geelong in March 1851 had 154 dependant women and children for every 100 breadwinners or people in work, but in contrast the main pastoral districts had only 69 such dependants for every 100 breadwinners. As the women and children in the towns needed houses and furniture, as they had to be clothed and fed and entertained, their needs gave rise to a variety of jobs in the towns.

The rising towns also mirrored the efficiency of the sheep lands. A traveller riding his horse in the 1840s on the Darling Downs and seeing the shepherds sitting beneath a tree and smoking a clay pipe while the sheep grazed might think the industry was inefficient. In fact, it might well have been the most efficient pastoral industry the world had so far known. The wool produced annually by the average employee of an Australian sheep-run far exceeded the wool produced by each shepherd in the most miraculous flocks of the Old Testament. Each Australian flock could not have been so large and profitable if the grasslands had been cramped, the climate harsher, sheep diseases more virulent, the dingoes more damaging, and if the flocks guarded by each shepherd had numbered only 80 instead of say 800 or 1000 sheep. If the sheep industry had been weighed down by these impediments, the income of both squatters and shepherds would have been far smaller, and

121

they would not have spent so much money in the towns. In essence the wealth produced by relatively few people in the sheep lands financed many jobs in the towns.

Everywhere in the world an essential stepping stone to the growth of towns at the expense of countryside is the increasing efficiency in the primary industries. Urbanization depends on the transfer of part of the workforce from primary industry to manufacturing, commerce, and the service industries. More efficiency in the rural workforce is thus a prerequisite. In Australia the wool industry was astonishingly productive by world standards, but the towns' industries were probably less so, and required more hands for a smaller output; that contrast in efficiency is part of the explantation of why so many people worked in towns in the pastoral era.

If we had been able to question an alert merchant in Adelaide in 1850, and enquire why he thought so many people lived in his town, he might well have offered a different set of reasons. South Australia's thriving towns were a curiosity: Adelaide had not been a convict place, the whaling ships had rarely called, and the sheep lands were not as important as in the colonies to the east.

It is likely that the Adelaide merchant might have pointed to several factors which applied to most of the towns in Australia but applied strongly to Adelaide. It was probably more middle class in origin than any Australian city. A high proportion of South Australia's first settlers were white-collar migrants, professional and mercantile people and artisans who, possessing little rural experience, stayed in Adelaide rather than ventured into the country. A favourable inflow of capital enabled these English settlers in Adelaide to import much of their food and most of everything else. Adelaide survived – until the depression struck in the early 1840s – without an adequate rural hinterland. Adelaide thus displayed in extreme form what other colonies experienced as more and more free settlers arrived: the doggedness with which migrants from the British Isles clung to the port at which they first landed. Again and again in the 19th century many jobs were available in the outback when no unskilled jobs could be found in the ports, but most migrants struggling in the cities were reluctant to move to outback regions which were hotter, lonelier, provided with cruder houses and few amenities, and in appearance unlike any place in the British Isles. Most of our migrants came from the most urbanized land in Europe, and here they also preferred the towns. They would have shaken with fear if in their first night in the bush, they had heard a twig crackle or a kookaburra laugh or a bullock cough.

If the intelligent merchant of Adelaide had scratched his head and sought another reason for the size of the cities he might have mentioned one final fact which was probably common knowledge at the time but rarely recorded in writing. Nearly all the Australian towns straggled. The compact squares of shopping streets were surrounded by lightly settled suburbs and villages. Many of the towns thus enclosed market gardens and orchards, the occasional paddock of wheat or oats, small farms with a few milking cows and – so long as the gum-trees remained – the huts of the axemen supplying firewood. The Australian towns counted in their own population, rather more than did the compact English towns, many inhabitants who followed rural pursuits. In addition the towns held, for part or most of the year, the richer squatters and their families. They held shepherds on the spree and stockmen waiting to collect a mob of cattle. At the census of 2 March 1846 at least one in every twenty breadwinners in Melbourne said that their occupation was grazing, farming, or horticulture. In the same census one in every twenty-five breadwinners in the 'urban population' of New South Wales said they followed rural occupations.

The strength of the towns came partly from their small factories, mills and workshops. Tasmania alone, in the late 1840s, had between 70 and 80 flour-mills – worked by steam, wooden water-wheels, or by canvas sails that caught the wind. In the year 1849 Tasmania had 16 candle factories, and the imports of foreign candles had virtually ceased. The island had 46 breweries – compared to a mere

123

14 in Victoria – and much of the malt they used came from local malthouses. About 40 Tasmanian tanneries turned hides into a distinctively red leather – the redness coming from the local wattlebark which had replaced English oakbark in the curing process; the leather was used by local bootmakers and saddlers who sat stitching and cutting leather all day in tiny workshops. Many workshops made ploughs and harrows and simple harvesting implements for local farmers. In quiet inlets where the forest came to the water, Tasmanian shipwrights were building ships from lcoal timber. At Battery Point in Hobart in 1847 they completed the *Tasman* of 560 tons, and a shipyard on the Tamar launched the *Harpley* of 547 tons – wooden ships capable of crossing the world. The first marine steam engine built in Australia drove a small paddle-steamer that plied between Hobart and New Norfolk from 1834, and that engine was the proud product of a Hobart foundry. A Tasmanian labourer could wash himself with Tasmanian soap, wear hats and boots made of the products of local tanners and furriers, read locally printed newspapers by the light of a Launceston candle, travel in a Hobart-built coach or ketch, and – if unfortunately sentenced to death – be hanged by a rope made in a Hobart workshop.

9 Mysteries of a New Land

The discovery of Australia went on apace. The explorers and the sheepmen found new rivers and the dry beds of rivers. Botanists and geologists found new specimens and marvelled at their oddness and gave them names. Some gathered Aboriginal vocabularies, customs and implements. Others discovered the fury of the hot north wind and the might of bushfires. We are inclined to see these explorers as the monopolists of discovery, but they were only the advance guard.

2

Everyone who came to Australia was a discoverer. The immigrants had to learn that the seasons were upside down, that Easter came in autumn and Christmas in summer, and that the whole calendar of gardening was different. Those who spent time in the bush were slow to reach the stage where they knew instinctively that at midday here the sun was in the north. A few knew that the stars were a guide when they were lost, and so they made and carried mental maps of the new southern sky. 'If I only see one fixed star through a cloud-break I know where I am,' said one bushman who had learned his bushcraft from Aboriginals. Those people building houses or laying out gardens and planting hedges had to learn that whereas in Europe the hot wind came from the south, here it blew more often from the north or north west.

Nature was seen as freakish here. How could newcomers explain a tree which retained its leaves but shed its bark, or a swan which was black or rich soil which was treeless and poor soil which nourished large trees? And on what plan did Nature design the kangaroo? Barron Field, judge and poet, gave this unexpected answer:

> She had made the squirrel fragile;
> She had made the bounding hart;
> But a third so strong and agile
> Was beyond ev'n Nature's art;
> So she join'd the former two
> In thee, Kangaroo.

So the kangaroo, it seemed, was the result of divine surgery, a successful transplant operation.

The French naturalist, Peron, decided that here many of the doctrines of science stood on their head. On 7 October 1802 he saw and heard a storm which he believed had no equal in the annals of meteorology: a calm, sunny Sydney afternoon was ruffled by flat black clouds arriving from the north west, a quick soaring of the temperature, thunder and lightning on the grand scale, winds blowing from every point of the compass, and then the crashing of hail. Even the hailstones were strange, being elongated and prismatic rather than round. Peron, still marvelling, was told that such storms were not rare in New South Wales. What other land, he asked himself, makes such law-defying weather? In his book of travels he reported that on the Hawkesbury River a monstrous Nile-like flood was more than 40 feet high. Such floods, he reported with wide-eyed exaggeration, rush down ten or twelve times in certain years. In this land of miracles his expedition collected greedily seeds, reptiles, birds, plants and minerals – 23,000 of them – which merited study. They returned to France with, in addition, about 100 living animals: no large ark had ever travelled so far. Decades later, Peron's idea that the weather in Australia was a law to itself can be seen in the writings of intelligent men. Thus W. H. Archer, Victoria's statistician, reported in 1854 that careful tests of the temperature on the hill and in the valley at the lunatic asylum at Kew supported the theory that the valleys in Australia were, unlike England's, cooler than the mountains.

3

The sea had to be explored. The discovery of the coastline of Australia was slow and dangerous. Tasmania was not found to be an island until ten years after the first settlement had been placed at Sydney. The possibility that a wide river might open a passage from the northern coast to the centre of Australia was still cherished by the British Admiralty thirty years after Sydney was founded; and indeed Captain P. P. King was sent by the British Admiralty in 1817 to north-west Australia 'to discover whether there be any river'. The remarkable charts drawn of much of the Australian coast by the brilliant explorer, Captain Matthew Flinders, were only the first phase of coastal exploration. Countless rocks and reefs close to the sea lanes still lay uncharted as late as 1850. Many bays and estuaries which could harbour ships were still unknown or unsurveyed.

Even when knowledge was accumulated it was not easily dispersed. Few lights shone on the Australian coast. The first lighthouse marking the entrance to Sydney Harbour was erected to the design of Francis Greenway in 1818, and its white lamp burned whale oil and could be seen on a clear night more than 20 miles from South Head. Australia's second lighthouse, manned by convicts on Iron Pot Islet at the mouth of the Derwent, was not built until 1832. More than half a century after the first settlement, the two main sea straits, Torres Strait and Bass Strait, carried no lights. Lighthouses in Bass Strait were essential because most sailing ships saw no land all the way from England to Bass Strait; and as they could not be certain of their exact position when they approached Bass Strait, they were in danger of running ashore when they believed they were still far out to sea. The western entrance to the strait, between Cape Otway on the mainland and Cape Wickham on King Island, was 48 miles wide but in thick and hazy weather, or when wild seas were running, it could be hazardous. No lighthouse stood on the capes which guarded the entrance, but hardly a day passed in which no ship sailed by. In May 1835 the *Neva*, carrying female convicts from the Irish port of Cork, struck a reef off Cape Wickham early one moonlit windy morning. A high sea was running, the ship was pounded to pieces in eight hours, and 219 people were drowned. Of the twenty-two who safely reached the shore, seven died of cold and exhaustion. All the children on board – and most were the children of female convicts – were drowned.

Ten years later, in August 1845, the ship *Cataraqui* approached King Island from the west. She had left Liverpool three and a half months earlier with more than 400 emigrants and crew. She was bound for Port Phillip and the long voyage was almost over and passengers could probably smell land – the strong, earthy smell which was carried in the wind far out to sea. The weather in the last few days had been stormy and the captain could not ascertain the exact position of the ship and believed he was 60 miles further west than in fact he was. Early on the morning of 4 August, amidst heavy rain and a strong wind, the ship ran into a reef close to the shore of King Island. In the first light of morning the shore could be seen but nobody could reach it. All day the waves broke over the ship, washing adults and children overboard, smashing the lifeboats and breaking the wooden ship apart. Eight of the crew and one migrant eventually reached the barren beach. It is believed that 399 were drowned: most were buried in mass graves, dug by a sealer near the beach. To this day no greater civilian disaster has occurred in Australia.

At last in 1848 a lighthouse was erected in the wilderness at Cape Otway, on the opposite coast, and the light which flashed every three quarters of a minute was the first to be seen by an east-bound ship on two thousand miles of coast. King Island was still dark at night, possessing no light or beacon of warning. Eleven ships were wrecked on the island in the 1850s; and even after a circular lighthouse with a fixed light was erected at Cape Wickham in 1861, many other ships were wrecked. The eastern end of Bass Strait trapped more ships. In the 19th century, around the coast of the continent, thousands of passengers and sailors were drowned because knowledge of the winds and currents, shallows and rocks, was inevitably patchy.

For any colony a crucial discovery is the shortest route to and from the homeland. The West Indies, North America, India and South Africa found that route easily because no major alternative existed. For remote New South Wales the question was more vital but less easily answered. We know now that the westerly winds dominate the colder seas of the southern hemisphere and that they virtually circle the globe, brushing past the south of Africa and the south of Australia and New Zealand and Cape Horn near the tip of South America. Between those capes ran a racecourse for east-bound sailing ships but existence of the racecourse was not appreciated in 1788. When the new town of Sydney became nervous about its food supplies, Captain John Hunter was ordered to sail in the *Sirius* to Cape Town to buy grain. Governor Phillip, knowing that the shortest distance to Cape Town was to the west of Tasmania, suggested that Hunter follow that route. Hunter, however, placed his trust in the strong winds and chose instead the longer route past Cape Horn and so east to Cape Town. He proved that the westerlies made the longer route the speediest. His loaded ship returned to Sydney – again with the westerlies – in May 1789, having circumnavigated the globe.

The knowledge of the strength of the westerlies was slow to reach chart-makers. When the French sent out Captain Baudin in 1800 they instructed him, after he had looked for the mouth of a great river in the vicinity of the present South Australia, to sail west to Cape Leeuwin, taking advantage of the winter easterlies. The British Admiralty's sailing directions half a century later recommended that for seven months of the year – from 1 September to 1 April – ships bound from Sydney to Europe should sail west past Cape Leeuwin and the Cape of Good Hope and in winter they should sail through Torres Strait. Sydney navigators, however, soon learned that, with the exception perhaps of January to March, a ship sailing against the wind might spend more than a month between Sydney and Perth. Thus

129

when the colony of Western Australia was founded in 1829 it was isolated from Sydney not only by a lack of useful commerce but by the strength of the winds. The difficulty of sailing from Sydney to Fremantle during most of the year more than offset the swift passage in the other direction; and if there had been plans to federate the scattered Australian colonies before the coming of steamships, Western Australia would probably have remained outside the federation. It was then more remote than New Zealand. Indeed a ship from Sydney sometimes reached Cape Horn in the same number of weeks as a ship sailing in the opposite direction reached Fremantle.

It became the custom on the England-Australia route, until the coming of steamships and the opening in 1869 of the Suez Canal, for ships to sail here by way of the Cape of Good Hope and to sail home by way of Cape Horn. They thus harnessed the reigning westerly winds on the two long legs of the round voyage of 27,000 sea miles. Even after that route became accepted, valuable discoveries were still to be made. From the late 1840s a few ships and in the 1850s most ships sailing to Australia followed a modified Great Circle route between the South Atlantic and Bass Strait, thus shortening the physical distance by about a thousand miles and also harnessing the stronger winds of the roaring forties and fifties. A Liverpool marine examiner, John Towson, and the superintendent of the National Observatory in Washington, Matthew Maury, were the promoters of this route which, in Maury's words, harnessed the wildest of west winds:

> The billows there lift themselves up in long ridges with deep hollows between them. They run high and fast, tossing their white caps aloft in the air, looking like the green hills of a rolling prairie capped with snow, and chasing each other in sport. Still their march is stately and their roll majestic. The scenery among them is grand, and the Australian-bound trader, after doubling the Cape of Good Hope, finds herself followed for weeks at a time by these magnificent rolling swells.

The new route and the improved design of sailing ships helped to shorten the average voyage of the faster ships by at least a fortnight between England and Australia in the late 1850s. The fastest ships were occasionally sailing from Liverpool to Melbourne – with not one port of call – in ten weeks or less.

On the homeward passage past stormy Cape Horn clipper ships began to sail a modified Great Circle route in the early 1850s. The dangers of the icebergs which they often met in summer were lessened as the flow of the drifting icebergs became more predictable. One little-known mapper of icebergs was George Neumayer, a scholarly German who sat in his Flagstaff Observatory in Melbourne and collated the information which had been recorded in the logs of ships. Faithfully he plotted the route of the clipper ships. He noted those which saw no icebergs. He observed *The Champion of the Seas* which on a fine day in the Pacific in January 1863 glided into a field of towering icebergs and then a chain of smaller bergs that extended for a hundred miles in a latitude more northerly than Cape Horn. In an era when many ships followed the latitude of 48, 50 or 55 degrees, hoping thus to avoid the summer icebergs until they had to veer south to round Cape Horn, Neumayer argued that they would meet fewer icebergs if in summer they followed the southern latitude of 60 degrees. There, he explained, the winds were more favourable and the summer days were longer, and so a lookout for ice was more effective. Neumayer's conclusions rested on the willingness of sea-captains to experiment – with their ships and cargo and passengers at risk – in finding or following new routes. The global routes of the sailing ships which for long were our lifeline were the result of countless mishaps and observations made in the space of a century by countless men on sea and land.

4

The faraway interior was for long a mystery. What if it should prove richer than the coastal valleys? The idea was widespread that in the heart of Australia lay a sea or lake and that perhaps on the shores of that sea, or beyond the dry bed of that sea, lay the Iowa or the Mississippi Valley of Australia. Between 1829 and 1845 Charles Sturt travelled – even carrying a boat overland – in 'search of the inland marshes or sea, and Eyre looked for it before he followed the coast westwards to Albany. Leichhardt and Major Mitchell looked for the great north-flowing tropical river in the north east of the continent while Grey sought it in the north west. We remember only the failure of these journeys and forget the enthusiasm with which they commenced and the optimism which survived their return. Several of these expeditions were like long street-processions. Ludwig Leichhardt set out in 1847 to cross Australia from east to west with eight men, 15 horses, 13 mules and a pile of provisions and equipment. He was also accompanied by 270 Queensland goats, 180 sheep, and 40 bullocks – a travelling abattoir. 'They must have greatly encumbered his march,' noted John Forrest, a frugal, Australian-born explorer who led one of the parties which failed to find traces of Leichhardt.

With few exceptions the most valuable journeys of overland exploration did not go far inland. As most of the fertile land lies in a boomerang-shaped area following the south-eastern coast, the long inland journeys were unlikely to succeed. The courageous expeditions travelling far into the centre rarely had much effect on our history.

The names of the explorers are printed on the map but hundreds of journeys of discovery left behind no reports or travel books. While the official explorers, usually equipped by a government, were the first to move into many new regions, each region had to be explored many times. It had to be explored in summer as well as winter, in dry years as well as lush years. It had to be explored by men whose minds worked like a theodolite and by men who were experienced with sheep and cattle, by men who searched for minerals or exotic plants and birds, or engineers planning a road.

Australia was a museum which breathed. The explorers gloried in the novel birds. The white Torres Strait Pigeon was seen near Cape York by the Spaniard, Luis Torres, as he sailed west in 1606. At the end of the century, the existence of black swans astonished the Dutchman de Vlamingh and from the Swan River he carried three black swans to Djakarta as curiosities. Once the British settled in New South Wales, the discoveries of birds and animals were accelerated. An emu was shot by a convict in February 1788 near the present site of the Central Railway Station in Sydney; and the second emu to be captured was said to taste like beef, and thereafter emus were hunted. The first wombat, the naked-nosed wombat, was found by ship-wrecked sailors at the eastern edge of Bass Strait in 1797, and in the following year the former convict John Wilson led a small exploring party which found the first mainland wombat as well as the first lyrebird. The lyrebird was discovered on the tableland at Bargo, near the present highway between Sydney and Canberra, and aroused such wonder that a grandiose name was sought: the Botany Bay Pheasant or the New South Wales Bird of Paradise.

Australian wallabies, echidnas, platypus, emus and other strange creatures were captured for shipment to Europe. Ships were fitted with deck pens, and kangaroos knew sea-sickness as they rounded Cape Horn on their way to the private zoos of European monarchs and zoologists. George Harper, reaching Sydney in 1827 as a young man with a letter of introduction from the king of living novelists, Sir Walter Scott, returned home in some disgrace six years later. But he carried in the ship *Portland* the feathers and skins of 1675 native birds. He also carried live emus, and offered two to Scott who was happy to accept, for he thought an emu was a coloured parrot.

Explorers found novelties far inland. Others explored Australia from the safety of Sydney. The southern sky was as mysterious as southern land, and in a new observatory by the Parramatta River in 1822 the governor Sir Thomas Brisbane busied himself on starry nights with his telescopes. In June he saw one of the most exciting sights ever presented to a sky-gazer. A young German astronomer Johann Encke had predicted that a faint comet first seen in

1818 would reappear in 1822, just as Halley's comet had reappeared in the predicted year; and with his own eyes Governor Brisbane saw Encke's comet march across the sky – only the second comet ever to reappear at its predicted time. The brilliance of the night sky in the temperate zones of the Pacific Coast, and the infrequency of fog and mist and rain compared with European cities, made Sydney a wonderful place for astronomy. A new sky was discovered, named and mapped. One early fruit was the publication, at Greenwich in England in 1835, of a Parramatta catalogue listing 7385 southern stars.

The geology of Australia offered surprises. In the 1790s earth was sent from Sydney to England for testing as a likely pottery clay, and the famous potter Josiah Wedgwood examined it and proclaimed it a new chemical element. Fewer than thirty elements were then known to exist: the finding of the new element which he named Sydneia was a notable event. In 1798, alas, the new element was found to be merely old Sydney clay.

A year later a more valuable mineral, the first consignment of Australian black coal, was shipped to Bengal from the new-found coal seams near the river mouth at Newcastle. Of the useful minerals, coal was the most common on that coast which was first settled. The finding of payable base and precious metals came much later when pastoral settlement moved beyond the very young sedimentary rocks of Sydney and the central coast. One of the influential events in Australian history was the simple fact that Sydney and Hobart happened to lie further away from rich metalliferous deposits than did the later-settled capital cities of Brisbane, Adelaide and Melbourne. If Melbourne or Adelaide had been the pioneer settlement of Australia or had been settled soon after Sydney, the sequence of major economic changes would have been very different. Rich gold and copper mines with all their social and economic implications would have been found decades earlier.

5

A new continent was expected to yield new plants as useful as those which the Americas had yielded in the preceding three centuries. The hopes which some scientists pinned on Australia were even higher than those which their predecessors had pinned on the Americas. As America had yielded an incredible harvest of new plants, it was inconceivable in 1800 that Australia would not yield its own version of the potato, peanuts and maize, and the prized tobacco plant.

The land was expected to provide drugs and medicines and ointments. Here, it was expected, Europe would find a capacious botanical garden with gaudy flowers, valuable food-plants, new fibres and dyes and ornamental useful trees which could be transplanted to Europe. The first British governors in eastern Australia had hoped to use two new raw materials – the pine and the flax plants from Norfolk Island – to enhance British naval power. They believed that other valuable plants were certain to be found as the explorers went inland. For this was an era in which Nature was still seen as the great inventor. Whereas many of the new substances of the 20th century have come primarily from laboratories and research stations, in earlier eras they commonly were found almost ready-made in nature. Nature was seen as a great laboratory of research and development. To discover a new large land was therefore to enter a laboratory such as not even a huge corporation could maintain today.

Timber was one of the early products of this laboratory. Such fine shipbuilding timbers as the blue gum and the Huon pine were found. The noble cedar of coastal New South Wales was cut in sawpits in the coastal forests. The bark of wattles was stripped by hundreds of men and used in local tanneries or shipped to England. The black wattle tree was transplanted to South Africa, and supplied tannery bark and eventually ran wild in Natal.

The eucalypt was probably the Australian equivalent of America's tobacco and maize – our most pervasive contribution to the useful plants of the wider world. It eventually flourished in so many parts of South Africa, Brazil and California that it was viewed by most inhabitants of those lands as a native. It found its way to dry expanses in North Africa, to southern parts of Europe, and even – under the personal patronage of Stalin – to the Moscow district and the Black Sea.

Nothing did more to exalt the eucalypt than its aromatic oil. In Sydney's first year, eucalyptus oil was steam-distilled from the leaves of the peppermint-gum, *Eucalyptus piperita*, a species which can still be seen on the sandstone bluffs overlooking Sydney Harbour. The oil, vouched as more effective than peppermint oil imported from England, was swallowed to ease 'gouty and cholicky pains and disorders arising from wind'. In the 1850s a druggist named Joseph Bosisto who had emigrated from Yorkshire to Victoria, proclaimed his own eucalyptus oil as an elixir. His bottles became well known in the British Isles and in the infirmaries and magic shops of the Orient where a parrot on a yellow label was his trademark. In his opinion the eucalypt was 'The Fever Destroying Tree', and a forest of such trees was believed to destroy 'fever-germs and poisonous exhalations', especially malaria. Today, Australians visiting the ruins of the port of ancient Rome are surprised to see the slender branches of eucalypts waving above the site of marshes which were once malarial.

The early scientists who visited Australia would have been disappointed had they known that the continent was to yield no new beast of burden, no useful animal, and no new fish or table-bird which was deemed worthy of breeding. Of the thousands of birds and animals and butterflies found in Australia, the only creature which was exported in large numbers was the dainty parrot known by the Aboriginal name of budgerigar. In the 1840s so many budgerigars were shipped to Europe that a decade later a bird-dealer in London could supply the birds in their thousands, while aviaries in Germany and France were breeding them for eager customers.

The continent which had promised the world so many new and useful creatures and products had hatched, after a century of British incubation, little more than the odour of eucalyptus oil, cages of bright budgerigars, wattle bark and the macadamia nut. Far more was offered than was taken by the outside world. If Australia had been discovered before the Americas, then it would have created more surprise: it would probably have exported a native tobacco, many useful drugs, and useful fibres and dyestuffs. Australia too would have added other products if the Aboriginals in many districts had not died out so quickly. The Aboriginals, being nomads and not hoarders, did not conspicuously display their foods and medicines to Europeans; and much of their botanical knowledge was not observed by Europeans. Curiously, one of the decisive events in the history of Europe – the invasion of France in June 1944 – was to be influenced by Aboriginal pharmacology. Many of the troops who crossed the English Channel to Normandy on D-Day were dosed against sea-sickness by a little known Aboriginal drug – the hyoscine from the Australian corkwood tree.

Botanists exulted in the variety of native plants, of which about 14,000 have so far been found. They collected them, dried them and classified them. Most of their specimens eventually lay desiccated in the basements of distant museums.

There was another kind of discovery of native plants, and it was more permanent and affectionate. Increasingly settlers – especially the women and children who had no access to a botany book or a museum – saw with their own eyes the beauty and delicacy of the living plants. Miss Elizabeth Macarthur, one of the first hundred native-born children, told an overseas friend that in her family's garden near Parramatta the English oaks and the Australian evergreen trees were both beautiful in season. The unique native wildflowers in their brilliant colour were also a delight. 'I wish it were possible', she wrote in 1818, 'to convey to you some of our flowering plants.' There was no way of conveying them – no air freight, no ice, no colour photography. Only a watercolour by a sensitive artist could hope to catch their colour and delicacy. More native-born children played each day on the fringe of the bush and gave flowers their own pet names – purple bells, spider orchids and Easter plants. 'How well we knew the wildflowers of the bush; how little we knew their names,' recalled a woman who lived as a child in a Gippsland bark hut. Sometimes the teachers and tutors tried to divert this joy in the wildflowers. We were compelled, complained one small girl of the 1830s, to draw with plain pencils the trees depicted in English books 'while our much-loved wildflowers were left unnoticed and our paint boxes set aside.'

Parents and children gathered seeds and cuttings and entire seedlings and transplanted the prettiest into their fenced gardens and hoped that they would survive: many did. The native plants cost nothing. They were capable of surviving the hot summers, especially on farms and station homesteads which could not always spare water for the vegetables, let alone for the flowers. The annual year books and colonial calendars began to offer advice on how to transplant them. Take them up in December, 'roots and fibres entire', and plant them in well-prepared soil, noted Melbourne's Almanac of 1841. The native bushes were the favourite decoration on Christmas Day, and in many cottages the veranda was decked with fresh-cut boughs and the dining room festooned with leafy branches and native vines. In public parks and the gardens of the rich, selected native plants made a stately entry, especially those which seemed European in stance and foliage. Sketches of Sydney Harbour about 1850 reveal a skyline pierced here and there by the towers and cupolas of the Norfolk Island pine and Bunya Bunya pine.

Late in the century the enthusiasm for native plants wilted. Perhaps it was the move of people to the cities, perhaps it was the more plentiful dams and water-pipes which enabled thirstier species to flourish, or perhaps it was a change of fashion. The strongest revival of enthusiasm for native shrubs was to come in the new outer suburbs in the 1970s, where they mirrored a new nationalism.

An early farmer, carpenter or fisherman – on reaching Australia – had to learn part of his own craft afresh.

Farmers had to discover the deficiences of the soils and the local pests and diseases. Thus the seed sown for Sydney's first crop was eaten in the ground by 'a plague of mice', presumably a native species: even the question of whether the mice were a plague or in normal numbers was a potential topic of debate, since nobody in that first year knew their normal numbers. In several seasons much of the harvest was destroyed by fly moths laying eggs in the stored wheat. As it was widely believed that swarms of insects were caused by lightning, no practical preventive was at hand. Many plants which flourished in cooler, moister English summers were bowed by disease in Australia. The slow-maturing English wheats were planted along the Hawkesbury river flats and were subject to blight and rust. The maize – the Indian corn – was less vulnerable, and in the early 1800s it covered half as much ground as the crops of wheat. The selecting and breeding of cereals for the various Australian conditions was a vital task but slow, for waves of farmers arrived with English and Irish preferences which were cemented by nostalgia. Significantly, when William Farrer at the end of the 19th century bred his prolific Federation wheat he utilized varieties of wheat from India, Galicia, and lands which were warmer than England.

Craftsmen and handywomen had to learn to use new materials to make furniture and utensils. In making their own chairs, kitchen tables, milking stools, crutches, wooden hay forks and harvest flails they found by trial and error which local timbers were suitable. The daily work depended at first on the simplest home-made equipment, and any tool that was easier to use or broke less readily was a valuable innovation which lessened the chances of hunger. Early colonists made their own leather from green hides and their own hats from the leaf of the local cabbage-tree. They devised new ways of cooking in a land where firewood was plentiful and became skilled at cooking in the bush in makeshift fireplaces. They slowly learned how to build with local timbers and to roof with eucalypt bark. Hundreds of long-forgotten men and women must have made those

139

numerous small discoveries – how to bake a better damper, how to make the handle of a stockwhip – which eased the daily burdens.

The search for raw materials had to be made afresh at every new settlement around the coast, for the varieties of timbers and clays and building stones differed. Sydney became the home of building in sandstone and Adelaide of freestone. In Melbourne no sandstone quarries were near and the abundant basalt or bluestone – while ideal for foundations, cobblestones, gutters and walls – was considered too sombre and expensive for most public buildings. The search for building timbers was likewise vital. Queensland carpenters had to discover that the beautiful close-grained coachwood was fit for making cabinets and the woodwork of horse-drawn coaches, that the tall turpentine tree was suitable for railway sleepers, that spotted gum could be relied upon by the wheelwright, and that the native cypress pine could resist the attacks of white ants. Only time and error could tell Queensland's early builders that the Moreton Bay pine, so durable in dry conditions, quickly decayed when it was exposed to alternations of dampness and dryness.

Any new country settled from afar has its Time of Hope and Mishap. So much has to be learned and unlearned. Much is seen but not yet appreciated. The mistakes are often most costly at the very time when the untapped resources of the new land – its soils, grasses, timbers, fisheries, minerals and virgin beauty – are there for the taking.

6

The climates of Australia were a mystery and an impediment. Sydney had been settled in the mistaken belief that its climate and soil would provide a paradise. The climate proved more attractive than the soil and appealed to many, perhaps most, newcomers. The tempo of work for convicts was rarely quick, and so the summer was not too exhausting. The convicts, coming from European cottages where fuel in winter was scarce, must have found the most trying days of a Sydney summer less oppressive than the coldest days of a Dublin winter. Indeed the attitude to Sydney's climate in 1800 seems to have been more favourable than it was two generations later. The mental attitudes to climate sometimes change, though we do not know much about those changes. Climate is more than a physical and measurable fact: its geniality or harshness depends much on how people adapt their minds and habits.

The first settlements were placed in hot climates in the year 1824. The tiny Fort Dundas on Melville Island, intended as a new Singapore but never as busy as a church bazaar, coped with the steamy heat when the summer monsoon blew in from the Timor Sea. A sister outpost, created at Raffles Bay in Arnhem Land in 1827, was stricken by scurvy and fevers. The main casualty of these attempts to colonize in a warmer climate was Brisbane.

When the first soldiers and convicts settled beside the red cliff on the shores of Moreton Bay in September 1824, the botanist Allan Cunningham accompanied them and supervised the planting of the seedlings shipped carefully from Sydney's botanical gardens: the bananas and pineapples, mangoes and guavas, loquats, plantains, oranges and lemons. Soldiers in their spare time dug the soil and planted french beans, cabbages, lettuces, pumpkins and turnips on the banks of the Humpybong Creek, while the commandant beamed on all this activity from his prefabricated house on the site of Redcliffe's present Anzac Parade and vowed that he needed only bullocks and plough to make gardens and fields of maize on the grand scale. His oasis soon shrivelled. The sandy soil soaked up the water carried by hand. Most of the seeds did not germinate and those which sprouted were scorched by the sun. Sickness set in, but the cupboard of medicines was bare by Christmas and was not restocked from Sydney for another eight months. In every isolated settlement in Australia the process of learning was painful.

Redcliffe on the bay was abandoned in May 1825 and a new camp was founded up the winding Brisbane river. More convicts arrived from Sydney, and at the end of the decade nearly 1000 convicts were at work – or sick. They spent the nights in crowded barracks, the hygiene was poor, their drinking water was sometimes polluted and they were prey to tropical infections. As the maize crops did not flourish at first, the convicts had meagre rations. They ate no greens and fresh fruits, for the gardens were a failure and nobody seemed to learn from Aboriginals which native plants were edible. The sticky flies clustered around the faces and eyes of the convicts in summer, and trachoma became an epidemic. Through malnutrition the scurvy set in, and the people were vulnerable to epidemics. The mortality rate was possibly aggravated by the heavy reliance on maize which lacks tryptophan, which in turn is necessary for the production of vitamin B. A diet consisting overwhelmingly of maize can lead to the disease known as pellagra, with its debility, digestive disorders and diarrhoea. In 1829 a disease diagnosed correctly or incorrectly as dysentery was devastating, and during that year one in every nine convicts died.

Whereas today Brisbane records considerably more deaths in winter than summer, the season of epidemics at the convict camps was the summer. The hospital, however, was often crowded in summer and winter. If cities in Australia in 1980 were to find a similar proportion of their population in hospital the whole health service would collapse, and the admissions to hospital in Brisbane alone would exceed one million a year.

In the hope that purer water and more fertile farmland would restore health, an outpost was laid out in 1829 on the site of the present Eagle Farm airport and racecourse. It grew maize prolifically, and those rows of tall green stalks along the river flats gave new heart. Nearby, however, were swamps and the mosquitoes bred. For several years Eagle Farm was stricken by a fever which was almost certainly malaria. For the first time the soldiers suffered almost as much as the convicts from a disease.

Slowly Brisbane Town mastered the seasons and the soil, the heat of summer, and the diseases. In its tenth year the grave-diggers were no longer busy, the maize and sweet potatoes and other crops grew in numerous small fenced paddocks, and the town itself had those bare, treeless slopes which reassured everyone who was frightened of Australian vegetation.

7

The cabbage-tree hat became one of the early signs of adaptation to the warm climate and to the local raw materials. Made from the dried leaves of the cabbage-tree palm (*Livistona australis*) the hat had a low crown and a broad, floppy brim. First worn in Sydney as early as 1799 the cabbage-tree hat became almost as popular as jeans today. In the Californian gold-rushes in the late 1840s this shady hat was often the hallmark of the Australian digger, and it even entered the United States' vocabulary: a 'cabbage hat' was the rhyming slang for a 'rat', an informer. In that same decade in Sydney the young larrikins loitered around the doors of Sydney theatres and made a point of molesting any man who wore a respectable black hat by tugging it down over his eyes. Known by their hats, the street loiterers were called the 'Cabbage-tree Mob'. In their skylarking they were early nationalists, the spiritual ancestors of rowdy larrikins at the big cricket grounds in the 1970s.

The veranda was the cabbage-tree hat of the early architects. Within forty years of the beginnings of Sydney the verandas were shading many new buildings in the town and the country. The idea of the veranda probably came from India and other tropical colonies – the West Indies or the southern seaboard of the United States – where naval and military officers had served earlier in their wandering careers. The high ceiling came with the veranda and both were answers to a warm summer. Soon the wide veranda with its neat wooden posts was the distinguishing mark of colonial buildings. Where no veranda was built the roof commonly overhung the walls. These wide eaves were designed mainly to protect the brick walls from the cascade of water during heavy rain. For Sydney was seriously short of lime for the making of mortar, and so mud and clay were often used instead of mortar between the bricks, and these soft materials and the hand-made bricks were easily damaged by pouring rain. Probably one function of the veranda was protection for fragile brickwork as well as an umbrella against the hot sun. In contrast, Tasmania had plentiful limestone for the making of mortar and a milder summer; and so the eaves and verandas were less necessary and indeed were unusual until about the 1870s when fashion rather than hot weather fostered them.

How to build for a new climate was a problem, and each colony found its own answers. In the new towns of Perth and Fremantle the summer had more of the hot, clear days than Sydney, and the surviving paintings depict those early towns awash with brilliant light and the shimmer of heat. They show houses of pale limestone which, no doubt, were cooler in the first two days of a heat wave and insufferably hot thereafter. The houses, curiously, had no verandas and no eaves. The builders of these houses sought protection more against the straying cattle and goats and geese than against the most pervasive intruder – the hot sun.* They preferred the picket fence to the veranda. The builders of Perth, coming direct from England and presumably knowing nothing of the colonial architecture which was already flourishing two thousand miles to the east, climbed their own slow ladder of discovery. Somewhere they eventually found the veranda. Well before 1870 verandas shaded many new Western Australian houses.

By the end of the century, verandas were almost everywhere in Australia, though many faced the wrong direction. The strong reaction of the writer Henry Lawson, on first seeing London in 1900, was to exclaim: where are the verandas and awnings? In Australia the veranda had become to the house what the hat had become to the people.

The more capacious verandas which shaded the house-

---

*When the climate had been discovered, news of it spread slowly and erratically. A well-known school geography book late in the 19th century affirmed that around Albany and Perth and Geraldton 'the temperature is like that of England, but somewhat higher'! It added vaguely that in Western Australia snow and ice 'are said to be rarely if ever seen'.

walls like a hat brim were a protection against the hot wind. Somewhere, in a morning or afternoon, could be found a stretch of veranda which was away from the hot sun and wind. Nothing was more feared, climatically, than these gusty hot winds. The source of these winds puzzled the first settlers in Sydney. Some people supposed that they blew from 'vast burning forests' in the interior: that theory was particularly convincing to those who believed in a wide inland sea, because a forest would only grow in a moist climate. Others supposed correctly that the heat of the winds was borrowed from the hot arid region through which they had passed. Charles Darwin, as a young scientist, felt the burning wind in 1836 when he rode his horse through a swirl of dust between Sydney and Bathurst: to him 'the wind felt as if it had passed over a fire'. The hot winds displeased nearly every newcomer, particularly those boisterous winds which carried gritty dust into every house, so that footprints were visible in the dust on the floors and stairs.

Sydney suffered less from the hot winds than did later towns such as Perth, Adelaide and Melbourne. The temperatures measured there, with imperfect instruments, were astronomical. At the public offices in Adelaide one day in the 1840s a thermometer registered 158 degrees Fahrenheit. In the same decade Charles Sturt, venturing further into the interior than any man, carried a thermometer which was graduated to 127 degrees. One sweltering day he took the instrument from its box and to his astonishment noticed that it registered 125 degrees. Placing it in the fork of a tree, away from sun and wind, he returned an hour later and found that the mercury had risen to the top and had burst the glass bulb. On that day the birds sat still, the horses could hardly lift their heads, and the dry leaves of trees fell in showers. 'I sought shelter behind a large gum tree', wrote Sturt, 'but the blasts of heat were so terrific that I wondered the very grass did not take fire.'

A wind-driven bushfire was completely beyond the experience and imagination of new settlers. They were careless with fire and Aboriginals were careless with fire. The bushfires and grass fires were specially devastating in south-eastern Australia where the summer grass was long and yellow and the eucalypts highly inflammable, the air was dry, and the fanned winds were fast. On Thursday 6 February 1851, James Fenton was farming in heavily timbered country near Forth, in north-western Tasmania. Early in the afternoon black banks of cloud approached, the light of the sun became eerie, and a strange silence and stillness descended. The fowls sat on their roost and birds flew about in alarm. Ashes began to fall on the ground, floating down in light clouds from the north. Many of the ashes retained the outline of leaves, suggesting that a great bushfire was burning. The darkness rolled in from the coast, so Fenton ran a mile to the beach, expecting to see a fire but finding only the darkness. The ashes were still floating down and the sea and the horizon were black. The darkness of this summer afternoon became so dense that settlers, by now sheltering inside their houses and huts, had lit candles. Some thought that the end of the earth, a catastrophe much predicted in the 1840s, was at hand. A neighbour known as Old Charlotte expressed the running fear. 'My word, missus, I never prayed before, but that brought me on to my knees.' She prayed until daybreak.

Nobody knew that the clouds of smoke and ash had been blown by a strong north wind across Bass Strait from the Port Phillip District where the bushfire of Black Thursday was ablaze. On that day a chain of bushfires extended 300 miles from Portland to Central Gippsland. Hundreds of thousands of sheep must have burned or suffocated. Half a million lambs, it was estimated, had died or would have to be killed. Dead magpies and parrots littered the roads, after dying from the heat. A Scottish woman and her five little children who lived in a bush hut at Diamond Creek, north east of Melbourne, were amongst the victims. The husband George McLelland was carrying the oldest boy Johnny through the flames to the creek when the blackened boy died. The father was so burned that at first he was not expected to survive.

Slowly settlers learned to reduce the devastation of most bushfires. They planted lucerne and potatoes and other green crops around their haystacks. They burned fire-breaks around their pastures to protect their flocks. They were more careful in choosing the day for burning the stubble of their wheatfields and in setting fire to dry, ringbarked trees. But new settlers, fresh from Devon or County Clare, continued to arrive and learn the lessons through their own painful experience.

The lesson of the sudden floods was also discovered slowly. Settlers built their huts and surveyors laid out the main streets of country towns close to the banks of rivers which could in twelve hours rise and drown the intruders. The little town of Gundagai, nestling in the shapely valley of the Murrumbidgee, had seen countless flocks of sheep pass through to stock the plains of northern Victoria. In June 1852 the river rolled over the town, drowning eighty-nine people. The great floods in Melbourne in 1934 and Brisbane in 1974 were far less lethal than that winter flood in little Gundagai. Bush ballads sang often of the danger of floods in this land of drought; and it is easy to understand why floods were so damaging, because few people could swim, they had no fast method of carrying warnings in the early outback, and the grazing and tilling of the valleys probably silted rivers and aggravated the flooding.

8

Australia offered clues to those scholars absorbed in the question of the origin of life. Were the present species of plants, birds, fishes and animals made by an all-powerful Creator, or did they slowly evolve? Was the universe, as the Old Testament stated, created about 6000 years ago, or was it the slow and unintended creation of billions of years? Did human beings progressively evolve and, if so, was the present civilization merely the precursor of a wiser, more powerful civilization? Those who were trying to answer these questions saw the Aboriginals as an example – perhaps the most valuable in the world – of a people in the earliest stage of social and perhaps of physiological

147

evolution. Were they a bench-mark by which to measure the progress of Western Man? Likewise the unique fauna and flora of Australia seemed to offer its own precious clues about the history of the universe.

The young naturalist, Charles Darwin, came in the ship *Beagle* to Sydney in 1836: an unknown scientist who had published virtually nothing. He had begun the voyage from the English port of Devonport with the belief that everything had been meticulously made by God in that swift act of creation recorded in the Book of Genesis. Viewing animals and plants in South America and the diverse finches of the Galapagos Islands in the Pacific, he began to question his own orthodox views. Crossing the Blue Mountains in the furnace heat of a dry summer, the sight of platypuses swimming in a river made him marvel that such an 'extraordinary animal' should exist only in Australia. Was this the water rat of Europe, but different in shape and build? Charles Darwin thought to himself the heretical surmise that someone who had never read the Bible, and had never been taught the existence of one, all-powerful Creator, would explain the presence of strange creatures in Australia by concluding that, in the beginning of the world, 'surely two distinct Creators must have been at work'. The sight, later that day, of an Australian version of the lion-ant seemed to confirm his thought. To suggest, however, that one God had made the northern hemisphere and that another God had made the southern hemisphere was, he knew, blasphemous. It was perhaps even more blasphemous than saying that there was no living God – a belief towards which he slowly inched his way. Only when Darwin returned to England, and thought and read and wrote, did he develop the theory that the various species of Nature had slowly evolved through a great struggle for survival in which only the best-adapted old species and new variants could survive. In 1859 his book, *On the Origin of Species*, set out his maturing view. Perhaps the most controversial book of the 19th century, some of its supporting arguments were culled from natural life in Australia.

When Darwin's book was impaled on controversy in the

early 1860s his strongest defender was Thomas Henry Huxley; and it is possible that Huxley's slow conversion to evolutionary views was aided by his own experiences as a circumnavigating scientist. Huxley had left England as assistant surgeon in the naval vessel *Rattlesnake* in 1846, and at the start of a long voyage he made a net with which to fish up sea creatures, examining them through a microscope which he lashed to a table in the ship's chart room. In Sydney Harbour in 1848 this 23-year-old scientist wrote his exploratory paper on the anatomy of the 'Family of the Medusae' – a kind of jellyfish – and that article provided the first layer of his international reputation. Huxley saw much of the Australian coast and saw countryside at places as far apart as Launceston and Arnhem Land. His future wife he met in a fine Georgian house over which a young Norfolk Island pine stood sentinel, in the outer Sydney suburb of New Town.

The birth of a plausible theory of biological evolution depended not only on the scientists who sailed from England to see foreign lands. The evidence used by Darwin and his early disciples came also from faithful field workers who sent plants and animals of the new world to herbaria, museums and individual scientists in the British Isles. In Tasmania, Ronald Gunn was one of those amateur collectors, a botanist and zoologist of titanic energy and patience. Born at the Cape of Good Hope, the son of a Scottish soldier, he became the police magistrate at Circular Head in north-western Tasmania – a bridgehead for trips into forests and mountains. Gunn began to collect plants and shells, animals and birds; and carefully packing them – using cotton, camphor or arsenic – he sent them by slow sailing-ship to the great botanist William Hooker, who was then a professor at Glasgow University. In 1832 he sent Hooker the results of his first six months' collecting, adding humbly that he was ignorant of botany, possessed no relevant books, owned neither a microscope nor a strong magnifying glass and was unable to purchase them in this backwater of science. He could not yet identify with ease the various mosses and lichens which he collected by shaded creeks or high summits. He was more familiar then with the Scottish Psalter than with any book of botany, but steadily his knowledge multiplied as he made, at his own expense, long journeys in search of botanical specimens. At a turning point in the history of natural science his remarkable collections would be extolled by an English scientist: 'There are few Tasmanian plants that Mr Gunn has not seen alive.' The great Hooker's son, Joseph Hooker, visited Tasmania in 1840 and 1841 as surgeon and botanist in a British naval expedition to the Antarctic. Gunn showed him kindness, taking him on expeditions or sending his personal servant to guide him, and showing him specimens of Tasmanian plants in his private library in Hobart. For years he continued to send hermetically-sealed glass cases of seeds and plants to the Kew Gardens near London where the Hookers, father and son, could examine them.

In 1850 Gunn sent a living Tasmanian tiger to the British Museum in London. He found and sent abroad so many species that today more than fifty plants bear a Latinized version of his name. Four species of shellfish, a bandicoot, and various landmarks in Tasmania were also named in his honour. The highest tribute came in December 1859 when young Joseph Hooker published his volume, *Flora Tasmaniae*, and dedicated it to the Tasmanians – Ronald Gunn and the pastoralist, William Archer. Gunn was not a theorist, and he would have evinced strong interest rather than delight when he read Hooker's suggestion that the distinctive plants in Tasmania could be explained most sensibly by Mr Darwin's new theory. Here, in fact, was the first book in the world to offer intellectual support for Darwin's controversial thesis.

Alfred Russel Wallace was a professional hunter of beetles and natural curiosities in South America and the Dutch East Indies. There he observed the marked difference between the Asian-type fauna of the western part of the Indonesian archipelago and the marsupials and monotremes in the Celebes, Timor and New Guinea: a difference now expressed in the name, Wallace's Line. In February 1858 he was staying in the port of Ternate, in that part of the Indonesian archipelago where the fauna is more Australian than Asian, when he reached independently the momentous conclusion which Darwin had made nearly twenty years earlier but had not yet published. Wallace had not visited Australia but he had experienced the uniqueness of Australian natural history. Is it merely a coincidence, at a time when only a handful of the natural scientists of Europe had visited Australia or its adjacent islands, that most scientists who were foremost in formulating and promoting the new theory of biological evolution had made such a visit?

In July 1858, at a small scientific meeting in London, the revolutionary theories of Darwin and Wallace were read to the world for the first time. Both papers stressed the harshness of the struggle for existence in Nature, a harshness such as naturalists who knew only tamed Europe were unlikely to imagine. 'Nature', wrote Darwin, 'may be compared to a surface on which rest ten thousand sharp wedges touching each other and driven inwards by incessant blows.' Both papers stressed that a knowledge of domesticated plants and animals – and the way they bred or flourished – was not a sure guide to life in the wilderness. These central conclusions could have been found by scientists who had visited central Africa, remote parts of South America or the jungles of south-east Asia; and indeed Darwin, Wallace, Huxley and Joseph Hooker had visited many of these other lands. Australia was not indispensable, but its long isolation had made it exceptionally provocative to an inquiring mind. Australia and the adjacent islands provided, more vividly than perhaps any other part of the globe, a clear impression of the variations among the species.

Meanwhile many students of the history of the human race turned to the Aboriginals, just as natural scientists had turned to the platypus and banksia. Australia might lack the magic of the Middle East, where man and civilization were thought to have originated, but it had its own fascination. Here perhaps was an early slice of human history, snap frozen. The iced specimen had to be studied quickly

151

because it was about to thaw and decay under the influence of European intrusion. Scholars thought that a study of the black Australians would illuminate the early stages of religion, the family, languages, and many human economic and social customs.

In scattered parts of Australia men and women busied themselves making lists and inventories of the Aboriginals. They busied themselves, believing that time was running out and that the Aboriginals would vanish from the earth. They collected vocabularies of several hundred Aboriginal languages, suspecting that day might come when these words would provide the strongest clue to the origins of these people. They busied themselves discovering Aboriginal myths, marriage rules, rites and initiation ceremonies. They collected Aboriginal skulls, for were not physiology and phrenology the sciences which ultimately might answer that perplexing question: where did they come from? Many influential books to be written in the second half of the 19th century – Charles Darwin on early man, Sir John Lubbock and E. B. Tylor on the origins of civilization, Lewis Morgan and Friedrich Engels' works on the origins of the family, James Frazer's *Golden Bough*, and E. B. Tylor and Andrew Lang on the history of religion – used evidence culled from Aboriginal life and thought.

The new continent was not only a laboratory and museum of human and natural history but was also a rich resource-bowl; and in 1851 it began to yield precious metals on a scale which would have astonished the Incas.

PART TWO
THE LONG HONEYMOON

10   Gold, Gold

The great rush began in May 1851. Centred first on gullies north of Orange and Bathurst, the gold seekers fanned out and found gold in creek after creek to the west of the Blue Mountains. The gold fever spread south, and far more gold was found in Victoria than in New South Wales. By the end of the year a long chain of gold-fields had been found, and in Britain the first ships loaded with intending diggers would soon sail for Melbourne. One of the world's great regions of gold had been opened so unexpectedly and swiftly that the events seemed like a miracle and seemed to defy rational explanation.

2

For decades settlers had been walking past the gold without seeing it, but that was not surprising. In a pastoral district people fix their eyes on the grass and do not easily see the signs of something more precious than grass. Most of the gold-fields of 1851 and 1852 had been crossed earlier by land explorers and by shepherds and their flocks; and some places rich in gold had been camped upon by drovers, shepherds, farmers, mailmen, dray-drivers and shearers. They kept their eyes open for Aboriginals, for pastures and waterholes and snakes and a multitude of things, but few looked for gold because they had no reason to believe that it existed here.

A few shepherds did find gold in the white quartz and they chipped away at the rock in their idle hours, taking a little gold to Sydney and selling it to jewellers. Coming from the British Isles where there was no tradition of alluvial gold mining they did not realize that over the ages the tops of large reefs of gold-bearing rock had been slowly eroded by weather and time and that the gold had broken loose from the rock and slowly eased its way down the slopes to the river flats and creek beds where it lay concealed amongst the gravel, clay and soil. In essence Nature had slowly done on a colossal scale the hammering and chiselling and levering which a few shepherds in the 1840s were attempting on a pigmy scale. Many river valleys therefore concealed, a few feet below the grass and river gravels, a vast quantity of alluvial gold dispersed in small grains, flakes and solid nuggets.

The first gold-rush would begin when somebody, by intent or accident, found the first grains of alluvial gold and applied efficient methods of separating grains of gold from the masses of gravel and clay. At least twice in the late 1840s that sequence of events almost happened. Near Amherst, north of the present Ballarat, a shepherd named Chapman found on a creek flat thirty-eight ounces of gold – worth about two years' wages – and attracted a small thwarted rush to a site which a few years later was to yield rich gold. Near the present town of Beechworth a young Victorian squatter named David Reid was digging a water race or ditch down to the water-wheel of his little flour-mill when grains of gold were seen but wrongly identified as mica. Two years later, in the foothills of the Californian mountains, an identical event – the digging of a race near a water-wheel – yielded the gold which began the greatest rush the world had seen. If not for a little ignorance, the Australian gold-rushes would probably have preceded the Californian, and the water-wheel mill at Beechworth would have become famous in international history. But squatter Reid, confronted by a workman who spoke the eager words, 'Master, this looks like gold', had simply said 'no' to the new tide of history.

Thousands of Australians sailed to California to dig for gold and many returned to see their own valleys and creeks with new eyes. In 1851 the big returning digger, Edward

Hammond Hargraves, visited the Bathurst district where shepherds had been known to find gold and requested to be taken to one such site; with his simple Californian skills of how to look and how to mine he found four or five grains of gold in the summer-dry creek. He continued the search, persuaded others to search, and by May hundreds of ounces of gold had been found in that place which Hargraves named Ophir, after the Biblical place of gold. The news created amazement, and people passing on word of the latest discovery repeatedly spoke of 'gold, gold' as if they had to assure themselves that the incredible was true.

The wool industry and its lines of communication aided discovery. Gold-bearing ground is more likely to be discovered if men happen to cross that ground in the course of their daily work. Understandably the first gold discoveries in Victoria in 1851 were close to sheep-folds, pastoral huts and upcountry roads. The first gold of Warrandyte was found near a hut. The first gold of Clunes was found in a quartz reef virtually in the backyard of a squatter's homestead; the reef was so handy to the squatter's vegetable garden that it had been originally considered more valuable as a source of gravel for the garden paths. At Buninyong, which was perhaps the largest inland village in Victoria, the first gold was found close to a road by the village blacksmith who had walked only a mile from his forge. The first gold of Castlemaine – the heart of the famous Mount Alexander field – was found in a bough yard where the shepherds kept their sheep at night. The first gold of Bendigo was found in a chain of water-holes near a shepherd's hut and stockyard. The first gold at Ballarat was found near an upcountry road. Everywhere in 1851 and 1852 the first gold on new fields was found where for years people had passed without looking.

By the law of England all gold belonged to the Crown, and that had been one reason why the shepherds who found gold in the 1840s had not publicized what they found. The law enabled the governments to regulate the new gold-fields minutely. Even gold found on private property was not legally exempt. Faced with the prospect of unimaginable chaos as people left their jobs in 1851 and hurried to the gold-fields, the Government in Sydney ruled that every digger must buy a licence at the exorbitant fee of thirty shillings a month, and the licence then entitled him to dig the Crown's gold. The high licence fee was ingenious: it was intended to tax heavily those who found gold and to drive back to their normal jobs those sailors, shepherds, clerks and road-menders who were unable to find gold. Devised on the spur of the moment to meet social dislocation of an extent which perhaps even Britain had not suddenly had to face in the previous century, the tax remained in Victoria and New South Wales even after the scarcity of labour had been turned into glut by the gold-seekers coming across the seas. A sensible tax in the crisis of 1851, it was to become a major cause of the crisis of 1854 when thousands of people unable to find work in the ports had to pay the tax simply for the privilege of struggling as diggers.

One forgotten reason for retaining the tax long after it should have been abolished was that temporary migrants dominated the diggings. They were birds of passage who were likely to fly away when they found rich gold, and the licence fee was seen in part as a special tax on them. The new diggers from Britain, California and later from China were in effect the multi-nationals of their day: they were the grasping intruders and the disturbers of the peace in the eyes of the officials, squatters, merchants and older colonists who now held power in Melbourne and Sydney. Nowadays it is common to see the noble Eureka flag and the rebellion of 1854 as the symbol of Australian independence, of freedom from foreign domination; but many saw the rebellion in 1854 as an uprising by outsiders who were exploiting the country's resources and refusing to pay their fair share of taxes. So we make history do its handsprings.

3

Victoria had the richest gold-fields, produced more than nine tenths of the gold in the 1850s and attracted the most immigrants. To Victoria came nearly half a million migrants, paying their own sea fare and tens of thousands more came overland, uncounted. Amongst these fare-paying migrants, males exceeded females by a ratio of about four to one. Another 86,000 migrants who arrived from the British Isles were subsidized, and most were women. Victoria soon passed New South Wales and held the lead for nearly four decades. Most Victorians were migrants of the 1850s.

When the gold-seekers from the British Isles came in sight of the Victorian coast they had usually been at sea for ten or fifteen weeks. They were not fit for the hard life that lay ahead of them. As soon as they landed at Melbourne or Geelong – the main ports for the gold-fields – they gathered equipment and set out to walk. The horse-drawn coaches were expensive and only for the wealthy, the businessmen or the women. To ride a horse was even dearer. Of those who went from a port to the gold-fields in the 1850s, perhaps ninety-seven of every hundred walked.

They carried as much as their arms, shoulders and backs would bear. Loading themselves with a small tent, blankets, pick and shovel and pan, cooking implements and perhaps a little flour, sugar and tea, they must have seemed from a distance like a laden donkey as they swayed on the road. If they had no strength and money to spare they soon bargained with the owner of a slow-moving bullock dray or faster horse-cart to carry much of their load. Many travellers were really hitch-hikers who walked alongside a dray or cart and took advantage, when the dray halted at nightfall, of making their bed beneath the shelter of the dray and sharing the camp-fire of the drayman.

Every road to the gold-fields was a news line, and travellers tramping towards the gold-fields halted those returning, to learn where was the latest rush. Until the connecting telegraph lines were built, gold-fields news published in the newspapers of the port was always stale: word of mouth along the road was the 'late extra'.

Each digger was allowed only a tiny claim or plot of ground in which to dig. Therefore more men were crammed into a golden valley here than in California where the mining claims were large. On the typical Victorian fields in the early 1850s one man received a square mining claim no larger than the floor of a moderate suburban bedroom or dining room. He dug down two or six or twelve feet with his pick, and the earth and gravel he threw up with his long-handled shovel formed a mound around his claim. If he was lucky enough to discover gold he carried the gold-bearing clay or gravel down to the nearest creek or waterhole where he washed away the waste and collected the gold. In a typical shallow field, a digger exhausted his ground in a few weeks and then looked for another claim. Distant fields were often enticing, and news of a discovery in a new region could draw ten or twenty thousand people, all rushing to select the most promising ground. Inevitably the majority arrived too late and, taking up marginal ground, spent sweat and capital in finding little or nothing.

The diggings were a casino but the prizes went more to men of strength and stamina. The acclimatized colonial was more likely to find gold than a labourer fresh from England; a barrel-chested labourer was likely to succeed more than a weedy clerk; and Cornish miners sank shafts 'twice as quick as new chums'. Here was one of the rare instances in modern history where a great natural resource was more freely available to the poor than to the rich, for the poor were more accustomed to hard work and only hard work could conquer the diggings. Whereas the first vital natural resource – the grasslands – had been apportioned in huge lots to a thousand or more sheep-owners, the second great natural resource was apportioned in tiny lots to tens of thousands of diggers. Not until the era of company mining began in the late 1850s did men of capital gain an advantage, and even then the working miners who sank the deep shafts or mined gold far underground were usually prominent as shareholders. The busiest Australian stock exchanges in many months were to operate in the open air at Ballarat and Bendigo, and most of their kerb-side clients were probably working miners. The democratic flavour of the 1850s came mainly from the wide dispersal of wealth and the widespread hopes of finding it.

In appearance the diggings were a forerunner of the European battlefields of 1915. They resembled lines of trenches and foxholes. Many were a chessboard of shallow holes and fresh piles of clay and soil. Near by straggled the vast encampments of thousands of tents and huts. Like a military camp the first diggings consisted mainly of men wearing a uniform of serge shirts, moleskin trousers and knee boots: 'thousands of the finest men I had ever seen', wrote a Southampton digger who walked to Ballarat. And like a military operation the diggings depended on a supply line that ran not only to the nearest port but right across the world. Much of the gold was spent in paying for that long supply line and for the thousands of draymen, carters, wharf labourers, wholesale and retail merchants, sailors and ship-owners who carried supplies. Even on the short journey from Geelong to Ballarat, the cost of cartage in the years 1851-4 probably consumed about one quarter of the value of all the gold mined at Ballarat, one of the two main gold cities. One day in June 1854, at the river crossing at Batesford, the traffic moving to the gold-fields was carefully counted; and if the figure were extended to cover the entire length of the muddy road, then on that one day there were at least 750 horse drays and 650 bullock drays, with about twelve or fifteen thousand horse and bullock hooves all pounding up and down at the same time. In the following month the road was so churned that a Geelong merchant riding a powerful horse had to dismount and lead the horse for three miles through the mud.

The diggers were fed from afar. Their tea came from South China and the sugar they spooned into the pannikin came from the island of Mauritius or from the West Indies. Much of the flour in their bread came from the United States and Chile, because the farmers here in the 1850s lacked the labour to grow sufficient wheat to feed a rapidly increasing population. Even the oats eaten by horses on the diggings came partly from England. The spirits drunk by diggers came from the other side of the world, and most of the beer, ale and porter came from England. The only important food which Australia could supply entirely was

161

fresh meat, and if we were able to piece together a list of the hundred men who in the 1850s made the most money from the gold-fields, butchers would probably predominate.

Gold had a glamour which for thousands of men became an obsession. Many who knew they could make high profits as carters and storekeepers preferred to dig for gold, digging year after year even though the rewards were small. The most exciting rewards were the huge lumps, the nuggets. Six of the ten largest nuggets recorded in the continent were found in Victoria in the 1850s; and perhaps several more were found, secretly broken with a pick, and sold quietly to a gold-buyer for fear that a publicized nugget would be stolen or the mine which produced the nugget would be raided. Canadian Gully near Ballarat yielded the first of the monster nuggets in 1853 and it was so heavy that its weight, when recorded, was usually in pounds rather than ounces: it weighed nearly 135 pounds under the troy measure of twelve ounces to the pound. It was found in a shaft about sixty feet deep, and two of the finders had been in Victoria only three months when they set off for England with their treasure.

The list of huge nuggets grew. In 1857 men were sinking a shallow hole only about two arms' length away from a hole abandoned a few years previously when they came across their 'Blanche Barkly' nugget. They measured it as twenty-eight inches long, described it as irregular in shape and brilliant in colour, and sent it from Kingower to the Crystal Palace in London where it was admired by thousands before the 1744 ounces of gold were melted down for a return of nearly £7000. At Ballarat, a year later, the Welcome Nugget was found by Cornishmen in a shaft 180 feet deep; it was probably the largest nugget found in the world until 1869 when the barely submerged Welcome Stranger was hit by a passing cart-wheel near the Victorian gold town of Dunolly. When rid of impurities by melting, the Welcome Stranger weighed 2284 ounces and earned a sum of money which would have been sufficient, at ruling prices, to buy eight farms, each a square mile in area with livestock and fences and buildings.

Monuments were erected later on the site of these two remarkable discoveries, and the grand monument to the largest nugget lies in the bush in a remote part of Victoria. It is a curious commentary on the allure of gold that a society should have erected monuments to these inanimate nuggets at a time when it had erected few monuments to its most celebrated citizens. And yet the massive nugget symbolized the excitement and hope of an era when every man had his opportunity. These were monuments to everyman.

4

For many years of the 1850s society seemed to sway on the brink of chaos. The inflation of prices was insane. Citizens and politicians were alarmed by the arrival in their thousands of convicts from Tasmania and diggers from Canton. Civil peace was threatened by the rebellion of miners behind the wooden fence of the Eureka Stockade at Ballarat, and more than thirty miners and soldiers were killed on the morning of Sunday 3 December 1854. A few years later politicians were worried that the gold might suddenly give out, stranding tens of thousands of people who depended on the diggings for their livelihood. And increasingly the controversial question of how the land should be divided between the squatters and the would-be farmers demanded a solution.

Inflation at first seemed insoluble. Great wealth had fallen into the hands of many people but not enough goods and services were for sale, and so prices soared. In Melbourne between January 1851 and January 1854 the price of flour and bread more than doubled, the price of poultry and fresh butter trebled, the price of hay for the cows quadrupled, the price of eggs and green onions was multiplied by six, that of carrots by twelve and that of cabbages by thirty. Cabbage soup, like a rented room in Melbourne, had become a luxury. The inflation created intense distress for migrants who landed and mistakenly imagined that they had enough money to travel to the diggings; for the old and the sick whose savings were small;

for the grass widows and children whose breadwinner had gone to the diggings and was unable or unwilling to send money home; and for people whose wages rose slowly.

In the first three years of gold, the cost of living in Melbourne must have increased by at least 200%. Inflation at such a rate makes later bursts of inflation seem innocuous. The worst periods of inflation in the First and Second World Wars totalled between 20 and 30% over three years. During the Korean War in the early 1950s inflation was about 51% for a period of three years, and during the three years of high inflation from mid-1974 to mid-1977 the index of consumer prices increased by 44%. In essence, inflation in the worst period of the gold rush was four or five times as rapid as in the worst period of the 1970s.

Inflation was said to be a haphazard blend of reward and robbery but another kind of robbery flourished on the dirt highways. Ticket-of-leave convicts and escaped convicts came from Tasmania and New South Wales in such numbers that most murders and highway robberies were attributed to them. In the early Victorian rushes one in every six men, it was alleged, carried 'the taint of convictism'. In an attempt to stem the violence the Victorian government in 1852 banned the entry of any convict whose sentence had not expired and who did not carry a pardon. Under this law at least ninety-one convicts were sent back to Tasmania, but hundreds remained at large.

For long the outcry against Tasmanian convicts was louder than that against Chinese – who arrived quietly in 1852 and 1853 and then flooded in, a total of about 18,000 reaching Victoria in the space of eighteen months. After Victoria imposed the first restrictions against Chinese immigrants in 1855 the ship-owners sailed past the new law by landing their Chinese passengers at the lonely port of Robe in South Australia. Of the square-rigged vessels which carried passengers from Hong Kong in 1857 to Singapore, San Francisco, Havana, Madras and other ports, more probably sailed to the little-known port of Robe than to any other port. Mainly British, American and Dutch ships, five sailed for Robe in January, six in February and eleven in March, and from the beach at Robe the processions of Chinese, with their belongings carried on long shoulder poles, jogged to the unguarded Victorian border and so to the Victorian diggings. In the late 1850s more than 40,000 Chinese lived on the diggings, and the larger Chinese camps were self-contained towns with their own shops, societies, joss houses, herbalists and doctors, opium dealers, gambling-house keepers and, in the town of Guildford, a Chinese circus and horse-and-coach company. Their way of life had little influence on the English-speaking diggers with perhaps two exceptions: they supplied vegetables on a large scale to towns which grew few themselves, and their acupuncture needles were taken up by some doctors and used especially in Ballarat to treat the sciatica of miners who worked in damp clothes.

The two cultures clashed, and there were episodes of violence and serious riots. The Chinese were looked down upon as heathen, as immoral, as flaunters of vices, as cheats and tax-evaders. At least half of the Chinese were opium-smokers and according to the sworn evidence of the official Chinese interpreters most were heavy gamblers. In the vivid words of Low Among of Daylesford, the Chinese gambler who loses 'steals like a mouse, and pilfers like a dog'. As gambling was also a widespread habit of the English-speaking Australians and as alcohol was the opium of the people, these charges against the Chinese were not entirely consistent.

It was the custom more than a century ago to place all blame on the Chinese but now, as if in guilt, it is increasingly the custom to place no blame on the Chinese and to see them as simply the mindless, passionless, voiceless, gutless and colourless victims of racism. The Chinese too had their views and prejudices, their own intense pride in their religion and civilization, and their own suspicion of strange ways. In their opinion the British spoke gibberish, imposed unjust laws, wore clothes which no self-respecting Chinese would wear, did not wash themselves often, worshipped a heathen god, neglected their ancestors, drank themselves under the table, ate barbarian foods, and stole like a mouse. Quong Tart, leaving Canton as a boy of nine to settle on the Braidwood gold-field near Canberra, said that the Chinese then commonly believed that the British were red-headed savages and that many were eaters of men and murderers of boys.

The tensions on the gold-fields were aggravated by the declining output of gold. More people were crowding onto the gold-fields but there was less gold and it was deeper and more expensive to mine. The output of gold was probably at its peak between 1854 and 1856 and then it declined steadily, falling in almost every year until the mid-1880s when it began to increase. In fact the decline was more gentle than many observers had feared, for in 1857 a Victorian commission of inquiry reported that the gold became poorer at depth and that the government should be wary of building railways to gold towns which might suddenly exhaust their gold and be deserted. In the frantic rush for a diminishing hoard of gold, diggers working in what they believed was a British land did not wish to compete with an army of hard-working Chinese. The prejudice against the Chinese persisted into this century and then waned dramatically in the 1960s and 1970s.

5

The prospecting went on apace. Every day of the week thousands of people going about their daily work in the bush kept their eyes on the ground in search of minerals, and thousands of others did nothing else but look for minerals. Throughout the 1850s gold was the craze; almost every Australian man in the countryside knew how to identify it and thousands of schoolchildren could tell a small piece of gold from something shiny and valueless, from mica or iron pyrite. Gold could be recognized by its heaviness and softness and usually by its colour. One small ingot of gold, held in a city strongroom in readiness for shipment to London, was found to be unexpectedly heavy for its size. Even a nugget no larger than a halfpenny felt strangely heavy in the cup of the hand.

Other payable minerals were ignored. The eyes looked only for gold. Promising lodes of copper and silver-lead were either not seen or were shunned in new pastoral districts. Valuable deposits of tin were walked over a hundred times and not even examined. At first people lacked the knowledge of how to identify the base metals: they did not realize that the heavy black grains which they sometimes found while working in creek gravel were tin. They did not know, when walking through grasslands in search of gold, that those surface rocks with vivid stains of green and azure blue and dull red often indicated the presence of copper.

The bush hotels were often the indispensable mineral academies, the clearing houses of knowledge, for those who wished to identify new minerals or learn where they might be found. Lonely little hotels had a place in the sequence of steps which led to some of the most significant finds. It is likely that Hargraves learned at an hotel about the place where in February 1851 he decided to look for gold; and he was in fact guided to that place by the publican's son. Similarly, the first important discovery of tin in Queensland was made in 1872 at the Quart Pot Hotel at Stanthorpe. There a sock of sand was used to prevent the cold draughts of winter air from passing through the crack at the bottom of the hotel door. The sand seemed curiously heavy to one visitor and on investigation was found to contain tin. Promptly men rushed to dig up the creek which had yielded the tin-bearing sand. Four years later the first silver-lead of the rich Broken Hill district was found near the shanty hotel at Thackaringa and the publican was the spreader of the good news and a promoter of the first vigorous mine. At the bush hotels the finder of strange minerals might show specimens to all who passed by and seek their opinion. There prospectors picked up rumours of new finds. The publican himself was eager to promote real or rumoured discoveries in the vicinity for he was the first and often the largest beneficiary of a sudden inrush of thirsty prospectors.

The gold rushes of the 1850s had transformed the land.

Gold had replaced wool as the leading export, and the margin was so large that even in declining years gold remained ahead: from 1851 to 1870 gold surpassed wool. The output of wool was not diminished despite the initial scarcity of labour, and the more enterprising squatters made so much money from selling livestock to the gold-fields and from selling wool at higher prices to England that they could outbid most competitors when their lands were put up for sale in the late 1850s and the 1860s. In the struggle between the sheep-owner and the farmer who wanted his own pocket-sized farm the victory for the sheep-owner in most areas was inevitable and desirable; most land at that time was fit for nothing but sheep grazing on a large and efficient scale. But in some districts which were ideal for small ploughed farms, the squatter was able to outbid and outwit the land-hungry diggers.

Gold enthroned Victoria and Melbourne. It accentuated the dominance of the south-east corner of the continent. It settled parts of the interior with a vigour which wool would never achieve and it so increased Australia's population that a wide market for all kinds of economic activities was ready once the severe dislocations caused by gold had been remedied. Gold spurred free immigration and ended transportation to Tasmania. Gold also made society more democratic and optimistic. In fact, a surfeit of optimism was to be one of the dangerous legacies of the 1850s.

From the end of the 1850s, eyes were more alert for other minerals. New gold-fields were now harder to find, for the surface of the settled districts of eastern Australia had been scoured by thousands of darting eyes. Moreover the inflation had halted, wages were falling, and new copper mines had a higher chance of earning a profit. Between 1860 and 1870 the rich copper-field of Wallaroo and Moonta was found near the sea in South Australia; the Queensland fields of Peak Downs and Cloncurry and Mount Perry yielded their first copper; and Cobar was discovered by Danish well-sinkers. Each of these copper-fields was to yield more than £1 million of copper in the following seventy years. Then in the 1870s tin became glamorous for prospectors. The silent, never-smiling bushman 'Philosopher Smith' found the massive lode of tin at Mount Bischoff in Tasmania, and the shepherd Wills found the first payable tin in New England. Rich tin-fields were also opened at Stanthorpe (being the site of the sandsock), around tropical Herberton, and in the cold valleys of north-eastern Tasmania. Those discoveries were scattered along the Great Dividing Range on a north-south line which spanned two thousand miles. They were so productive that Australia, a pigmy as a miner of tin in 1870, was by the end of the decade the world's main miner.

Meanwhile the spearhead of the gold rushes entered remote places. The main movement was in the form of a great anti-clockwise loop that ran for more than twelve thousand miles. The rushes which began in the south-east corner of Australia in the early 1850s were repeated in the South Island of New Zealand in the early 1860s, in Gympie in southern Queensland in 1867, in Charters Towers and the steamy Palmer River in north-east Queensland in the early 1870s, and simultaneously at the Darwin end of the Northern Territory. There the movement of prospectors around the continent halted for more than a decade, before leaping across to the north-west of Australia in the mid-1880s. Then followed in the next decade a sequence of rushes to the Pilbara, the Murchison, the Yilgarn, Kalgoorlie and the dry mulga country beyond. The circular movement of gold prospectors was virtually over. From Ophir to Kalgoorlie – from the south-east around to the south-west of the continent – the rushes had occupied a span of little over forty years. It was therefore conceivable for one man to have taken part in most of the main rushes which marked that anti-clockwise march, if only any man could have persisted so long in the face of so many obstacles and hardships and disappoinments.

The mighty men were those who prospected in rain forest or desert. They had to carry their own supplies, cut their own track through forest and find their own water in the near-desert. Their triumphs were in the mountain forests of Gippsland in the 1860s, in the heat of Cape York Peninsula in the 1870s and the cold of western Tasmania in the 1880s, and the dry interior of Western Australia between 1886 and 1895. In forbidding terrain they pushed inland with the aid of a series of stepping stones of their own making. Thus when gold was found in 1887 at Southern Cross in Western Australia it became the supply base for excursions to the east. Eventually, in 1892, the rich gold of Coolgardie was found and that became the supply base from which prospectors probed further east, and in 1893 the new Kalgoorlie became the stepping stone from which prospectors moved further into the interior.

Most of the mining fields lay near the coast. Of the rich fields found before 1880 few were more than 150 miles from the coast. What lay in the centre of the continent? The puzzle excited more and more explorers. The dryness of the interior did not necessarily matter because gold was now rivalling grass in explorers' dreams.

11 That's Where the Dead Men Lie

In 1860 the exploration of the land was far from over. Vast areas had been seen by no European. A jigsaw of gorges and forest was untouched by roads, hundreds of waterholes had not yet been stamped with the hoofprints of cattle, and the native grasses and shrubs in several large regions had never been nibbled by sheep. Many of the landmarks in the centre were still unknown to Europeans: the smooth, monumental Ayers Rock was on no map, and the scalloped tops of the Petermann Ranges had not been sighted through a European telescope. In 1860 the printed map in the best guidebook to Australia portrayed the centre as completely blank. Large areas were inscribed with no names and lacked even a wiggle to denote a river or dots to denote desert.

We now know how much of the country, through defects of climate and terrain and soil, cannot be ploughed or even sown with pasture. This dry core stretches from the Indian Ocean in the west to the plains beyond the Darling River in the east. It stretches from the cliffs of the Great Australian Bight in the south to the edge of Arnhem Land. This area has no name but it has a rough geographical unity. Late in the last century parts of it were colloquially called the Never Never. A vast, oval-shaped region, occupying more than half of Australia, it holds less than one hundredth of our people but now produces one fifth of our wool and one tenth of our meat.

2

In 1860 it produced virtually nothing. The weight of opinion suggested then that most of it was barren. Charles Sturt in 1845 had reached barren ground near the border of Queensland, South Australia and the Northern Territory, and had been turned back. Edward Eyre had travelled close to the shores of the Great Australian Bight and seen hungry land stretching north. The Gregory brothers had come to the edge of a furnace-like interior in so many places that Augustus C. Gregory, chewing over the evidence in 1856, decided that 'the remainder of the unexplored interior is a desert, or at least unfit for the habitation of civilized man'.

This topic was too vital, and too bereft of evidence, to give rise to unanimous opinions. For every learned man who envisaged a rolling desert in the centre, at least another hoped that out there, beyond the dancing heat, were provinces of well-grassed land. 'As big as Denmark,' said the cautious; 'bigger than France,' said the optimists. There was even space for that permanent inland sea which for decades had been one of the magnets of the explorers: an Australian Caspian. As late as 1865 the South Australian priest, Julian Tenison-Woods, concluded the second volume of his history of Australian exploration with the hope that the inland sea, if it existed, might become the centre of an empire.

Governments and private patrons were willing to finance expeditions in the hope of finding pastoral lands for overflowing flocks and gold-fields for idle miners. In 1860 Victoria sent out Burke and Wills in a slow-moving, lavishly equipped cavalcade of camels and horses. The leaders reached the muddy flats of the Gulf of Carpentaria but died near Cooper's Creek, by the border of Queensland and South Australia, in the winter of 1861. The search for Burke and Wills found more grassland than they had discovered.

South Australia, suffering from dry years between 1859 and 1861, and the best placed of the colonies for thrusts into the interior, had another reason for finding a route to the far northern coast. Many of her politicians hoped to attract the marvel of the mechanical age, the electric telegraph. Already the telegraph stretched overland from England to her greatest possession, India; and the Indian mutiny of 1857 showed the potential value of a telegraph for summoning ships and troops during a military crisis. A telegraph to Australia would not only strengthen the security of the Australian colonies – and the Russian war scare of the mid-1850s had mirrored that insecurity – but might also enrich the Australian colony which became the terminus of the telegraph. South Australia was determined to be that terminus. It sent forward the gritty Scottish explorer John McDouall Stuart in a series of journeys which ultimately led him across the continent. He washed his hands in the warm waters of the Arafura Sea – east of the site of Darwin – on 24 July 1862. A year later South Australia took over the area through which he had passed, and for half a century it was to be known formally as the Northern Territory of South Australia.

Stuart's journey provided a route for the overland telegraph. By 1872 the continent was spanned by a long line of wire, suspended between tall poles spaced sixteen to the mile. Along this north-south line between Adelaide and Darwin ran the telegraphic messages to and from the outside world. The towns of Alice Springs, Tennant Creek, and Darwin came into existence as repeater stations where operators, sitting beside their machines, tapped out the short, expensive messages and so sent them along the wires until, growing fainter, they were picked up and repeated at the next telegraph station. From Darwin the cable ran along the sea bed to the Dutch East Indies and so joined the telegraphic system of Asia and Europe.

The string of telegraph stations across central Australia, and the parallel cart track by which those stations were supplied, provided bases for the explorers. At last the unknown space, stretching more than a thousand miles from the telegraph to the Indian Ocean, could be explored. Here lay perhaps the largest tract of unknown, ice-free land in the world. Between 1872 and 1876 it was a magnet for explorers who were more successful than Burke and Wills but did not receive the same acclaim. The western explorers were too far from the cities of the east, and it is in those cities that folklore is most powerful and most history is written.

Wonderful sights and dismal sights were seen by these explorers of the western desert. W. C. Gosse, the South Australian, saw one of the most astonishing views less than 200 miles from the telegraph line. Travelling with his camels through the spinifex and the sandy rises in 1873, he could see in the distance a high granite hump. Suddenly, from the top of a hill, the complete rock was set out before him: 'what was my astonishment', he wrote, 'to find it was one immense rock rising abruptly from the plain'. He called it Ayers Rock, after an Adelaide politician, but its ancient Aboriginal name was Uluru, and that name is returning to favour. Gosse did not realize that it was an inselberg rather than a rock and that it was the remnant – wind smoothed and water carved – of a tableland. On Sunday 20 July 1873, Gosse and his Afghan companion Hamran looked for a way up its steep sides. Together they climbed and scrambled and puffed. Gosse took off his boots so that he could gain more grip, but his feet blistered and at the summit he could barely stand on his sore feet. The view and the exhilaration were compensation. 'This rock', he exclaimed when he returned a week later, 'appears more wonderful every time I look at it.'

The elderly commandant of South Australia's volunteer army, Colonel Peter Warburton, set out from the telegraph station at Alice Springs in 1873 in the hope of crossing the wilderness to Perth. With three Europeans, two Afghan camel drivers, an Aboriginal named Charley, and seventeen fat camels he thought he was prepared for a parched land. But he was not prepared for the extent of the dryness or for the time required to penetrate unknown country. Fortunately there was no war scare in Adelaide during his absence, because the colonel was away from the city for a year and a half, and for most of that time he was missing.

Warburton was driven off course by the scarcity of water. His long string of camels became shorter. One camel ate

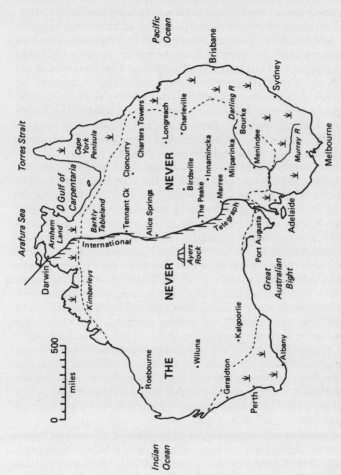

The Never Never – a vast area which can produce neither crops nor sown pastures.

poison, three became so weak that he had to abandon them, four ran away, and seven were killed to provide dried meat for the hungry men. Only two camels finished the journey, and on them Warburton heaped praise. Exhausted and ill, he reached the Oakover River in Western Australia and eventually the tiny port of Roebourne in January 1874. He had triumphed but had found nothing. The first half of his journey, to the north west of Alice Springs, can now be glimpsed by hundreds of thousands of people yearly on the flight between Sydney and Singapore. About three hours after leaving Sydney they reach his route; and in one effortless hour they cross the country on which Warburton and his camels laboured for four months.

'No horses could have lived with us,' said Warburton emphatically. John and Alexander Forrest would have agreed. They set out from Geraldton with twenty horses in 1874 in the hope of travelling east to the telegraph line. They knew that a camel might travel for twelve days without water whereas a horse might travel for only twelve hours and even then be in distress. The Forrests, however, were willing to spend much time searching for water. Using their two Aboriginals as water-finders, they rarely moved ahead unless they knew that water was awaiting them. So they moved slowly east, passing between the later gold-fields of Peak Hill and Wiluna but seeing no gold, and crossing a sea-barren country where they briefly clashed with Aboriginals. Finally, their sharp eyes saw a welcome sign on the ground: dry horse dung. They had reached the other side. They came to the telegraph station at The Peake, exactly six months after leaving the Indian Ocean. They had travelled 1800 miles, most of them on foot, and most of those miles marked barren country.

Wherever the explorers went, news of their journeys was awaited eagerly in the cities. They might find an inland sea. They might find a rich mineral field. They might find grasslands which stretched so far that even a man on the bordering ranges might, with a telescope, not see their limit. They might find a new overland route to a faraway port or region. At the lonely telegraph station at The Peake the news of the Forrests' arrival was telegraphed south where it created intense excitement. Their own slow journey towards civilization became a procession of triumph. After twenty-four days of travelling along the telegraph line they reached Jamestown, the first town on the route, where there were speeches and the drinking of toasts. At the railhead at Burra, where they placed riding horses and pack horses in the horse boxes of the train, they heard long speeches in their honour at a complimentary dinner. More speeches and celebrations followed at Gawler and Salisbury. Everyone shook the hands of the heroes, and at John Forrest's insistence his Aboriginal comrades were not forgotten. But all these receptions and banquets were mild compared to the parade of honour in Adelaide where people lined the roadside, crowded the balconies and rooftops, held up streamers and banners, rang church bells and cheered as the Forrests and their party rode their horses slowly towards the heart of the city – their horses now fit again, and the packhorses easily able to carry the waterkegs. And at the town hall the brass band played 'The Song of Australia' and the Aboriginal explorer Tommy Pierre made one of his short racy speeches and the sound of the cheering and the remembered emotions made older explorers who were present feel thick in the throat. This welcome was for bravery. The Forrests had found nothing.

If only one of the explorers could find, between the telegraph line and the pastoral country on the west coast, a corridor along which cattle and sheep could move between Perth and the eastern cities! Even if wells had to be sunk in the dry stretches of the track, even if the track were open only for four months of the year, it would break the isolation of Western Australia. Everywhere the explorers went – from the high cliffs of the Bight to the Tanami Desert – they found no evidence that such a stock route could be found. Even after the journeys of Warburton and the Forrests the hope remained.

Ernest Giles had gone to the fashionable London school, Christ's Hospital, the school where Coleridge of 'The Ancient Mariner' had studied. Giles himself became one of the great mariners, navigating the Australian sandy deserts. Infatuated with the romance of exploring he fixed his mind on the emptiness west of the telegraph line. It was a sign of the new sense of mission, the scientific sophistication of the last phase of exploring, that his main sponsor in 1872 was the Melbourne botanist Baron von Mueller. So Giles set out partly a plant-hunter. He also had dreams of that unknown space: 'There was room for snowy mountains, an inland sea, ancient river, and palmy plain, for races of new kinds of men inhabiting a new and odorous land, for fields of gold and golcondas of gems, for a new flora and a new fauna.' He also exulted that 'there was room for me!' At the start of his second journey, in 1873, he was about to leave the telegraph station at The Peake with his twenty loaded pack-horses and four riding horses when he was accosted by a moody young man who enquired whether he could come. Giles already had two mates but he could perhaps use a third. 'Well', Giles asked the newcomer, 'can you shoe? can you ride? can you starve? can you go without water?' Alfred Gibson said he could do them all. And did he mind if he were speared by the blacks? No, he said, he didn't mind. So Gibson rode off with them, carrying his small black-and-tan terrier. Far out in the desert country, a year later, when Giles and Gibson were on their own and water was scarce, Gibson was sent on a mare, with a patent compass he could not comprehend, to find help. A brother of Gibson had died while exploring with Sir John Franklin in the Arctic ice; and now, a quarter of a century after, in the desert which bears Gibson's name, he himself vanished without trace.

Giles was alone and far from help. Walking in intense heat, he was saved by his own stamina and perhaps by a mouse-sized wallaby which had been thrown from its mother's pouch: 'I pounced upon it and ate it, living, raw, dying – fur, skin, bones, skull, and all.' He never forgot the delicious taste of the animal.

Only when Giles brought camels to that harsh country did he conquer the 1300 miles of space between the telegraph and the Indian Ocean to the west. He conquered it twice before returning in 1876 in triumph to Adelaide and what he called 'the great family of civilised mankind'. Some said that the heroic age of exploring had now ended. It was always about to end, but in quieter ways it still continues.

These expeditions in the western half left few tracks on the ground. The territories of many Aboriginal tribes had been entered but few Aboriginals saw the white men. Occasionally there were incidents – a spear thrown or a shot fired – but both sides were wary. The small European parties, being far from help and fearing ambush, were eager to pass through in peace. At times the explorers were helped by local Aboriginals. Warburton, in a desperate plight, was given fresh meat, and all explorers used the small Aboriginal wells and waterholes. Here and there the explorers discarded equipment: an empty tin, a broken stirrup, a frayed piece of leather, a medicine bottle. Soon there was nothing in Aboriginal life to show that newcomers had ever passed by – except perhaps a spear point made from broken glass or the memory of the sight of a camel or a horse – animals far larger than any which the Aboriginals had seen. Occasionally on a rock face an Aboriginal artist expressed his surprise at what he had seen. On Ernest Giles's route at least one of those Aboriginal paintings was long preserved: it showed the extraordinary pattern, the hoofmarks of a horse.

Thirty years after that horse had passed, the Aboriginals' life in vast western areas went on as if the painted horse was surreal. The heroic burst of exploration had revealed that west of the telegraph lay nothing. The thread of wire which divided the continent in half happened to separate very roughly the marginal land from the hopeless land. While to the west lay nothing for a stock-owner, to the east lay vast carpets of country which were lush in a few years and marginal in most years and desperate in lean years. The trek of the pastoralists into that country was one of the quieter but more impressive events of the period 1860 to 1890.

179

3

The outward spread of the squatters before 1850 had been remarkable, but the invasion of grasslands and saltbush country and mulga after 1860 covered an even larger area, embracing nearly all the Never Never which could be occupied and some which couldn't. The expansion called for courageous pioneers – stockmen and shepherds, hardy mailmen, blacksmiths, well-sinkers and women who ran self-sufficient households and served also as doctors, padres, school-teachers and sewing mistresses. Courageous financiers living in the safety of cities often backed these remote ventures: so too did individual Aboriginals. Many of the white parties relied on Aboriginals who travelled with them and served as guides, water-finders, trackers, interpreters, finders of straying horses and searchers after lost white men. They were called 'black boys'. Any man who was thinking of settling in the outback was firmly advised by the popular manual of 1881, the *Australian Grazier's Guide*: 'A smart black boy, if one can be got, is almost a necessary adjunct to an exploring party.'

The procession of sheep and cattle into the Never Never was so persistent that by the late 1880s hardly any occupiable land in eastern Australia was not taken up. Virtually the entire route followed by the explorers Burke and Wills in their journey between Melbourne and the Gulf of Carpentaria was now grazed by sheep or, in the far north, by cattle. Not far from the place where they died, a town called Innamincka was born, and streets were optimistically laid out by surveyors in 1890. The plains of the Gulf of Carpentaria, the Barkly Tableland and the Channel Country were occupied. Alice Springs by that year had a few pastoralists in the vicinity. Darwin and its hinterland also had pastoralists, and C. B. Fisher's massive leasehold was as large as Tasmania though, he would have quickly added, not as green.

The mastermind of the Never Never was the drover and head stockman. Much of the interior formed a chain of intersecting drovers' routes by the 1880s. On most nights of the year a map of the drovers' camps – if such a map could ever have been compiled – would have shown an irregular chain of firelight stretching from the Kimberleys to Camooweal and Cloncurry and across to Longreach and Bourke and Wilcannia and Port Augusta and Oodnadatta. In hot weather or when waterholes were far apart, herds travelled at night, but normally they were halted near nightfall; and in watches of two to four hours the drovers took turns to keep awake, the red embers in front of them, the polished horns of the cattle occasionally reflecting the light, the strange moaning noise of the resting cattle rising and falling like the sound of distant surf. Overhead the black sky was dusted with stars. Like Clancy of the Overflow, as thousands once recited, they saw the sunlit plains extended and at night 'the wondrous glory of the everlasting stars'.

Most of the herds or flocks would have been driven fewer than 500 miles from station to station, or from railhead to outback station. Longer overland movement of flocks and herds were not uncommon. Cattle from the Barkly Tableland in the Northern Territory might walk slowly, painfully slowly, down the Birdsville Track to the settled districts of South Australia. Cattle from the Gulf country of Queensland might be driven in slow stages to the Wodonga saleyards in Victoria. Sheep in almost uncountable numbers might be driven – at six miles a day.

The skilled drovers were widely known. Nat Buchanan was a name known to nearly everyone in Never Never Land. In 1878 he drove 1200 cattle all the way – some 1400 miles – from Aramac in central Queensland to the Daly River in the Northern Territory, passing through difficult country in the late stages of the journey; his cook was killed while making damper. In 1880 he made an overland journey from St George near the border of New South Wales and Queensland, passing near Charleville and Hughenden and at last reaching Glencoe station, not far from Darwin. That expedition of two thousand miles would in itself have been remarkable if he had ridden alone but he reached Glencoe with 20,000 cattle – perhaps more than any man had previously driven on a long trip.

If such movements of cattle had been made in a well-watered country they might not have aroused curiosity; but in many parts of the inland the pools of water were not found easily for such large herds. In drought a stretch of sixty miles without water was frequent, and the thirsty cattle were not easily managed. 'They smell water from a long distance,' wrote one drover, and when they smelled it they were likely to break into a mad rush towards the water. It might be water which a drover or cook was pouring from his waterbag, it might be a private dam protected by a wire fence, or it might be a small, brown-coloured hole with enough water to serve only twenty of the hundreds of travelling bullocks. In a stampede the cattle could capsize a drover's waggon which held a barrel of water; they could knock down a horse and rider which stood in their way. Sometimes they thundered on, their sense of direction unfailing though most were half-blinded by the dust they raised. Rushing down the banks of a creek, the followers charged or jostled or fell on top of the leaders, and weaker cattle sank in the mud and were hopelessly bogged, and soon the small waterhole was puddled into soupy mud, leaving most of the cattle in thirst. Wonnamitta waterhole became a famous name after that night of 1883 when 1300 bullocks rushed its water. In the stampede about 600 bullocks were smothered by the weight of bodies and the sticking mud.

The best drovers were really generals out of uniform. Commanding armies of cattle and a small group of officers, they had to think of tactics, sending out scouts to see if sufficient grass lay ahead, where water could be found, or whether poisonous bushes might lie in wait. Drovers had to select their halting places with care, for they ran a military operation which called for watches throughout the night. They had to decide when they should move slowly if cattle were becoming weak, or press on in the knowledge that the weak would die. They had to count their cattle regularly, remaining alert for rustlers or for bush cattle which mixed with their herd. They had to keep up the morale and efficiency of their stockmen. The driving of sheep was usually, by contrast, an easier task because the sheepdogs were an invaluable ally, the flock moved slowly, camped more quietly at night, and was less gluttonous for food and water.

4

The new spearheads of settlement were aided by steam and steel. In 1859 Francis Cadell, a South Australian who had opened the Murray a few years earlier, steamed five hundred miles up the Darling in his paddle-steamer *Albury* and tied up beside a stout gum-tree near the Mt Murchison sheep station. He unloaded flour and stores and carried away a hundred bales of wool. In the same year Bourke, nine hundred miles up the Darling, was reached by steamer and became the port for a wide sweep of pastoral country which was opened in the 1860s. Whereas the opening of the Murray to steamers was valuable for commerce, the opening of the Darling River was indispensable because its steamers penetrated further inland. This narrow, meandering, tree-lined river was the first steam highway to the dry country.

Paddle-steamers, gathering their wood fuel from the steep banks of the river, provided the cheap transport so essential for remote country. Steam engines also worked the machines which bored for underground water. In 1879, on the million-acre sheep station Kallara, not far from the Darling River and the wool port of Bourke, a boring machine discovered artesian water. The water gushed high into the air and kept on gushing. The exciting news spread up and down the Darling and ran inland by electric telegraph and bush telegraph. In the following decade the strenuous drilling located a huge artesian basin. Small Queensland outback towns began to draw their water from artesian bores, stock routes at the back of Bourke were provided with precious water, and many pastoral stations filled dams and troughs with the water which gushed up – lukewarm or hot – from the boreholes. The finding of artesian and other underground waters began to generate over-confidence, and the day would come when large sheep-owners could point to dams full of bore water and surrounding plains which were eaten bare by sheep.

183

Corrugated iron – now that great ornament of the Australian landscape – began to find a home in the new interior. It had been first used on arched roofs in the London docks in the 1830s, and the iron was made more durable by the galvanizing technique invented in France in the same decade. By the 1850s it was being used sparingly in Australia. In the outer outback it offered clear advantages, being relatively cheap to carry, durable as a building material, easily dismantled in a dying town or deserted outstation, and verstatile in areas where building timbers were rare. In dry country those settlers who lived beneath a shingle or bark roof with no spouting and who collected their water in an old wooden barrel or a heavy square iron tank (usually a secondhand tank in which malt had come from England) realized quickly another benefit in corrugated iron. The iron roof and spouting collected rainwater and a round iron tank at the side of the house stored it. The new outback towns of the 1880s gleamed from afar, their 'tin' roofs and walls shining across the treeless plains.

Iron and steel began to provide the outback with its fences. At first there were shepherds or stockmen instead of fences but the high cost of labour and often the desire to keep out straying stock increased the demand for fences in the middle-distance country. As early as 1861 one sheep station in the Riverina built 54 miles of wire fence, stretching the wire between stout posts. By the 1870s the long wire fences could be seen on huge sheep-runs towards Barcaldine and Longreach, and boundary riders who patrolled the fences on horseback replaced the shepherds who had followed the flocks on foot. The wire fences were more popular in the sheep country but were less favoured by cattlemen because the heavy cattle could lean against the wires and – the early iron wires often corroding – break or bend them. After the invention of barbed wire in the United States in the early 1870s, it was tried in Australia. It was stronger than plain wire and the pointed barbs discouraged cattle from leaning against the fence.

For the kangaroos which had grazed on the plains for

thousands of years the wire fence was both prison and trap. Whereas they jumped the formidable log fences of the old days they hesitantly approached the thin strands of wire and halted. Red kangaroos who found themselves locked in a huge paddock would turn back and speed across the plains, sometimes in the formation of a great fan half a mile wide. Many ran headlong into the wire fence or tried to step under, entangling themselves. One nature-writer of the 1880s thought that in the Riverina the wire fences were as deadly as the professional hunters of kangaroos.

The stations in the Never Never seemed to possess a biblical simplicity, with their flocks and herds and riding horses and pack camels and slow bullock teams. Those who lived there – unruled by the clock – seemed to be barely touched by the industrial revolution. And yet many of these stations depended on the paddle-steamer, the steam water-boring machines and – from the 1880s – the refrigerating plants which at last enabled Australia's surplus meat to be frozen and exported. And increasingly they depended on wire for fencing and corrugated iron for shelter and water tanks.

Long railways even began to approach the edge of the Never Never. By the late 1880s only four of the long inland railways had reached towns more than 300 rail-miles from the coast: Barcaldine and Charleville in Queensland, Bourke in New South Wales, and the tiny Warrina, beyond Marree in South Australia. The longest inland railway was the line of 500 miles from Sydney through Bathurst to Bourke, the river-port on the Darling. Bourke seemed – to the coastal folk – to be the centre of the continent in those days, and one of its hotels was called the 'Central Australian' and one of its newspapers was called the *Central Australian and Bourke Telegraph*. In reality it was far from the centre, and travellers leaving the train at Bourke could go west nearly 300 miles – past Wanaaring and Milparinka – before they even reached the end of New South Wales. The inland railways were more like short shiny pins in a padded cushion. They were conspicuous and modern but did not go far.

From these outer railway stations the bullock teams set out with supplies for the far country. The five-horse coaches of Cobb and Co. or the mail man's buckboard or buggy carried the mails, small parcels and passengers, and those who could not afford the coach carried their swags. Where the bullock teams and the coach team finally stopped, the mail men with packhorses or the Afghan with pack camels took over. And so the furthest places were reached with letters and city newspapers which by then were stale.

Birdsville, a little pastoral town lying seven miles on the Queensland side of South Australia's border, was one of the busiest towns in the Never Never by the late 1880s. With just over a hundred people it was in its heyday. It had three hotels, two general stores, a butcher, a baker, and those indispensable shops of the outback – the blacksmith's and the saddler's. Birdsville had a court house but no church. It had a post office but no telegraph line. In the main street a few horses were tethered, the dogs sat in the shade and the bellowing of cattle was not far from earshot. The mail and nearly all supplies came by railway from Adelaide to Marree and then by camel or by a fortnightly coach across the Birdsville Track – a journey amounting in all to nearly 800 miles. The nearest telegraph town in an emergency was Boulia, a mere 257 miles to the north west by coach; and in a sustained emergency Brisbane was only 1300 miles away by the normal mode of travel through Bourke, Winton and Rockhampton. If we were to mark out a central rectangle embracing exactly one third of the continent, Birdsville in 1890 would have been the largest town.*

5

Many people now said the remote inland country was the real Australia. It had huge pastoral runs and few fences and

---

*In the late 1890s the fare by public transport from Adelaide to Birdsville was £10.6s, which equalled about four weeks' net income for the average Australian skilled tradesman. In 1979 one month's take-home income was sufficient to buy a return air-ticket to London. The return journey between Sydney and London can be accomplished more quickly now than the one-way journey from Adelaide to Birdsville in 1900.

The inland rivers were both pathway and barrier. A paddle-steamer towing wool barges along the Darling (c. 1884) and a punt carrying horse-vehicles across the Murray at Echuca in the mid-1870s.

University of Melbourne Archives

Edward Hargraves, the gold-finder of 1851, lived to see the gold rushes almost circle the continent. *Mitchell Library*

gates. It had few towns and few places which could even be called villages. Few of the towns had clergymen; the hotels were the main meeting places and their main drink was spirits; the men far outnumbered the women, and of course the working horses must have outnumbered the people. Hardly a newspaper was published in the entire Never Never but in the cities by the 1890s more and more was written about these hot places where a few people lived amidst adversity.

The life there was distinctive; it harnessed the heroic virtues and some of the mean as well. The life was close to the soil whereas more and more Australians lived in cities. It was often an adventure at a time when the daily life of perhaps half the Australians had little scope – outside the sports field or the larrikin bunch at the street corner – for acts of physical daring. It was a life in rhythm with the gallop of a horse at a time when the clock indoors was striking louder and louder. The most popular writers of the 1890s – Henry Lawson and Banjo Paterson – wrote about the Never Never or its edges. The daily newspapers gave space to the violent happenings and the natural disasters of the faraway places. And what is now called the Australian legend saw noble qualities – loyalty and mateship and courage – in the life and attitudes of swagmen, shearers, stockmen, windmill-repairers and boundary riders who lived out there.

In the attitude to the Never Never was hostility as well as romance. This hostility was displayed in the life and verse of a young stockman named Barcroft Boake. In appearance as in name he was distinctive: his nose was hooked, his right brow was deeply scarred and his dark face was waxy and unexpressive. In several photographs – his father was a photographer – Barcroft Boake has rather a Spanish appearance. Born in Sydney, loitering often as a child near the landing stage of the harbour ferries, he went to the bush as a surveyor's assistant and became a horseman in the era when the lively bush horse served the same emotional function as the racing motor-bike serves today. Often gloomy in the company of people, he revelled in horses –

the spirited bush horses. 'There is a pleasure in a mad gallop,' he exclaimed. 'There is a charm about this life always in the saddle,' he wrote breathlessly, on another day. He worked in the cold high country of the Monaro tableland, to the south of Canberra, and was also a stockman on the slow stock routes stretching as far north as Cunnamulla in Queensland. Like many bushmen he wrote poetry and he was in a surveyor's camp near Holbrook in New South Wales when he received a letter from the Sydney *Bulletin* disclosing that one of his poems would shortly be published. At once he wrote to his sister, apologizing for his elated mood: 'Tonight is the proudest moment of my life.' The tradition of the horseman-poet was powerful in the last quarter of the 19th century.

Barcroft Boake wrote verses which, perhaps more than any other written by an Australian, expressed hostility towards the pastoral lands of the remote outback. He wrote of the howl of the dingoes, the weariness of the 'never-sleeping drover', the skeletons of dead animals, and the skulls of men. He called his ballad, 'Where the Dead Men Lie':

> Out on the wastes of the Never Never –
> That's where the dead men lie!
> There where the heat-waves dance for ever –
> That's where the dead men lie!

In his view the far outback was hostile and treacherous: it could not be tamed. One suspects that Boake's view had been the common view amongst Australians in the 1870s but was a declining view amongst native-born Australians by the end of the century.

The cool high country of southern New South Wales is Barcroft Boake's paradise. On Easter Monday of 1892, moodily lolling about the shores of Sydney Harbour, his mind wanders southwards to the familiar highlands of the Monaro. He imagines its people preparing to go to the Easter picnic races. He hears the crack of the stockwhip as their riding horses are rounded up, he sees the women of the homestead buttoning their gloves and he seems to hear the stirrups jingling as the riding horses stamp the ground. In his imagination he sees the mists silvering the Murrumbidgee River, sees the willow trees shading the shallows where the horses ford the river, and glimpses the slaty yellow ridges sweeping 'proudly from the plain'. Here he sees the landscape and life of a kinder Australia and captures it in ten verses called 'An Easter Rhyme'. In the week when the verses are published in the *Bulletin*, he goes to Clontarf, a quiet inlet of Sydney Harbour, and with his own stockwhip hangs himself.

12 Juggling the Squares and Rectangles

Many decisions which shaped politics and society of today were made quickly on the banks of the Thames by a few politicians and civil servants. They largely made the political map of Australia. They determined how many colonies should exist and where their boundaries should run.

In the generation between 1825 and 1859 they were not afraid of drawing boundaries and proclaiming new capital cities. They created seven separate colonies in Australasia and abolished one, the now-forgotten colony of Northern Australia.* In 1860 the indications suggested that even more Australian colonies would be created. In the following third of a century the population increased from one to three million and that large part of the continent which lies in the tropics was settled for the first time, but no new colonies were created. Whereas the westward movement in the United States of America was accompanied by the creation of a jigsaw of new states, the vigorous extension into new territory in Australia between 1860 and 1900 created no new colonies.

2

The English government had long envisaged a string of separate colonies around the coast of Australia. It saw no

---

*The new colonies were: 1825 Tasmania, 1829 Western Australia, 1834 South Australia (but first settled in 1836), 1841 New Zealand, 1847 Northern Australia, 1851 Victoria, and 1859 Queensland.

reason why eventually tropical Australia should not also have a string of colonies as its population multiplied. It was even willing to create the first colony in tropical Australia before that vast region held even three hundred white people. In London in 1846 William Ewart Gladstone, the young secretary of state for the colonies, decided that a new penal colony should be centred on the coast of central Queensland. Colonel George Barney, a military engineer who in Sydney had begun the building of the present Victoria Barracks at Paddington, was sent to found the colony.

Colonel Barney was lieutenant-governor of a colony larger than Western Australia. His rule formally covered all of the present Queensland except the far south: the sandy beaches of Fraser Island were within his command but Gympie and the Sunshine Coast were just outside. His colony, moreover, ran as far west as Arnhem Land and Ayers Rock and Western Australia and as far north as Torres Strait. If it had remained – instead of the present Queensland – the main political unit of the north-eastern part of the continent then it would have had profound effects. That colony would have served tropical economic interests in a way in which a colony governed from Brisbane never could. It would probably have been a stronghold of indentured coloured labour even into the 20th century.

As the capital city of Northern Australia, Barney selected the site of the present aluminium-refining town of Gladstone, in the far south-east corner of his colony. There on 30 January 1847, in front of a small band of settlers and millions of hidden mosquitoes, he proclaimed the birth of a new colony. Northern Australia was elaborately planned; the members of the executive council and legislative council to assist him were formally named; and even the first government gazette was issued, in clear hand-writing. In equally clear hand-writing, in a sealed envelope in a locked despatch box aboard an Australia-bound ship, was another letter which – unknown to Barney – announced that the colony was to be abandoned. In London, Gladstone had been replaced by Lord Grey. It was almost as simple as that.

Lord Grey himself was not opposed to the general idea of making new Australian colonies. Indeed he had become entangled in the separation movement in Melbourne where electors in 1848 had actually voted him as their member of the legislative council which met in Sydney: a simple way of arguing that a man living 12,000 miles away could not be more useless than local men. Lord Grey and his advisers in London were willing to create new Australian colonies: the only question was when and where. In May 1849 in London a committee of the Privy Council had reported that the 'most cursory inspection of the maps and charts of these regions will sufficiently show' that, as the population spreads out, new colonies should be created. The committee could think of few greater social evils than the tendency for remote settlers to be virtually disfranchised if they lived far from the capital city. In calling for the creation of a new colony ('on which we would humbly advise that your Majesty should be graciously pleased to confer the name of Victoria') they noted that Sydney and Melbourne not only had different climates and differences in natural resources but lay at 'a great distance from each other'. On such arguments Victoria was created in 1851.

As even Melbourne and Sydney seemed to be far apart, there was a clear argument for creating additional colonies as the settlement leap-frogged around the continent. In July 1856 the British government gave notice that it would create a colony of Queensland. Better, it said, to run the risk of granting independence to a community which was immature than to run the risk, by doing nothing, of increasing tension and jealousy between regions. In December 1859 the new colony of Queensland held only 23,500 white people, and a larger but uncounted number of Aboriginals who would not vote or pay taxes. A precedent had therefore been set for the creation of many colonies. The new colonies, it seemed, would be set up in isolated regions but perhaps even in the settled south-eastern corner. In the 1860s Australia experienced a secession movement near the Victorian and South Australian border; and even the Riverina bellowed its threat to secede from New South Wales.

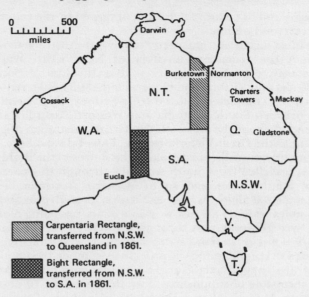

Carpentaria Rectangle, transferred from N.S.W. to Queensland in 1861.

Bight Rectangle, transferred from N.S.W. to S.A. in 1861.

The first parliament in Brisbane governed a colony which was smaller by about one sixth than the present Queensland. A long rectangle of territory in the far west of the present Queensland was still nominally part of New South Wales. The site of the Gulf port of Normanton was just inside Queensland, by a few miles. But the present Burketown, Camooweal, Mount Isa and Birdsville were part of that elongated rectangle which was still governed from Sydney rather than from Brisbane. No white people lived permanently in that Carpentaria rectangle and no black people cared who laid claim from a distance. Curiously, when the explorers Burke and Wills made their final dash northwards to the Gulf, they travelled through New South Wales rather than Queensland. They reached the salt waters of the Gulf in February 1861, one month before the site of their journey was transferred to

193

Queensland by virtue of a document signed by the colonial secretary in London.

While Queensland enlarged itself, South Australia took a bite of the remaining territory of New South Wales. Curiously, New South Wales – after the loss of South Australia and Victoria and Queensland – still held territory which was completely isolated from Sydney. One corridor ran between South Australia and Western Australia and extended from the head of the Great Australian Bight inland to the Great Victoria Desert. Thus Edward Eyre, in his brave westwards journey along the shores of the Bight in 1841, travelled from South Australia through this part of New South Wales and so to Western Australia. The rectangle was almost as large as Victoria, though only about 180 miles wide on an east-west line. Cars travelling along the Eyre Highway pass through it today in two or three hours. On the Indian-Pacific railway, five stations from Ooldea to Hughes stand within it. In December 1861 South Australia was granted this arid Bight rectangle, but the land was incapable of supporting more than a colony of ants.

South Australia then turned to the Northern Territory which was still nominally part of New South Wales. Stuart's journey of exploration had wrapped the Territory in the glow of wonder, and South Australia sought the permission of the British government to take it over. Queensland could have taken it but refused. In July 1863 South Australia was granted that vast mass of land, and in 1864 it sent Boyle Finniss, a former premier, as the first government resident in the Northern Territory. His first settlement at Adam Bay was abandoned in 1867, to be replaced two years later by Port Darwin.

Adelaide was willing to take over the Northern Territory, but willingness was virtually its only asset. By normal transport Adelaide was further from Darwin than was any other capital city. Even Hobart/was closer to Darwin by the normal sea route. Admittedly Adelaide had a land connection to Darwin but the distance was so long that the building of a railway was impossibly expensive. Even the building of a reasonable road was impossibly expensive;

and not until the Second World War did the combination of railway and made road link Adelaide and Darwin.

As the Northern Territory was governed from afar, it had nearly all the ingredients of a successful secession movement. But it lacked sufficient natural resources close enough to the coast to support a large white population in the 19th century. And without a white population of at least several thousand, its hopes of seceding were not high.

An east-west line drawn between Carnarvon in Western Australia and Bundaberg in Queensland divides Australia in half but all the capital cities still lay south of the line. The south ruled the north. This might not have mattered if the northern half possessed a similar climate and similar natural resources to the southern half. But the northern half was dryer and hotter; it was deficient in natural resources; and its climate was less conducive to European immigration. Its problems and obstacles were unusual and required their own solutions. And yet the entire northern half of Australia, by 1863, was governed by three cities – Perth and Adelaide and Brisbane – which were likely to prescribe southern solutions for northern problems. We have become so accustomed to the borders within Australia that we see them as unexceptional. Transfer them to the Mediterranean, and we would find Gibraltar governing Denmark, Rome governing Finland, and Cairo governing Moscow. Transfer our long longitudinal borders to North America, and we would see Boston in the 1860s governing Cuba or Vancouver governing northern Mexico.

For the first time, serious efforts were made to settle the more favoured parts of tropical Australia. Gold-fields, pearling ports and sugar plantations and pastoral districts were opened in scattered parts of the vast north. The question of whether separate colonies should be created there now rested with Australian governments in the south as well /as with the government in London. Without exception the Australian governments were reluctant to encourage secession movements in their remote tropical outposts. Each Australian colony was like a nation, proud of its territory and conscious of the wealth which might eventually come from empty spaces. The British government was also unlikely to encourage secession movements within tropical Australia if encouragement antagonized public opinion – the greater weight of public opinion – in the temperate zone of Australia. Moreover for London to encourage a 'home-rule' movement in the Northern Territory or in north Queensland would, by implication, be tampering with that more explosive issue: should Ireland be granted home rule? Accordingly a local agitation for a new colony in any part of tropical Australia had to be even louder than the separation crusades of the 1840s and 1850s.

Another series of changes in the 1860s and 1870s were quietening the discontent of those Australian regions which had the potential to be separate colonies. Telegraph lines were laid as far apart as Perth and the sweltering Queensland port of Normanton. The trunk lines of railways stretched out more slowly from the capital cities. In most parts of eastern Australia the mail coach drawn by fast horses linked outback towns at least once a week to the nearest railhead. Mail bags regularly criss-crossed the country. Even those outback squatters, storekeepers and politicians who shunned the coach could ride horses on long journeys, stabling them at night with a nose-bag of oats at the livery stable of a tolerable or intolerable hotel. From the isolated ports small steamships left regularly for the capital city. The local member of parliament could leave Townsville, boarding the ship at the roadstead three miles from the town, and be in Brisbane in a week. From the river-ports of northern New South Wales the local member could reach Sydney in the steamship in a couple of days. On the coastal routes steam offered a speedy, reliable service such as sail could never provide.

The most remote of the settled regions by 1880 were the pastoral lands and small pearling ports of northern Australia. Their isolation was still acute. In the Pilbara district of Western Australia, the main towns were Roebourne and the tidal port of Cossack, and in all they had four hotels, a few stores, several hundred people, and the services of a member of the Western Australia legislative

196

council whose electorate covered the whole north west of the continent. Lying more than a thousand miles from Perth these tiny towns had no telegraph line and no railway. The only means of contact – commercial travellers were informed – was 'by occasional coasting or pearling boats'. Further around the coast the few settlers were more isolated from a seat of government. In 1886 Darwin had about 200 Europeans and about 700 Chinese but the Northern Territory was not promised its own parliamentarian in Adelaide until there were a thousand electors. At least Darwin had a telegraph line running south to Adelaide, but the voyage to Adelaide required about three weeks of steaming in addition to the calls at many ports. If the Pilbara and the Northern Territory had had more people they might have launched successful secessionist movements. One reason why they had few people was their remoteness from governments which cared little for their interests.

The continent was shrinking. Every colony was compressed by regular, quicker, cheaper transport. By 1880 a London committee of politicians, happening to make one of its 'most cursory inspections' of the maps of Australia, could no longer argue that the 600 miles separating Sydney and Melbourne or the 1000 miles separating the parliament in Brisbane from the furthest electorates was a high electoral barrier. Indeed if Melbourne had not clamoured for separation from New South Wales until 1880, its plea would have been too late. In less than thirty years the old argument for a string of self-governing colonies around the coastline had been eroded by fast transport; and the time was coming when politicians proposing a federal parliament for all the colonies could no longer pretend that the remotest electorate would be hopelessly disenfranchised by distance. They could no longer accept the astute observation of 1849 that the people living in remote regions had no alternative but to be represented in parliament by city residents 'who possess but a very slight knowledge of their constituents and a faint sympathy with their peculiar pursuits and wants'. So had come about a sharp change in the theory and folk-wisdom of remote representation; and the main instruments of change had been less the political philosophers than telegraph operators, postmen, railway men, coach-drivers and ostlers, lighthouse keepers and steamship captains. Their daily work had shrunk the political and social distances.*

The cheap public loans arriving from Britain might also have stemmed the desire of isolated regions to form themselves into separate colonies. An uneven trickle of money in the 1850s, a waterfall in the 1880s, it financed railways, harbours, reservoirs, public buildings and those amenities, the absence of which had once launched secessionist crusades in the provinces. Whereas in the 1840s and 1850s the secessionist movements often complained, with justice, that they paid more than their share of taxes but received less than their share of public works, such complaints were not voiced so readily when British loans increasingly supplied the railways and improvements for which the outlying provinces clamoured. A province is most likely to seek independence if it believes that it is unfairly deprived, to the point of hardship, of the magic technology of the age. The British loan market numbed that sense of deprivation. Moreover, by financing railways and telegraphs and stronger roads, British loans now numbed that sense of isolation which had been so crucial in the Victorian and Queensland secession campaigns during the middle years of the century.

4

In North Queensland in the 1880s arose the kind of separation movement which, had it existed thirty years earlier, would have had quick success. The narrow strip of North Queensland, running from Mackay on the Pacific

---

*Even in 1849 the members of the London committee which reported on the need for new colonies in Australia were perhaps a little behind the times. They did not realize how in the new world long journeys were less forbidding than in the old, and that 600 miles to an Australian was a shorter step than 600 miles to the average Londoner. The fear of another rebellion on the North American pattern was still with them.

Coast around to Normanton and Croydon near the Gulf of Carpentaria, was one of the success stories of colonization. The first squatters moved into North Queensland in 1861 and the first sugar-cane was treated near Mackay in 1867. More sugar farms were cut from scrub on the tropical river flats, and Pacific Islanders were recruited to work them. They were known as Kanakas, and their death rate was high, but they enabled Queensland to outstrip New South Wales as the heart of the sugar industry at a time when white labour was believed to be unfit for hard work under the tropical sun. A string of sugar-ports and gold-ports arose along the northern coast. Mackay was a sugar town, Townsville was the site of a boiling-down works and then the port for the pastoral country and the deep gold-field of Charters Towers which, discovered in 1872, became Queensland's second largest town. Further north in the 1870s Cairns was founded by a publican as the port for the Hodgkinson gold-field and Cooktown became the port of the Palmer gold-field with sixty-two grog shops for the white diggers and a host of Chinese business houses for the Chinese diggers who dominated the most northerly gold-fields.

The secessionists became strong and vocal in North Queensland. Mainly sugar farmers and people of the sugar towns, they knew that their industry depended heavily on low wages and coloured labour. They were alarmed when in 1885 the parliament in Brisbane gave notice that the importing of Kanaka labour would eventually cease. In 1885 a petition with 10,006 signatures was sent from North Queensland to Queen Victoria pleading for a separate colony. The British government ignored arguments which, a few decades earlier, would have been most persuasive. Its final reply was that a region should not be permitted to secede unless the colonial parliament gave its consent. In terms of such a reply neither Victoria nor Queensland would have gained self-government.

In North Queensland perhaps the most dynamic politician was a small, pale-faced intense Irishman named John Murtagh Macrossan who had come to the northern gold-fields to mine and had become successful as a businessman, newspaper-owner and cabinet minister. He tended to favour coloured labour on the coastal sugar lands and white labour on the inland gold-fields, and so was capable of speaking for the divided north. In 1886 he spoke for secession, eloquently and intelligently. In August 1886, in the legislative assembly, his motion was lost by 40 votes to 9. In 1890 he lost by 32 votes to 26. Slowly the tide was turning. In 1892 the assembly voted in favour of separate lower houses for north and south Queensland with a common upper house to which each would send representatives. This bill, however, was defeated in the legislative council in Brisbane.

An acute sense of isolation had been one of the mainsprings of the earlier breakaway crusades in Australia. Transport had so improved that an acute sense of isolation did not inspire the North Queensland secessionists. The petitions for separation used isolation as one of their arguments; but it was far from as prominent and persistent a grievance as it was when Queensland itself had broken away from the parliament in Sydney. Those 1400 people of Charters Towers, Townsville and other places who petitioned the Queen against separation did not take the argument very seriously. They believed they had demolished it in one sentence. They simply pointed to the telegraph lines which ran from Brisbane to every town in North Queensland and concluded that 'for all practical purposes of communication', Brisbane is as 'near and accessible as any other place can possibly be'. The crux of the breakaway movement was not isolation but the difficulty of growing sugar with expensive unacclimatized white workers on the tropical coastal corridor. If the parliament in Brisbane were to allow coloured labour to work in those sugar fields, most of the northern cane farmers would cease to be secessionists. On the other hand, most supporters of the new labour movement at Charters Towers and Townsville were not secessionists so long as the parliament in Brisbane banned coloured labour. When in the early 1890s that parliament became more tolerant to coloured labour, thus reversing its policy, the labour movement became secessionist and the sugar districts became silent. North Queenslanders thus lacked a binding loyalty to their own region. They were too divided, and that division nullified their hopes of seceding.

The refusal of the British government to create a separate colony of North Queensland in the late 1880s was probably a turning point in our history. At the time it seemed a decision of no great importance but it probably prevented the emergence of a seventh colony which could have become a stronghold of coloured labour. For in a new colony the first parliamentary elections would have been a tense struggle between the sugar interests and sugar towns and the large pastoralists on the one side and the miners, shearers, wharf labourers, railwaymen and other white wage-earners on the other side. Mackay was the spiritual home of the one group and the gold-field of Charters Towers the home of the other. A victory for Charters Towers would probably have led the new colony into the new Commonwealth in 1901. A victory for Mackay's cheap-labour party might have led to sustained recruiting of coloured labour not only for the cane-fields but ultimately for the underground gold-mines and the sheep and cattle properties. If Mackay won power – and it probably had an even chance of winning – the new colony would probably have remained outside the new Commonwealth of Australia just as Newfoundland remained on the edge of the Canadian federation. North Queensland might have become a version of Rhodesia or the old American Confederacy of cotton states, with eventually its Ian Smith or Jefferson Davis defiantly facing the black world beyond Torres Strait and the white world beyond Rockhampton.

Events Which Might Have Happened:
A Chronology of the New Colony of North Queensland

1888:   New colony of North Queensland formed.
1889:   First election is stalemate between Sugar and Labour.

1892: Narrow victory for Sugar Party in elections and vigorous recruiting of coloured labour for cane-fields.

1894: Unions strike at Charters Towers and Ravenswood in fear of attempts to introduce Chinese and Indian labour. Long strike ends in deadlock, and white miners begin to move from North Queensland.

1897: Redistribution of electorates favours Sugar Party which wins strong majority at polls.

1900: North Queensland refuses to join new Commonwealth because cheap coloured labour would thereby be banned in its cane-fields, mines and shearing sheds. More white miners and labourers migrate south to the free colonies.

1904-09: 27,000 Indian and Chinese labourers arrive on contract to work in Cloncurry copper-mines and Charters Towers' gold-mines, to build inland railways, and to work in the booming sugar industry.

1910: North Queensland tries to buy Northern Territory but negotiations halted by Commonwealth and British governments.

1911: The Commonwealth of Australia places a prohibitive duty on imports of North Queensland sugar in order to preserve the Australian market for sugar grown in sub-tropical Australia by white labour. North Queensland imports more coloured labour to work on wharves, in sugar mills, on railways and ships, hoping thereby to cut costs of producing sugar and so compete on the world market.

1913: Indian, Chinese, Japanese and Polynesian population of North Queensland exceeds white population by six to one.

1914: North Queensland – along with Australia – declares war on Germany, and its geographical position enables it to lead attack on German New Guinea and occupy it.

202

A mail coach, heavily loaded, on the Cloncurry road.

Cobb and Co., Toowoomba

Many prospectors in arid country were using pack camels and riding camels by the 1890s.

A Kalgoorlie wedding party of 1910, drinking beer and lemonade made of water pumped from the distant coast. When the man in the foreground was born, Kalgoorlie and more than half of the continent had never seen a white man.

W.A. Museum, Kalgoorlie

1919:   German New Guinea becomes the Mandated Territory of North Queensland.

1920-27: Low price of sugar encourages farmers to diversify into rice, tobacco and cotton.

1929:   Mines at Mount Isa are opened with Indian and Chinese workforce and British capital. New railway opened to a new dredged port in the Gulf of Carpentaria.

1933:   Trade agreement with Japan.

1938:   Silver Jubilee of North Queensland opens with tentative promise to give voting rights, in next ten years, to all Asians who are literate and own freehold property.

To set out a chronology of events which did not happen hardly seems appropriate in a history book. And yet we easily forget that every statement we make of why events happened is in part speculation. In looking at history we have to ask: what might have happened? Every time we affirm the profound importance of a particular event – whether the finding of gold in 1851 or the failure of the North Queensland separation movement in the 1880s – we unmistakably imply that such an event was a turning point and that society – but for that event – would not have changed direction. There can be no discussion of a powerful event without realizing that it is like a traffic junction where a society is capable suddenly of changing direction. In writing history we concentrate more on what did happen, but many of the crucial events are those which almost happened. The born and the unborn may seem completely different but essentially they have to be analysed and discussed in the same way.

5

In the century after 1859 no new colonies or states were created. The colonial borders became rigid, except for the transfer of the Northern Territory from South Australia to the Commonwealth in 1911. The political geography was becoming crusted, like the geological landscape. Few events in the second half of the 19th century had such effects on our history, but this event is still little studied.

The existence of six instead of, say, ten colonies in 1900 helped to ensure that all the colonies entered the federation. For in the absence of a crisis it is easier to reach a compromise – and a federal constitution is a compromise – between six than between ten colonies. The rigidity of the colonial borders also helped to eliminate the possibility of a Rhodesia in northern Australia.

Aboriginals gained, too, from the encrusting of the borders. Back in 1860, in nearly every region of the northern half of Australia, the old Aboriginal life was virtually unchanged except perhaps for the arrival of an infectious disease, a blunt tomahawk or those fragments of glass which served as a knife blade or a spear point. Sometime in that decade – probably late in the 1860s – the traditional way of life ceased to be the prevailing way of life on most of the physical surface of Australia: it now occupied less than half of the land. Elsewhere the Aboriginal society was collapsing, the old ways of gathering food and honouring rituals and following ceremonies were in decline. And yet the pace of decline would have been more rapid if the white settlement of tropical Australia had been more vigorous.

In Western Australia as late as 1881 more than half of the land was completely occupied by tribal life. Aboriginals there had the good fortune to live in an economically backward colony but in the following two decades that good fortune vanished as gold men and cattlemen pushed into the arid areas. In the Northern Territory the Aboriginals far outnumbered the Europeans and Chinese and many Aboriginal adults had not even seen a European and not heard the sound of a gun or seen the hoofmarks of a horse or wheelmarks of a dray. In 1901 perhaps three of every four Aboriginals in the continent lived in the Northern Territory and Queensland, and thousands of them were alive largely because those long north-south colonial borders enabled the south to neglect the north.

13 The Rivals

The towns continued to fatten. In 1850 four of every ten Australians lived in cities and towns and by 1890 at least six of every ten lived within sight of a public clock or streetlamp. Victoria and New South Wales were the heart of the urbanizing process but even in Tasmania in the 1880s seven eighths of the increase in population took place in towns.

Some of the older influences strengthening towns – for instance, convictism and whaling – had given way to new influences. Some politicians deplored the drift to the cities as a sign of natural decline but it was more a sign of efficiency. The rural industries and the transporting of their products were becoming so efficient that they called for no large part of the workforce, thus leaving the rest of the population free to produce other goods and services. The efficiency of the primary industries underwrote the increasing workforce in the secondary and tertiary sector – in other words, the city sector. The rising standard of living increased the demand for biscuits and hats and other manufactured goods which, of course, were made in the towns; and increasingly they were made in Australia rather than imported from English towns. The mechanization of farms and inland transport increased the demand for ploughs and railway locomotives and other equipment, and they were made in cities. So the cities and towns grew as the factories and workshops employed an increasing part of the workforce. Commerce boomed, and it created work for bank clerks, stockbrokers, merchants, and warehousemen in towns. Administrative and professional jobs multiplied, though still at a tiny pace by today's standards, and most of the civil servants, teachers, clergymen and lawyers, doctors, nurses, policemen and barristers worked in towns.

The strong mining industry also promoted the tendency to live in towns. In the 1850s the shallow gold-fields had given rise to moving camps rather than towns but ultimately gold-mining sustained small and large towns. An urban economist recently argued that the gold-rushes had created no 'new urban centres', but as late as 1891 four of the ten largest cities in Australia sat on mining fields. As late as the First World War eight of the fourteen main towns in Victoria were, in origin, gold towns.

2

While the cities grew faster than the countryside, the capital city of each colony usually grew faster than any rival city. To possess a parliament house and a civil service was to possess the hormones of growth. By the late 1880s Adelaide and Melbourne were more than ten times larger than the largest rival town in their own territory. Sydney and Brisbane were more than seven times larger than their nearest rival. Occasionally the second-largest city of a colony would challenge the capital, but the challenge rarely lasted long.

The puffed-out capital cities puzzled many travellers from England. Even London, traditionally seen as a great wart on the clean rural skin, was not as dominant as were the Australian capitals. The statistician Timothy Coghlan said almost annually in the 1890s that the progress of our chief cities 'has no parallel among the cities of the old world'. Here, 'perhaps for the first time in history', he argued, 'is presented the spectacle of magnificent cities' growing not only with dazzling rapidity but embracing within their own suburban boundaries one third of the population of the colony they governed. After his annual huffing and puffing he added quietly that he disapproved of this spectacle. Most people were probably proud of their capital city. It was a symbol of what the settlers had so quickly achieved. It was a boast in brick and stone.

The Rivals

The ability of the capital city to outgrow rivals was aided usually by its site. Most of the capitals stood in the centre of a coastline on which other natural harbours were rare. Australia had no wide navigable rivers and lakes on which, far inland, a new commercial city – an Australian Chicago or Minneapolis – could grow outside the sphere of influence of the coastal capital city. While the atlas shows Australia to be close to a square in shape, the inhabitable Australia is a long ribbon of land, occasionally bulging and always following the coast. Australia was thus designed for coastal cities, and the capitals usually sat on the prime sites. Once a capital city had arisen it could use its political power to retard rivals. The civil servants were gathered in the capital city. There too the government financed a water supply, the improving of harbours, and the building of railways. The railways radiating into the hinterland from the capital city were often seen as weapons with which a capital city speared a rival but it is doubtful whether this was a crucial weapon. The radial appearance usually came later – the finishing touches to a system which originally consisted more of separate railways, each running from a port to the inland mining towns or sheep lands. Even if the railways of Australia had been built by private companies or railway magnates, the outline of the routes would probably have been similar.

The cargoes themselves favoured a central port; our main exports were wool and gold, and were so valuable in relation to their weight that they were carried from the interior to that port which promised the quickest shipment to London or Liverpool. Quick shipment of these cargoes was essential, and so they rarely waited at Portland, Port Augusta, Rockhampton or a minor port for an English-bound ship to arrive. A bulky and cheap cargo such as wheat or coal, on the other hand, could not afford to be double-handled. So the tiny wheat-ports of South Australia could flourish at the expense of Adelaide, and the coal-port of Newcastle at the expense of Sydney. These cargoes were the exception. The capital cities dominated the imports as well as the exports.

When manufacturers decided to set up a factory or mill or foundry most chose the coastal capital. It had more customers than any other town, and was convenient to several railways pushing inland as well as to the wharves. By 1891 Melbourne and Sydney were the great factory cities, and Melbourne had two of every three factory workers in Victoria. Likewise nearly all immigrants came ashore at the capital city; and when too many migrants landed in Brisbane or any other capital the government often undertook public works near the city in order to give them work. So the city grew.

Such were the influences that combined to build one towering city in each mainland colony. These influences were uncommon but not unique in colonies which had grown rapidly in modern times. In many new tropical nations today the same towering capital city can be seen.

3

Melbourne and Sydney were far and away the largest. Their rivalry was almost neurotic. It is probably normal for two large competing cities to display animosity, envy and good-natured derision towards each other; and it is probably the weaker of the two cities which feels its lesser position the more keenly. Thus Sydney in the 1880s was more likely to express resentment of the leader Melbourne, and a century later Melbourne was more likely to feel slighted by Sydney. The contrasts between the two cities were stronger a century ago than today. Those observers who ridicule the rivalry between Melbourne and Sydney as a mere veneer perhaps do not realize in how many ways those cities differed late in the 19th century. The difference between institutions and ideologies of Melbourne and Sydney were, a century ago, probably as deep as the contrasts between the Liberal and Labor parties today.

While Sydney had been founded as a place for convicts, and Melbourne newspapers often took pleasure in recalling that fact, Melbourne was essentially a free city. Melbourne, however, conveniently forgot that thousands of former convicts had flocked to Victoria during the gold-rushes and had probably remained there. While the politics of Sydney in 1880 were largely in the hands of men who had been born in Australia or lived here for a long period, the parliament in Melbourne was ruled more by British migrants who had arrived during the gold-rushes. This contrast of origins was symbolized in March 1856 in the first cricket match played between the two colonies; the winning team from New South Wales, with one exception, was Australian-born but all the Victorian players were migrants. In an era when the climate of Australia was seen as energy-sapping, Melbourne had the more bracing climate; and alert English visitors thought they detected more energy and drive in Melbourne's streets and business houses, and they contrasted the Yankee push and bustle of Melbourne with the languor of Sydney. In religion the rival colonies and cities were also dissimilar. In Victoria the Presbyterians and Methodists and other nonconformist churches were popular and, in all, had slightly more adherents than the Anglican church, but in New South Wales they were only half as strong as the Anglicans. And in political theology the colonies were far apart, the free traders ruling in New South Wales and the protectionists in Victoria.

The economic differences between New South Wales and Victoria and their capital cities were also wider than now. The pastoral industry was perhaps three times as productive in the wide grasslands of New South Wales as in Victoria by 1880. On the other hand the small farmers who ploughed the land, their own land, were far fewer in New South Wales; and the acreage of sown crops was dwarfed by Victoria's until the end of the century. So, in Victorian attitudes and politics, the independent farmer had an influence lacking to the north of the Murray. Likewise Victoria was much richer in gold, and that speculative mining industry possibly gave to Melbourne, as to San Francisco, an economic bravado that permeated attitudes to business and building. Melbourne was capable of being intoxicated on the mere sniff of a commercial risk, and the word 'risk' was at times synonymous with certainty. A whiff of the wet ink on the prospectus of a new gold-mining company, or the sight of a land-auctioneer's marquee in an outer suburb, was like a bag of smelling salts to many middle-aged and old Victorians. They had paid their own fare to cross the world to take part in an enormous lottery in the 1850s and it would be surprising if such adventurous people kept their savings, nearly a generation later, in a bag of sovereigns in a pit in the backyard. Melbourne's mercantile classes had a higher ratio of speculative investors, and they sometimes infused the city's commercial climate with the ozone of recklessness. Most of these economic contrasts would in time be painted out by the rise of similar manufacturing and service industries and the waning importance of primary industries in both New South Wales and Victoria. But in the 19th century the rivalry rested on concrete foundations.

The rivalry between Melbourne and Sydney impeded early hopes that the six little Australias would federate into a Commonwealth. Even those politicans who in spirit saw themselves as Australians were often caught in the undertow of animosity. Alfred Deakin, the young Melbourne politician who perhaps more strenuously than any other in that city was to campaign for federation, wrote a private essay which reveals the intensity of rivalry. Deakin noted how James Service as premier of Victoria attended an intercolonial conference in Sydney in 1883, and on his return gave a banquet in the new Queen's Hall in parliament house. Service was one of the few major Victorian politicians who was a free trader, and so he could be expected to show some sympathy to Sydney's point of view. But in his speech at the banquet he announced how 'he had found Sydney asleep and how with the help of his friends who rallied around him he had awakened the slumberers'.

When the speech was tapped along the telegraph to Sydney, politicians there were angry: all the more angry, confided Deakin tartishly, because Service had spoken the truth. In hot retaliation the politician Sir John Robertson

said Victoria was a mere cabbage garden – obviously an
allusion to the small area of Victoria. Another Sydney
politician announced, amidst cheers, that New South Wales
was as far above Victoria as heaven was above the earth.
Deakin, normally a generous man, wrote some confidential
remarks about the personality of those New South Wales
politicians who, he hoped, would someday support a
federation. He remarked that George Dibbs, thrice premier
of New South Wales and a paragon of prejudice, was almost
obsessive in this hatred of Victoria's commercial supremacy. As for Sir William Lyne, 'he appealed at all times to
the narrowest Sydney and New South Wales provincialism
by the pettiest and meanest acts and proposals'.

In the rivalry between the two leading colonies, one
source of contention was Victoria's aggressive commercial
empire. From the 1860s Victorian promoters and
businessmen cast their net far beyond their own coast and
far north of the Murray. The expedition of Burke and Wills
in 1860 was in part a search for remote pastoral lands and
minerals in the hope that the restless Victorian population
could exploit them. The lands found by their expedition
and by the rearguard of search parties were more than
three thousand miles by sea from Melbourne, but no sooner
did news of the grasslands reach Melbourne than promoters planned to occupy them. Burketown, near the Gulf of
Carpentaria, was one result. Many Victorian pastoralists
took up huge estates in northern Queensland in the 1860s
and ran them in addition to their own home stations.
Victorian expeditions went to the dry north west of
Australia, and one syndicate sent nine shiploads of settlers
and livestock from western Victoria to Camden Harbour,
not far from the present town of Derby. The hungry land
around Camden Harbour was soon abandoned, another
Victorian ruin. Twenty years later Victorian promoters
were again magnifying the fertility of the region, and
occupying five million acres on Cambridge Gulf.

In the Riverina district of New South Wales many
Victorian squatters and selectors moved in, and Melbourne
drew down most of the trade of the Riverina through the

new Echuca railway. Even the new copper mines of Cobar, though closer to the Queensland than to the Victorian border, sent away its bags of copper ore in the 1870s in a wide outback loop involving bullock drays to the banks of the River Darling, paddle-steamers along the Darling and the Murray to Echuca and then railway to Melbourne. As late as 1878 more than one third of the wool grown in New South Wales came overland to Melbourne's wharves, and of course the supplies that were sent back to those faraway sheep stations came mostly from Melbourne merchants and manufacturers. To capture that traffic of wool and general stores, Sydney in 1878 began to lay railways westwards to Hay on the Murrumbidgee and Bourke on the Darling. This was a costly military thrust designed to cut off one of the lesser supply lines of the enemy: Melbourne was that enemy.

The railways did not go west rapidly enough to prevent another prize from falling into the hands of Victorians and South Australians. The rich silver-lead lode of Broken Hill, perhaps the most productive so far found in Australia, was discovered in 1883 by a boundary rider working on the sheep station of Mt Gipps. The station's leased land lay in New South Wales but was owned by a syndicate in which Victorians were prominent; Sir James McCulloch, four times premier of Victoria, was a member of the syndicate. Victorians tended to be mining gamblers, and Victorians owning or managing sheep stations in the district quickly bought up shares in the rich lode at Broken Hill. Melbourne was the city to which they had the strongest ties, and to Melbourne they retired when the mine made them rich. When other companies at Broken Hill were floated, Melbourne as the great mining casino supplied much of their capital. Melbourne thus became the head office of most of the rich mines, including The Broken Hill Proprietary which became eventually the largest and most diversified firm in Australia. Broken Hill was a windfall for Melbourne and confirmed it as the financial hub of Australia. In the 20th century much of the industrial expansion north and south of Sydney – including the steelworks at Newcastle and Port Kembla – was controlled by that Melbourne company which itself had arisen from the rocks of western New South Wales.

Sydney financiers were vexed to see Melbourne stetching its claws to faraway places. Melbourne capital was busy in Fijian sugar plantations, New Caledonian nickel mines, the new sugar belt in the far north of Queensland, the Kauri forests of New Zealand, pastoral stations in every part of the country, and the mines on the west coast of Tasmania. Melbourne was also the main tap through which British capital flowed. In Melbourne were the main Australian offices of those English banks and pastoral money firms which specialized in Australia. Melbourne had by far the busiest stock exchange in Australia and was easily the largest trader in mining shares – except for coal shares which were Sydney's preserve. As Melbourne was the main port for the European mail steamers and a central place for wholesale merchants to distribute imported goods to many parts of Australia and New Zealand, Melbourne's role as a commercial and financial depot gave work to thousands of warehousemen, wharf labourers, railwaymen, and clerks.

A simple way to describe the Melbourne sphere of influence, as distinct from the Sydney sphere, is to map those towns and regions which adopted Australian-rules football rather than another winter game. By 1880 that code of football – first played in the Melbourne parks in the 1850s – was played in Victoria, Tasmania, the Riverina and Broken Hill districts of New South Wales, South Australia and Western Australia with brief outposts of popularity in Dunedin and the gold-fields of the South Island of New Zealand. Those were, presumably, the regions where Melbourne wholesale merchants and their commercial travellers did business, where Melbourne banks were more likely to open branches, where Melbourne promoters and emigrants and investments were more likely to be found, and where Melbourne-owned ships were more likely to ply. That Sydney and its commercial hinterland did not take to Australian-rules football was partly a reflection of Sydney's suspicion of any game devised in Melbourne.

There was one irony about Melbourne's long commercial fingers. While they seemed to denote success, they were also a sign of its imminent troubles. The city could not find the resources, the investment outlets, and the markets in Victoria itself. The smallness of Victoria was driving out capital and skills. The cabbage garden could not fatten its own white moths.*

4

The prosperity which had run high since the gold-rushes reached a golden crest in the 1880s. There was a boom in the main cities, and especially in Melbourne, which was still the biggest of all. Melbourne's population soared: it was 268,000 in 1881 and 473,000 in 1891. In that year a few women and men, walking the streets without even the aid of a walking stick, could remember the Melbourne of their childhood, a new village with green hills running down to the clear River Yarra. Few cities in the world had grown so swiftly. Old residents were proud of that fact, and their pride was inflated by any visitors who expressed admiration that a city should have burst from bare earth like a mushroom. In 1885 the visiting English journalist, George Sala, named it 'Marvellous Melbourne'.

Many people who settled in Melbourne in the 1880s came from declining gold towns and from farms where new machines now ploughed and harvested, thus dispensing with labourers. Tens of thousands of newcomers came from the British Isles or other colonies. Melbourne's poulation also gained through the strange delayed effect of the gold-rushes. For in the late 1850s, the main rush for gold being over, the single men who were the typical

---

*It is revealing to see the directions in which Melbourne's and Sydney's financial institutions extended. Sydney banks were more likely to advance north into Queensland. Melbourne banks tended to advance west to South Australia, Western Australia and Broken Hill. Thus the Commercial Banking Company of Sydney had a branch in Rockhampton sixty years before it opened a branch in Melbourne. The National, a Melbourne bank, opened branches in the tiny port of Fremantle and the Indian Ocean sugar island of Mauritius about two decades before it opened one branch in Sydney. In contrast, big insurance companies were more national in their spread of business.

gold-diggers tended to settle down and marry. The result was a strong increase in the birth rate in the late 1850s and early 1860s, a token increase in the 1870s, and another dramatic increase in the 1880s when the gold-rush children reached marriageable age. There were about 5000 marriages in Victoria in the year 1879, but about 9200 in 1889. The children of the late gold era were marrying, and as they needed houses the building industry boomed. The suburbs fanned out to Malvern and Camberwell, Preston and Moonee Ponds and Footscray, and steam railways were built to serve them. From 1885 Melbourne built a suburban web of cable tramways, like those in the hilly cities of San Francisco and Dunedin. As the population increased, the price of city property jumped, doubling in the decade to 1885 and continuing to rise. In the main streets, taller buildings were now needed in order to earn sufficient rent to recoup the purchase price of the site. Baby skyscrapers were built: eight storeys, ten storeys, and even one of thirteen storeys which still stands in shabby splendour at the corner of Elizabeth Street and Flinders Lane. These tall buildings had thick brick and masonry walls – the steel frame building had not yet arrived – and passenger elevators which were driven by high-pressure water supplied by a special pump house in West Melbourne and a grid of seven miles of street pipes. Many lift cars were ornate with padded seats for the passengers: only the conductor stood. In 1890 no city in Europe had such tall office buildings.

The flurry of building extended to everything – factories, wharves, railways, mansions, terrace houses, suburban villas, schools, churches, town halls, grandstands, banks and shops. The building industry was the largest employer in the city; and in the mornings one saw the carpenters, bricklayers, tilers, slaters, tuckpointers, plasterers, wall-paperers, house-painters and all the tradesmen carrying their tools to work, for work-tools were too precious to be left overnight on a building site. In the outer suburbs one saw the 'for sale' signs on rows of new houses, standing on the edge of paddocks and on Saturdays the flags of the auctioneers and the white marquees signified where subdivisions would be auctioned. The land sales went on at such distances from the heart of the city that even in London, the world's largest city, the twenty or thirty miles from the city would have seemed too far. There were subdivisions at places as far away as Frankston, Ferntree Gully, and the plains near Laverton where one land-alligator spoke of building a pier to enable intending residents to travel to the city by fast steamer. Glib promises, rash prospectuses, false balance sheets, defalcations and embezzlements were so common that when the boom ended and the investigations and prosecutions were accelerated, the reputations of hundreds of trusted people were destroyed.

In the mid-1880s, builders had been serving people who wished to rent or buy houses. By 1888 the middle and outer suburbs had become a Disneyland where subdividers, builders, hardware merchants, brickyards, estate agents, auctioneers and landlords shared the fantasy that families would somehow arrive to occupy the rows of new houses and shops. The peak of the boom in Melbourne was 1888. The following slump was at first not dramatic. But by 1890 the building boom was definitely over. The hammers and trowels and hand-saws were silent in many streets of unfinished houses. Soon the hammer of the auctioneer, selling the property of bankrupt estates, would tap-tap the end of the boom.

The optimism made the stock exchange a symbolic institution of the 1880s. So much business fell into the hands of members of the main Stock Exchange of Melbourne that rival stock exchanges were launched to share in the profits. In the first three months of 1888 – until the Stock Exchange of Melbourne called for a long Easter break – the buying and selling of Broken Hill silver shares verged on lunacy. Fortunes were made with ease: the losing of them would be as easy. In the space of twelve months 62 new silver companies were floated on the Stock Exchange of Melbourne, and investors borrowed heavily in order to traffic in silver shares and in the shares of the 113 new gold companies floated. As land prices in Melbourne were still soaring, dozens of new land investment companies and land financiers were also floated on the stock exchanges. The trading in their shares also became a form of frenzy until, in the second half of 1888, land prices fell.

The boom in mining shares was initially justified. Broken Hill was the first major silver-field in Australia and was rich even by the standards of such great gold-fields as Bendigo and Ballarat. Who would tell whether other Broken Hills might not be discovered in that arid country which prospectors were now penetrating? In the late 1880s at least two mines, which were undiscovered when the decade commenced, were paying a larger sum in annual dividends than the greatest Victorian gold-mines had paid in their whole lifetime. One was Broken Hill Proprietary and the other was the new Queensland gold-mine, Mount Morgan, and those names were magic. Indeed if all the investors in Australia had been questioned in 1889, and had been asked what they thought was the value of these two new mines, they would have said emphatically that they were worth more than the assets and prospects of operating in Australia – worth more than the English-owned and the Australian banks added together, worth more than all their grand city and country offices, their reserve funds, their city and pastoral properties, and all their anticipated profits of the future. This question was not actually given to the investors but we can be certain of their answer; for the valuations which the typical investor actually gave to every mine and bank were recorded, and can be compared with ease.

There were valid reasons for the boom in mining shares continuing after the boom in land had fizzled. In November 1889 the share market jumped again, and was high for six months. The names of Broken Hill shares were bandied about in thousands of households as if they were family friends. In 1890 the volume of business on the main stock exchange in Melbourne was far higher than in the year of years, 1888, and was probably not exceeded until the 1920s. By 1891, however, the silver shares were sagging. Everything in Melbourne was sagging.

No visiting phrase-maker christened Sydney as the spectacular or sensational city of the decade but it was growing nearly as fast as Melbourne until 1888, and thereafter faster. In the decade to 1891 its population almost doubled to 400,000; and that growth rested solidly on the development of the farms, sheep-runs, country towns, and mines which used Sydney as their manufacturing and commercial and administrative centre. The sight and smell of black-coal smoke from tugs, launches, ferries, wharf cranes, coastal and ocean steamships dominated the harbour, for Sydney was now a city of steam. Cheap coal was one of those advantages which enabled New South Wales to reduce Victoria's lead until, about 1890, they were level in population. That Sydney would likewise overtake Melbourne seemed almost certain to observers – except those in Melbourne.

Brisbane almost trebled its population in the 1880s and was now the fourth largest city in Australia with close on 90,000 people. In the one decade it had passed Ballarat, Newcastle, Bendigo and Hobart and its city streets were reminiscent of New Orleans or Charleston with their wide verandas, colonnades and airy promenades, and the Indian blinds on the walls and slow fans on the ceilings of the larger hotels, clubs, offices and banking chambers. Adelaide was the other large city, with nearly 120,000 people, but in the 1880s it had grown only by one third. That rate of growth, spectacular if it had happened in a European capital city, seemed paltry in Australia.

And yet Adelaide, alone, had the crucial amenity of a modern city. Whereas in Melbourne and Sydney the nightcarts clattered along the streets, removing the nightsoil even from city hotels and skyscrapers, in Adelaide the main suburbs were sewered in the 1880s. In other colonies the capital city was unhealthy, and babies and young children had a greater chance of remaining alive if they lived in the country, with its poor medical services, its scatter of small hospitals, and the hazards of the bush. In New South Wales between 1871 and 1886 the death rate of children under the age of five was twice as heavy in Sydney's suburbs as in the country. In the heart of Sydney the death rate of children under five was even higher. Here was a sunny, well-drained site for a city, but on the healthy site sat an unhealthy city. In one terrible year, 1875, the city of Sydney lost one in every eleven children under the age of five through diarrhoea, pneumonia, bronchitis, measles, scarlet fever, diphtheria and other illnesses and mishaps.

Sydney was sufficiently alarmed to begin driving sewerage tunnels in the early 1880s, but the work was slow and the city spread out far ahead of the new tunnels and ditches. The septic tank was still untried in any suburb. Sydney, at least, was a decade ahead of Melbourne where the mains of the sewerage system were not commenced until 1892. Melbourne on 15 August 1897 had a population of half a million and one sewered house, the first. Melbourne could boast of its high skyline and its healthy sea winds and spacious parks and wide streets, but the deaths from typhoid even in the 1890s showed that sewerage tunnels should have preceded skyscrapers.

14 Where Merchants are Princes

In London, Berlin and Brussels those editors and politicians who wondered about the future watched with surprise or dismay the experiment in democracy in Australia. What kind of men would voters elect? What crazy laws would their parliaments pass? Some observers feared that the daily round of commerce, the operation of the law courts, the rights of free assembly and private property, and respect for learning would be endangered by a form of government which entrusted ultimate power to people, of whom many could not write, many owned no property, many had served long criminal sentences and most had probably voted in no previous election. Here was an adventure which our generation can more easily appreciate: it resembled, in some ways, the recent granting of the franchise to every adult in new nations in Asia and Africa.

The last of the convict colonies, Tasmania and Western Australia, were not democratic; and Western Australia did not even have a fully elected parliament until 1890 and Tasmania's older parliament did not grant every man the vote and the right to stand for the lower house until 1900. In the other colonies the lower houses or assemblies were amongst the most democratic in the world. South Australia granted the vote to nearly every adult man in 1856, and Victoria and New South Wales quickly followed. By the year 1859 the colonies holding more than 90% of the continent's people were governed by politicians for whom nearly every man could cast his vote.

2

The democracy in the new parliament houses was not snow-pure. Every man in theory had to vote at elections for the lower house but most did not use that right. The owners of property used that right more diligently than the wandering shearer. The businessman in the city used his vote more than the digger on the gold-fields. Votes were available only for those who registered themselves on the electoral roll, and many did not bother to pay the shilling or sixpence which the enrolling entailed. The electorates were unequal, and so a rural vote usually carried more weight than a city vote. A labourer probably found it difficult on polling day to record his vote, for the polling booths in rural Victoria even as late as the 1890s were open only from eight in the morning to five at night. Moreover while nearly every man over the age of 21 had the right to vote, those who owned property had the right to cast one vote in every electorate in which they owned property. At least there were no postal or absentee votes, so they could vote only in those electorates which they could personally visit on the day or days of polling. Plural voting remained normal in most colonies until the end of the century: and in swinging seats the plural vote could be decisive. Women of course received no vote, and in fact no nation then allowed women to vote.

The lower house was elected on the popular vote but there was also an upper house – a legislative council – which was elected on a narrower franchise. The upper houses were houses of review: they were like a House of Lords without the lords. An upper house could occasionally thwart or impede the lower house. In most colonies the upper houses were elected only by the professional and propertied people though property owners in Australia were unusually widespread. In New South Wales and Queensland the members of the upper house were nominated for life, and in Victoria and South Australia their initial term was ten or twelve years, and so they were less sensitive to rapid changes in public opinion. Whereas the lower houses were to become more democratic, the upper houses were slower to change. As late as 1963 three of the five surviving upper houses still did not acknowledge adult suffrage.

In the new democratic era the governor, residing in his stately house in the capital city, no longer governed but he did restrain as the Imperial Agent. Infrequently he did reserve his assent to a bill which had been passed by both houses of parliament. Even if he assented, the government in London had the right – infrequently used – to disallow the bill at any time in the following two years. Moreover the governor was not entitled to assent to colonial bills which legislated on such topics as divorce and coinage, or which contradicted England's treaties with foreign nations or facets of her commercial policy. Such bills he had to send to London where they might or might not receive the royal assent. The bills passed by the new colonial parliaments were, after the 1860s, rarely deferred or challenged by the governor and by the colonial office.

3

In the democratic wave of the 1850s one Australian reform aroused intense interest throughout the English-speaking world. This was the secret ballot. A Chartist idea, it was widely supported in England in the 1830s and 1840s but was shunned by Westminster as revolutionary. The normal practice at parliamentary elections was for the electors to declare publicly for whom they were voting. Accordingly a progress count of the votes was available throughout polling day, and when the contest was close the rival candidates used inducements to persuade voters to hurry forward and cast their vote. It was practicable to bribe a voter, because the briber could stand at the polling place and see how the voter actually cast his vote. The practice of public voting also encouraged landlords to intimidate their tenants, or employers to intimidate employees who possessed a vote. Understandably the democrats thought the secret ballot was vital. What was the point of pleading for an extension of the franchise if those new voters, either through fear or bribery, did not use their vote in their own interests?

Thousands of new British immigrants had been persuaded of the importance of the secret ballot. In Victoria the strong supporter of the secret ballot was William Nicholson who came from the north of England in 1842, becoming a rich grocer and mayor of Melbourne at the age of 34. In parliament he fought for the secret ballot: it was almost an obsession. In Victoria, by a narrow majority, the secret ballot became law in March 1856. In South Australia it became law a fortnight later and the ballot paper designed originally in Adelaide is now the typical Australian ballot paper, being ideal for the preferential system of voting which became common in this century. By 1859 the five self-governing colonies, including the new Queensland, had adopted the secret ballot.

Many useful reforms are first introduced in lands where the reform is not of great importance. A reform is more likely if its opponents suffer lightly rather than heavily by the change. In Australia the traditional method of open voting – of affirming in public one's current political loyalty – was less prone to abuse than in England. Australia in 1856 did not have an army of tenant farmers, and those tenant farmers who did exist were not duty-bound to doff their hat to the owner. If they did not like the owner they could simply move on to other areas. Usually they felt no social obligation to vote in the way their landlord directed, because the landlord in Australia was not necessarily more literate and of higher status than the tenant. The different attitudes in England and Australia can be seen in a diary kept by a Yorkshire girl, Sarah Midgley. Her father, a tenant farmer about eight miles north of Leeds, disagreed with his landlord about his right to vote independently and emigrated to western Victoria where he bought 120 acres of chocolate soil. In November 1855 he went from Koroit to the port of Warrnambool to cast his vote for the legislative council and he noted that in this last election before the secret ballot became normal, voters had to wear coloured ribbons to signify for whom they voted. He also observed, in this district which held a high proportion of tenant farmers, that few landlords tried to suggest how their tenants should vote. The secret ballot, in essence, was less revolutionary in Australia then in England.

Many Australians were proud that their land was a political laboratory. Even some who at first had spoken against political experiments were pleased to proclaim them successful. Hugh Childers was one of those ambitious Englishmen who viewed Australia as they viewed India, a valuable place for experience on their upward path: he was a political jackeroo. Educated at Oxford and Cambridge he reached Melbourne with his bride on the eve of the gold-rushes, became the inspector of church schools, in which many of the students were not much younger than him, and then became the chief of the audit and customs departments. As a nominated member of the council which framed Victoria's constitution he opposed the secret ballot, but soon he was a convert to this method of voting.

Returning to England to contest a seat in the House of Commons for the Yorkshire market town of Pontrefact, he saw once again the bribery which open voting encouraged. At about three o'clock on the afternoon of polling day he was running neck and neck with his opponent. The poll was to close at four, and those electors who had not yet voted knew their bargaining position. In the space of an hour some sixty voters offered to sell Childers their vote. He decided not to buy, and he narrowly lost the election to the highest bidder. Appealing against other irregularities in the poll he won the new election, and his first speech in the House of Commons in 1860 set out the virtues of the 'Victorian ballot', explaining that the traditional British method of voting was hardly fair because it often proved that an elector's vote was not as valuable at eight in the morning as at three in the afternoon.

Childers later became the First Lord of the Admiralty; he was thus minister of the world's largest navy when he had barely passed the age of 40. When in 1872 the House of Commons divided more than sixty times on the controversial bill to introduce the Australian ballot, Childers

224

supported the bill. In August of that year he stood in the first election in Britain ever held under the secret ballot, a by-election, and won; and nothing pleased him more – except his victory – than reports that election day lacked the drunkenness and uproar which had marked many of the open elections. That was the verdict in New Zealand, Belgium, Canada, the United States and wherever the secret ballot was adopted.

4

Those conservatives who wondered how Australia could ever be governed effectively when the miner, cobbler and wood-cutter could vote, might have been slightly reassured if had they known that in the first forty years of self-government most of the cabinet ministers were men of property. The typical premier of a colony was likely to be a self-made, self-employed man of moderate wealth and – to critical English eyes – of scant polish. He was likely to be a merchant, general businessman, land-owner or lawyer. As members of parliament in most of the colonies were not paid until the 1880s, only men of independent means could afford to sit in parliament. Moreover there was a belief, expressed at election meetings, that a man who had proved successful in business was more likely to succeed in conducting the larger business of the state. The men often exempted from this popular belief were the large land-owners. Some were likely – it was thought – to be too successful.*

In 1880 the premiers of the five self-governing colonies were, in their economic background, typical of the colonial premiers of that era. South Australia's premier was Sir William Morgan, aged 51, son of a Bedfordshire farmer;

*The election of Malcolm Fraser as prime minister in 1975 was unusual because he was popularly though erroneously seen as a squatter. A squatter stood little chance of becoming premier of a major colony late in the last century or prime minister of the Commonwealth in the first half of this century. Squatters became politically respectable when their economic power had faded.

Morgan had worked briefly on the Victorian gold-fields before returning to Adelaide to become a wholesale and retail grocer and then a merchant. He was a founder of the Bank of Adelaide and a heavy investor in the nickel and copper mines of the French colony of New Caledonia – an investment which so entangled his financial affairs that he was to resign as premier.

In Hobart the premier was a 39-year-old son of the town, William Robert Giblin, a successful solicitor who seemed eager to do good works rather than make money; he founded and taught in a Congregational Sunday School and founded and presided over the Hobart Working Men's Club. He was an oarsman on the estuary and a walker in the mountains, marvelling at the sunlight on the treetops at a time when many Tasmanian politicans marvelled more at the price of the real estate enclosing the tree roots. Lawyer premiers were not uncommon in Australia even in Giblin's day, but the Deakins, Bartons, Reids, Kingstons, Downers, Turners and Griffiths had not yet made the law rather than the merchant's office the home of the most successful politicians.

Victoria's premier in 1880 was James Service, a tall, 56-year-old Scot who came out in the gold-rushes as resident partner for a Glasgow tea and coffee house. In politics he was a Chartist, an ultra-democrat, and in business he was a driving individualist whose merchant house in Melbourne sold the popular Robur tea and Bryant & May matches. Service was a founder of what became the most ebullient bank of the 1880s, the Commercial Bank of Australia, and he was its chairman at the same time as he was premier of Victoria. The name of this Scot who made a fortune from groceries is commemorated in the border town of Serviceton, long celebrated for its small railway refreshment room. Victoria's second premier in 1880 was Graham Berry, who was a draper in the London suburb of Chelsea before the gold-fields attracted him, just as they had attracted Service. Berry was a storekeeper and seller of wine and spirits in South Yarra, then an owner of newspapers in Collingwood and Geelong. Not a very wealthy man, he did acquire money through mining speculations and his salary as minister of the Crown. He was to fall on poor times in his old age.

Service and Berry were typical of the successful politicians of the late-colonial era. They were migrants; they were self-made men. Many of their political views reflected more their humble economic status when they reached Australia rather than their elevated status of 1880. Had they remained in the British Isles, they would have had little opportunity of amassing wealth or of entering parliament. Here they were merchants – primarily importers – and that occupation was important and often rewarding because Australia had a narrow range of factories and so it imported heavily. The occupation also led easily to parliament, for the business of a Melbourne or Brisbane merchant depended heavily on government facilities and policies: on import duties or their absence, on the post office, and especially the telegraph which linked them to their buyers in London, on lighthouses and dredged harbours, and on the upcountry railways built by the governments.

In Sydney the premier in 1880 was Henry Parkes, an unsuccessful businessman, who enjoyed five terms as premier. His common portraits display a very broad nose, a drooping, mouth-obscuring beard and long white hair breaking over his ears: an imposing face which resembled a lion or sometimes an old Aboriginal. One forgets that he was once a young man, full of the normal uncertainties. The son of a failed farmer and handyman, Henry became an apprentice to a bone-and-ivory turner, and he practised that craft briefly in Birmingham before he and his wife sailed to Australia as subsidized migrants. Parkes reached Sydney in July 1839. His first surviving son was born in 1839, on the second last day of the voyage, and his last surviving son died almost a century and a half later – in August 1978 – so that this one generation of Parkes' children covered three quarters of the European history of Australia. The young Henry Parkes knew how to shape, with saw and lathe, the tusks of elephants into the handles of knives and forks and a variety of luxury articles ranging from combs to false teeth: bone and ivory, in many of their uses, were the costly precursors of plastics. It was an inappropriate trade for a Sydney immigrant because ivory and bone goods could be imported cheaply from the lands where skilled labour was cheap. Parkes worked for wages in his first six years in Sydney, mostly as a tidewaiter – a minor customs official on the waterfront. In 1845, with the depression clearing away, he opened a shop in Hunter Street, Sydney, and made bone and ivory articles for the few who wanted them, and sold imported fancy goods and luxury knick-knacks over the counter. He opened branches in the big provincial ports of Maitland and Geelong, but drifted into financial straits. In 1850 he started again in this land of start-again as editor and owner of the radical *Empire*, a newspaper which launched him firmly into politics.

In business Parkes was a Rip Van Winkle who seemed to sleep for long periods and then awake with a shock to find that his customers had vanished. In 1858 he became insolvent. After a visit to England as a high-paid recruiting agent for immigrants, he set up again in Sydney in 1863 as an importer of Birmingham fancy goods but by 1870 he was again insolvent. That did not prevent him from entering a period of political success, in which he enjoyed a salary as premier. He again became an importer of ivory goods from Birmingham in the mid-1880s, became insolvent for a third time, and became premier for a fourth time. He must have been a financial ninny: his name as a politician was a commercial asset, and the economic climate of the 1880s should have been sunny enough to ripen money even in the pocket of a Parkes. His fifth book of verse, appearing in 1889, was called *Fragmentary Thoughts*: probably he himself was a fragmented man, and was unable to concentrate on commerce with that single-mindedness common at that time.

Parkes was a big man, a fox, an actor, a weather-cock of the unsettled political sky, a speaker capable of noble oratory as well as the mud-slinging of the stallkeeper. The rising politician Alfred Deakin, a watchful observer of older politicians, said that Parkes often wore in old age a 'far-away expression of the eyes, intended to convey his remoteness from the earthly sphere'. The debacles of his business career also conveyed that remoteness.

The essence of Parkes' philosophy in the heyday of his career was free trade. He believed that free trade could revolutionize the world. Since the 1840s Britain had removed import duties on virtually every commodity, and Parkes had tried to implement the same policy in New South Wales. In March 1890, addressing a breakfast rally in the old court room at Berrima, Parkes proclaimed amidst applause that England under her policy of free trade 'had made more bounding advances than any other nation on the face of the earth'. Nobody, said Parkes, could refute his argument. To attempt to refute it would be as futile as an attempt 'to put a tarpaulin over the sun and light the world with a tallow candle'. That strange, down-to-earth metaphor, interrupting the soaring oratory, typified his generation of versatile, part-time politicians. They were statesman at breakfast and shopkeepers by mid-morning.

Of the political leaders of 1880, the most spectacular as a businessman was the Queenslander, Thomas McIlwraith; he was then 45 years old. In the first week of that year he must have wondered often about the steamship *Strathleven*, which was then in the Indian Ocean not far from the Red Sea. The ship had been chartered by McIlwaith's brother, Andrew, and the premier himself was one of the courageous private backers of this first shipment of Australian frozen meat to cross the equator – the beginning of a trade which was to be as important as anything McIlwraith himself did during an energetic political career. McIlwraith was a man of push and presence. 'He carries with him a dignity that would make an impression in any Chamber,' commented a Canadian writer who was to sit in the House of Commons in Westminster for eighteen years. McIlwraith was to become a kind of tropical Parkes.

McIlwraith had migrated to the Victorian gold-fields at about the age of 19, and dug for gold at Bendigo and worked as an engineer in the building of railways. We do not know the steps by which he became rich. He had been in Australia less than a decade when he provided £3000 of his own money for his brother's lead-sheet mill in Melbourne and for the stocking of pastoral runs in Queensland. Like many businessmen-politicians he became in 1874 a director of a bank, the new Queensland National Bank, which became the government's own banker. After making a fortune from sheep and cattle runs he turned to more risky financial ventures. At one time in the 1880s he was probably a millionaire – using the common definition of a million US dollars – and a variety of mining companies, land syndicates and breweries absorbed his funds.

Whereas Sir Henry Parkes dealt in delicate ivory trinkets, Sir Thomas McIlwraith was willing to gamble with the tusks of entire herds of elephants. There was something of the big-game hunter in the way he stalked, the scale on which he hunted and the breadth of his plans for his own business empire and for Queensland. Whereas Parkes dealt privately in terms of rods and perches, McIlwraith dealt in thousands of square miles. In the 1880s he tried to push through a railway project which would link Brisbane and Roma directly with the Gulf of Carpentaria. He was the premier who in 1883 ordered the annexation of Papua; and one of the motives of this migrant from cramped Scotland was the belief that such a large tropical land must offer mercantile opportunities for the brave and the bonny. His third period as premier was to end in 1893, and by then he was in deep trouble. His overdraft with his favourite bank ran to the colossal sum of £251,000, only one quarter of which was adequately secured, and his political career was now as insecure.

Thus in 1880 five of the six men who held the office of premier were merchants or general businessmen. They were developers in a decade when development would be the popular slogan, but when the development eventually turned to disaster the McIlwraiths and other merchant princes would not again be so prominent in parliament.

5

People walking past the parliament houses did not necessarily think that there lay the great seat of power. Some thought it lay inside the newspaper offices. A city newspaper not only told the public what the politician said; it increasingly told the politician what he should say.

Even in 1850 the newspapers had numbered about fifty and stretched from Perth to Maitland and Brisbane: eleven were still alive a century later. Here newspapers already had an independence which was wider than that enjoyed by the press in many of the leading nations of Europe. In France, Austria, Russia and Prussia in the 1850s the governments frequently censored newspapers, taxed them, hounded them, and closed them. Even England collected a tax on every copy of every newspaper until 1855. Australia, in contrast, had neither newspaper taxes nor censorship at a time when it lacked self-government.

During the gold-rushes, businessmen could make fortunes if they snatched the latest English commercial news before their rivals were awake. There was money in news, both for those who supplied it and those who read it in those long lean columns. The news of the Crimean War was read eagerly by the patriotic who craved for a Anglo-French victory against the Russians, by those who feared that the Russian navy might suddenly appear out of the haze near Sydney Heads, or by those merchants who knew how the war could suddenly affect their supply of goods for the booming Australian markets. Between 1854 and 1856 the *Sydney Morning Herald* and its rival the *Empire* were quick to send small boats out to intercept sailing ships arriving with the English news. They would buy the latest English newspapers from officers or passengers, race back to the city, and issue an 'extraordinary edition' – ('Extra, extra!') – which printed, almost word for word, the latest news from the home newspapers. That the news was eighty or ninety days old made it no less exciting.

In 1853 the Fairfaxes had installed perhaps the first steam newspaper press in Australia for their *Sydney Morning Herald*, and other daily newspapers adopted new techniques. The telegraph, the steam printing press, and new newsprint – made cheaply from wood pulp instead of old rags – were revolutionizing the newspapers. As the circulation increased, the price of each newspaper fell. In the mid-1850s the main Australian dailies were selling for threepence or sixpence a copy and by the 1870s certain newspapers sold for one penny. The city newspapers quickly attracted readers from the countryside as the railways and the fast coaches of Cobb and Co. made their daily journeys inland. In several colonies the post offices became the ally of the city newspapers; by 1860 several million newspapers were carried free through the post. In some colonies, postage was eventually charged but as late as the 1890s three colonies allowed newspapers to pass free through the post. New South Wales went further and allowed people who had read their newspaper to wrap it up again and post it, without affixing a stamp, to friends within the colony.

Most newspapers were still sombre by present standards. The pages were large and served as a hiding place to those who read them on suburban trains. The headlines were small and few. The editorial was long and written in such a tone as to suggest that it should be read only in a room where silence prevailed and the half-drawn blinds provided a funereal light. Few concessions were made to young or backward readers; and in 1880 no illustrations appeared in a daily newspaper and even the illustrated weeklies used black and white sketches and not photographs to depict dramatic events – the safe return of an explorer or the wreck of a ship. Daily newspapers carried no comics or cartoons, no crosswords or other diversions, no page for women or children, no chatty comments on eating or drinking, and few notices of birth or death or marriage.

Spectator sport was taking more space in newspapers by 1880, just as the news of shipping was slowly declining in importance. The two trends were probably linked. The arrival of ships was now less important partly because the telegraph – opened between Australia and London in 1872 – had replaced the ship as the fastest carrier of news.

Moreover the ships themselves were safer and so less newsworthy. Many of the dangers of the sea had been mastered by stronger ships, steam engines and by the calmer routes and more accurate charts followed by the steamships. There is a sense in which the spectator sport of the cities provided the excitement and danger, the heightened role of chance, which the normal hazards of shipping, overland travel and daily life had once provided. Spectator sport catered for a town existence which was becoming safer, ruled by the clock and other routines, and increasingly anonymous. The secret ballot reflected in part that emphasis on anonymity.

Politics filled many of the columns in newspapers. An able newspaperman was essentially a reporter: he reported what politicians said rather than what he himself thought. He was skilled in shorthand, and took pride in his accuracy. The *Argus* of Melbourne – the argus was a mythological person with a hundred eyes – lived up to its name with its long and wide-eyed reports of political speeches. When parliament was sitting, the *Argus* placed six reporters in the press gallery, and they wrote in relays, and messengers carried their reports down the hill to the printing office where a row of compositors stood in the late hours of the night. The compositors painstakingly picked the various metal letters of the alphabet from the tray in front of them and so – like an eternal game of scrabble – set up the speech in cold type. Most of the morning dailies in the cities bathed in a sea of political reportage.

The newspaper editors were themselves politicians, trying to shape as well as to express public opinions. The editors on the main newspapers were more articulate and more skilled in handling ideas than most of the new politicians elected under adult franchise. They also reached wider audiences than could be reached even by those politicians energetic enough to address public meetings on six nights of the week.

David Syme, a lean young Scot who mined for gold in California and Victoria in the early 1850s, joined hands with his brother Ebeneezer in buying the insolvent *Age* newspaper in Melbourne. The paper at first sold few copies, but they lowered the price from sixpence to threepence in 1860, and David Syme as editor began to argue popular economic policies with moral earnestness and calm logic; he was a long-faced theologian who had lost his faith in God. In a time of unemployment he called for a protective tariff against imports, and was later acclaimed as the 'Father of Protection' though he was more the tireless midwife of protection. The circulation of his daily increased steadily. It became a penny paper in 1868, and the low price and popular liberal views attracted readers. Politicians began to realize the power of this man who was rarely seen at a political gathering, was unknown to almost every man in the street, spoke at no public rally, and was not seen in church on Sunday. How much power he possessed over politicians is impossible to gauge but it was large. In 1877 he regularly advertised his newspaper by saying it sold twice as many copies as any other daily paper in Australia. In 1890 he could proudly announce that the *Age* sold more copies than any other daily in the British Empire, except a few famous newspapers in London.

Syme thought it was a mistake to accept the public meeting and the press as an accurate guide to what the public was thinking. They were educators of the people rather than voices of the people. As instructors, wrote Syme, the public meeting and the press had no rivals: 'But for the platform and the press not one of the great reforms of recent times would have been carried.' The penny newspaper was really a penny school.

The scholar and politician Viscount Bryce, who served Britain in cabinet and as ambassador in Washington, described in his massive book *Modern Democracies* the high standards and the strong influence of the serious Australian newspapers: 'In the later decades of the last century, the three or four greatest newspapers in Sydney and Melbourne exercised more power than any newspapers then did in any other country, being at times stronger than the head of the political parties.' His view was held widely. Moreover reasons can be offered why certain newspapers in Melbourne and Sydney were likely to capture a power which was unusual by European or North American standards. They appeared in capital cities which held a high proportion of the parliaments' electors and were unusually strong in leisure, literacy and wealth – thus enabling readers to buy, understand, and dawdle over the newspapers. These too were cities in which virtually every man had the vote. Melbourne and Sydney thus offered, to daily newspapers, advantages such as no city in Europe and few in North America possessed. They also had another advantage which even New York and Chicago lacked: nearly all the adults spoke the same language.

By 1890 the large newspapers were possibly reaching the peak of their political influence though their readership was far from the peak. They were read by the majority of people who on polling day accepted their responsibility and voted. They held almost a monopoly in intercolonial and international news. They saw politics as the main business of life and were not yet forced to compete strenuously with racy, snappy tabloids for whom politics was only one course in the daily banquet of news. In offering news and sober entertainment they did not yet face competition from newsreels, movies, radio and television. In an era of self-improvement they were a powerful educational influence and might well have achieved, in the average year, half as much as all the schools and colleges achieved: the purpose of most daily newspapers and their readers was serious.

The influence of the city newspapers was probably enhanced by the absence of a rigid party system. Admittedly political groups and factions operated, and parties had existed intermittently before 1890 in Victoria, New South Wales, and Queensland; but so long as political loyalties remained less rigid the newspapers played a special role. A large city newspaper was often a party in itself, with its clear policies, its warning to ministries, its political propaganda, its occasional pre-selection of candidates and its how-to-vote instructions on the eve of elections. So long as political groups and parties were organized inadequately, the newspaper with its mass audience was in a powerful position. The rise of the Labor Party and a tighter party system at the turn of the century inevitably weakened the role of the big newspapers.

The political heyday of the newspapers coincided with the heyday of the self-made businessmen in politics. The self-made businessmen, especially the city merchants, were probably at the summit of their power in the 1880s. In that decade thousands of voters familiar with the Book of Isaiah's description of ancient Tyre as the city 'whose merchants were princes' and whose traders 'were the honoured of the earth', could see that Tyre had been reborn in Australia. The merchants were now the princes. But they were not all-powerful, being dependent on the popular vote, nor were they simply promoters of commerce and rapid economic development, for they were capable of passing radical laws on taxation and land, schools and mines which in style seem to belong more to the Labor era than to the pre-Labor era of politics.

The dominance of the merchants, shopkeepers, land-owners and self-made businessmen was about to be challenged. The long waves of prosperity since the 1850s had launched them in their thousands, but the end of that prosperity was almost in sight. The bank failures and the revelations of the 1890s would harm their public reputations. The introduction of the payment of members, the rise of a Labor Party, and the increasing power of the public companies and their boards compared to that of the individual magnate – these changes also were to undermine the hustling, self-made businessman and his political opportunities. He was to flourish much longer in state parliaments than in the Commonwealth, where in the first eighty years no McIlwraith or Service – nor even a Henry Parkes – was to become prime minister.

15 Rich and Poor: The Economic Whirlpool

The main aim of most migrants was still the making of money. James Graham, a migrant fresh from a Scottish bank, wrote home the simple truth in 1839: 'In this country money is the great idol, and for it they will do anything or undergo any hardship.' Exactly half a century later the desire to make money was said to be almost a passion in Australian cities; and a Catholic priest, lamenting the respect paid to possessors of wealth, observed that ordinary men preened themselves simply because their hand had been shaken by a rich man. The comment is revealing. The wish to touch the hand or frock-coat of a rich man was in one sense the superstition that some of his business luck might be magically transmitted.

It was – until the great break in the economic mood in the 1890s – a fine land for making money. The enterprising, the thrifty, the shrewd or the shifty had an opportunity to amass fortunes. There was pride at the high proportion of people who, by the standards of Europe, owned property, but at the same time much wealth was clustered into few hands.

2

The rich Australians were perhaps not so conspicuous as the rich Americans or Englishmen. They did not travel around the city in carriages whose drivers were gaudily dressed. The scarcity of able domestic servants, male and female, tended to limit the number of rooms in their mansions. Many of the rich men were pastoralists whose main house was in the country; and most of those rural mansions were not in sight of railway lines or main roads or, if within sight, were soon shielded by banks of English trees and tall gums. This is not to say that the cities lacked houses which were pretentiously large. Moreover the contrast between the mansion of a rich merchant and the poky cottage in a narrow lane was probably greater then than the contrast in large and small houses in the same cities today. Nonetheless an English domestic servant who migrated here would probably have noticed a relative lack of visible wealth amongst the very rich and – to her eyes – a surprising number of possessions held by the poor. We, looking back from a different viewpoint, are more inclined to see the opposite.

Another fact hid the very rich from the public gaze in the 19th century. Many of the rich returned home and spent their last years in the British Isles. Perhaps they still held property here but spent the income overseas. In 1880 a small *Who's Who* could have been compiled of the wealthy Australians who now lived in England and Scotland.

In Europe only a young man with capital, a trusted surname, and thrift, energy, and commercial acumen had a chance of making a small fortune by the age of 60. In Australia, however, a new migrant could land with no money, a name so disreputable that he changed it, and a feckless improvidence that seemed a liability; but even he had an opportunity of becoming rich. Of all the migrant groups the young Scot, if he migrated to Australia, possessed probably the stronger likelihood of making a fortune, as the Scottish names of mansions and pastoral properties still testify. And yet even a feckless misfit of a migrant, simply by being present in a new gold-field at the right hour, could also make a lot of money. The statistical chances of him being in the right place at the right time, sober and alert, were not high.

The optimism was buttressed by the knowledge that the unexpected event influenced the distributing of wealth in a new land. Fortunes were made from gold and minerals. Traders, especially in the outback, might earn windfall sums if they were the first to set up a shop or workshop in a new town or a construction camp. Money was easily made from central blocks of land in those towns which quickly prospered. The rise and fall of the price of wool, wheat and copper on world markets reshuffled wealth. The caprice of the weather could reward some and harm others. Even in drought there were gainers as well as losers: farmers with large haystacks, for example, gained rapidly because in a drought they could sell their hay dearly. The huge business of importing goods from overseas was also affected by erratic gluts or scarcities of goods. There was a strong touch of the lottery in commercial life in Australia. Speculation was unavoidable and in prosperous times the speculator was often rewarded.

If we could piece together a history of the host of people who failed in business ventures and then started again, starting even a third and fourth time, their history would explain more about the persisting optimism of society than a story consisting solely of spectacular successes. Large numbers of the insolvent and the impoverished, the bruised and the pummelled, believed that by their own efforts they would rise again; and in the period 1851 to the end of the 1880s that belief was widespread and flavoured society.

3

On the warm plains of the Wimmera lived two Victorian settlers who, if they had met in the late 1880s, would have recounted stories of similar ups and downs and restless wanderings. Thousands of other settlers could have repeated variations on the same theme.

Thomas Williams was born in 1826 at Ryde, within three hours' walking of Sydney. After working for twelve years as a carpenter, boy and man, on sheep and cattle stations as remote as the Clarence River in the north and the Canberra district in the south, he set out as a forty-niner for California. He spent twelve months on the gold-diggings where, he said later, he did 'well'. That poker-faced adverb even then was often an understatement. Back in Sydney in

1851 he crossed the Blue Mountains to the first rushes near Bathurst. At the end of the same year he must have been one of the first diggers on Bendigo where gold gleamed in shallow holes: in seven weeks he made £3000. If as a boy carpenter he had heard from a fortune-teller that he would earn such a sum in the course of his entire working life he would have been jubilant and here at Bendigo he had dug that sum in seven weeks.

It was well known that more fortunes were made from buying and selling than from gold. Williams next became a merchant, buying farm produce in Sydney and selling it at his new store in William Street in Melbourne.

'How did you get on, Mr Williams?' It is probably his own phrase which has survived: he 'made money'.

Perhaps even more money could be made in a hotel. So Thomas Williams opened the Golden Fleece Hotel. That was when Melbourne was a kind of canvas Las Vegas, with fortunate men from the diggings squandering gold sovereigns and bank notes in hotels and saloons. In one year the new publican made more than £10,000 – more than three carpenters could have hoped to earn in a lifetime of 60-hour weeks.

This quick movement from one occupation to another and from one town or colony to another was typical of the times and especially of single men. Anyone who failed in one job or one town believed he might succeed at last in another. Opportunities rushed in, calling for takers. Williams then moved from the hotel to a wine and spirits business, where his run of luck ceased. Perhaps he gave too much credit. Possibly he bought gin and brandy in large amounts when it was very dear in Melbourne and was caught holding much of it when the cheaper imports flooded in from Europe during the mid-1850s. He lost £14,000 – a fortune – in two years. The buffetings of his career were far from over.

Meanwhile a young English immigrant was passing through a similar apprenticeship of success and failure. Edward Usher was a Kentish man who migrated to Adelaide in 1849; he was probably crossing the Indian

Ocean to Adelaide when Williams was crossing the Pacific to California. Usher had made bricks at home, and in the village of Norwood, near Adelaide, he set up a brickyard and baked bricks, at first with some success. In his own guarded reminiscences he did not mention what happened to the brickyard, but it seems likely that so many builders went to the Victorian gold-fields in the early 1850s that nobody wanted new houses or new bricks. His business must have slumped, so he too set off for the Victorian gold-fields. At the Bendigo diggings during seven months he did 'fairly well'. We would actually need to hear him speak that phrase to know what emphasis he put on those words: probably he was very successful. He returned to Adelaide, to learn that his wife had died while he was away.

With the aid, perhaps, of his Bendigo gold he bought himself a wagon and team, loaded it with South Australian butter, cheese, bran and oats, and travelled the 400 miles to Bendigo. There he found the market for farm produce was dead, because many miners and storekeepers had just left for the Ovens gold-rush. How much he lost on that speculation as a carrier he did not reveal. Back in Adelaide he took another wife and made bricks again. He cannot have prospered because again he set out for the Victorian diggings, that place of perpetual hope. 'And how did you get on, Mr Usher, in your four years on the Maryborough gold-field?' His answer, not recorded, was probably: 'Not quite so well'.

Usher was next heard of about 100 miles to the south. At the farming towns of Birregurra and Colac he followed his old trade as a brickmaker, and many of his bricks can probably still be seen in old farmhouse chimneys. Unfortunately he fell once more on poor times. Injuring his knee and unable to make bricks, he took up shoemaking to support his growing family. How does a brickmaker take readily to shoemaking? One can only marvel at colonial ingenuity. One can almost overhear Mr Usher enquiring of a new customer: 'Do those new boots fit you, sir?' And one can almost hear the answer: 'Not quite so well'.

About 1870 he turned to that new colonial panacea, the

small farm. He took up land towards the Otway Ranges and also made boots and shoes in his spare time. After seven years, with his sons growing, he decided to find a larger farm, and in the new wheat belt between Warracknabeal and Jeparit, with not a high hill in sight, he grew wheat on the large scale. Being an experienced jack-of-all-trades, he presumably made boots for the children, bricks for the fireplaces and, of course, carted his own wheat to the railway station. By the late 1880s, justifiably proud of his success as a colonial battler, he paid a small fee – along with thousands of other Victorians – for his life story to be published briefly in a massive who's who of Victorian citizenry, a book as heavy as a family bible and fingered with reverence by many whose names were inside.

There, on the same page, could be read, in small print, the final lines of the erratic story of Thomas Williams, the young Sydney carpenter who had found his way to Melbourne by way of California in the 1850s. After winning and losing small fortunes in the liquor trade, Williams became an auctioneer. Old patrons of the Golden Fleece Hotel must have been surprised to hear his voice extolling the merits of a horse or an armchair but soon the loud voice was going, going, gone. After the failure of that venture he went fifty miles away to the gold-diggings at Mt Blackwood and built a hotel. That also failed. The fruits of a run of luck that had followed him all the way from California to the Golden Fleece Hotel in Melbourne must have now been entirely consumed.

Williams trudged to that mecca of the unconquerable, the newer gold-rushes; and for five years he sank shafts at various fields. At Chinaman's Flat, near Maryborough, with money either won from gold or borrowed, he made the unpredictable decision to build a theatre. The one-time carpenter could easily build a theatre but running it must have been riskier. He 'did well for a time', we learn. Chinaman's Flat today not only has no theatre but also has no audience; and the initial decline of population probably closed his theatre.

Thomas Williams moved from place to place like a

re-addressed letter. New gold-rushes occasionally beckoned him. He spent five years in the solid gold town of Ararat but his stay cannot have been very successful. He returned to the hotels, keeping the Bulls Head amongst the vineyards and diggings of Great Western. Finally, in 1875, he went beyond the end of the railway line, and in the tiny wheat town of Rupanyup 'he built the hotel which he now conducts, and in which he is doing a good business'. That was the report of his affairs after thirteen years in the town. He had never been so long in one place. Now he was probably seen as the epitome of solidity, the stay-at-home whose flittings in past years were unimaginable. Of his personality no clue is available except that he must have been gregarious and cheerful, the eternal promoter and impresario. He was the kind of man who kept on climbing even when the ladder was falling.

We leave brickmaker Usher and his sturdy sons at his wheat farm at Pepper's Plains. We leave carpenter Williams presiding over the bar or the prim dining room of his hotel at Rupanyup. Their struggle to be independent, and the manner in which they bounced back after reverses, were repeated in thousands of lives. Many settlers made more money than these two had made. Even more of the settlers had made less money and security. But most – irrespective of whether they finally won or lost the material contest – could remember long periods of hope.

Australian men could be divided into two groups: those who worked for themselves or in their family's business, and those who relied on daily or monthly pay. In 1890 the independent breadwinners were outnumbered, about two to one, by those receiving wages and salaries, but the two groups overlapped. People moved often from wages to independence or back to wages. Many small farmers or their sons would leave home to earn money by shearing sheep, or working for wages for a few months in gold-mines, on travelling threshing-machines, and as railway navvies. These small farmers, after returning home, might even employ labour for a few months of the year, paying a passing well-sinker to sink a well, or hiring a labourer to stook the sheaves and cart the hay. Similarly many men who called themselves wage-earners ran their own small venture on the side. In the country many employees of a mine, railway or flour-mill owned a few acres with a cow and pigs, a hen coop, a vegetable garden and potato patch, twelve or twenty fruit trees, and a stack of firewood which they had cut in nearby bush. They thus had a modicum of independence and security.

Initiative, thrift, and self-help with a dash of luck were widely extolled as virtues. The idea that the government should often intervene was not held widely. Most people believed that by their own efforts – as small owners or as wage-earners – they could make a living and keep self-respect. At times there was the hope that they might become rich. This optimism relied partly on the existence of gold-fields and occasional new rushes. This optimism relied also on fertile Crown lands which could be bought on time-payment. The optimism depended too on plentiful jobs, so that people – if they fell or failed – could at least earn reasonable wages while they wondered where next to throw their dice. The small farms, shallow gold-fields and the abundant town opportunities were a source of social security, or the hope and feeling of security, in colonies whose parliaments so far had provided little security. The other source of social security was the abundant jobs. Remove these sources, and part of the optimism and individualism would fade from society.

Even before the depression of the 1890s the typical small business venture outside the large cities was losing some of its attraction. Mining and farming now required more capital. In contrast, the attraction of wages' jobs seemed to be rising, especially in the large cities where the hours of work in the skilled trades and hard labouring jobs were declining. As the governments built most of the railways and as they were pressed to improve working conditions, the government jobs set the pace for conditions and wages. In essence many secure government and city jobs became more attractive than the long hours and risky livelihood of the small farmers, independent gold prospectors, small shopkeepers and hawkers, firewood cutters, charcoal burners and the carter owning his own dray or cart.

4

Those who were capable of working, whether for themselves or for others, coped well by British standards. Those who fell sick, suffered serious accidents, or grew too old to work did not cope well unless they had managed to save money for an emergency. It was not necessarily a favoured land for the needy.

The governments provided few social services. There were no pensions for the old, for widows, for crippled breadwinners, or the unemployed. The official view was that charity was not needed in the land of plenty. In most colonies, officially, poverty did not exist. In fact it did exist and could be seen in the inner suburbs of large cities. It could also be seen around the countryside, especially amongst those small selectors whose farms were a failure, or who themselves were failures as farmers. But poverty in Australia in the period 1850 to 1890 was less common – though not less humiliating – than in any country in Europe. In England in 1850 nearly 6% of the population were so poor that they received indoor or outdoor relief from public funds, but destitution on such a scale was unknown in Australia: it was unknown and unthinkable.

In England many breadwinners and their families were poor even in times of full employment because wages were low by Australian standards. Poverty was often acute in English occupations filled by casual labour, but here casual labour often was highly rewarded because of the general shortage of labour. In England a large family of young children was especially prone to poverty, but in Australia it was easier for the children of a large family to find work after school, easier for the husband to grow vegetables and gather firewood, and easier for the wife to find part-time work as a domestic servant.

Similarly, our climate was an asset. The strong building industry here did not decline in the very cold months, thus throwing builders' labourers and bricklayers out of work.

Moreover these Australians who were destitute suffered less from the effects of the climate. They needed fewer clothes: they could more easily survive a winter without fuel – in fact their stove might not even lack fuel, because firewood was easily obtained or scavenged in most Australian towns. Winter in northern Europe was a shivering nightmare for the poor. An Australian winter was more tolerable.

As household help in Australia was scarce, and therefore paid more than in the British Isles, an Australian widow had a slightly better chance of keeping her family together by going out to work or taking in washing or lodgers. It is also reasonable to suggest that an Australian widow had a much stronger chance of remarrying and thus finding a new breadwinner because of the shortage of women of marriageable age.

For these reasons the governments in Australia had probably less need to provide social welfare services. Those services they did provide were mainly in institutions – lunatic asylums, hospitals, benevolent asylums for the very old, orphan schools, and homes for the deaf and dumb and the temporarily destitute. Most institutions received a large part of their income from the government, though many hospitals relied almost as much on voluntary donations as on government support in New South Wales in the 1860s. Curiously, that government in 1864 was paying more towards the salaries of clergymen of the four main sects than towards the running of hospitals. Most of these public institutions printed a long list of commands which dictated the inhabitants' hour of rising, what they could eat, when they could smoke, when they could visit their dormitory, and what work they had to perform if capable of work. People tried to keep away from these institutions unless they were weighed down by misfortune and illness and were devoid of hope.

Many of the colonial misfits were old people who had held senior offices in Europe but were unable to cope with a new society. A Melbourne journalist of the 1870s wormed his way into the Benevolent Asylum as an inmate for three days and found, wasting away in the dormitories and dining hall and grounds, an old Oxford-educated clergyman, several retired naval officers and an officer's widow, surgeons and lawyers, a clerk from the War Office in London, a former officer of the Swedish army, an ex-master of a merchant ship and a shopkeeper from Oxford Street in London. Old Tasmanian convicts and people from many English and colonial backgrounds were also there – the driftwood from floods and storms. Even two Chinese, conspicuous with their long pigtails, lived in the asylum. Many more of the sick, stray and senile were waiting for vacancies to appear in asylums. In these barracks of the helpless the advantages outweighed the defects, for the inhabitants received shelter, enough to eat, and a free coffin when they died.

Old people and invalids suffered unduly in Australia. Large numbers of men and women had no relatives in the whole continent: in severe sickness or in old age they were thus thrown on to public charity. Tasmania was first to face this question because it had an unusually high proportion of old people by the last third of the 19th century. The Tasmanian government simply placed the old and the infirm in invalid depots.

The prevailing creed was that people should be encouraged, through their own hard work and thrift, to save for the rainy day. If the government cared too generously for the old, it would be fostering extravagance in those who were young. When it was alleged that the bedding at the Brickfields Invalid Depot in Tasmania was miserable, a Royal Commission of 1871 retorted than an attractive poor-house or invalid asylum would punish those who had been thrifty. It would compel 'the honest self-denying workman', who shunned the public house, to pay an additional tax in order to support those old folk who had once revelled in the public house. This generation was convinced that most of the poor people had only themselves to blame. Their poverty was blamed upon alcohol and other forms of self-indulgence. 'What is the cause of all this pauperism?' enquired a visitor who observed 800 old and decrepit Tasmanian men and women at the asylum at New Town. The reply of the superintendent was emphatic: 'Drink, unhesitatingly, drink.'

Since 1890 academic explanations of poverty have tended to swing from the extreme position of placing virtually all blame on the poor and unemployed to the other extreme of placing all blame on society. A century ago such a swing of considered opinion was inconceivable. Society then could probably not yet afford to undermine those incentives to hard work and thrift because the standard of living relied on those incentives.

Poverty was to be expected in a proportion of people, but was on no account to be encouraged: otherwise the poor might multiply. Thus the Hobart Benevolent Society set up a woodyard, and unemployed young men who sought help were simply handed an axe and paid a few pence hourly for the wood which they chopped. This method was said to sift the energetic poor, who deserved help, from the lazy poor. In two hours, it was said, the wood-chopper could earn enough to buy a day's food for his family, and then for the remainder of the day he was free to look for work. In 1871 the Tasmanian govermment seriously considered compiling a list of all those who were receiving charity, and publishing it as a warning in newspapers and even posting it on the walls of police stations.

If all the public and private gifts and good works bestowed on the orphans, the poor, insane, sick, old, and the deserted could be added together, the private donations possibly would exceed the government's contributions, one century ago. Many churches helped members of their own congregations who were in need. In every town the clergyman carried out many functions – the listening, the reassuring and visiting – which professional social workers and doctors now fulfil at the government's expense. In the larger towns benevolent societies gave help to the old or homeless; and public subscription lists were opened when a mining disaster, shipwreck or a bushfire caught the public imagination. In depressed years groups of citizens collected old clothes, ran up new clothes, opened soup kitchens, or distributed loads of firewood. Occasionally relief money went overseas: in 1846 a large sum was collected in New South Wales towards the relief of the famine in Ireland and Scotland; and in the early 1860s another large sum was collected to relieve distress in Lancashire when the American Civil War disrupted cotton supplies and closed the textile mills. The severe famine in India in the late 1870s led to relief funds in all the colonies and the contribution of at least £65,000 by February 1878: the sum seems small today but it equalled the weekly wage for about thirty thousand Australian working men. An appeal to relieve the famine in China yielded the equivalent of some four thousand pay packets in the same year.

In hundreds of towns and villages and workplaces the custom was to send round the hat and collect money for those neighbours in trouble. At the back of Bourke about 1890 a lanky shearer named the Giraffe was sometimes taking around his wide cabbage-tree hat and collecting banknotes and silver coins for the latest casualty or cause: the woman whose husband was drowned in the Bogan flood, a bullocky who was so drunk that he was run over by his own wagon, or the sick jackeroo who could no longer work and had no money to take home to his wife and children in Sydney. Henry Lawson wrote a story about the warm-hearted Giraffe, and the story provided the title of one of his celebrated volumes of short stories, *Send Round the Hat*. While the hat was being passed from man to man, the women often had their own version of sending around the hat: hot food, plates of sandwiches, bundles of clothes, the nursing of the sick, the caring for neighbour's children when a new child was born. In the farmlands, neighbours might club together to bring in the harvest for a widow whose husband suddenly died. In many towns at least one storekeeper gave struggling customers an amount of credit which was far beyond the call of duty and the guidelines of good business; and this may help explain why grocers were usually high on the list of bankrupt occupations. By the end of the century a social philosophy applauding mateship and kindness was widely held or applauded or nodded to in the

249

outback, the mining fields, and in thousands of city houses. Many *Bulletin* writers spread that message. Adam Lindsay Gordon, who had died in 1870, did not so often preach it; but the lines of his verse which were most widely remembered by 1900, and appeared again and again in autograph books and keepsakes, affirmed the message:

> Life is mostly froth and bubble,
> Two things stand like stone,
> Kindness in another's trouble,
> Courage in your own.

In the outback for several generations most of the pastoral properties unfailingly gave food supplies to swagmen and sundowners – more often called 'travellers' – who called at the station in the course of their travels. In the Riverina in the 1870s the stations gave a minimum of one pound of meat and a pannikin of flour to all travellers, irrespective of whether they were searching for work or dodging work. In some stations in the 1890s sugar and tea were often supplied. The allowance of fresh rations was known as *the dole*, which suggests that it is the origin of the word widely used today to denote the government's payment to the unemployed. It is said that in the eastern Riverina one man lived for thirty years on the pastoralists' dole. He did no work except to carry his swag from station to station, tramping along one bank of the Murrumbidgee and returning along the other bank. From Gundagai to Hay, and back again, was his itinerary, and he completed it every twelve or fifteen months. At isolated sheep stations at certain times of the year as many as thirty or fifty men might arrive about sundown to receive free rations.

The camaraderie, the rituals of duty, were occasionally extended to Chinese, Kanakas and Negroes in the bush. Many of those men who in life were treated as outcasts were given a respectable burial. William Lockhart Moreton, a pastoral pioneer, was riding towards Wilcannia in 1870 and chanced to call at a lonely grog shanty just after the Creole cook had died. The cook was a Catholic and, in his last

250

hours, had requested that he be buried in the Monaro Hills near by and that his body should face the sunrise. The four men at the shanty dutifully placed the dead man in a coffin made of thin planks of white pine and buried him – not on the hill because it was rocky – but in ground at the foot.

The Aboriginals received many kindnesses but many acts of meanness. Their need for help and compassion and a little understanding had never been stronger. In Tasmania the last full-blood Aboriginal died in May 1876. Named Trucanini she had lived in comfort in Hobart in her last years, smoking her pipe and drinking at bedtime her hot spiced ale, a dignified woman who stood no more than 4' 3" tall. Several other full-blooded Tasmanian women still lived in obscurity on Kangaroo Island and it was there that Sukey died in the centenary year of the British settlement of Australia, her death unnoticed amidst the speeches of those who described how a wilderness had been tamed in one century.

Almost everywhere the Aboriginals were diminishing and it was widely said that the race would be extinct within a lifetime. In the dry interior tribal Aboriginals still lived their traditional life over vast areas but most Aboriginals were in contact with the whites and lived in relative poverty, camping on sheep and cattle stations and sometimes receiving rations from the owners, clustered in government camps and forlorn reserves, living in flimsy shelters on the edges of outback towns, the children rarely attending school and few fathers working for wages. In one sense they were a people lost in their own land but in another sense they were still sustained by intense family and tribal loyalties. A willingness to share what they had helped them cope with distress more easily than most British Australians: moreover they probably knew less loneliness.

The governments treated Aboriginals with a mixture of neglect and concern. In Victoria where the Aboriginals by the 1880s were few, they received more generous help than the poor whites. Indeed the recent burst of fierce criticism of colonial ministries of a century ago and of their 'racist' policies towards the blacks is not always fair, for it neglects

to say how those same ministers treated the destitute
members of their own race.

5

The popular view, until at least the 1890s, was that most
people could provide their own welfare services. Australia
was infinitely more favoured than England for the fulfilling
of this dream of self-supporting families and individuals
who, only in the harshest emergency, would seek help from
a government. But even in the 1850s this dream was tinged
with fantasy, and the fantasy increased as more and more
Australians lived in cities. In 1891 only 23% of the
workforce lived on the land, though many more had made
the attempt and failed.

In the cities the lodges and friendly societies provided
funeral benefits and a pension for a widow or a small
income when a breadwinner was sick. The purchase of a
house was another form of security practised more widely
in Australian cities than in England. In 1891 four of every
ten Melbourne householders and three of every ten Sydney
householders owned or were buying their houses.

Australia had become a parade ground for hawkers and
door-knockers who sold life assurance. After the creation of
the Australian Mutual Provident Fund in Sydney in 1849, a
co-operative company owned and directed by Australians,
the policies slowly began to multiply. Other new mutual
societies entered the chase, and in the 1870s they pioneered
new forms of insurance which gave the policy-holder a
protection such as no society in any other land provided.
They eliminated much of the small print which had forced
new clients to forfeit policies when, through sickness or
poverty, they were unable to continue their quarterly
payments. Presbyterians set up the Australian Widows'
Fund and the Rechabites set up the T & G Society to enable
abstainers to receive more generous benefits. The big
Australian co-operative companies with their branches in
every colony and New Zealand outbid the old British
companies for new members; and in 1886 the Colonial

Mutual Life Society, a Melbourne youngster, even began to sell policies in London.

Travelling salesmen and lecturers spread the message that insurance was the way to prepare for old age. At one meeting John Templeton, pioneer of National Mutual Life, spoke on the comforts of life insurance in Hobart Town Hall to the governor, most cabinet ministers and more than a thousand people. Three American companies, hearing about this land where a higher proportion of the people took out insurance policies than in the United States or Canada or Great Britain, entered the market in the 1880s. The Equitable Life suggested that it would stay in Australia by spending £363,000 on a block of land, perhaps the most expensive block of land ever purchased in Australia. In the 1890s, at the corner of Collins and Elizabeth Streets in Melbourne, arose its granite and marble palace of thrift and forethought.

When New South Wales sent a contingent of 800 to fight in the Sudan War in 1885, those soldiers who held life policies in certain Australian companies were permitted to run the risks of war without paying higher premiums. The co-operative societies could afford such patriotic bonuses. They had calculated their table of risks and their premiums on the assumption that the death rates of clients would be as high as in England; but the death rate of clients in the AMP Society's first thirty years was only two thirds of the predicted rate. Curiously violence – whether drowning, accidents, murders or suicides – accounted for one sixth of the recorded deaths in the members of one society.

In 1888 in Australia and New Zealand there were sixty-five insurance policies for every thousand people. As most of these policies were presumably registered in the name of heads of families, perhaps one quarter of the population was covered by life insurance. In Great Britain and Canada in contrast only about twenty-five policies had been taken out for every thousand inhabitants, and in the USA a mere fifteen. Clearly the chattering, buttonholing entourage of insurance men had signed Australian clients of an income-level rarely insured in other English-speaking lands. Often the travelling insurance salesman was accompanied by his doctor, ever ready to examine a client to see if his health justified the granting of a policy. Too often the salesman was a huckster who, according to a New South Wales judge in 1886, pestered a client all day and would not give up until he had taken 'the very coat off your back and the very boots off your feet'. For most people, however, an insurance policy did provide a coat for their back. When the economic storms blew in the 1890s that coat protected tens of thousands of people, but even more people lacked a coat.

The government was the helper of last resort; and until its taxation system was transformed it could do little to ease social and economic distress. And the taxation system was not likely to be reformed quickly because most people believed that high taxes discouraged savings and self-reliance.

We are so accustomed to the idea that the rich should pay much higher taxes than the poor that we forget that the idea was a latecomer to Australia. Whereas the United Kingdom imposed an income tax on the wealthier citizens and imposed estate duties on the landed gentry, Australia in 1860 collected nearly all its taxes indirectly. The main taxes were the import duties on opium, tobacco, alcoholic spirits and other luxuries, the excise duties collected from Australian distilleries, and the tax which was collected from those who exported or dug for gold. Few of these taxes weighed more heavily on the rich than on the labourer.

The largest single source of government revenue was the windfall income which each colony gained from the sale of its public lands. That income could not last forever. Indeed the decline in revenue from land sales was often the spur to collecting new taxes. Victoria, Tasmania and South Australia were the first to see their revenue from land sales dwindling dangerously, and significantly they were quick to impose new taxes on the assets and income of the rich.

Five of the six colonies also imposed death duties on the larger estates – Tasmania having introduced the first permanent succession duty in 1865 – but these duties generally were mild. When Victoria in the late 1870s imposed a tax of 10% on those deceased estates worth more than £100,000 the tax was regarded as extortionate but was not so large that wealthy people went to great pains to evade it. Most of the wealthy men in colonial Australia had made rather than inherited their own fortunes and were proud of their success; they imagined the public's astonishment when it was announced, after their death, that they had left behind £200,000 or £500,000. They were not too willing to forgo that seal of colonial success, that sable knighthood of death, simply to save probate or succession duty.

If the rich could be taxed after death, perhaps they could also be taxed while they lived. The big squatters were an obvious target, and Victoria in 1877 was the first colony to impose a small annual land tax on the larger rural properties. Edward Jenks, an early professor of law, described this land tax as a vicious piece of class legislation because it taxed only the larger rural properties and completely ignored those city frontages which were becoming as valuable as vast sheep stations. South Australia followed in 1884 with a tax which, being based on the principles of the American reformer Henry George, tried to confiscate part of the increase in the value of unimproved land. By 1890 three colonies collected land taxes and three collected that tax which made some rich men mumble and others explode – the income tax.

Tasmania has for long been singled out by historians as an unusually conservative colony in the late 19th century but it initiated the income tax. In 1880, faced by a heavy deficit, Tasmania imposed a tax of ninepence in the pound – or roughly 3½ % – on incomes earned from dividends and rent. South Australia in 1884 went a step further and imposed the first Australian tax on income earned through personal exertion as well as a tax on income from property. Businessmen and civil servants and a wide range of salary earners were liable to pay income tax, but wage-earners were exempt because the minimum income which attracted the tax collector was £300 a year. The citizens of the two most populous colonies, Victoria and New South Wales, were spared the income tax until 1895, a year of depression when any new source of revenue was tempting to hard-pushed governments. Even then the average wage-earner paid no income tax. In New South Wales, where a citizen was exempt from paying taxes on the first £300 of his income, he had to earn an annual salary of £500 – five times a labourer's income – before his rate of taxation reached 1%.

Most of the colonies earned their main revenue from the customs house and the land sales, but the direct taxes on wealth were growing. Negligible in 1860 they yielded perhaps one eighth of government tax revenue by 1881 and about one fifth by 1901, and were to supply more than half by 1941, a war year. But death duties, land taxes and income taxes were not welcomed by a wide array of observers who believed that society as a whole gained more by providing incentives rather than deterrents to money-making. One politician in New South Wales saw the proposed income tax as the gift of Satan. 'If', he said, 'the Devil had sent a representative here to institute a means of destroying the morality of the people, he could have found no better instrument than an Income Tax.' He was simply suggesting in an exaggerated way that the thrifty, diligent and enterprising people provided jobs and created wealth and that an income tax was a theft of their hard-won wealth.

Capital, enterprise and technology, working in partnership, had contributed heavily to the high standard of living of Australians and deserved their reward. Labour likewise deserved its reward and captains of labour now strode forward to claim it.

16   Sharpening the Shears

By 1875 there were dozens of trade unions in Australia, but most were small exclusive clubs rather than loose alliances which preached the brotherhood of labour. Many coal-miners of the Hunter Valley and many gold-miners in Victoria were trade unionists. In the printing shops, in iron foundries and many of the metal trades, amongst the stonemasons and bricklayers, trade unions could be found. A unionist passing along a city lane and suddenly detecting the sour smell of colonial leather in the large workshop of a saddle maker or bookbinder could expect to find a few unionists inside. In the countryside a trade unionist was a rarity. If he existed he told nobody of his existence: he might be sacked. Amongst women who worked in factories or as domestic servants in homes and boarding houses, a trade union was unknown in the 1870s. Amongst unskilled labourers who worked with pick and shovel on the railway embankments or the site of buildings, the union was uncommon. Amongst the white-collar men, amongst the clerks and officials in banks and government offices or importing houses, the very thought of joining a union would have been almost as rash as the thought of arriving at work without a hat.

Most unionists in Australia in 1875 were craftsmen or tradesmen. They had served an apprenticeship and had learned a skilled trade. Their trade union was not only a defence league but also a social club and minor welfare agency. Before the governments began to fulfil welfare functions, most trade unions collected a weekly due from their members and so accumulated a small kitty of money which might help a member who was too ill to work or might help his widow on burial day. Occasionally a trade union conducted a strike in pursuit of shorter hours of work or to prevent wages from falling, but the strikes rarely lasted long. Few union leaders in Australia in the 1870s could foresee the day when a strike could dislocate a city or a whole industry. Few leaders of unions could probably conceive of the day when unionists would be the most powerful group in a strong political party.

The trade unions in the 1870s embraced only a small fraction of the employees in the land. We do not know how many people formally belonged to unions in 1875 but they were probably far fewer than those who were formal members of each of the main religious denominations. In 1875 even the fourth or fifth most important church would have had more influence on society than all trade unions added together. No leaders of unions were national or colonial figures. It is likely that in Adelaide or Sydney in the 1870s the man in the street, if asked for the name of a prominent unionist or a prominent preacher, would have selected a preacher with greater ease.

2

William Guthrie Spence was probably the first unionist to become a national name. He had come to Victoria as a six-year-old from an island in the Orkneys – forty miles beyond the northern tip of Scotland – and on the gold-fields he lived in a tent with his parents. In the early years of the rushes he was a child shepherd, a gold-digger, and a butcher. His formal education was brief but as a young man he read resolutely and gained a fluency in writing and in public speaking. Most of his early years he spent around Creswick, a gold town which lay on the fringe of bare green volcanic hills to the north of Ballarat. He often climbed or walked around those rounded hills, he saw them on hundreds of mornings, and he worked in some of the rich mines which arose in the 1870s at the foot of the volcanic hill called Spring Mount. That hill epitomized this man of enormous drive, and the way in which he was to inflame emotions in every part of eastern Australia.

In July 1878 Spence decided to form a trade union on the new deep alluvial gold-fields near Spring Mount. Other unions had been formed on Australian gold-fields and coal-fields, but most of their branches were either weak or dying. Provoked particularly by the attempt of the mining companies to cut wages from 7 shillings to 6s 6d a day, Spence called a meeting of miners one winter's night at Thomas Dibdin's wooden hotel in Broomfield Gully, a town then booming but now almost deserted. Guided along dark tracks by lanterns, 150 miners crowded into the hotel, heard Spence speak of the advantages of forming a union, and elected him secretary and the publican as treasurer. Two evenings later Spence conducted a rally in the nearby town of Creswick. The union was organized with such skill and aroused such support that the mine-owners did not reduce the wages.

Spence, then in his early thirties, became a missionary for the union. He encouraged the opening of new branches or the revival of old branches in many other Victorian gold-fields. He had an instinct for strategy and tactics. As he knew that the union would rarely win a strike unless it could prevent outside miners from acting as strike-breakers, his committees tried to insist that only unionists should work in the Creswick mines. His union set up accident funds whereby members or their widows could receive compensation in the event of accidents in the mines; and by insisting that every miner should help pay for these benefits he virtually banned non-unionists. The mine-owners applauded the accident fund, especially as they did not have to finance it. Perhaps they also realized that so long as the accident fund dominated the finances of the miners' union, the union could not afford long strikes: a long strike used up so much money that it robbed the accident fund. In fact, in its first two decades the Amalgamated Miners' Association throughout Australia spent more than nine tenths of its revenue on compensating the victims of accidents or their families.

Spence knew how far he could squeeze the shareholders of the mines. Unlike many men who later were to lead unions, he knew minutely the economics of industry. It has long been forgotten that when he organized his union at Creswick he was not a miner working for his daily wage. Soon after the union was formed he and some mates took over a gold-mine under the tribute system and worked it for three years on a profit-sharing basis with the owners. He was thus a share-miner, the underground equivalent of a share-farmer. Likewise, scores of members of his union were share speculators who used their inside knowledge of particular gold reefs to buy and sell shares on the stock exchanges which then flourished in the mining towns. They knew therefore that if wages were unrealistically high the low-grade mines would have to close, thus depriving unionists of work.

The miners' union spread across Australia. It linked up with the coal-miners in New South Wales. It formed branches on the gold-fields of New Zealand. By 1890 it had members as far apart as cold Zeehan in Tasmania and the dry heat of Croydon near the Gulf of Carpentaria. Its roll of members probably exceeded 23,000, the biggest union in the Australias.

If travellers happened to see Spence, standing in the refreshment room at the Ballarat railway station during one of his journeys as an organizer, they would have noticed nothing unusual in his appearance, manner or speech. Spence's indignation might run hot but it rarely approached boiling point. A quiet negotiator, he was inclined to see a strike as the last cartridge in his belt. A clear and strong stump-orator, he was not the author of catch-cries and long-remembered phrases: indeed, there was something of the lawyer in his approach to an argument. His appearance, like his speeches, aroused few emphatic comments. The painter Tom Roberts observed simply that Spence's head had 'more height above the eyes than the average'. Spence was a highbrow, walking in heavy working boots.

Though he travelled far as an organizer and negotiator in

the 1880s, Spence spent most days in his home town where the Amalgamated Miners' Association had its headquarters. In Creswick he was known as a family man and a good citizen. He drilled with the volunteer militia, sat on the town council, and spoke at meetings of the debating society. On Sundays he stood on the platform of the Presbyterian Sunday School, and on some evenings he preached in the local chapels of the Primitive Methodists and Bible Christians, which found most of their support from working people, especially miners. Significantly, these churches saw nothing inherently evil in capitalism or private property. They believed that the highest obstacle to the reform of society was not the present economic system but the mote in everybody's eyes.

By present standards, the powerful Amalgamated Miners' Association seems conservative, and indeed is sometimes derided by historians because it was not socialist. But Spence would probably have achieved nothing if he had preached socialism. He would have stood alone on his tree stump, just three feet above the earth. He stood high because he climbed the ladders which already existed.

3

The miners' union became so powerful by 1886 that a few shearers wondered whether William Spence might be the crusader who could organize shearers into a union that spanned the continent. The shearing of sheep in the second half of the year was the equivalent of the annual harvest in Europe, for wool was again supreme in Australia; providing more than half of the export income.

The large pastoralists who owned most of the country's sheep employed roaming teams of men who arrived on the eve of the shearing season, set up camp not far from the shearing shed, and then worked strenuously six days a week until the whole flock had been shorn and the wool had been pressed into the great bags or bales made of Indian jute. The larger pastoralists ran sheep on a colossal scale. I doubt if any people in the history of the world had ever owned so many domesticated animals as were owned on the vast estates of these Australian pastoralists. Their wool sheds, some of which were noble high buildings of bluestone and sandstone, could have easily been mistaken for a steam-locomotive shed at a railway junction or the civic hall of a flourishing town. In rules and in discipline some of these large shearing sheds were like factories. Indeed many were old-style factories, with a hundred or more shearers who began work on the stroke of six in the morning, halted for meals and the regulation smokos, and worked exactly nine hours on every day except Saturday. Nearly every shed imposed fines on shoddy workmanship: a foreman observed any sheep that was carelessly shorn and marked it with a 'raddle' of red ochre, and for that sheep the shearer was not paid and might even be fined.

While many sheds were organized with a minimum of rules – so long as the sheep were shorn with skill – other shearing sheds fined men who swore or were rowdy. The rules posted on the walls of the Mt Eba shed in South Australia in 1887 carried the killjoy sentence: 'Singing, whistling, swearing and noise prohibited'. Moreover any shearer dismissed for an infringement was paid less than the standard rate for the sheep he had already shorn, even if he had performed that work faithfully. At a station in western Victoria in 1886 the rules provided that a shearer who was drunk or who brought back grog was liable to forfeit all money owing to him for the sheep he had already shorn. Naturally a pastoralist who was too eager to use the red ochre or to invoke the rule book would find himself short of shearers in a season when work was plentiful.

It is not simply poverty or a deep sense of injustice which leads to a revolt by workmen. The stories of the rise of the shearers' union neglect to notice that most shearers were paid more than the larger army of rural labourers who worked as ploughmen, fencers, potato diggers or hay-makers. Moreover shearers worked a shorter week, especially in summer, than the farm labourers. What distinguished the shearers from other rural workers was an ability to organize themselves, for they lived and worked together, relatively isolated from outside influences. They were also distinguished by the belief – usually but not always true – that their employers could easily afford to pay them more. The shearers slept in rough huts and ate rough-cooked meals and worked until the sweat could be wrung from their clothes. The typical owner of the big station lived in a large homestead, or mansion, was waited on by servants, rode everywhere on a fine horse or in a painted carriage. He might have a second house in the city, where he lived closer to the smell of claret and whisky than to the yolky smell of new-shorn wool. The young bushman Barcroft Boake, in his poem 'Where the Dead Men Lie', reflected anger towards these owners. In his last verse – excised from many anthologies of his poetry – he described old Moneygrub, wallowing in luxury in the city while his stockmen died of thirst or privation on his cattle station far outback.

> Moneygrub, as he sips his claret,
> Looks with complacent eye
> Down at his watch-chain, eighteen-carat—
> There, in his club, hard by:

Each link of his watch-chain, said Boake, was invisibly engraved with names of men who had died on his outback station. The metaphor was highly exaggerated but had some truth.

Many sheep-owners were not prosperous. The price of wool by the mid-1880s had fallen and the seasons were perhaps less reliable. In the dry interior – and it was the most recently settled and the riskiest of the sheep regions – many of the big pastoral runs were sliding deeply into debt. The city banks and the large pastoral houses acquired mortgages over tens of millions of acres. By the mid-1880s the annual interest owed by many individual sheep stations equalled one third or even one half of the value of the annual wool clip, and five years later the lower wool proceeds of many stations could not even meet the interest bill owed to the city finance houses. The sheep-owners naturally searched for savings, and in 1886 in some districts they tried to lower their payments to shearers. The shearers saw the visible homesteads and mansions of the pastoralists, not their invisible mortgages, and were indignant at the attempts to cut their pay.

At Creswick, the unionists' mecca, a young gold-miner named David Temple was accustomed to go shearing each winter; and when he heard that a shearer's pay was to be lower, he wondered whether all his travelling from shed to shed, his back-stiffening work with the shears and the petty rules devised by some of the owners, made the job worthwhile. When he told his mother, a level-headed Scot, she said simply: 'Why don't you go to Mr Spence?' David Temple spoke to Mr Spence and explained his grievances as a shearer. Spence decided that he would back the forming of an Amalgamated Shearers' Union. An office was rented in Ballarat, an inaugural meeting was held at a hotel in Sturt Street on a cold Saturday night in June 1886, and with Spence as president the union began to enrol members on the eve of the new shearing season. Organizers were sent around the countryside to sign on shearers at an annual fee of five shillings. Organizers also went to New Zealand and, printing the union rules in Maori as well as English, enlisted more than 2000 shearers there by the end of 1886. Whereas Spence's unions had no time for Chinese or other Asiatics he accepted Maoris as well as American Negroes and Aboriginals.

Other men had tried to rally shearers into a trade union before Spence took up the task but he galloped where others had stumbled. Perhaps no union organizer anywhere in the world had so succeeded in uniting the wanderers of such a vast area. Spence must have had fine colleagues and a sense of teamwork. He also knew that an occupation where the workmen worked side by side and lived side by side could be easily organized. He knew that the pastoralists themselves were rarely organized, and cleverly he made them compete with each other for shearers. Those pastoralists who agreed, at shearing time, to employ only union members were given the pick of the shearers and treated with respect. Other pastoralists who refused to give in to Spence's demands were in effect picketed and deprived of shearers.

Many pastoralists recruited non-union shearers in country towns and gave them free tickets to the railhead nearest their wool shed. The union, however, was often waiting for the arrival of the tainted shearers. Spence's men would camp by the road leading to the sheep station and refuse to allow shearers to pass along that road. Sometimes Spence's men arrived in force at the shearers' huts and kidnapped men who did not belong to the union. Years later, when the battle had been won right across the grasslands, Spence used to recall the ruthless exploits against the non-unionists. 'On many occasions their hut was rushed at night, and they were taken away to a Union camp,' said Spence. An angry pastoralist might go to the nearest police station to complain that his shearers had been abducted. The policeman then accompanied the pastoralist to the union camp under the big gum-trees near the billabong, but the abducted shearers were rarely willing to say what had actually happened. Many found it simpler to join the union. When questioned by police they usually vowed that they had chosen to live voluntarily in the union camp and would remain there until the pastoralist agreed to employ only union men in his shearing shed.

Spence had no hesitation in picketing a sheep station for weeks, knowing that if the owners wanted an income from wool they could not afford to wait too long. Sometimes the union surrendered, for it ran out of cash with which to buy food and tobacco. Sometimes the pastoralist gave in, especially if the season were dry. In a dry spring the grass-seeds quickly ripened and wormed their way into the thick fleece of the unshorn sheep and so lowered the market price of the wool. 'This fact', recalled Spence, 'helped the Union to win many a shed.'

Distance was the main obstacle facing Spence's lieutenants as they rode their horses from shearing shed to shearing shed in the far outback. Distance, we now forget, was also their ally. The big shearing sheds, being far from the railway lines and the big towns, were also far from the large police stations and soldiers' barracks. At times, when hundreds of unionists assembled in an outback town and defied the local police, reinforcements of police or soldiers were sent by train from the coast; but that happened only in a grave emergency. In the cities the police were numerous and were usually on the side of the employers during industrial skirmishes, but in the outback the helmet sat on the head of the unionists. Far outnumbering the policemen and the volunteer militia of the bush towns, the union could quietly impose its own law and order.

Some unionists believed that the big landholders should be rubbed in the dust. One sheep-owner entered a village hall beyond Moree one evening in the late 1880s to hear a union leader and he was astonished at the message. If I had my way, said the unionist, 'every man in New South Wales should have one pound a week, and nobody should have any more'. Many members of the union, however, were small farmers who believed ardently in private property. In that great curve of pastoral country stretching from Goondiwindi and Bourke around to Port Augusta, perhaps half of the shearers in the 1880s were small farmers or the sons of men on small farms. Their concept of paradise was a grassy plain, fenced into neat farms where the owners proudly tilled their ground and doffed their hat to nobody. Such men were not radicals: they might be shearers for only four or eight weeks of the year, and so did not see themselves as employees as distinct from owners. Many such men were at first reluctant to join the union.

Spence's union did not try to insist that all shearers should earn alike. His union did not penalize the shearers who set a fast pace and earned three or four times as much money as a railway ganger or stockman. Ironically the sheep-owners had traditionally insisted that no man should shear too many sheep on the one day, and 110 was a common limit until the union abolished the limit. The 1890s were to become famous for shearing records. In some districts small crowds gathered at out-of-the-way shearing sheds to see the champions working with their remarkable stamina and dexterity. The daily tallies of the

266

best shearers were discussed in hotel bars, argued about and fought over. One of Australia's new folk heroes was the shearer and unionist Jacky Howe, and in October 1892 at Alice Downs station in Queensland he shore a daily average of 259 sheep during a five-day run, and on the sixth day he shore 321 ewes in less than eight hours – the most remarkable burst of blade-shearing in the history of the sheep.

The shearers' demands for more money in the 1880s seem to have encouraged the creation of the first shearing machines. Frederick Wolseley had come to Australia as a 17-year-old during the gold-rushes and had become an employee on a sheep station and then an owner. With financial help from his brother, Field Marshal Sir Garnet Wolseley, he developed a shearing machine which could be powered by shafting from a steam engine. His improved machine was shearing sheep at Walgett in New South Wales with some success in 1885. Accordingly, at a wool warehouse in Melbourne, he arranged a public test between an Australian blade-shearer and a Sudanese man operating a Wolseley sheep-shearing machine. The hand blades were faster but the machine succeeded in removing more wool from the average sheep. In 1888 a large wool shed near the Darling River installed forty machines, and more of the big stations installed Wolseley machines in the hope of cutting costs and in the belief that a semi-skilled man could handle the machine shears more easily than the hand blades. The machine would thus weaken the bargaining position of the unionists by opening the work to thousands of newcomers. Such motives, arising from industrial conflict in Australian shearing sheds, were to affect the new automobile industry in England, because Wolseley set up a factory at Birmingham to make shearing machines on the large scale, and in 1895 he diversified and made the first Wolseley motor cars; and soon the young Melbourne engineer who managed his factory decided to make his own car, the Austin.

4

At the end of 1886 Spence's Amalgamated Shearers' Union

of Australasia had about 9000 members. By February 1890 his union had most of the shearers in Victoria and New South Wales and, in all, some 20,000 members. His union spread far outback and as far north as the shearers travelled in their annual circuit. Under the new name of the Australian Workers' Union, adopted in 1894, it was to be the largest union in the land for about three quarters of a century.

At first the rising power of trade unions seemed to have no limit. A wide span of opinion was sympathetic to the aims of unions and to the right of working men to hold their head high, though not too high. In 1889, when about 150,000 dock workers in London went on strike, the financial aid which came from Australia was virtually sufficient to enable them to remain on strike until they won their dispute. Here were the carriers and the heavers of the world's largest port, carried to victory by donations which came from every large town in Australia, from lord mayors and judges, from working men who sent around the hat, from the gate receipts of football matches and recitals, from stock exchanges and scores of conservative members of parliament, as well as from trade unions. The £37,000 raised in Australia was a sign not only of the strength of trade unions here but also of the high standard of living which made many Australians marvel that dock labourers in London were paid so little. In helping these Londoners, Australians were consciously proclaiming the success of their own society as a creator of wealth. Curiously, 1889 was almost the last year in the 19th century when Australians could make such a proclamation.

In August 1890 the upheaval was virtually transferred from the waterfront of the Thames to wharves in Australia. The officers of coastal ships, the seamen and wharf labourers went on strike in Sydney and Melbourne. The Maritime Strike eventually embraced shearers far inland – those from Spence's big union and those from the small Queensland shearers' union – and the coal-miners of Newcastle and the silver-lead miners of Broken Hill. Here was a trial of strength between unions who were sensibly

268

trying where possible to make membership of a union compulsory and employers who were sensibly trying to control their working costs and their future.

In Melbourne and Sydney the strike provoked dramatic episodes which were talked about for a generation. In Melbourne at the end of August 1890 the government feared disorder, partly because the erratic supply of coal for the gasworks could snuff out the street lights but more because a mass meeting of strikers and sympathizers had been called for Sunday 31 August. As a precaution the government mustered the mounted volunteers of the militia in Melbourne, and in the barracks Lieutenant-Colonel Tom Price told a section of the Mounted Rifles that if a riot occurred and it was ordered as a last resort to fire at a crowd: 'Fire low and lay them out.' His men did not have to lay them out – they did not even leave the barracks – but Price's instructions were engraved so deeply into the minds of people that folklore sometimes recalled mistakenly that the troops had actually confronted the masses and threatened to fire. Price was, in fact, a son of that commandant of Norfolk Island who, renowned for his own harsh treatment of convicts, was battered to death by convicts in a prison hulk near Melbourne in 1857. In the popular imagination the reputation of the father had been visited, a generation later, on the son.

On 19 September 1890 in Sydney, employers and their supporters took the reins in their own hands by driving drays and wagons of wool to the deep-sea berth at Circular Quay. The strikers who declared the wool to be black lined the route and several tried to halt the procession of wool carters. At Circular Quay, just a century after the first convicts had been taken ashore, many of the descendants of those convicts were now insisting that in this land the master was no longer the master. At the quay the crowd seemed so huge and menacing that the Riot Act was read aloud to them and they were told to disperse. It was like ordering the salt water to run out of the harbour. Accordingly the constables on horseback scattered the people. As the wool was to be carted to the ships by strike-breakers and loaded by strike-breakers, the supply of wool from the country was cut off by a strike of the shearers. The blades were silenced and the country's main export was endangered. But the unions – even the shearers' union – were not yet powerful enough, and economic conditions were not buoyant enough, to favour the strikers. Moreover the strikers received no generous flow of funds from English working men, judges, football crowds, and members of the House of Lords, nor from many of those Australians who only a year ago had supported the striking dockers of London.

Everywhere the strikers were defeated, and unionism declined. The next advance in the strength of unionism had to wait until the following decade. One far-reaching effect, however, is attributed to the strike. The entry of the labour movement into parliament is said to have sprung partly from the defeat in 1890 and the realization that labour would always be struggling in industrial disputes unless it could enlist police, soldiers and statute book on its side. There might be some truth in this argument. And yet it is also plausible that, had the unions won their strike in 1890, they might have entered parliamentary politics with even more energy in the confidence that in unity lay strength.

5

There were already signs that the labour movement would show its strength in parliament as well as in workplaces. Charles Jardine Don, an Australian stonemason, was perhaps the first working man to take his seat in a parliament in the British Empire, but he was a generation ahead of his time. As a young Scot he had educated himself at night in debating clubs and mutual improvement societies, had read widely and learned apt quotations from William Cobbett, Tom Paine and Adam Smith, and taught himself how to speak in public. Migrating to the Victorian gold-fields at about the age of 33, he dug for gold at Ballarat and became a stonemason in Melbourne. He also chiselled away at society, campaigned for the eight-hour day and for the opening of lands which squatters occupied. In 1859 he won the seat of Collingwood in the legislative assembly, and is said to have worked as a stonemason on the walls of the new parliament house in the day and to have spoken inside at night. Charles Don could not tap any deep sense of solidarity amongst working people, for society was still mobile and optimistic and most working men did not resign themselves to the idea of remaining manual workers all their days. Nor was the colony's social distress acute by Scottish standards.

In his five years in parliament Don received no payment as a member; this vital innovation came to most colonies only in the period 1887 to 1890. As a politician Don therefore had to keep himself partly from his earnings as an inner-suburban publican, and his death at the age of 46 was probably hastened by occupational hazards faced as a stonemason and publican. He deserves to be remembered, but has no memorial.

Twenty years after Don was dead, few working men sat in the colonial parliaments. And then in the early 1890s, almost overnight, they became prominent in the legislative assemblies, first in New South Wales in a season of prosperity and then in other colonies as the depression deepened. Payment of members now enabled workmen and small employers to give up their normal job and sit in parliament. There was increasing unease with the perfor-mance of the self-employed, middle-class politicians who traditionally held workmen's electorates, and in January 1890 the Trades and Labor Council in Sydney voted overwhelmingly to campaign in the hope of winning seats for the labour movement at the next election. Economic changes made more employees realize that they would always be wage-earners. New ideologies from the northern hemisphere increasingly favoured the redistribution of wealth from rich to poor, and the success of trade unions in the 1880s and even their success in mounting though not winning the Maritime Strike of 1890 suggested that through political organizing and a sense of solidarity Australian workmen might win what had previously seemed unattainable. In New South Wales in June 1891, to the astonishment of many experienced politicians, the new

Labour Electoral Leagues won 35 of the 141 seats in the legislative assembly.

The appearance of the first Labor party in parliament house in Sydney rather than in another city was in itself a surprise, for in the preceding twenty years that parliament had perhaps passed fewer radical economic bills than any other east of the Nullarbor. In one sense then the surprise was only to be expected: the scope for a party of reform was stronger in New South Wales. There the ruling ideology of free trade, once a radical ideology, now seemed tame because radicalism in Europe was increasingly expressed more in collectivist and less in individualist terms. Free Trade had proclaimed: let us all work and trade together to create unparalleled abundance. And now came Marx, Henry George, the Fabians and others who said in their various ways: let us attack those who have cornered this abundance.

The platform on which Labor in New South Wales fought that first election was, by the standards of the time, quietly radical. It promised to fight for free education beyond the primary schools – a fight which it was to abandon or conduct half-heartedly when eventually it came to power. It promised to fight for the eight-hour day as the maximum working day in all occupations, and kept the promise in the cities but not in the country. It called, often with success, for safety in mines and factories. It successfully called for a fair electoral system in which no man could vote more than once, in which policemen and soldiers could at last be permitted to vote, and shearers, sailors and other wandering workers could have a chance of registering an absentee vote on election day. The new party's affirmation that each man – but not each woman – should have the vote accompanied the argument that the people should elect their own magistrates, an idea which has not yet been adopted. Economic nationalism but not an acid-tongued nationalism flavoured Labor's policy. Any Chinese who made furniture in the colony would be compelled to stamp their timber with a confession that it was made by Chinese labour, thus warning buyers who preferred to see the plane

and chisel held in a white hand. Any government contract –
whether to build a locomotive or to supply ink for the
schools – would be carried out by New South Wales
employers and workmen. At the same time the Labor
candidates supported the federation of the Australian
colonies.

The idea that the law courts and the armed forces should
not be the special instruments of employers in settling
industrial disputes was one of the reasons accelerating the
rise of a Labor party. Hence the policy of 1891 sought not
only the election of magistrates but also the substitution of a
volunteer army for the professional army: a 'purely
volunteer' army, presumably, was seen as unlikely to march
against workmen engaged in demonstrating or picketing.

If we had to seek the philosophers whose thoughts
underlay that first Labor platform, the finger would first
point not to European reformers but to the populist
American, Henry George, who had spoken to vast crowds
in Australia only the previous year.* This San Francisco
messiah argued in *Progress and Poverty* that governments
should impose a single tax on land and that the tax should
be based on the fact that the market value of most land grew
largely as a result of the increase of population, the building
of railways and public works, and other indirect improvements for which the owner of the land could take no credit.
There was merit in George's scheme, especially for a new
country where the price of land quickly multiplied. And in
the 1880s, during that bellowing boom in which real estate
soared in price, the Australian governments could in fact
have abolished all taxes and concentrated their taxation on
that 'unearned increment' which the rising value of land
provided.

His main idea was not new to Australia and versions of
the idea had been shaped and popularized here in the
1870s, especially by William H. Gresham, a Yorkshireman

---

*Henry George was aged 50 when he visited Australia in 1890. He had
visited Melbourne as a sailor when he was a teenager and his wife was a
native of Sydney. He still has followers, and occasionally they stand for
parliament.

who arrived in the gold-rushes and worked as a ship-chandler and merchant at Port Melbourne and as a maker of safety fuse at Footscray. In spare hours Gresham lectured on land reform and wrote pamphlets. He was also owner of a small vessel which he called *Felix Holt*, in honour of the radical hero of George Eliot's new novel, and in that vessel he set out from Port Melbourne before dawn on 13 May 1875 to make sales to incoming ships. The vessel ran into a fierce bay storm, and he and his two boatmen were not seen again. Gresham's pamphlets on taxing the land were read widely and Henry George himself read one with approval five years before he published his own book on taxing land in 1879.

George's ideas had a brief vogue in South Australia and then in New South Wales, especially in a string of linked towns extending from Lithgow to Wagga: eight of the first nine branches of the Henry George movement in New South Wales lay west of the dividing range. By the end of the 1880s George's disciples were meeting in more than seventy ·different organizations in various parts of Australia. As he supported free trade his ideas were particularly appropriate in New South Wales. As he supported private enterprise while believing in what that first Labor platform described as 'the natural and inalienable rights of the whole community to the land', his moderate stance suited those critics of society who did not wish change to go too far. George's influence presumably explains why the Labor party did not at first believe in the income tax. Only one tax was needed – a tax on land.

The sudden entry of Labor as an important minority party in New South Wales in 1891 was followed by less spectacular success in other colonies. Labor won ten seats in Victoria in 1892, and eight in South Australia a year later. In Queensland in 1893 Labor was almost as successful as in New South Wales two years earlier, winning nearly one quarter of the seats in the assembly. Whereas most Labor members in South Australia came from the city, in Queensland most came from the outback where the tropical gold towns of Croydon and Charters Towers gave them their strongest support. Generally the new party in the 1890s did not build on its initial success but in December 1899 in Queensland it briefly sipped power. Probably the first Labor government in any country, it ruled Queensland as a minority ministry for a total of six days. When the house resumed sitting, the ministry lasted only a few hours. Its 36-year-old leader, Anderson Dawson, was born in Rockhampton, the son of poor parents, and the story of his courageous rise from a Brisbane orphanage and the gold-mines of Charters Towers to the front bench of parliament was to be repeated many times in the early history of the labour movement. His ultimate quarrel with the Labor party was also a story repeated often.

The rise of a Labor party in the colonial parliaments delighted hundreds of thousands of people and worried or frightened older employers, property owners both rich and poor, and a small army of professional people who saw politics as in part a school of elocution in which the dropped 'h' should earn an automatic disqualification. In time to come the emergence of this new party would be seen by many as the most important event in Australian political history and the source of the well-being of several generations of working people and their families. The party had fine achievements but prosperity was not necessarily one of them. The favourable standard of living of the average Australian was visible long before a Labor party was visible. Labor was elevated from a minor party to a major party largely because that standard of living ceased to grow; but the first half century of the party's existence, both in power and in opposition, was to be marked by relatively little improvement in the way of life of the average Australian.

6

Spence entered parliament in Sydney in 1898 as one of the Labor members, and became even more a national hero and villain. Legends and gossip clung to him like burrs, and those which he brushed off were replaced by others. Once strong rumour alleged that by pilfering the union funds and by making deals with sheep-owners Spence himself had become a great sheep-owner. Some pastoralists were said to have spread this rumour as a means of undermining support for Spence's union. For a time, at outback gatherings, men used to recite five verses which mocked the idea that Spence owned a sheep station far out west. Successive verses began with the lines:

> He owns five hundred million sheep of Lincoln Leicester breed
>
> and
>
> His shed is roofed with beaten gold, brought from the planet Mars
>
> and
>
> He got eight million pounds, we've heard, by pinching Union funds . . .

Spence had integrity in financial matters, but the rumour that he owned a vast sheep station in some faraway place where 'droughts and flood are both unknown' might have been more than simply the result of malice. He was a wheeler-dealer: like many a skilled negotiator he did not discourage the idea that he had the magical touch and the mercury tongue. He had the conjurer's gift of producing, at conferences, a lamb from the lining of his hat. In such an air of mystery it was not difficult to conceive that Spence's own station might have been another outcome of those secret deals.

He saw the union – or, as it eventually became known, the Australian Workers' Union – not only as a means of sharing more of the wool industry's profits amongst the shearers. He also saw his union as an instrument of moral change. The men who joined his union would become less selfish and more interested in their fellow men. Membership of the union, wrote Spence, makes a man a 'better husband, a better father, a better and more active citizen'. In one sense Spence remained the superintendent of a Sunday School that spanned the outback.

The dramatic expansion of the miners' union had probably been aided by links with the churches. Those links would become weaker, being challenged by radical movements which argued that Christianity did not tackle the real issues of an industrial society. One sign of the changed mood could be seen in 1891 in a small ceremony at Creswick where the miners publicly showed their appreciation of Spence. They presented him with a copy of a book which few in Australia had heard of, because it had been translated into English only five years previously. The volume was called *Das Kapital* and was written by a man named Marx.

Spence had been the leading man in the creation of the two most powerful unions in Australia. As an organizer and tactician he must have been remarkable as well as ruthless. He made his share of mistakes but it is doubtful whether many Australian businessmen had overcome more obstacles. It may well be that few, if any, union organizers anywhere in the world had hitherto created unions which successfully marshalled so many workmen from so many isolated places. The great man in the early history of the labour movement, his fame seemed imperishable but was not. In the First World War, when Australians were divided on whether young men should be compelled to join the army and go overseas to fight, Spence decided as a minister in the federal cabinet that he should place the interests of the nation, as he perceived those interests, above the commands of his party. He was not forgiven.

17   The Veiled Maid of Adelaide

Many people noted the unity of Australia and the dearth of strong differences between the colonies. The differences, however, existed and were sometimes strongest where least expected.

South Australia in a quiet way retained many of its early characteristics. It held the smallest proportion of people of Scottish and Irish descent but to compensate for the Celtic deficit it had the largest Cornish communities. With Queensland it also held the largest settlements of Germans. In religion it was also the main deviant, being exceptionally strong in the nonconformist churches. In the 1880s it had a higher proportion of Methodists than any other colony and also a higher proportion of Baptists, Congregationalists, Lutherans, Unitarians, and members of the Church of Christ and Salvation Army than any other colony. Adelaide was often likened to Christchurch in New Zealand, for both cities had been founded loosely on the Wakefield principle of planned colonization and were essentially English, but Christchurch was Anglican whereas the real cathedrals in Adelaide were chapels in which the candle and cross were taboo.

South Australia had received no convicts and quietly reminded other colonies of that purifying fact. Its growth was more even because it lacked after the 1840s those great mineral discoveries which suddenly lifted the population of the other colonies. The characteristics of its population persisted, for no flood of later migrants swamped the old settlers. It was remarkably orderly and had no riots, rebellions or social upheavals. It was even deficient in those minor folk heroes, the bushrangers. They were less likely to flourish in a colony whose highways carried no valuable gold, except the escorts from Victoria in 1851 and 1852. Above all, the colony did not have those mountainous or heavily timbered regions which aided the guerilla activities of the bushrangers. The geography of the colony definitely favoured law and order because the settled districts formed a long coastal corridor and so were not difficult to police.

2

It is also likely that South Australia had less visible and less pronounced extremes of wealth and poverty. In origins it was perhaps more middle class than any other colony. It was weak in the Scottish who tended to be the fastest money-makers and weak in the Irish who tended to be the fastest money-losers in Australia. Of all colonies it became strongest in the farmers and they were neither rich nor poor as a group. It did possess a group of very wealthy sheep-owners but the wool industry in South Australia was not strong; nor were the early pastoralists, though rich, seen as such enemies of the people since their land could easily be resumed by the government. In essence there was a lack of wide extremes in economic and social life in South Australia. Women were unusually plentiful and here in 1855, for the first time in Australian history, was a colony where they were not in a marked minority.

South Australia was also shaped by an oddity of geography. Here the dry interior came down to the sea and a long tongue of sea also poked into the dry interior. The Adelaide Plains, so close to the cheap transport of the sea, had the dry summers which were ideal for wheat-growing, and such a climate was not experienced by wheat farmers of Victoria and New South Wales until railways enabled them to grow wheat beyond the Great Dividing Range. South Australia quickly became Australia's granary and the pioneer of mechanized farming on the bone-dry plains. The northern dint in the coastline gave South Australia early access to rich copper deposits. It also served as a launching pad for explorers of the interior.

As the long tongue of sea was closer than were Brisbane or Sydney to many parts of New South Wales and Queensland, it became the terminus of long droving routes followed by the skinny cattle of the far north. For the same reason South Australia acquired the Northern Territory and also became the terminus of the long telegraph line which came all the way from London and Calcutta through the Dutch East Indies and the centre of Australia. As Adelaide was close to the mouth of the Murray, it used that long artery to tap the commerce of other colonies. And so in the last third of the century South Australia was more closely in touch with the outback than were Brisbane, Sydney, and Melbourne. In the streets and hotels and saleyards of Adelaide could be seen Broken Hill miners, drovers from Birdsville and the Barkly Tableland, captains and stokers whose paddle-steamers chugged nearly two thousand miles along the inland rivers to load bales of wool, telegraph operators who had served in Tennant Creek or Alice Springs, and station-owners whose flocks grazed so far in the dry interior that the wool was sent south on the back of camels. South Australia, understandably, was federalist in sympathies because it leaped over all borders in its search of a commercial hinterland.

Economic and social structure also made this colony unique. Her economic chronology was also different and, like New Zealand, she slumped in the 1880s. In a decade when most other colonies were soaked by showers of English capital, South Australia suffered from drought and from a scarcity of new natural resources; and for a time she had reached the limits of growth. This helps to explain her bold political phase which began about 1884 and continued for just over a decade. The first place in the world to apply Henry George's taxation reforms and the first in Australia to place an income tax on income from personal exertion, South Australia was also the first to open children's courts and the first to attempt the compulsory arbitration of industrial disputes. She was an early crusader against excessive alcohol, and in 1894 she led Australia and almost every part of the world in granting the vote to women.

3

The early movement of democratic reform in Australia had largely ignored women. The privileges of the 1850s were not for them. They did not vote or sit on juries. They rarely wrote to or for the main newspapers and magazines. They had no hand in the learned professions. Speakers looking down from the platform at a public meeting did not often see a woman's hat in the rows of bare heads. Women were paid less than men even when they did exactly the same work; and the costly task of providing a school place for every child in the main colonies in the 1870s, when education became compulsory, was therefore financed in part by the lower salaries of women teachers.

The names of plants illustrated the prejudice against women. An inferior Australian beech was called the she-beech and the timber cutters called an inferior native pine the she-pine. The *casuarina* tree was called the she-oak, for its grain was like English oak but its timber was deemed inferior. There was a time when the beer brewed in the colonies was mockingly called she-oak to indicate its inferiority to English beer which presumably came in oak kegs. Once colonial beer became respectable it was usually given masculine names: it was often called shearer's joy, and in Sydney the tallest glass of beer was known as a Bishop Barker, after the tall Anglican bishop, a man of 6′ 5½″, who arrived in 1855.

In some issues and areas women had the privileges. Many laws were more lenient to women than to men, and a man convicted of civil and criminal offences was more likely than a woman to be sentenced to prison. Many colonial hardships, for instance life in the far outback, were experienced by relatively few women. The divorce laws, viewed from some angles, were extremely unjust on women but these laws were of minute relevance because in Australia in the 1870s only one divorce or judicial separation was granted each fortnight, and even by the

1890s they averaged only one a day. A few laws which were preposterously unjust to women were modified in practice. Under the English law still ruling in Australia a married woman's grip on her own property and income was precarious, but according to a well-informed Melbourne merchant in the 1860s 'hardly a marriage takes place without a summons to the lawyer – from all at least who can afford the cost': the lawyer then drew up a document which circumvented the law. Soon the marriage lawyer was redundant. Between the 1860s and the early 1890s each colony passed its own Married Women's Property Acts which gave women virtually the same property rights as men. As the British mode of government depended on the principle that ownership of property conferred political right, and as many married women now owned property and paid rates and taxes, it seemed that their full political rights would soon be conceded. But there was a now-forgotten obstacle to the slogan of 'no taxation without representation'. Some men were deliberately excluded from the vote not because they were insignificant but because they were significant. New South Wales in its electoral law of 1858 precluded all members of the army, navy and police force from voting and even from attempting to persuade an elector on how he should vote. In some colonies a clergyman could not stand for parliament. In such a climate it was possible for politicians to agree upon the importance of women and still withhold from them the vote. Their place, it was said, was in the home; and rarely had the home been so venerated as in the reign of Queen Victoria.

The educational reforms of the 1870s also suggested that women would soon receive the vote. When education was made compulsory for most Australian children, girls and boys were treated equally. Likewise universities in New Zealand and Australia were opened to women students once a few girls' schools and parents applied pressure. A woman graduated at Auckland in 1877, two women graduated at Christchurch in 1880 and one at Melbourne in 1883, while in 1885 the first women graduated at the universities of Sydney and Adelaide and Otago in Dunedin. A democracy which called itself enlightened could hardly continue to give the vote to illiterate nomadic men who had no stake in the society and had lived here only a year but refuse the same vote to intelligent, educated women, some of whom were born in Australia, had a stake in the country, paid taxes and followed the controversies of the day.

Already many women were voting in municipal elections in various parts of Australia. A Victorian loophole allowed four women to vote at an election for the Richmond council in May 1855, and other women voted at later elections, and in 1863 parliament confirmed the right of female property holders to vote though not to stand at municipal elections. South Australian women in the 1860s won the same right. If certain women could vote in municipal elections it was hardly logical to exclude them from the polling booth at parliamentary elections. The logic was strong, but few women and even fewer men called for the logic to be expressed in a new law.

South Australia led the campaign for votes for women. Why it should have been so far ahead of most other parts of the world – and a generation ahead of Britain – is not fully clear; but its strong nonconformist churches probably sensed that women's votes would strengthen moral crusades and moreover its whole history as a colony had been more sympathetic to family life and the role of women as a civilizing force. That it entered about 1884 a phase of political reforming – when other colonies were more sedate – made women's franchise more attainable. In 1886 Edward Stirling, a young surgeon, first persuaded many members of the lower house that propertied women should vote. The upper house in South Australia, always more democratic than in other colonies, eventually was the stronghold of the women's cause. The campaign became strong in 1893, especially after New Zealand had granted women the right to vote though not to sit in parliament; and in December 1894 South Australia went even further and granted women the right to sit in parliament as well as the vote. They first voted at a general election on 25 April 1896 and were expected by many to be conservative in tendency but the result suggested they were not.

4

It was easy for a woman to enter a polling booth and exercise her new privilege. It was not so easy to stand for parliament or any legislative body. A wall of traditions had limited the opportunities for women to become prominent in public life. When secondary schools and universities were first opened to women they attracted women, but the opening of the first parliaments to women was a token victory. One reason why no women entered parliament is obvious: formal education took place in the years when women were still single whereas a seat in parliament was open only to women of an age when most, being married, lacked the liberty, time or ambition to stand. Above all, the profession of politics required a public apprenticeship, from which women for too long had been excluded.

Catherine Helen Spence was the first female political candidate in Australia and perhaps in the British Empire. The daughter of an unsuccessful Scottish banker, she had sailed as a teenager in 1839 for Adelaide, where she spent the remainder of her life. Twice marriage was proposed to her but she said firmly, 'no'. One reason for her firmness was her Calvinistic fear that children whom she brought into the world might have no hope of eternal salvation. By the time she was 30 her religious gloom had evaporated but her prospects of marriage and perhaps her desire for marriage had also evaporated: 'People married young if they married at all in those days.' The single aunts donned their old-maid caps at the age of 30 as a 'sort of signal that they accepted their fate'. Miss Spence did not wear a cap but accepted her fate. Moreover she had work to do, a talent to use. In 1854 a London firm published her two-volume novel set in the half-deserted South Australia of the gold-rushes. She understood that she was the first woman to write a novel with an Australian setting but at first she earned no public praise, for a woman writer was usually anonymous.

284

The Veiled Maid of Adelaide

A nameless inhabitant of a man's world, Catherine Spence thought women should serve in public life. Women could not only express the needs of women and children on legislative issues but also possessed an intelligence and morality which no society could afford to neglect. In her quiet ambition Miss Spence was aided by unusual advantages: a critical mind, a clear style of writing, wide intellectual interests, and a small private income. In Adelaide her family possessed a network of useful though not powerful connections, so that she was able to enter the male occupation of occasional journalism without leaving her home. Nonetheless the obstacles which prevented her from entering public life were still high.

It was difficult for women even to acquire experience in that quintessential of public life, the making of speeches. When Miss Spence returned to Adelaide in 1866 from an overseas tour she was invited to give a public lecture on her impressions of England, but the idea that she herself should deliver the lecture occurred neither to her nor to the organizers of the lecture. Intellectual women were to be heard, not seen, and she did not attend the meeting at which her friend, a newspaper editor, read her script. Five years later, when she was in her mid-forties, she decided that she should personally read the lectures which she had been invited to write on the poets Elizabeth and Robert Browning. Her motive for delivering her own lecture, she said, was to ease the way so that any woman who had something to say could henceforth stand up and say it.

On the chosen day she was nervous. She had received no tuition in elocution and no lessons in that gesturing which was then an important accompaniment of platform speaking. ('I never speak in public with gloves on', she wrote later. 'They interfere with the natural eloquence of the hand.') She could not call on women for advice, for she knew no woman in Adelaide who had spoken formally to a large mixed audience. We forget, moreover, that before the microphone was invented, the ability to project the voice to the corners of a large hall was a vital skill. She could not feel sure that her natural voice was strong enough to reach the

back seats of the hall. Fortunately the young barrister
Samuel Way offered to sit in the back row and raise his hand
if her voice became indistinct. The lecture began. Miss
Spence felt nervous, very nervous. Her knees seemed about
to buckle as she stood. A spinster of steel, she gave no
outward sign of her apprehension. What the women in the
audience thought of her performance and of the fact that
she was performing a man's role, she herself did not reveal.
Many women were amongst the staunchest enemies of
women's liberation.

Originally a Presbyterian, Miss Spence became an
Unitarian. That most intellectual of all the sects in Australia
was not averse to women preaching. In Melbourne, Miss
Martha Turner was elected by the wealthy Unitarian
congregation as one of their pastors in 1873, and for about
seven years she conducted most of the duties of the
ministry, performing marriages, composing and publishing sermons, and preaching from time to time in a clear
blue-stocking style from a raised desk in the church. Twice
Martha Turner visited Adelaide to conduct a series of
Sunday services in the Unitarian church in Wakefield
Street. There in the congregation sat Miss Spence, all ears
and eyes, for she had not heard a woman preach in that city
of churches. 'I was thrilled', wrote Miss Spence, 'by her
exquisite voice, by her earnestness, and by her reverence.'
She was pleased to hear Martha Turner read the lessons
from the scriptures with such intelligence and sensitivity
that she seemed to uncover a new layer of meaning in
several of the passages. Suddenly Miss Spence thought how
much the world had lost, through so many centuries, by its
refusal to allow women to preach. She resolved, if the
chance arose, to become an occasional preacher. At first she
was merely invited to read a printed sermon but later she
wrote her own. In the following thirty years she preached –
in Adelaide and other Australian and North American
cities – more than a hundred sermons. She liked the drama
and theatre of the pulpit and public meeting, and her
delight is visible in her autobiography.

Most Australians as late as 1890 had not heard a woman

preach in church or even speak from a political platform; 'Women as platform speakers were unheard of', wrote Miss Spence. Even the idea of women writing political letters to the newspapers was seen as uncomely by many editors; and Catherine Spence decided that the safest way to forward her belief in proportional representation was to write under a man's name. For thirty years she wrote political letters under the name of her brother. Her first two novels were anonymous, and her controversial book of 1884, *An Agnostic's Progress from the Known to the Unknown*, was also anonymous. Here was one of Australia's most thoughtful citizens, conscious that on the serious issues of the day she would remain powerless unless she disguised herself.

In 1897 an election was held to select ten delegates to represent South Australia at the convention which would frame the new federal constitution, and Catherine Spence came forward as a candidate. She argued that the federal constitution should be so arranged that minorities and independent members could flourish alongside the large disciplined political parties: hence her plea for proportional representation. Now in her early seventies, white haired and plump, this effervescent woman spoke often in public in her slowly fading Scottish accent. Her supporters wondered whether she could overcome all those impediments, specific and subtle, which society had placed in the way of female candidates. Could she overcome the insistent statements, made by her opponents, that even if elected a woman would not be eligible to sit in the federal convention? Polling day came, an important day in the history of the emancipation of women. Miss Spence polled 7500 votes, an impressive tally for a woman and especially a woman preaching an unfamiliar cause, but she was not amongst the ten leading candidates.

Ironically, a woman then sat on the English throne. In her last years Queen Victoria was extolled as the greatest of the sovereigns, and the extolling was boundless in 1897, which was the year of her diamond jubilee and also of Miss Spence's candidature. 'Those who object to women entering Parliament', wrote Miss Vida Goldstein, 'should logically object to a woman occupying the exalted office of Sovereign.' Miss Goldstein found that such logic was not sufficient. She stood in Victoria for a senate seat in 1903, one of three women to stand for seats in the Commonwealth parliament at the first national election in the world in which all women were free to stand or vote. She did not win but she received more than 50,000 votes – just over half of the votes polled by the man who headed the poll. The day of the female politician seemed about to dawn.

The resistance to the idea of women sitting in parliament remained as emphatic amongst women as men. 'Even angels are pictured to look like women', wrote May Vivienne in her book *Sunny South Australia*. She concluded with skatty logic that women should 'keep their proper sphere'. While she was happy if women excelled in literature, the arts, science and economics, she explained that the posts of mayor and cabinet minister *rightly* belonged to men, though by what right she did not specify. She was delighted to hear the retort of a woman who, in conversation with a politician, was asked which party she favoured. 'The wedding party,' she said promptly. And the wedding party won every election until 1921 when Mrs Edith Cowan, in her sixtieth year, won a seat in the Western Australian lower house. But Australia was far ahead of Britain where all women did not even have the right to vote until 1928.

Much of the opposition to women participating in politics was simply a belief that marriage and the family were more important than public meetings and parliament; but the opposition went to absurd lengths when it insisted that not even one woman – not even the most talented individual in the nation – should vote or sit in parliament.

18   Pistons of Prosperity

In the forty years since the discovery of gold the economic progress – progress was an incantation more than a word – had been swift. The population was now three million, having been muliplied by seven. Parliaments, juries, and free institutions had taken root in a land which back in 1850 still received British convicts and still bowed, on most major issues, to decisions made in London. The new machinery and the gadgetry of ease could be seen everywhere – in the railways that stretched far inland, the tall blocks of offices in larger cities, the ships and cranes at the wharves, the gasworks and refrigeration chambers, and the hydraulic power which propelled the passenger lifts to the upper floors of the new hotels. The standard of living had so improved that a housewife in the larger cities, with such household amenities as gas and running water and a sewing machine, probably had more comfort than the typical housewife in almost every city in the world. The thousands of schools and churches, the high circulation of daily and weekly papers, the abundance of leisure in the towns, the relative sense of social security, the ease of travel in steamships and trains, the larger, more weatherproof houses – these were all advances which, added together, were to dwarf the slow material gains of the following half century.

2

An unusual blend of circumstances had created this age of prosperity. Perhaps the strongest piston of prosperity was the abundance of new natural resources. Australia's pace of development owed much to the wide grasslands, the virgin soil ready to grow cereals, the untapped deposits of gold and copper, coal and tin and silver-lead, and to the forests which yielded building materials and firewood. Here was a bonanza, and most of its choicest parts were used for the first time between 1840 and 1890. These natural resources had been little used in the Aboriginal epoch but in the half century to 1890, they were exploited, often with energy and ingenuity. Rarely in history had people explored, occupied and used such a vast terrain so quickly.

The strenuous application of new techniques was possibly the second piston of the long era of prosperity. Much of the prosperity came from fatter cattle and heavier fleeces and more appropriate breeds of wheat. It came from hundreds of labour-saving devices, from the post-and-rail fences which replaced the shepherds, from the wire fences which replaced post-and-rail fences, from the corrugated iron spouting and water tanks, from the artesian bores and the creaking windmills which supplied underground water on the plains, and the new irrigation schemes of the 1880s. Fewer hands produced more wheat because of the devising of new ploughs, strippers, mechanical harvesters and the travelling steam threshing-machines. At harvest time, in the kitchens of the larger farms, the dining table seated perhaps only ten men where once there were thirty, and those ten men with the aid of horsepower and steampower did more work each day than the vanished team of thirty.

An old miner who visited a large gold-mine in 1890 would hardly have recognized the mode of work. Thirty years ago he had climbed down ladders to reach his working place but now he was whisked down the shaft in a fast safety cage which travelled more rapidly than a lift in the latest city building. Powerful pumps unwatered the workings; dynamite and other powerful explosives had superseded the old blasting powder; and in the latest mines the mechanical rockdrills were beginning to replace the hand-hammers in the drilling of holes. That the new rockdrill was filling the still underground air with particles of sharp dust and ruining the lungs of many miners was not yet recognized.

Almost everywhere steam was doing work which was once performed by the sheer physical strength of teams of workers. Visitors to the mills and factories saw the steam or smoke from a distance, heard the throb of the pistons and crushers and mills, and once inside they saw a criss-cross of overhead belting which conveyed the energy from the working engine to the scattered machines. Those who did not visit factories knew, from the advertisements in newspapers and the painted signs on delivery carts, that this foodstuff or that commodity was now miraculously made by labour-saving machines driven by steam. Eat our steam biscuits. Take your suit to our steam laundry. Most steam was produced by firewood in the interior or coal on the coast, and nearly a thousand ships a year by the 1880s carried the coal away from Newcastle. There on the crowded wharves the handling of the coal was increasingly mechanized, as readers of *A New Geography for Australian Pupils* learned in 1885: 'The noise is stunning, for yonder come trucks of coal running down to the edge of the water. Great cranes seize them, whirl them into the air, swing them over the hold of the vessel, turn them upside down, and so empty coal into the ships below.'

Transport had been transformed since 1850. In that year many travellers had to walk long distances, the roads were poor, and strong horses were few. Even the horse-drawn mail coach did not make long journeys. The strength of the wind was far more important than the steam engines in propelling ships and not one mile of railway was open. By 1890 the fast steamship dominated the passenger routes to Europe, and the long and often-stormy voyage past Cape Horn had given way to the calmer passage across the Indian Ocean to the Suez Canal and the Mediterranean. The international telegraph had replaced the mail steamer as the fastest way of sending important news, and the mail steamer itself was twice as rapid as the fast sailing ships of 1850 in crossing the world. Within the larger cities the trams, trains and cabs provided cheap and regular

291

transport in streets where, in the late 1840s, nearly everybody walked and only the wealthy could call on riding horses or a horse and carriage. And in capital cities the first telephones were installed in the decade 1878 to 1887 though calls outside the city were still impossible. Mechanized transport now saved human labour on a huge scale.

In a continent possessing few navigable rivers and no inland canals, the railway was the great miracle. It filled old pioneers with wonder. Whenever a new railway was opened, old settlers were there, sitting stiff-backed on the platform amongst the top hats, and reminiscing how they had been amongst the first white men to ride through country where the black locomotive now rushed. When the railway between Melbourne and Sydney was completed in 1883, and a banquet of food and speeches was set out in the locomotive shed at Albury, the new Edison electric light shone on an old man who had crossed the silent Murray in 1824 with the explorers Hume and Hovell. Stand up old man and tell them how you rode your horse through these ranges nearly sixty years before the iron horse arrived. Others are eager to reminisce beneath the blaze of electricity. The New South Wales premier Alexander Stuart recalls how thirty-one years ago that very month – yes, that very month – he had ridden horses day and night in order to complete the overland journey from Sydney to Melbourne in six and a half days. To return, he recalled, was harder. The coastal steamship had already left Melbourne, so he sailed home in a clipper ship, was becalmed day after day, and reached Sydney after sixteen days at sea. His audience laughed, because now the iron horse made the journey in twenty-four hours.

The sense of wonder at the railway comes down clearly over the years. But the wonder was not simply at its speed and its predictability. The railway so cheapened the cost of transport that it created industries where previously there were none. It gave birth to distant wheatlands and new dairying districts, and opened forests to the timber-miller. The railway enabled low-grade or remote mining fields to treat ores which, without a railway, were unpayable. It saved pastoral districts in time of drought and sent their wool quickly to market. Between 1875 and 1891 the railways grew from 1600 miles to more than 10,000.

There were also gains from using ancient modes of transport more effectively. Draught horses of improved breeds replaced bullocks on most farms and farmers used large teams to pull the plough, thus reducing the labour costs for each acre. In the dry outback the camel was introduced at first by explorers and then by carriers. Sir Thomas Elder, a rich pastoralist, imported 124 camels and 31 'Afghan' camel men in 1865 from the port of Karachi in the present Pakistan, and the pack camels increasingly became carriers of wool, station supplies, mining equipment, and food and alcohol in the dry outback. At one time half of the continent and its sparse, struggling population relied on pack camels.

In 1850 the central streets of only one city, Sydney, were illuminated by gas lamps, but by 1890 most towns of a few thousand people were lit by gas. In smaller towns the household lamps burning kerosene – a word coined in 1854 – supplanted the old tallow candles in the sitting room. A whole range of night meetings and activities had become more convenient, night work had become safer, and in most houses people could read or sew at night without undue strain to their eyes: gaslight and kerosene lamps were thus the allies of compulsory education. By the early 1880s the electric light was the latest fashion, and audiences at the Opera House in Melbourne marvelled at the electricity, less because of the way it illuminated the stage than because it was cooler than gas and caused fewer headaches. The reading rooms at city libraries changed to the incandescent electric lamp, and librarians claimed the rooms were cooler in summer and that electric light – unlike the fumes from the gas lamps – did not weaken the bindings of books. Tamworth in 1888 was probably the first town to be lit by electricity but the era of electric power still lay ahead.

We had our own inventors, mostly men of little schooling who fastened their mind on new problems and would not

293

let go. In the farmlands, hundreds of part-time inventors devised new or improved old machines. South Australians between the 1840s and 1870s invented a range of simple and effective machines which prepared and tilled and harvested the wheatlands with more speed and less labour. They invented the stripper which, drawn by horses through the tall wheat crop, combed the wheat from the stalk and partly threshed it. They invented the Mallee roller which rolled over the Mallee scrub and so saved much of the slow work of using the axe or the grubber. They invented the stump-jump plough which neatly jumped over buried roots still left in the roughly cleared ground. They devised and manufactured, at small foundries and the wayside shops of implement-makers, the ploughs and the drills which were more suited to hard dry soils than the damp soft soils which their European ancestors had farmed. Victorians in the 1880s led in developing the combined harvester. In the slow evolution of this machine which now harvests much of the world's wheat, Australians contributed the most.

Even in those problems which European inventors where facing, Australians working patiently in isolation still had hopes that they would transform the way the world did its work. In Geelong the newspaper editor, James Harrison, was a brilliant pioneer of mechanical refrigeration but was almost too far ahead of his time. His important cargo of hard-frozen meat was shipped to London in 1873 in the sailing ship *Norfolk*, which possessed no refrigerating plant and so could not adequately preserve the meat. In the 1870s a young Melbourne watchmaker, Louis Brennan, invented a retrievable torpedo which he eventually sold to the War Office in London for the huge sum of £110,000. In Sydney in 1893 Lawrence Hargrave, son of a Sydney judge, made a vital step in aeronautical engineering when he invented the box-kite, thus advancing knowledge of the vital question of how a flying machine could be made stable while in flight. And a decade later the young Melbourne engineer, A. G. M. Michell, was working on his revolutionary device, the thrust bearing, without which the huge ocean liners and oil-tankers would be impracticable.

3

A willingness to use and experiment with machinery was thus one of the causes of the high standard of living. A large volume of commodities produced by few hands: that was the secret of colonial Australia's prosperity. In turn the willingness to import machines or even invent machines was spurred by the frequent shortage of labour and the abundance of capital. British capital financed much of the mechanization, including the railways. By 1890 at least nine of every ten miles of Australia's railways had been financed by long-term loans raised in London at 3, 4 or 5%. If Australia's small population alone had had to finance the building of the railways, dams and walls, harbours, roads, fences and many other private and public amenities, the standard of living in 1890 could not have been so high. Part of our prosperity rested on hire-purchase: the final purchasing and the strain of paying came later.

Other factors promoted the prosperity of Australians. The years 1850 to 1890 were unusually peaceful; Britain fought in only one major war, the Crimean War of 1853 to 1856, and the war was short and victorious. All the dislocations of a major war were thus avoided. Moreover in this long period most of the expense of defending Australian ports and sea lanes was still paid by the British taxpayer: ironically Britain collected an income tax but no Australian colony tried to collect an income tax from its citizens until the 1880s.

Economic life experienced boom after boom, and after each boom the slump was short. Tasmania was the main exception, and was relatively stagnant from the 1850s until the early 1870s. The absence of major economic slumps is one of the unusual facets of the period, and part of the explanation is simply luck. The banks possessed, if a crisis should arise, no central bank and no emergency legislation to help them through the troubles; and yet somehow until the 1890s the network of banks was spared the panics of depositors and those financial nightmares which were felt in England, France, Germany, Austria and the United States in almost every decade. The willingness of the colonial governments to spend money on public works in lean years and the willingness of British investors to lend that money at low interest also helped to give economic life an unusual level of stability. Above all, gold was a wonderful insurance in economic life. Whenever the economy began to slump, the search for gold and the mining of gold were intensified. The price of gold was fixed internationally at £3.17s an ounce and so gold was attractive when the price of wool, copper, wheat, or other exports declined. Gold was ballast in the storm: it provided stabilizers for the ship.

One spur to the high prosperity was not appreciated at the time. From the late 1840s to 1890, the main rural districts experienced favourable weather, measured against the following half century. We are only now beginning to realize how favourable was the climate in the south-eastern corner of Australia for those grazing and cropping industries which were so important then to economic life.

Some of these advantages promoting material progress were squandered. Some were counterbalanced by adverse factors in the period 1850 to 1890. There was a zest for taking risks which leaped beyond the bounds of common sense. Thousands of useless mining shafts were sunk on the basis of airy hypotheses and blind rather than reasoned speculations. Again and again expensive crushing mills and steam engines were installed at mines which possessed no ore to crush. Thousands of new farms were large enough for England but too small for Australia and much of the work on those farms was wasted. The deficiency of phosphates in our soils, and the speed with which wheat crops exhausted that phosphate, led to the abandoning of thousands of farm houses. In good years in the far outback, pastoralists were tempted into country so poor that in the end they had to retreat. In vast expanses of poor land too many sheep and cattle grazed, and the pastures and the scrub deteriorated. Railways were built to districts which did not have enough traffic – and never would have enough – to pay for the railway. Breakwaters and stone harbour works and long piers were built for ports which then faded away. Permanent towns were built on gold-fields and then the gold ran out, leaving fine churches, schools, banking chambers, shops and even town halls to serve only a fraction of the people for whom they were built. Noxious weeds and pests were introduced and flourished, wiping out part of the hard-won gains of pioneers. All such miscalculations formed debits which partly offset the credits from the abundance of new natural resources and new techniques. Risks were inevitable in the process of opening new natural resources but many of the risks taken were extravagantly risky. In the cities the mistakes were also made, perhaps even on a larger scale, but a normal city can cover up its 'ghost towns' and abandoned ventures. In Melbourne, however, the ghost suburbs were too widespread to be concealed when the gargantuan building boom of the 1880s came to a halt.

The standard of material life would have grown even more quickly but for a changing rhythm of work in many jobs. The hours of work in city jobs and in mines and in railway camps were tending to decline. Many people had reached the stage where they preferred more leisure to more money. The warm summer climate placed a premium on leisure. So too did the high proportion of single men who, having no family to care for, could live comfortably on their wages so long as they remained in work. The preference for leisure often raised the enjoyment of life and here the spectator sports had a popularity which was virtually unparalleled. A crowd of 100,000 is said to have seen the running of the Melbourne Cup in 1888, and 84 special trains carried spectators to the racecourse. Two years later a crowd of 32,600 saw a football match at the Melbourne Cricket Ground: no larger football crowd had yet assembled in a European city. Inevitably the attitude to leisure permeated the attitude to work. This is a fact to be observed rather than deplored, for there was no reason why people should continue to work their heart out simply because, in the British Isles, that had been the only way in which an honest man could feed and clothe his family.

In the 1880s, perhaps more than ever before, there were two distinct styles of work. One group of people worked

297

shorter hours and many of them worked in a more leisurely way during those hours. Another group was working as hard as their parents had worked. The declining tempo of work was most visible in the cities though not yet in a majority of paid occupations there. The grinding, exhausting labour belonged more to rural occupations, to people who were still their own bosses, and to housewives. A strong farm labourer who thus moved to a town soon found he had more leisure than he had known.

Observers in the cities detected a waning pressure of work. Sir Richard Tangye, owner of a large engineering works in Birmingham, made his fourth visit to Australia in 1886; and in his observant but over-emphatic diary he expressed unease at the casual approach to work in what he called 'the land for my lord the workingman'. He claimed that in the city the workman did a small amount of work each day. The word that fell from his frothing lips was 'scandalous'. It was a time of mild economic slump in Sydney and he was vexed to hear the unemployed, in calling on the government for work, demanding the standard wage of 8 shillings a day. He said that they should be willing to work for less. When the government arranged for a free train to convey the unemployed to the country to grub out tree stumps, more than half of the train was empty. Where, he enquired, were the remainder of 'these scoundrels'? Tangye thought that he knew where they could be found: 'lying on the grass in the public parks, and smoking short pipes'. He noted in his diary that the unemployed here prefer to pick and choose rather than to pick and shovel. In contrast, he heard with pleasure of an 18-year-old Essex migrant who was rising each morning at five o'clock to groom four horses, driving a cart to market to collect greengroceries, eating no breakfast until he returned to his master's shop, and finishing his day at eight in the evening.

Visitors who saw the working habits of many Australians were peeping into the future and not liking it. Admittedly, Tangye had the bias of an old man and a factory-owner. He was also more likely to see idleness when he was overseas than in England where workmen, knowing who he was,

Carting hay in the 1880s when chaff and hay were the petrol of the day for large parts of rural Australia.

A tiny farm in the forest, with shingle-roofed hut and bush fences of the mid-1870s.   *University of Melbourne Archives*

Unemployment in a land of plenty:
unemployed maritime workers in Adelaide, c. 1890

S.A. Archives

fruit barrows in Swanston Street, Melbourne, c. 1902.

worked busily in his presence and then perhaps slowed down after he had been escorted from the factory floor. And yet he could not be dismissed as an unsympathetic observer of working men. After all, he had been one of the first owners in Birmingham to give his employees a holiday on Saturday afternoons.

4

The forty years had been blessed by an unusual assortment of advantages. We had virgin soil, rich mineral deposits and many untouched natural resources to reward the first comers. We did not have to depend on one dominating export, and so we did not stumble if the price of that export fell. We were quick to adopt or adapt the new ideas of a great era of invention in the North Atlantic. We were at peace with the outside world, and in the more populous parts of the country the weather was relatively favourable. Throughout the forty years the world's richest money-lender, Great Britain, sent out capital, enabling us to enjoy a high standard of living at the very time when we were spending heavily on railways and reservoirs, on opening up the land, the building of towns and a variety of debt-incurring works.

Through hard striving by people in every section of society and through an unusual combination of conditions the country had achieved much. But now the striving in boardrooms and in offices as well as on workfloors was easing a little, at the very time when the other advantages were falling away. And the pride in the forty years of achievement was itself an increasing hazard, because serious setbacks were virtually unimaginable and therefore would be more damaging when eventually they came.

19 The Rabbits are Coming

They set out to change and to manage the landscape, and almost everywhere could be seen signs of their success. In their zeal to import grasses, flowers and vegetables, fruit trees and shade trees and hedges, they also imported weeds. Some weeds came as stowaways and some as assisted immigrants. They came in the hair and tails of imported animals. They came in packing materials, they came accidentally in the packages of seeds, and they came in the ballast which sailing ships brought out in their bottom and unloaded on waste lands near ports. Many were deliberately imported and sown and tended with care: there was no thought that they might someday be called weeds.

2

A weed was more likely to arrive if it flourished near a port on a route to Australia. Cape Town was a frequent port of call for early ships, and moreover its climate was not unlike that of Perth and Melbourne. From South Africa came the boxthorn, originally favoured as a hedge because its sharp thorns would keep cattle and sheep from straying. From South Africa came the boneseed plant and onion grass; only a few tiny bulbs at first, the onion grass then multiplied by the million and took over pastures and garden plots. By design rather than accident the yellow-flowering capeweed was introduced to Victoria as fodder, and it covered the paddocks with gold in spring and died away in mid-summer, leaving paddocks bare. As its name suggests, it came from the Cape of Good Hope or Cape Town and was originally given the courtesy of a capital C. Later the courtesy was withdrawn.

Poisonous weeds arrived and a few spread like an infection. The Cape Tulips – naturally from South Africa – were carried to Perth and Adelaide and planted in home gardens where their orange and rose flowers could give pleasure. With their large bulbs they spread to the pastures where they ceased to give pleasure: they poisoned the livestock. Similarly in the 1870s a German woman living in the gold-fields of north-east Victoria planted innocuous German seeds in her garden. The seeds flourished: everyone admired her display of St John's Wort. The plant spread to the Bright racecourse and flourished. It took to the hills and half a century later covered hundreds of square miles in Victoria and patches of ground in four other states, its poison endangering cattle which brushed past, and its deep roots defying cheap methods of eradication.

Many alien weeds lived quietly, each in its small corner. One species of the *Oxalis bifurca* is believed to inhabit only the Campbelltown cemetery in New South Wales, where it has lived quietly since the 1850s. Another oxalis occupies an area equivalent to a large paddock near Grenfell and is not known to flourish elsewhere in New South Wales. But any weed with a pretty flower was petted and favoured, transplanted and watered, and so given opportunities to find the soil and climate and botanical niche where it might eventually run wild. The Mediterranean herb known in England as viper's bugloss had bell-shaped flowers of vivid purple. Finding its way to a few Australian flower gardens, it became a runaway weed in many parts of the temperate zone from Holbrook in New South Wales to the Great Southern Railway in Western Australia. In mid-spring it spread itself like a rich purple mat, a glorious sight on the grasslands. In Victoria and New South Wales it came to be known as Paterson's curse – the accursed Paterson is said to have been a home gardener in Albury – and in South Australia it was called Salvation Jane and in Western

301

Australia it was the Lady Campbell weed. It destroyed nutritious pastures and could not be rooted out.

As ships called at South Africa on their way here and at South American ports on the way to England, the South American plants were less likely to arrive here accidentally. But there was some direct trade with the Americas. The Bathurst burr is said to have come from Chile in the 1840s, its seed clinging to the tail of imported horses. It soon ran wild, especially on the grasslands around Bathurst, and by the 1850s was a pest. By the 1860s the Noogoora burr of North America was also common; the sharp spines of these burrs stuck to the wool and lowered its value. No more costly horses have ever entered Sydney than that Chilean consignment.

Plants from tropical America seemed to be even slower to take root in Australia, partly because our sub-tropical and tropical regions were settled late. The decorative plants were the most troublesome once they had arrived. The lantana was tended carefully in gardens all the way from Sydney to the furthest tropical ports but eventually it escaped and strangled vast areas of countryside, its berries attracting birds which spread and fertilized the seeds. The water hyacinth and its shiny leaves and mauve flower attracted gardeners. It was soon floating on the warm rivers and in January 1911 the Clarence River at Grafton – one of the few important navigable rivers in Australia – was closed to steamships by the pontoon of hyacinths.

Already the prickly pear was a pest further to the north. It had reached Australia from the Gulf of Mexico, probably by a roundabout route. One bush is known to have grown from a pot plant near Scone in New South Wales as far back as 1839. Its tough prickles made it a promising hedge in the days when, the cattle and sheep being so plentiful, the 'living fence' or hedge was eagerly cultivated. Cuttings were taken by other landholders, and the hedges of prickly pear became mildly fashionable. The plant was carried north into Queensland. By the mid-1880s the prickly pear, in many areas, formed a straggly fortification about five feet high and extending for miles. The patches of prickly pear were to spread all the way from the Hunter Valley, its first Australian home, to Mackay in north Queensland, swallowing up land probably equalling the entire area of Victoria or the present West Germany.* In 1925 the prickly pear occupied more land than all the cultivated crops and orchards in Australia.

As late as 1890 few botanists could predict the vigour with which weeds would establish their salients in Australia. Many of the weeds, ranging from blackberries in the south to prickly pear in the north, were seen as pleasing curiosities, as forget-me-nots for the homesick. The country seemed to have more than enough land for every use, and moreover many of the weeds were more successful on the poorer grasslands, the steep hills, and the bush. In contrast, when a weed took root in rich farmland the farmer and wife and children attacked it with sheer grit and sweat, and usually controlled it with their own hoes and scythes and bare hands. But the time would come when weeds would occupy far more land, and when rural profits were so deteriorated that the loss of that valuable land was serious, and when widespread drought would provide fallow ground which helped new weeds to establish themselves.

For certain insects and lice, and for animal diseases, the long journey to Australia offered some quarantine in the era of the slow, wallowing sailing ship. Certain insects evaded the quarantine. The vineyards of Victoria had become almost as extensive as those of the other colonies combined when in 1887 the phylloxera insect was detected in a vineyard near Geelong. Thereafter, as in France, vineyard after vineyard had to be destroyed in the hope of eliminating the insect; and Victoria was quickly outstripped by South Australia in the production of wine.

In the tropics the cattle tick, first identified on cattle near Darwin in the early 1870s, had moved along the stock

---

*The prickly pear (*Optuntia inermmis*) was eventually conquered in the period 1925-33 by the introduction of an Argentinian tunnelling caterpillar, *Cactoblastis*. An Australian insect had already triumphed in California. There citrus orchards were endangered by white scale until, about 1890, they were saved by the Australian ladybird beetle.

routes into Queensland and would ultimately infect cattle which were more than 2000 miles away from Darwin. The tick fever killed as it made its slow journey. Some said that the tick had arrived from Java with cattle which fed the men who were building the overland telegraph, but it is possible that the tick had immigrated much earlier on cattle landed at Port Essington or other small tropical military settlements of the period 1824-47.

3

Even the sheep, whose coming to this country proved one of the most successful transplants in recorded history, were not completely successful. The Aboriginals were partly a victim of the sheep. There were other victims, because sheep disturbed the topsoil and the life of plants, animals and birds. Millions of hungry sheep, no matter how light their step, could not leave the land unscathed, though opinions differed on how and where they scathed the land.

John Robertson was one of the successes of squatting, for he had arrived as a migrant in Hobart in 1831 with 3 shillings in his pocket and twenty years later was rich enough to think of retiring to Scotland. He admitted to himself, however, that his land had deteriorated. When his first flock of a thousand ewes reached the Wannon district of western Victoria the tender grass was a rich green, for a bushfire had recently passed through, followed by rain. 'I could neither think nor sleep for admiring this new world,' wrote Robertson. Slowly his new world lost its sappy freshness. The original plants and grasses were replaced by shallow-rooted grasses, the ground began to crack, the sides of creeks eroded, and deep gulches were opened by heavy rain so that he had trouble riding his horse across his pastures.

In the Monaro, the high country to the south of Canberra, unexpected changes were also noticed. One blade of grass, reported one historian, eventually grew where once were two. The Polish explorer and natural scientist, Strzelecki, mistakenly vowed that the flocks and axes and tinder boxes, by destroying the forests and undergrowth, were actually making the climate hotter and dryer. Many disagreed that sheep and cattle were like locusts. Many believed the pastures had actually been improved in their district since the arrival of the sheep.

Who could tell with certainty what had happened to the land, and why it had happened, after twenty years of grazing by sheep and cattle? We often think of the Aboriginal lands as lying unchanged for thousands of years: the primeval eternal landscape. But the evidence is accumulating that the lands were not static. Climate was not static, Aboriginal man was busy making his living, the dingoes he had introduced were hunting. Fires were frequent, and plant diseases were probably not unknown.

In each district the first settlers often assumed that they had arrived in a normal year but some arrived in mild drought, some in a lush Indian summer, and some when the new shoots of grass were sprouting after a bushfire. Many of the first squatters were not observant about wildlife and grasses. Most who were observant penned no notes or left the district, carrying away their knowledge beneath their cabbage-tree hat. Even in those rare districts where detailed notes were made of the grasses, the herbaceous bushes, the wildflowers, nests of birds, the kangaroos and possums, the flow of the creeks and the level of the swamps, that description caught only the moment when the pioneers arrived. That picture did not tell whether certain species were already in decline, or even in the last phase of decline. Thus the white-footed tree-rat lived in the hollows of trees over a range of country from southern Queensland to Victoria and South Australia. Now extinct it was probably declining before the settlers arrived. Even if we could be certain that it was declining before the first flocks moved in, the causes of its initial and ultimate decline would still be a puzzle. Was the decline of these handsome rats hastened by the feeding of the sheep, the decline of certain native plants, the decline of Aboriginal-lit fires, the death of the Aboriginal hunters and vegetable-foragers, the coming of European hunters and dogs and cats, slow changes in climate, the importing of grasses or diseases, the work of ring-barkers and axemen, or a causal chain involving the interaction of several of these agents of decline? Sheep were not blameless in this wilderness of 'ifs' but they did not have an adverse effect on all species.

Perhaps the larger species of kangaroo owe a vote of thanks to the sheep. The kangaroo is sometimes said to be on the brink of extinction; and some of the warnings come from Americans who seem to possess field glasses capable of looking across the Pacific. In many large regions, however, kangaroos seem to be far more plentiful today than when the first sheep arrived. Explorers in the north west of New South Wales and central Queensland observed, before 1850, a scarcity of kangaroos in places where they are now a pest. In some regions the invasion of sheep led to the destruction of low bushes and shrubs and to the replacement of coarser and longer grasses by shorter grasses; and in the new vegetation the larger kangaroos flourished more than ever before. The new water dams were welcomed by kangaroos. They lived side by side with the sheep but ate different plants except in the very dry seasons.

The thinning out of the tussocky grasses and the low shrubs did imperil the smaller marsupials. Bandicoots, rodents and wallabies nested and foraged in the coarse grasses, and their native hearth was soon overturned to make woollen singlets for Europe. From vast regions some species of small marsupials simply vanished, and not one specimen has been captured or even sighted there in recent decades. Similarly birds which lived on the coarse grasses were disturbed and driven out by sheep. The squatter pigeon was decimated in the eucalyptus woodlands of the outback and the flock pigeons which at times flew in myriads on the Barkly Tableland suffered from changes in the pastures. In Tasmania certain of the larger creatures of the open country were hunted to extinction. The Tasmanian emu, which laid a dark-green egg that weighed as much as a dozen hens' eggs, was soon extinguished. The Tasmanian tiger – the striped, meat-eating marsupial – was hunted by the sheep-owners and was extinct probably by the 1930s.

Cages of English birds were imported. Hutches and deck-pens of foxes and deer and other animals were brought out in the hope that they would multiply for the delight of the homesick hunter. The 1860s was a busy decade for Acclimatization Societies which met in the cities and planned the introduction of all kinds of useful creatures. Through the work of these societies the house sparrow, the English starling, and the Indian myna arrived and soon they prospered. The mania for acclimatizing was in one sense a reflection that people themselves were still unacclimatized. They longed for reminders of home. Victoria had the most vigorous Acclimatization Society partly because it held the highest proportion of foreign-born adults in the 1850s and 1860s. Facing rural problems – plagues of grubs or caterpillars – they thought of the remedies of home, not realizing that one fine remedy often set up a new ill.

4

On Christmas night of 1859 the elegant Liverpool clipper ship *Lightning* reached Melbourne with passengers and a small consignment of livestock. It is doubtful whether any cargo loaded at any port in recorded history was to prove more fecund than the small animals which were carried ashore. The 24 wild rabbits – along with five hares and 72 partridges – had been shipped from Liverpool to the English-born squatter, Thomas Austin, and were promptly carried past Geelong to his estate of 45 square miles at Winchelsea, on the undulations of the western district. Austin was a sportsman and employed his own gamekeeper to care for the consignment. The partridges were placed in an aviary and later they were joined by English blackbirds and thrushes. At least thirteen of the rabbits were imprisoned inside a paling fence and they too began to multiply. Though the popularity of the phrase 'to breed like rabbits' belonged to the future, it really commemorated the activities of Austin's rabbits.

In earlier years many sportsmen had tried to acclimatize rabbits in Australia. Austin, however, put his mind and his land to the breeding and protecting of the rabbits. Soon so many rabbits ran about his sheep-run near Winchelsea that he invited friends to join him on shooting excursions. His hunts followed the English country tradition, and he employed men as beaters to frighten the rabbits and drive them within range of the hunters' guns: on some days the sound of gunshot must have been incessant. In the year 1866 he and his guests shot 448 hawks, 622 native cats, 32 tame cats and a total of 14,253 rabbits. Austin now lived in a huntsman's paradise of his own making. Two years later he enclosed part of his land with a type of fence that was unfamiliar to many who passed by: the fence was wire-netting and was to become eventually a symbol of the war against rabbits. But Austin's fence was not trying primarily to control the rabbits but to prevent the stray cats from attacking his Ceylon partridges.

Austin gave rabbits away to his friends; and strangers probably stole a few from his land. Thirty miles to the west the rabbits became plentiful. The mighty sheepman, William Robertson of Colac, realized in 1869 that the protected pets were now a plague and spent part of his fortune trying to eradicate them from his rich chocolate soil. He was too late. On his sheep lands the warrens formed an underground city which must have housed more rabbits than Australia held people. The rabbits were now established securely on the grasslands that seemed heaven-made for their support, and these grasslands ran without a break or barrier to South Australia and New South Wales and even to Queensland.

Years later, when the rabbits were a pest or plague in about half of the continent, the popular belief in Australia was that Austin was solely to blame for the terrible invasion. Austin had been a squatter, and so he was a suitable target. His elaborate shooting parties had been described in the newspapers almost shot by shot, and it was common knowledge that he had bred thousands of rabbits, so he was more conspicuous than other landholders who had quietly imported or bought rabbits in South Australia as well as Victoria. It was also the popular belief that the rabbits – by then respected as a foe of herculean strength and fertile mind – had spread of their own will all the way from Austin's land to new warrens as far as two thousand miles away. Recent investigations suggest that the rabbits possessed many human allies in their first years. They were at first welcomed as free meat, not feared as rivals to the sheep. Englishmen nostalgic for home applauded their appearance. Many land-owners and labourers carried the rabbits in hutches and baskets and boxes to their own homes and hoped that they would multiply. That they did multiply was aided by the succession of favourable seasons: droughts were infrequent during their period of rapid advance. The security of the early rabbits which hopped about in open country was possibly aided by the success with which land-owners had used strychnine to eliminate dingoes, native cats and eagles. Seen as enemies of newborn lambs, the dingoes and these other native creatures were also enemies of rabbits. The decline of dingoes, eagles and native cats probably assisted the encroachment of a species which, by eating the grass and ringbarking the young trees, was to become a more powerful enemy of sheep than the feared dingoes had been.

The plains of western Victoria were the zoological garden from which the main horde of rabbits moved north towards the Murray, but South Australia had sufficient rabbits in 1875 for parliament to enact a law designed to curb them. Even then the dangers of the plague were minimized. Rabbits were pets as well as pests. People in one district, hearing of the spread of rabbits a hundred miles away, dismissed stories of the multitude of rabbits as rural exaggerations, as boastings. Old men nostalgic for England hoped that rabbits would come to their district but come in eatable numbers not in devouring numbers. Farmers who were respected for their common sense pointed out optimistically that rabbits would not flourish in the hot, dry plains and would be easily evicted in the dry wheatbelt by the energetic small farmers. Naturally the rich pastoralists with their county-sized lands would be troubled in keeping down the rabbits but that was their responsiblity, the price they must pay for greedily taking more land than they could care for. So everyone fiddled while the rabbits spread. In 1874 the rabbits were already a pest in several large pockets of the western half of Victoria but the secretary for agriculture did not mention them in his annual report to the Victorian parliament. He warned of the dangers of caterpillars in crops, of the phylloxera in vineyards, of parasites in sheep, but on the deadliest of all the parasites he was silent.

The rabbits in favourable years now spread at lightning speed. One or two rabbits suddenly appeared as if making a reconnaissance, and yet the nearest known colony of rabbits might be fifty miles away. Along the Darling River in the early 1880s the unexpected arrival of the first few rabbits made some pastoralists wonder whether they had been dèliberately released at river bends by people travelling in the paddle-steamers. Occasionally their hunch was true: the river was a highway, and all kinds of people travelled it, sportsmen, swagmen, friends of squatters, and foes of squatters. Usually the rabbits simply moved at such speed that all kinds of human agencies were erroneously considered as the culprits.

'The rabbits are coming, the rabbits are coming.' That became a familiar warning in dozens of districts in the last third of the century. Many flock-owners who were warned of the coming horde made their own precautions. George Riddoch, a South Australian with sheep-runs in three colonies, lost so much money when the rabbits overran his land near Swan Hill that he took pains to defend another of his sheep-runs north of the Darling River about 1883. He knew the nearest rabbits were still a hundred miles away and so he had time to prepare his property at Weinterriga. He gave orders that men were to be employed on his boundary as patrollers. Their task was to watch for any trace of rabbits – any dung, fur, or scratchings in the ground. When the traces eventually were found he paid the men a bonus of 2 shillings 6d for each rabbit which they caught.

'The rabbits are coming, the rabbits are coming.' And now the rabbits came, a great grey tide. Riddoch's men were soon catching so many rabbits that if he had not reduced the bonus he would have gone bankrupt paying it. By the first month of 1887 he employed 125 rabbiters. More of his employees were now catching rabbits than were, presumably, carrying out all the station's other tasks put together. By the end of the year on that one property, his rabbiters had caught more than a million rabbits.

All the time the search went on for the remedy that would sweep the species from the land. In the hope of reducing the pest, they used iron traps, cats and ferrets, hunting dogs, guns, nets, fumigants, and all kinds of concoctions and devices. Bushmen soon had as many recipes for poisoning rabbits as housewives had for cooking them. A mixture of phosphorus and sugar and cold water was added to pollard and left on the ground as bait for the rabbits. Another tempting mixture contained phosphorus, flour, and wheat or oats. Many farmers mixed baits of chaff and arsenic, or quinces and strychnine, or arsenic and carrots. The doses were often large; the Victorian government's official recipes, as told by the high-titled 'chief inspector of vermin destruction', instructed small farmers to mix 60 pounds of the best grain with phosphorus. For rabbit poisons, only the best ingredients were appropriate. The potion 'jam and strychnine' called for eight pounds of manufactured jam and half an ounce of powdered strychnine. The mixture was to be spread on strips of bark and small pieces of wood which were then placed in the furrows of a ploughed paddock. The jam had to be spread as late in the evening as possible because ants might find the jam; and it was well known that the taste or sight of ants was 'objectionable to the rabbit'.

The poisoning of rabbits in a prolific season was on a colossal scale. The stench was sickening. Up and down eastern Australia a total of one million rabbits could be killed in one night. Near Wilcannia, on the two great pastoral runs owned by the Adelaide firm of Elder, Smith & Co., 120 trappers were employed in some months of the

1880s. As incentive payment the owners paid so many pence for each rabbit scalp, and so they kept accurate records of the rabbits caught and scalped. In the last half of the year 1887 their trappers caught 618,000 rabbits on ground where probably not a rabbit lived only four years earlier. When that fine newspaperman C. E. W. Bean was travelling through the same district several decades later he was told that at one waterhole on Momba, three million rabbits were poisoned in the space of a week. The tally had been computed by counting the number of carcasses in a few square feet and then multiplying it by the total area in which the carcasses lay. The figure, though probably an exaggeration, showed how the outback had learned to count in millions. On very large sheep-runs, in the years when the grasses were juicy and when some mechanism seemed to favour unusually the proliferating of the rabbits, there were probably enough rabbits to feed a city the size of Sydney for several months, but none of those remote rabbits found their way into a Sydney pot or oven.

5

By the early 1890s the rabbits were entrenched or emburrowed in most parts of Australia south of the tropics. They were at home in the hot half-deserts where a furry creature seemed the most unlikely inhabitant. They flourished on the steep hill country. They thrived on the river banks and in the sandhills. They revelled in the plains and ran on to the colder tablelands. Even where the grass was scarce they could flourish because they ate the saltbush and other low plants or the bark from mulga, sandalwood and stunted trees, effectively ringbarking and slowly killing these trees. As the leaves of these trees were a reserve of fodder for sheep and as the trees stabilized the soil, their destruction was costly.

In the hope of containing the rabbits, long rabbit-proof fences were built by governments. They were possibly amongst the longest fences in the world, but they were not a sure defence against rabbits. One fence ran for about 500 miles close to the border of Queensland and South

Australia. Western Australia built a fence along a line stretching 1139 miles from the Southern Ocean, near the port of Esperance, to the tropical Eighty Mile Beach, beyond Port Hedland. It hoped that rabbits would be confined to the central desert. That fence was built too late, and when the wooden posts were in place the rabbits had already slipped by and were feeding in the fertile strip of Western Australia.

How the rabbits reached Western Australia puzzled many people. The evidence is powerful that the ancestors crossed the dry Nullarbor Plain, not far from the ocean. On several of the harsh stages of that journey, kitten rabbits had probably been carried in the billy of swagmen, to be released by a waterhole and a patch of green grass, there to multiply. The westward run of the rabbits had crossed the border into Western Australia by the early 1890s, and rabbits were plentiful around the gold-fields of Coolgardie and Kalgoorlie in 1901. In the history of prospecting, those pioneering Australian rabbits who prospected for grass, their finds preparing the way for the great rushes, were as impressive as the men who prospected for minerals.

The rabbits had an unexpected effect on the way income was distributed in the grazing districts. Rabbits indirectly were a form of welfare legislation. They transferred money from wealthy squatters to rural labourers. Thousands of professional rabbiters with their dogs, traps, nets, and poisons often made a high monthly income by destroying rabbits on the large pastoral stations. They were paid piecework rates – fivepence or threepence or even one halfpenny for each rabbit they killed. At the peak of the rabbit invasions the king rabbiters must have been earning more than the fastest shearers; moreover they were their own bosses and worked in their own way with little outside supervision. Hundreds of these rabbiters then turned from poisoning the rabbits to trapping them for the English market, and in the year 1906 Australia was to earn more by shipping away rabbit meat and skins than by shipping frozen beef. In that year twenty-two million frozen rabbits were exported, mostly to London, and hot rabbit pie was probably eaten in cottages close to the English woods where the progenitors of the pie had run wild only half a century previously.

It was ironical that in the last quarter of the 19th century, none of the laws directed against the unpopular squatters – none of the land taxes or the higher rents imposed on their leasehold runs – were more damaging than the rabbits. The orators who had stood with waving arms on the platforms at popular rallies and called for the cutting up of the big sheep estates and for vengeance on the squatters thought that the statute book was their weapon; but in the end the leading slayer was the conjuror who quietly produced a rabbit from the hat.

We can speculate about, but not compute, the losses caused by rabbits. Undoubtedly the money earned from rabbit skins and from fresh or frozen rabbits was small compared to the wool income which rabbits devoured. The dispersal of rabbits should be seen as an economic event of similar magnitude to the invention of the refrigerated ship or the rise of the butter industry towards the end of the century. It is possible that the devastation of the rabbits outweighed, financially, the gains from a mining field as rich as Broken Hill. The written history of a new land is, understandably, so centred on applauding the innovations that lead to swift material progress that the innovations retarding progress are overlooked.

In many years perhaps one twentieth of Australia's potential income from wool was devoured by rabbits, and in bad years rabbits perhaps reduced the wool income by one eighth or more. On individual sheep-runs the financial losses attributed to rabbits varied widely, ranging from small losses to the virtual abandoning of the sheep station when the first armies of rabbits arrived. One sheep-owner in the Cobar district began with 16,000 sheep but in the year 1892 his flocks were reduced to a mere 1600. Asked for the explanation he replied in three simple words: 'the rabbit invasion'. On scores of large sheep stations the rabbits, after the first year or two of bedlam, were rarely a plague but rabbit trappers made a living there in nearly every year

Women at a political meeting were a rarity as late as 1902: a policy speech at Nhill in Victoria with the platform crowded and the long press table at the speaker's feet.

In central Australia a sharp-edged stone was skilfully used to cut a coolamon or carrying dish of bark. By 1900, Aboriginal life in most regions was eroded by the great coolamons of western technology – wagons and drays, ships and trains, pipelines and gasometers – and their pervasive effects.

Robert Edwards

until the 1950s, when the myxomatosis disease began to decimate the population of rabbits.

6

Much of the early history of Australia is a story of the lottery of transplantation. The Austin family knew the variations which this theme could play. The first Austin pioneer was a young Somerset convict, who had stolen beehives and honey. In Tasmania, after his sentence expired, he acquired farms, a big orchard, an inn, and a most profitable river ferry. He was childless and his nephews who came out inherited his money. Several of the younger Austins, James and Thomas, moved across to Victoria with the first sheep and prospered.

James Austin returned to England in 1856, and bought the abbey house and the famous ruined abbey at Glastonbury. He presided over the place where King Arthur was said to have been buried and where pilgrims came in medieval times to see the famous thorn tree, which they believed had been planted by Joseph of Arimathea. According to legend, Joseph had come to England as a missionary and had placed his priestly staff in the ground at Glastonbury and it had sprouted as a thorn tree, flowering twice a year, the symbol of the miraculous and the power of the transplant. On this sacred site the returned Australian settled down as proprietor. It was he who arranged in 1859 for the cargo of rabbits to be sent to Liverpool for shipment to the Australian estate of his brother. When as an old man James Austin made a last visit to Australia he must have been astonished to see how the thorns had multiplied.

PART THREE
WHERE IS PARADISE?

20 The Banks Crash

It was inconceivable in 1891 that the prosperity of Australia should fade. But the promised land was about to forget its promise. Not until the quarter century 1945 to 1970 did Australia fully recapture the buoyancy and the increasing prosperity which had marked the period 1851 to 1891.

2

The economic collapse came in three stages – a moderate slump followed by bank crashes and then by drought – and each stage deepened the depression. The first stage was visible in many towns in 1891, being marked by unemployment, a fall in new investment, and an air of uneasiness. Such slumps had come occasionally in the previous thirty years – usually when export prices were falling – and they had been falling in the 1880s. Such slumps also came when the boom in the share market had gone one puff too far, and in the late 1880s the boom had gone several puffs too far. So the intoxicating optimism gave way to a mood of sobriety in which people hesitated and waited.

The slump also owed much to the increasing wariness of those British investors who had created so many jobs by subscribing to the loans of the six Australian governments, by placing deposits in the London and Scottish offices of Australian banks, and by buying shares in Australian mining, pastoral and finance houses. In some years of the 1880s one fifth of Britain's new overseas investments came to Australia. Here was the great financier of the world pouring money into a continent holding fewer than three million people. Australia could not hope to absorb sensibly so much capital so quickly. Between 1885 and 1890 Australia's borrowing from overseas averaged £20 million a year, but in 1892 it fell to £7.5 million. The fall was sufficient to throw tens of thousands of Australians out of work and to make the teeth of businessmen chatter.

The second stage of the depression was a shock to almost every Australian: the banks were suddenly besieged. No private institution was so respectable, so monumental and so powerful as the banking houses. Banks had more prestige here than they had in England, the United States, France and probably almost any country in the advanced world. In most Australian cities the noblest buildings were the churches and the big banks. Indeed the head offices of most banks were built like temples with vast banking chambers decorated with Italian marble, fine-grained woods, chandeliers, and even stained glass in gothic windows. From the internal balconies the head banker could look down on a scene of splendour and extravagance financed partly by the people's thrift. Whereas in the New Testament the money-changers were driven from the temple, in Australia the money-changers built their own temples.

The big banks were public companies whose shares were prized. They held more assets than any other Australian organizations and their dividends were regular and generous. They promoted much of the economic development of the continent and their branches could be found in every town: usually two-storeyed buildings with an ornate facade which would have pleased an English provincial city. Four of the biggest Australian banks held, between them, more than 600 branches, a statistic which must have flabbergasted English bankers if they had realized that it was true. Their general managers received princely salaries which dwarfed the salaries of the permanent heads of government departments. On the boards of the main banks sat not only rich men but many of the leading politicians. As each colony did not yet have its own state bank it entrusted its own substantial business to one or two of these banking

319

companies. The banknotes which circulated in every colony were issued not by the government but by the banks, and printed in colours as bright and in lettering as grand as the dignity of the bank would permit. As bankers did not believe that their activities should be closely regulated by governments, and as they had been remarkably free from disasters, the banks were regulated less than those of almost every country. This more than anything was to be the cause of their collapse. The bankers and politicians could not foresee a serious banking crisis, and were unprepared when crisis came.

The lifeblood of an Australian bank – and any bank in the era when the gold standard dominated finance – was gold coin and bullion. Every bank had to keep sufficient gold in its safes and vaults to pay, without prior notice, any customer who wished to withdraw a deposit or to cash a banknote. A bank which happened, on one busy day, to be short of gold coins could not compel a customer to accept paper money. Banknotes were not legal tender, and every note carried in flowing script a guarantee signed by the bank's own manager: 'I promise to pay the bearer on demand ONE POUND sterling'. In law £1 sterling was a gold sovereign.

During economic uncertainty the banks had to keep a higher proportion of gold in their coffers, but they could only build up their stock of gold sovereigns at the expense of the money which they lent to the public. The temptation to skimp on the hoard of gold and to lend out as much money as possible was always present. And yet if the day came when a bank, through miscalculation, was seriously short of gold, then it had to close its doors, reconstruct its business, and thereafter incur odium. Indeed, it might never reopen its doors. In Europe in the 19th century many banks failed not because they were unable to meet their obligations but because they could not meet those obligations instantly.

Depositors in Australia occasionally panicked and rushed the banks and demanded their money in gold. These runs or rushes on banks were usually met with ease. Once the customers found that the bank calmly paid out as much gold as was required, they themselves became calm. In the following weeks they quietly and shamefacedly returned their money to the safety of the bank. If the news became public that a bank had made unsound loans to businessmen, then customers naturally feared for the safety of their own deposits in the bank and withdrew them permanently. Curiously, in 1885 there were fears that the Russians might invade Australia, and the branches of some banks were almost emptied of gold by nervous depositors. Presumably they buried their sovereigns in the garden or behind the bricks in a fireplace or a wall. Obviously gold could be hidden and hoarded with more safety than paper money because gold did not catch fire, could not be destroyed by damp and could not be nibbled by mice or washed away by floods. To hoard gold at home was therefore common. The danger of the hoarding habit was that it could jeopardize the safety of banks and indeed the economic prosperity of everyone.

3

In 1891 a shiver ran through every Australian banker. For the first time since the 1840s a large bank was rushed by panicking depositors and was bled to death. The Bank of Van Diemen's Land had been founded in 1823 when the name of Tasmania was little used, and its business was sound until the late 1880s when it lent heavily to Tasmanians who gambled in silver shares. In August 1891 it closed its doors throughout Tasmania and attempted to meet its debts by offering all its banking premises as prizes in a lottery at one pound a ticket.

Like many banks which were to close, it seemed to be a fortress of respectability until the liquidators and the funeral directors of high finance began their post-mortem. Its managing director was a self-made Tasmanian, William Henry Burgess junior, whose name inspired trust. He had risen from his father's grocery shop and the teachers' roll of the Wesleyan Sunday School to become treasurer of the colony when only in his thirties; and he seemed to look after his own affairs and the colony's affairs with such skill that many people marvelled at the bank's good fortune in having such a fine managing director. Later, after the bank had failed, and its last misleading report had been scrutinized, it was learned that Burgess had borrowed from his bank the large sum of £74,000, of which half was unsecured. Carelessness, corruption and fraud were uncovered or suspected in so many of the small banks and finance houses that public confidence even in impeccable firms became brittle.

In April 1892 the Bank of South Australia was assailed by rumours of mismanagement which were partly true. Founded in London, it had been the first bank in South Australia and had commenced business in a tent on the beach at Glenelg when the colony was just beginning, and had financed many of the great families and many of the main enterprises in the colony. Two months after it had closed, the New Oriental Bank, a London house which was once strong on the Victorian gold-fields, closed without creating severe hardship. Then came a pause of ten months in which only the small Federal Bank went into liquidation. So far the only banks to fall had not been amongst the top twelve, had not operated throughout the continent, and even in their home colony were viewed sometimes with suspicion by the banking fraternity. If the eliminating of the weak banks had gone no further, only good would have resulted.

In the autumn of 1893 one of the most vigorous banks fell under public suspicion. The Commercial Bank of Australia had been founded in Melbourne in 1866, and in an era of racial and sectarian loyalties it was especially strong amongst Methodists and popular with the Chinese for whom it printed special banknotes. It eventually held a remarkable network of branches spreading from Collingwood to Darwin and – the price of growing so fast – also held many risky accounts which older banks had eschewed. To finance its multiplying customers it gathered deposits in Scotland and England on a massive scale. In Melbourne, the heart of its business, it was an over-generous supporter of individuals and building societies gambling in land.

Just before the Easter of 1893, people passing the head office of the bank in Collins Street began to notice that business seemed very brisk: people were entering and leaving in surprisingly large numbers. Customers of the bank, knowing that their own savings would be endangered if the bank ran out of gold, joined the queues at the great counters of polished wood. By withdrawing their deposits in gold they did not realize that they hastened the event which they feared – the closing of the bank. Rumours swept through the country that the bank was about to close. The rumours sent more people hurrying to the bank, and they withdrew their money and thus guaranteed that the rumours would be proved true. On 5 April 1893 the bank suspended payment. Behind the locked doors lay about £11 million of depositors' funds – the sum sounded colossal in those days – and ledgers which revealed very risky business deals.

The failure of a large bank turned the suspicions onto other banks, and people wondered which bank would be the next to close? Some of the fickle depositors decided that a London-owned bank which had operated in Australia since the gold-rushes was vulnerable. The English, Scottish and Australian Chartered Bank – known amongst bankers as 'The Scotty' – soon paid out so much gold that the directors closed the bank before all the gold had gone. This became the common pattern of behaviour. Once depositors began to panic and to endanger a bank, the directors closed the doors before all the gold ran out. In many of the banks which closed, less than one tenth of the total deposits had been withdrawn in the panic; but that was enough.

During April 1893 five banks closed. The streets and hotels and clubs and vestries were full of rumours. The new telephone wires that now linked the larger business houses within a city sagged under the weight of the gloomy news, gossip and rumours they carried. Rumours were printed gravely in city and country newspapers: it is reported that, our correspondent understands that, the latest intelligence

323

indicates that, a certain bank will not last long. The telegraph lines carried warnings and fears to every corner of the country. They also carried coded messages from isolated banking chambers to the head ofices calling for more and more sovereigns to be railed urgently to quell the panic. The head offices in turn sent secret cables to England and to New Zealand, ordering gold sovereigns to be shipped by the fastest route to Australia. Several banks closed when the precious sovereigns they had ordered were in fast steamers in the Mediterranean, the Suez Canal, or the Indian Ocean.

A bank could be bled to death with astonishing speed. The National Bank of Australasia was first assailed by panicking depositors at its relatively unimportant Perth office on Monday 17 April 1893, two days after 'the Scotty' was closed. The run on the National Bank in Perth was launched or accelerated by a rumour that there was a run on the head office of the bank in Melbourne. In fact there was no such run, but now rumours and fears were racing backwards and forwards across the continent. In the last fortnight of April the National Bank at its many branches paid out nearly 45% of its gold. On Monday 1 May the bank's doors remained barred.

In Brisbane it was unthinkable that the colony's greatest financial institution, the Queensland National Bank, could fall; and in Sydney the idea of the old Commercial Banking Company of Sydney failing to meet a request for gold seemed sacrilegious; but these banking houses were about to fall. The impact on the mind of the faithful was as if the spire of a cathedral had been struck repeatedly by lightning.

4

The governments of Victoria and New South Wales probably could have halted this chain of events at an early stage. Unfortunately, in Victoria – the centre of banking – a new ministry had won office in January 1893, just when the collapse of the Federal Bank signalled the start of the panic. The new premier was James Patterson, a gold-rush migrant

who had become a slaughterman and butcher on the
gold-fields and then an auctioneer in Melbourne suburbs.
His treasurer, G. D. Carter, a gold-rush migrant now in his
early sixties, had been a wine-merchant but knew something of banking because he sat on the board of the Bank of
Victoria. Patterson and Carter had no rational notion of
what to do when Melbourne was gripped by hysteria. In a
last twitching gesture they went in a special ministerial train
to the bayside town of Frankston on Sunday evening 30
April and, at a hasty meeting of the executive council in the
holiday house of the acting governor, instructed him to sign
a proclamation which closed all the banks in Victoria for a
week. The proclamation advertised to the world that
Victoria was in a state of crisis: it did nothing specific to ease
the crisis.

Two large banks – the Union and the Australasia – defied
the governor's proclamation of a banking holiday and
opened their branches throughout Victoria on the Monday
morning and the Bank of New South Wales reopened in
Victoria on the Tuesday morning. It would have been
preferable if, instead of opening, they had first devised a
scheme whereby the surviving banks would help each
other. If New South Wales had likewise proclaimed a bank
holiday, the pause might have been useful. But to make
New South Wales and Victoria co-operate was even more
difficult than making the various banks co-operate. The
individualism which during the boom had edged many of
the banks towards disaster was never more pronounced
than in 1893, when a common policy might have averted
disaster.

In Sydney many politicians were tempted to see the crisis
in banking as largely a Victorian event, a punishment for
reckless optimism. This view was complacent, for the panic
was already visible in Sydney where the powerful Australian Joint Stock Bank had closed. Fortunately for Sydney
its premier, George Dibbs, had been longer in office than
the Victorian premier, and knew more about the ways of
banks. Born in Sydney in 1834, the son of a sea-captain who
that year disappeared at sea, George Dibbs realized how

devastating a bank failure could be. In 1866 he was living in the Chilean port of Valparaiso, buying wheat for shipment to Australia, when he heard of the failure of the London bank known as Agra and Masterman's; and for the next eight years he was virtually bankrupt. He raised himself up again, won the West Sydney seat in parliament in 1874, and was twice premier for short periods before beginning in 1891 a full term of office. As his older brother Thomas was general manager of the strong and respected Commercial Banking Company of Sydney, Sir George Dibbs was not unaware of banking policies and dangers, and he also probably realized that almost every nation in Europe and North America possessed what no Australian colony possessed – a simple law which permitted banks to drown a panic with paper money when a state of emergency was declared.

Sir George Dibbs also held firm views on how to behave in a crisis. When, on 10 February 1892, depositors clamoured for their money at the Savings Bank of New South Wales in Barrack Street, this burly politician went to the bank, stood at its doorway, and urged the customers to go home. The bank, he said, was safe. With his own hand he wrote out, and pinned to the door, a notice affirming that his own government would guarantee the safety of the deposits. Fifteen months later, when far larger banks were besieged in Sydney, he acted just as sensibly. On 3 May 1893 his government passed a Bank Notes Act, and on 15 May it declared that for the following six months the act would be in force. In effect the act permitted banks in New South Wales to pay out their own printed banknotes instead of gold. The banknotes were now legal tender, and anybody in New South Wales could pay for food, land or any goods and services simply with banknotes. Only at the main office of each bank in Sydney could people convert banknotes into sovereigns, but the need to convert notes into sovereigns was less urgent because notes were now accepted everywhere. This sensible act instantly eliminated the scarcity of gold coin, a scarcity which had so devastated the savings and property and livelihood of people.

Unfortunately the new law was first enforced only after the huge Commercial Banking Company of Sydney closed its doors. While it therefore failed to save the bank which was managed by Dibbs' brother, it probably prevented the panic from engulfing Sydney. Moreover it released stocks of gold which, no longer required in New South Wales, could reinforce endangered banks in other colonies.

Throughout Australia only three important banks remained open. The oldest in the land, the Bank of New South Wales, was still doing business; so too were the London creations of the 1830s, the Union Bank and the Bank of Australasia, which later were to come together to form the present ANZ Bank. These three banks had, on the whole, been managed soundly during the boom. Fortunately they also owned a string of branches in New Zealand which in 1893 was relatively prosperous and so could release gold for the banks' needs in Australia. Although it is now believed that these banks survived solely because they were sound, no bank anywhere could hope to survive a crisis of such intensity unless governments intervened. But for the good sense of Sir George Dibbs they would also have closed their doors; and that would have put such pressure on the six smaller banks which still carried on business that they too would have fallen. These smaller banks traded only in the one colony and therefore could draw on local loyalties, but those loyalties would have vanished if the panic had continued.

People were numbed by the run of events. In 1892 in Melbourne some of the denominations had called for days of prayer, fasting and self-denial as the depression became serious. On 4 May 1893 the Anglican Bishop of Melbourne, Dr Goe, called for people to observe a Day of Humiliation and Prayer on Wednesday 17 May, and between the issue of his call and the actual day of prayer another seven banks were to fall, two of them on the official Day of Humiliation. 'Multitudes of unemployed men throng the streets of the metropolis, and there are many silent sufferers, who have lost the savings of a life time through the collapse of trusted institutions,' said the Bishop; and within a fortnight the multitude had grown larger. Thousands of Australians, laymen and clergymen, agreed with him that the depression was a divine punishment. 'And all has come', wrote one of the oldest of the Australian-born clergymen, a son of Parramatta of 1820, 'because of so wildly making haste to be rich, and forgetting the Lord our God'.

At the start of the year, we had twenty-two note-issuing banks. By the end of autumn, thirteen of those banks were closed and were receiving legal and financial repairs. In Victoria and in Queensland two thirds of all deposits were locked up in those closed banks. In New South Wales more than half of all deposits were locked inside those banks which had closed. In Australia as a whole every second customer was debarred from a bank.

Nothing in the history of English banking could match our disaster of 1893. I can find nothing in Germany, France or Holland to compare with this collapse. Even in the United States, where one-branch banks were almost as plentiful as tobacconist's shops, I doubt whether a disaster of such magnitude had occurred. In 1893, the United States also experienced a dangerous panic of depositors, but in the whole nation the total liabilities of the banks which closed were less than those of the banks which closed in Australia. In the United States in the banking crisis of 1893 the proportion of the nation's savings which was locked up was small compared to the proportion in Australia.

A throbbing nervousness hung over the country in June 1893. Nobody knew when another run on the surviving banks might suddenly begin. Nobody could be sure how many of the banks which temporarily were closed would re-open. Outside the banking system, thousands of business transactions were postponed. Debts which fell due in the normal course of business could not be paid. People who had borrowed money from banks could not be sure when their loan might be recalled: they only knew that if it were recalled too soon they themselves would be ruined. The market in shares and real estate was groggy, and a buyer with ready cash could buy shares and land at bargain prices. But, all values being chaotic, what was a bargain price?

328

Some investors who bought shares at bargain prices found later that the shares were worthless.

Out on the distant plains many of the sheep stations transacted their banking business not with the orthodox banks but with pastoral or dry-grass banks. The dry-grass banks were large finance organizations with a London board on which might sit lords or retired colonial governors, with branches in many Australian towns and ledgers full of mortgages. These banks tended to do business in the more arid country especially in western New South Wales and in central Queensland where they invested their own capital and the money they had borrowed in providing fences, dams, new flocks, and working capital for sheep stations. As the mortgage-holders of vast plains, the dry-grass banks were now endangered by the collapse of commercial confidence as well as by a fall in the price of wool. The three largest were Dalgety, New Zealand Loan, and Goldsbrough Mort; and in the middle of 1893 two of the three suspended all payments and even Dalgety could not be sure of survival.

No Australian could escape these events. It was true that no savings bank had closed in the crisis but in those days the savings banks were relatively small and possessed few branches outside the capital cities. In dozens of towns the labourers, blacksmiths and domestic servants kept their savings in the note-issuing banks rather than in savings banks, and so became victims of the crisis. Even the banknotes which were held in pockets or tills were exposed to the banking disaster. In Victoria anybody who carried banknotes could feel safe, for the Victorian law insisted that banknotes issued in Victoria would be the first charge on the assets of the banks which issued them. In South Australia anybody who held a banknote could not feel so safe, and in New South Wales the banknotes were not specially guaranteed until Dibbs changed the law in May 1893. In fact, the banknotes circulating in 1893 were – probably without exception – redeemed eventually but in the first weeks of the crisis nobody could be certain of the value of those pieces of coloured paper. Many people, made

329

jittery by the rumours, preferred twelve silver shillings in the hand to a £1 note in the purse.

One by one the banking companies which in 1893 had closed their doors prepared to reopen them: the exception was the small Federal Bank. Each bank had to reconstruct its business, compelling its shareholders to subscribe more capital in order to strengthen the bank and meet any losses. Each bank had to meet its depositors in Australia and Britain and persuade them to agree to withdraw their money slowly and sometimes on less favourable terms. Each bank finally had to submit its scheme of reconstruction to the highest courts for approval.

The first bank reopened five weeks after it had closed and the last bank nineteen weeks after it had closed. Many people still recall how the fortunes of their ancestors were 'ruined in the bank crashes' but few people were ruined by the actual failure of a bank to repay deposits. Nearly all the deposits were largely or entirely repaid, and usually with interest. Some people – perhaps numbering several hundred – were probably ruined because, as shareholders in banks, they had to pay heavy calls on the shares they owned. In contrast, those who had borrowed money from banks were generally treated leniently: to have pressed them too hard would have lowered economic confidence even further.

The crash of the banks in 1893 could almost certainly have been averted by sound government policies. But those bankers, editors, politicians, borrowers and lenders who in their own ways had contributed to the crisis had learned a lesson. After 1893 the main banks were conducted with more caution, with higher reserves of gold, with a reluctance to gather deposit in the British Isles, and with less emphasis on high dividends. No lesson, however, is learned permanently and this lesson had been learned too late.

Though the banks were alive, the crisis had shattered confidence and created even more unemployment. Over-seas investors lost confidence in Australia, and at the very time when Australia needed investment for public works and private projects, money was being withdrawn. The ebb of funds was acute, and in the worst year the staggering sum of 40% of Australia's export income was eaten up simply in paying interest on those overseas debts which had been incurred in the balmy years. So the end of 1893 was marked by far more distress than the beginning. The unemployment was more serious than people had ever known, and the depression of the 1890s would remain the great scar in the country's history in that long period between the convict days and the massive casualties of the First World War.

21 Retreat from Paradise

The year 1893, in the memory of Victorians, was the great time-barrier. The phrases 'before the crash' or 'after the crash' appeared in hundreds of conversations and printed reminiscences. Before was prosperous and proud and after, for many people, was humble.

New suburban streets were lined with new houses in 1893 but nobody wished to rent them and no night-watchman came to guard them; and their window sills, internal walls, gaslight fittings, water pipes, and floorboards were systematically pilfered until only the brick shell remained. In South Melbourne in 1894 one charity organization alone was supplying bread, meat and vegetables to 800 people, most of whom were the wives and children of men who had gone upcountry to seek work. People who had lived in style during the boom were not always willing to trample on their pride. 'I have known people to eat orange peel rather than ask for bread,' said one charity worker. No old age pension and no sickness or unemployment benefits were available for those in need.

The government of Victoria was forced to reduce drastically its spending just when legitimate appeals for relief were loudest. The only teachers' college, a palatial college with stone griffins surmounting the fresh red walls, was closed because new teachers were no longer needed; the government simply economized by instructing many outback teachers to divide their week equally between two small schools. Parliament house, a palace of stone, was not closed but some of the grand ministers who had dispensed millions during the boom were now scrounging shillings from humble jobs and no longer sat in parliament. One recent premier of Victoria, said to be a millionaire in the boom, was riding his bicycle along suburban streets in order to erect auction hoardings on vacant houses. A minister of railways who during the boom placed new railways on the map with as much ease as a man doodling with a pencil was now insolvent and running a small farm near Port Fairy.

2

To the teeming builders of Melbourne the heart of the city was now almost as quiet as a cemetery. New skyscrapers stood like tall stucco headstones, and many headstones were blank. Some of the tall offices became boarding houses, and the new lodgers walked along the uncarpeted corridors, their footsteps echoing, to rooms which were furnished frugally and lit dimly. The owners of other skyscrapers let out the upper floors as residential rooms and the lower floors as offices, but even the cheap rents did not attract businessmen. When in 1899 the government thought of rebuilding the central railway station at Flinders Street and adding large offices, they were reminded by one engineer of the hundreds of office suites which, standing within a few minutes' walk from the station, had not housed one tenant. Mentally walking along Collins Street, the engineer named building after building, the upper floors of which had never been occupied. Turning down Elizabeth Street he came to the Australian Building, once one of the tallest in the world. 'I suppose', he said, 'that two-thirds of that building have never been used.'

The glut of skyscrapers was less painful than the glut of bricklayers, slaters, tilers, tuck pointers, stonemasons, carpenters, cabinet makers, architects and surveyors. Fifteen years after the cessation of the building boom, Victoria still had a surplus of building tradesmen; and when the earthquake shook San Francisco in 1906 many hundreds of them sailed away to rebuild that city.

Melbourne remained the biggest city in Australia but it was now only a question of time before she lost to Sydney the supremacy she had held since the first gold years and which her people so prized. For many years of the 1890s Melbourne lost population. In modern times it is rare for a country's largest city actually to decline in population, and Melbourne's decline was made more galling by the sight of hundreds of her own citizens moving to Sydney. But most people leaving Melbourne went west rather than north. The long shipping lane across the Great Australian Bight to Albany and Fremantle became one of the busiest in Australia, as tens of thousands of people went to Western Australia where even today many of the shops and villas built in the 1890s have the style of Auburn, Moreland and the Melbourne suburbs of the land boom.

Another stream of Victorians went to Durban and so on to the booming gold city of Johannesburg where Australian-rules football was regularly played at the turn of the century. On the eve of the Boer War so many Victorians lived in the vast region between Rhodesia and Cape Town that news from South Africa was reported in many of the four-page weeklies of the Victorian country towns. The students from one middle-class Melbourne school became so numerous in Western Australia, Cape Town and Johannesburg that the school old boys' song, written in 1907, devoted two of its five verses to old boys living in those regions.

So many people sailed from Victoria in the coastal steamships or in the overseas liners in the 1890s that the gains of immigration in the recent decades were wiped out. Victoria had gained heavily through net immigration between 1861 to 1890, but that gain was exceeded by the net emigration in the following fifteen years. In essence, between 1891 and 1905 Victoria lost, through migration, a greater total of people than she had gained through migration in the previous thirty years. As the young people led the exodus from Victoria, the marriage rate and then the birth rate declined. As the old people stayed behind, the death rate ultimately increased. For sixty years after the bank crashes Victoria persistently had the lowest rate of natural increase – the excess of births over deaths – of the

six Australian states. We can only guess how many families
in Victorian towns in 1890 were broken up – the older
children travelling to faraway places, the parents remaining
– and did not meet again. The families so dispersed must
have numbered thousands.

3

Governments made hurried plans to entice the city
unemployed into the country. Frightened of political
violence if hungry men remained in the cities, and certain
that these men could learn to grow their own food, most
governments provided free land and money for rural
co-operatives and peasant settlements. In South Australia a
chain of village settlements sprang up near the Murray
River. Queensland in 1893 provided land for any rural
co-operative possessing more than thirty adult members.
Each member could lease up to 160 acres of Crown land
and borrow £20 to buy tools, seed, and food until the first
crops were ripe. By Christmas 1893 more than two
thousand Queenslanders were settled in rural groups. The
optimistic names of the groups – Excel Pioneers and Nil
Desperandum – were soon a mockery. Members of groups
quarrelled. The poor land which they farmed increased the
tension.

Victoria in September 1893 set aside timber reserves and
town commons on which poor people could settle on a few
acres for a small rent. If the men could find seasonal jobs
nearby as harvesters and timber-cutters they managed –
with the aid of the grain and vegetables from their own
allotment – to survive the worst years and keep their
self-respect. In ten years Victoria set up at least seventy-
eight village settlements, each with a managing committee.
These settlements stretched from the banks of the Murray
to the tall forest of Noojee and the Gippsland Lakes.

In 1894 the village settlements were scattered between
the southern Tasmanian village of Southport, which was
founded by the ladies of Hobart, to the radical Queensland
communities at Roma. Their members, numbering
perhaps 20,000 at the peak, were scavenging a rural living

335

with less land and humbler equipment than most of the selectors of earlier days had used in their struggle to survive. On most of these settlements the people worked their own paddock but on a few they shared the land and plough and working horses. A few other larger settlements, modelled partly on a Berlin experiment, gave food to men who were willing to do simple bush work.

The Leongatha Labour Colony, Victoria's largest, was a block of forest where unemployed men from the city could clear the scrub in return for three substantial meals and a little pay. The men chosen in Melbourne had to be able-bodied, of good character, and destitute. As a wife and children were not allowed to live at the labour colony, married men tended to come only if they could find no work elsewhere. Leongatha was thus a workhouse for the single men and for men in their sixties whose spirits had sunk or whose energy was sapped. In Melbourne they were given a free railway ticket, and they travelled the ninety miles in the morning train and then walked from Leongatha to the labour colony where they lived in tents or huts, the tall forest hovering over them. Eating in the communal dining hall, and using knives and forks supplied by the colony, each man received a daily allowance of 1½ pounds of boiled meat, and a total of 2½ pounds of boiled potatoes and bread. Hot tea and a little sugar were served at two of the three meals. Men were also paid trifling sums of from threepence to eightpence a day, allowing them to save a little and perhaps move away to find work elsewhere, but only the strong found work elsewhere.

On railway stations in Victoria, bold yellow and black posters invited employers to write to the labour colony if they wished to hire labourers. Few bothered to write. At first a labour bureau, the colony became simply a haven for unemployed in the days before governments offered social security.

At the colony the short working day, the long dinner break, and the cheerful smoke-ohs where the men could yarn were superior to life outside. The hard work of clearing the scrub, tending the bonfires of the cleared

336

timber, and grubbing out the green stumps of giant eucalypts was not done with professional skill or the breathless tempo of the farmers of the neighbourhood. When inquisitive neighbours emerged from the forest to see what was happening behind the post-and-rail fences they were often astonished at the colony's slow progress. And yet in the first six years a total of 3500 men had worked at the farm, staying on average about three months; and many had been restored to that 'spirit of self-dependence' which was high in the aims of those who had founded the colony at a public meeting in the Melbourne Town Hall.

Overhearing the conversations at the colony's dinner table, or at the burning-off fires where they yarned on cold mornings, a visitor would have easily patched together the common experience of so many Australians of the last three decades – the mounting prosperity and the growing leisure, the pride in seeing the cities rise and railways span inland, and the optimism of a land which seemed to promise everything. Then suddenly the promise faded; and there they were, living a version of the spartan life once lived by rural labourers more than half a century ago. The rural life had even less appeal to those who, having achieved the white-collar dream, were counter-salesmen and commercial travellers in the boom years when almost everyone could sell anything in this land of easy business.

Even now we can overhear William Wallace, almost a regular resident of the labour colony, talk of his experiences. In 1900 he could look back on three years in the labour colony, helping the cook in the kitchen, for he was not a muscular man. He could also look back even further to the boom years when his collar was white and his suit was neatly pressed and every customer was greeted as 'madam' or 'sir' with that tone of voice which perhaps hinted that he himself was also 'sir' in this land where all men were almost equal. He had worked as a draper's assistant at Hordern's in Sydney in the days when every draper's assistant knew how to dress well on a smallish salary. (And now in the camp kitchen one can almost see the flour specking his jacket and smell the potato peel on his hands.) He had come to

337

Melbourne in the worst year of the depression and had sold Pearson's sand-soap on a commission for two years, one of the procession of hawkers and canvassers. The owners decided that there were better ways of selling working men's soap at a time when more hands than ever were dirty with hard work, and so he lost his job. His clothes became shabby because he had no room in which to sleep, let alone to wash and dry and iron his clothes. In the end Wallace slept wherever he could find shelter. Perhaps on a dozen nights he slept in the open – 'sleeping about the streets' was the expression of the day. Finally he went to the labour colony.

In 1900, with business in the city reviving, he thought of becoming a draper's assistant again: 'I intend to when I get sufficient money to clothe myself properly. There would be no use in my attempting to do so without that.' One can almost hear his indignation at the naive idea that a shop assistant could apply for work in a shabby suit. 'I have some friends in Sydney', he added, 'and if I go in a proper condition to them, they may be able to do something for me.' Whether he again unrolled the cloth and cut it on the long draper's counter is not known. The life of tens of thousands of people, and their own self-esteem, did not recover from the blows of the depression.

4

Everywhere people seemed to be in retreat. Thousands were forced to leave the cities for the country, and thousands left Australia. Nothing is more disillusioning for a new country which has spent heavily in attracting migrants than to see them going away to new lands of opportunity.

William Lane was a perpetual migrant and in 1893 he was preparing to move again. Born in Bristol in 1861, the son of a landscape gardener, he had first migrated to North America where he worked as a printer's devil, linotype operator and newspaper reporter. Returning in 1885 to England he decided to follow his brothers to Australia. Here he became an editor of radical newspapers, and in

338

1890 he founded the Queensland *Worker* with the motto of 'socialism in our time'.

Lane had visions of founding a communal settlement in Australia or across the seas. In 1891 he was a promoter of the New Australia Co-operative Settlement Association which eventually attracted scores of shearers and other bush workers from Queensland and New South Wales as well as a smaller band of Henry Georgites from Adelaide and Albury. That Lane's association should attract virtually no support from Victoria is a curiosity not easily explained, though part of the explanation may simply be that Victorians tended to ignore organizations which were not Victorian.

Lane's socialism was more like the intense communion of a small religious sect than the socialism set up by a government. He was not primarily a supporter of the sweeping five-year plans that re-shaped a whole society. He was more the preacher than the planner and more the teacher than the man of action, though he preached action. Furthermore the golden age which he saw lay perhaps as much in the past as in the future. He saw merits in each man being his own employer. He preferred rural life to the fattening cities and he hoped that the outback would supply him with the ideal recruits – men who were strong and straight and who possessed 'the manliness which town life destroys'.

The main aim of Lane's association was to set up a colony based on communal ownership. Men and women were to be equal. Members were to remain teetotallers until the colony had been founded and the hazardous stage of settlement was over. Coloured people could not join the association. Nor could people of bad repute, people who lived together but remained unmarried, and traitors to the labour movement. The very poor were also excluded, no matter how white in skin, pure in morals, high in reputation, or steadfast in their radical loyalties. They were excluded by the fact that the membership fee was £10 or equal to about four or six weeks' wages.

In 1889 William Lane thought South America might

339

provide the area he was seeking. It was far away, like every utopia. It might also offer a sharper climate than the sweaty Brisbane where Lane worked at his journalism and where the summer lethargy made commentators and visitors doubt whether the Australian race would ever achieve greatness. This was an era when many intellectuals attributed much of Britain's greatness to a bracing climate, and Lane doubted whether any great society could arise out of a sea of perspiration.

It so happened that one of Lane's colleagues had lived in Uruguay before coming to Queensland to edit the Maryborough *Alert* (apt title for a newspaper in a town that was sweatier than Brisbane), and Lane sought his opinion about sites on the high tablelands of South America. 'We must go high, I think, to get the true Aryan climate', wrote Lane. He had strong ideas on race, ideas which were then intellectually more fashionable. He believed that utopia could be built only with people of a chosen race living in a chosen climate. If he could succeed in building his socialist colony and then spread the news of its triumph, he hoped that 'a world-wide revolution would speedily be brought about'.

South America was then in closer contact with Australia. Every week sailing ships left Newcastle with coal for the Pacific coast of South America. Other sailing ships carrying Australian wheat, copper, timber, and cheap cargoes to Europe usually sailed past Cape Horn and sometimes called at ports on the Atlantic coast of South America. It was therefore easy for Australians to visit South America. Three of Lane's colleagues made the visit, and eventually found half a million acres of free land in the inland republic of Paraguay. By acquiring so much land so easily from a poor nation, Lane's society resembled those Australian squatters who were the targets for many of his editorials: the squatters had moreover paid for their land but Lane had not. No utopians can escape the dilemma that in founding their utopia they need many of the business skills of the way of life which they are rebelling against.

The plans to create a new Australia in Paraguay caused

excitement amongst hundreds of people who were disillusioned with Australia's prospects. On 8 April 1893, when many banks in Australia were about to topple, Lane's supporters were informed that a sub-tropical Garden of Eden awaited them: 'We think that an acre cleared in Paraguay will produce as much as two in most other countries.' On two important issues, however, the promoters were in error. They thought that Paraguay was politically stable, but ten revolutions came in the next two decades. They also had not learned one of the lessons of Australia's history – that any settlement remote from markets pays heavily for that remoteness. Their land was a long dray-ride from the nearest railway station, and even if their products reached the railways and then the river-port of Asuncion those products still had to pass through Argentinian territory before reaching the south Atlantic. Remoteness was to be one cause of the early crisis in the New Australia settlement, and yet that same remoteness was one of the settlement's attractions to many Australians.

In Sydney in 1893 the promoters of paradise bought a sailing ship of 598 tons. She had been built of blue gum and bloodwood in an isolated shipyard on the Nambucca River in New South Wales and had made many voyages across the Pacific with cargoes of timber. The only flaw was her name; *Royal Tar* was not the most appropriate name for a republican vessel. And now the settlers of New Australia began to arrive from many parts of eastern Australia: outback men, many of whom had not sniffed a salt wind for years; city families, some of whom had not lived for long in Australia; and people who had never been to sea. When the ship was about to sail, the passengers numbered 120 adults and 100 teenagers and children: a few others had been taken ashore at Balmain with measles on the eve of the sailing. On the last Sunday which many of them were to spend on Australian soil an outdoor rally of 10,000 people assembled on the Sydney Domain and wished them well. The chairman of the rally was John Christian Watson, and he was to become, eleven years later, the first Labor prime minister of Australia, leading the kind of ministry which –

341

had it existed in 1893 – would have dissuaded many passengers from leaving Australia in the *Royal Tar*.

On the morning of 16 July 1893 the Sunday ringing of church bells along the south shores of Sydney Harbour was followed, off Garden Island, by the sound of a sea-shanty:

> We're homeward bound I heard them say,
> Goodbye fare ye well!

The starboard anchor of the *Royal Tar* was being hauled up by the crew, and soon the bare-masted barque was towed down the harbour by a steam tug, with small vessels of farewell sailing behind. One accompanying launch carried the union leader William Guthrie Spence, and at the Sydney Heads the people in Spence's launch and those on the crowded decks of the *Royal Tar* sang 'Auld Land Syne' before the final parting and the raising of the sails. In retrospect it was a timely song, because after the ship had slipped over the horizon the past was perhaps the only possession shared by Lane and Spence, and shared by those who sailed for New Australia and those who stayed behind.

The *Royal Tar* passed icebergs near Cape Horn and reached the port of Montevideo and transferred passengers and cargo to a river steamer. The barque then sailed for Adelaide where she was to take on more settlers. Meanwhile Lane and the pioneers slowly travelled 800 miles up the wide river to the city of Asuncion where the president of Paraguay waited on the wharf to welcome them. By steam train and then bullock carts they travelled east to a deserted orange grove in a grassy clearing, and in that small corner of their vast estate they built and thatched their huts, made bricks, chopped trees and dug gardens, and put up fences and stockyards. And in their New Australia they also quarrelled. The disputes centred on those who drank too much or worked too little, or on the leadership of the generous but tetchy Lane, or the question of how communal their utopia should be. More than one third of the settlers left New Australia even before the second contingent arrived from Adelaide.

The rift was so deep that Lane and his more ardent followers decided to found their own commune sixty miles to the south. The followers were mostly bachelors and Queenslanders. They supported his puritanical socialist ideology or were gripped by his personal magnetism. Together they formed a new colony at Cosme on land bought from a railway company, and for several years Cosme flourished, a hard-working, frugal brotherhood amidst the cane-fields. The brotherhood, however, was rarely extended to the parent colony at New Australia and Lane's men even refused to play New Australia in cricket, thus leaving them with only one other Paraguayan cricket team to play against.

The British Embassy, reporting on Paraguay in 1896, described Cosme as perhaps the best-run and most orderly of all the European settlements there. But it was not a material paradise. Many of its members were lonely and restless, and its idealism slowly sagged. By the year 1899 William Lane was disillusioned, and he sailed down the river and took a ship to Australia. A photograph of this bushy-moustached man in the disillusioning years shows big eyes looking through small, thin-rimmed glasses, like two microscopes examining the frailties of this world.

The two rival settlements, sixty miles apart, became alike in their new economic outlook. Communal ownership gave way to private ownership, and property and livestock were divided amongst those who remained. Families tilled their own farms and ran cattle, and even today the Smiths and Jones and Kennedys and other Australian names can be found in the region. Their new society ultimately failed, and did not light that beacon which Lane had hoped all the world would see, but they had settled the land with perhaps a ratio of success close to that achieved by new farmers in Australia in the 1890s. In failing as utopians they possibly became more a part of Australian folklore than if they had succeeded; and New Australia has quietly taken its place with Eureka, Cooper's Creek, Glenrowan, and Gallipoli as a tantalizing failure, as a nationalist legend appealing to an unexpectedly wide range of people.

Those who remained in Paraguay were quietly absorbed by their new land. Inevitably most of the second generation spoke Spanish and the native Guarani, married into Paraguayan families, and replaced their secular attitudes with Catholicism. But as late as the First World War a loyalty to Australia and England resurged in many of the young men, and sixteen of them rode away as volunteers to enlist in the British forces. When the war in Europe was over, the fifteen survivors were offered the chance of being repatriated to Australia. They chose Paraguay: it was no longer utopia but it was their land.

William Lane was proud to hear that they had enlisted. Now editing a newspaper in Auckland he denounced those militant unionists whom he once would have praised, and he gloried in the British Empire and was proud that his son, one of the boys from New Australia, had given his life at Gallipoli. Lane himself died in 1917, and in time the news of his death reached the remnant of his former followers in Paraguay. But news from Australia arrived less and less frequently. In 1940 one of the Paraguayan-Australians named Juan Kennedy decided to give the settlement of New Australia the name of Nueva Canberra, but the formal letter which he wrote to Canberra seeking permission was not answered. So the bond with Australia was slowly dissolved.

5

Most people who found a utopia in the 1890s found it on a mining field. The mining industry was revitalized by a new era of discovery in the 1880s and early 1890s. A string of mining camps arose all the way from Tasmania to the Kimberleys in north-western Australia, Croydon near the Gulf of Carpentaria and Chillagoe in the hills behind Cairns. Even in New South Wales, which had been scoured for forty years by prospectors, two major gold-fields were found in 1893 at West Wyalong and in 1894 at Mount Boppy. The spearhead of mining had moved into the ancient rocks of the Precambrian zone, where many of the lodes were massive and the rewards for large companies

344

were high. Most of the successful mines were now owned in Britain but Britain also owned hundreds of unsuccessful shafts which, by providing work, did much to ease the depression.

Western Australia was the utopia of the 1890s. A chain of gold-rushes, beginning in the far north west in 1886 and reaching Kalgoorlie just one month after the bank crashes in 1893, provided work or hope for thousands. Indeed the timing and the magnitude of the main gold-rushes in the Coolgardie and Kalgoorlie and Leonora districts were influenced by the deepening depression on the eastern colonies. Labour and capital, previously idle, poured into Western Australia to search for gold and to develop promising gold lodes. The more indications of gold they found, the more labour and capital poured in to intensify the search and to hasten the building of towns and railways and the sinking of shafts. In one year alone, 1896, the increase in Western Australia's population was 36,000, and that equalled the colony's total population of a decade earlier. Between 1894 and 1897 the population doubled, and straggling gold towns of hessian and calico and canvas arose on dry plains where not a white man or a horse travelled a decade earlier. In 1898 the West passed Victoria as the leading producer of gold, and so rapid was the rise of the West's gold-fields and so strong the revival of gold-fields in other colonies that in 1899 Australia produced more gold than in the richest year of the gold-rushes of the 1850s. Measured by the annual output of gold, Australia's golden age was to run from 1899 to 1908, and every one of those years was to produce more gold than the peak year of the 1850s gold-rushes.

Thousands of people also moved back to the land. The small farms multiplied; they clung to steep hills and sat on the plains and small clearings in forest and scrub. With the aid of the new cream separator the output of butter soared and for the first time Australia became a steady exporter of butter to Britain. As in the depression of the 1840s the low price of wool and livestock encouraged the production of tallow, and in the space of three years the workers in

345

abattoirs and boiling-down works doubled. And so much frozen mutton and beef was sent away in the refrigerated chambers of steamships that during the 1890s as a whole frozen meat exceeded wheat and flour as an export.

In the long-distance movements to mining fields and farmlands, Victoria and South Australia were the main losers of people and Western Australia and Queensland were the main gainers. As these two colonies held more than half of the continent, and as their natural resources seemed infinite in the minds of promoters and pamphlet-writers, they seemed invincible in the long term. In 1860 they had held less than 4% of Australia's population but at the end of the century they held 18%. Queensland had recently passed South Australia to become the third most populous colony and Western Australia had passed Tasmania to take fifth place, and both seemed certain to continue to overtake New South Wales and Victoria; but surprisingly the rankings would not alter in the long period from 1900 to 1980.

In a land which exulted in collecting statistics because they had been the neon signs of progress, most statistics of the 1890s were gloomy. The population statistics were the gloomiest of all. The birth rate was falling, partly because the depression was postponing marriages and partly because contraceptives were increasingly used. Commentators and provincial prophets, not sure of the causes of a drastic fall in the birth rate which seemed as cataclysmic as France's, thought that the falling birth rate was an insult to patriotism. 'No people', said the Sydney statistician Timothy Coghlan, 'has ever become great under such conditions.' The colonies had been proud of their favourable birth rate in part because it bandaged a wound in their pride. The statistics, until recently, had firmly rebuked those who assumed that a society founded on convicts was unlikely to multiply and that people of British stock were unlikely to flourish in a warm climate.

The fat official year books and handbooks disclosed that the abrupt decline in immigration was also checking the growth of population. In the fifteen years to the end of

1890 Australia's net gain through migration was more than half a million people. In the following fifteen years the gain was a mere eight thousand, and in some years more people sailed away than arrived. The financial crisis had created one exodus, and now in the first years of the new Commonwealth the long drought was driving more people away. In Australia in the first five years of this century more people left than arrived, and even Queensland experienced an exodus as the drought desolated the country.

22   The Long Drought

Mining fields and farmlands gave clear signs in the mid-1890s that the recovery from the depression might be quick. Then unexpectedly the recovery began to falter. A drought of unprecedented severity slowly settled on that part of Australia which produced most of the rural wealth. The drought showed how little the Europeans, as distinct from the Aboriginals, had so far learned about the erratic climate. They had explored the land: the climate they had barely begun to explore.

Most farmers in 1890 lived in regions where reliable knowledge of the weather did not go back more than thirty or forty years. In many districts the records of rainfall and temperatures went back only a few years to that important day when the local postmaster was issued with a barometer, rain gauge, and wind gauge and instructed to telegraph his daily recordings to the capital city. Every district had already experienced arid seasons but a drought was considered by most landholders to be abnormal. On the eve of the greatest drought there was widespread optimism that such a drought was impossible.

2

Thousands of men who had sowed grain on the remote plains before 1890 were buoyed by the faith that the climate was on their side. They built cottages, barns and stables, wells and dams, and an endless frontier of post-and-rail fences. At dusty crossroads they built their weatherboard or stone churches where they met on Sunday afternoons. At

348

first, in most districts, they probably didn't have to pray for rain.

In the leading wheat colony, South Australia, farmers had come to believe that rain followed their ploughs. Marvelling that such dry land should yield plentiful crops they leaned to the conclusion that their own iron ploughs, by breaking up the soil, were indirectly changing the climate. They argued that the ploughed ground was much more capable of absorbing and conserving the rain than the virgin ground. Moreover the slow evaporation of that moisture could induce more regular rains. In the mid-1870s the minister for agriculture in South Australia officially blessed the theory that rain followed the plough. Here was one of the rare instances in western civilization where the drays and wagons of the pioneers carried not only bibles, axes, seeds, blankets and the paraphernalia of the kitchen but also a new climate.

A few influential scientists used another line of argument which was equally optimistic. Occasional droughts, they said, were to be expected but the climate of Australia in the long term could be improved. They believed that forests, not the horse-drawn plough, would change the local climate. Plant trees, they argued, and the rain will follow the trees. The study of ancient civilizations seemed to support their theory, for many scholars blamed the destruction of forests and vegetation around the Mediterranean for the turning of fertile land into desert.

Conservationists stepped on to the public platform with the message that civilized man, though a vandal, could repair his damage by planting forests. An early friend of the earth was the first United States' Minister to Italy, George Perkins Marsh, a versatile scholar whose published grammar of the old Icelandic language and whose books in praise of the camel were followed in 1864 by the influential *Man and Nature*. Marsh argued that careful observations in Australia could help to confirm this vital proposition that trees would change the climate. Marsh soon had disciples in South Australia and northern Victoria where farmers were hand-sowing wheat on the dryest land yet cultivated in

Australia. In Victoria a board reported to parliament in 1867 that the systematic planting of forests and the conserving of existing bushland would increase the humidity of the air and lead to 'a more continuous rainfall in districts that are now subject to long and excessive droughts'.

In Adelaide in 1870 the director of the botanic gardens read a learned paper affirming the 'Influence of Forests on Climate'. In 1878 the young Scottish forester who had come to Adelaide as the official Conservator of Forests made the astonishing announcement that a scarcity of trees had made inland Australia an arid place. Few farmers, at first, took notice of these theories. They carried their axe wherever they went, chopping or ringbarking the larger trees. They were determined to sow grain on every inch of soil they could clear. Let the neighbours plant the forests that would bring down the rain.

When three dry seasons hit the farms beyond Port Pirie and Port Augusta early in the 1880s, and three successive harvests along 150 miles of wheat belt did not exceed five bushels to the acre, the South Australian government at last applied the theory. They set out to plant trees to bring the rain. The trees planted along the railway line beyond the dusty town of Quorn had not grown high before wheat farmers in the vicinity were retreating, beaten by the climate. South Australia's wheat belt tasted a run of dry seasons in the 1880s, a decade before Victoria's and New South Wales' wheat belts had that experience. Meanwhile in the small-town newspapers in the shade of the pepper trees which grew beside farmhouses on bare plains, the controversy about climate went on. The idea that man could, by his own plantings, increase the rainfall of his own region was far from dead. In the three decades before 1890 no single invention in farm machinery was probably more influential than those notions that ploughing and tree-planting could attract more rain. These notions were like bagpipes which enticed farmers into marginal land, soothed them in the first years, and then fell silent in a season of unexpected dryness.

In the outer country the richer pastoralists were optimistic enough to build stone wool sheds which were as spacious and lofty as the town halls of a middling gold town. Tens of thousands of miles of fences were built, dams were scooped out, and the sheep or cattle multiplied on plains where not enough grass and scrub would survive – if lean years arrived – to feed one third of the livestock. The kind seasons of the 1870s and early 1880s also favoured the spread of the imported rabbit across the grasslands, so that rabbits were competing with the same livestock for herbage. And yet for the present the grasslands could usually feed them all.

Long-term forecasts of the weather were accepted readily. Hucksters and witches stepped forward with their predictions. Old English sayings were imported. Red skies at night became a shepherd's delight, and a wet year in England was reputed to parallel a dry year in Australia. As the statistics of climate were accumulated, strange correlations and clues were discerned. From 1871 to 1906 the River Nile tended to be in high flood at the very time when, thousands of miles away, the rainfall in Chile was low. It was also observed with some validity that between the mid-1890s and 1910 the far inland town of Cordoba in the Argentine followed a zigzag of summer temperatures similar to those of Alice Springs. In Australia for many decades the main disagreement was not whether a cyclical pattern in the weather would be found but which pattern would prove to be correct.

In the 1870s a few colonists claimed that the dry seasons in New South Wales seemed to come every 6⅔ years, exactly when the comet Biela passed the earth. Many other settlers argued that the dryest years in the colony came at the end of a decade. Was there a ten-year cycle?

Some said that the Australian climate ran in an eleven-year cycle, under the influence of the sunspots. Some said the weather was influenced by Jupiter and followed a twelve-year cycle. And there was reportedly, under the influence of the moon, a weather cycle of nineteen years. The belief that weather tended to repeat itself every few years was soothing because it subtly implied that Australia was not likely to encounter droughts of greater severity than the older settlers had already experienced.

The nineteen-year cycle was espoused by Henry C. Russell who was possibly more influential than any other Australian meteorologist of his day. Born in 1836 on the banks of that great flood river, the Hunter, Henry Russell graduated from Sydney University and became at the age of 34 the government astronomer and the head of the observatory in Sydney. Perusing the records of rainfall, ransacking the diaries of old colonists and collecting the weather stories told by the Aboriginals, Russell produced in 1877 a large book on the climate of New South Wales. Inside its watery-grey covers he presented a tidy pattern of rains and drought. This year's weather, he said, would by and large repeat the weather of nineteen years ago. If 1860 was a wet year in Sydney, 1879 was likely to be wet. Just as there had been fierce droughts in the past, so those droughts would come again.

Lake George, near the rural village of Canberra, was one of Russell's weather-gauges of the past. Aboriginal stories suggested to him that this largest inland lake in New South Wales was dry in the 1790s or perhaps earlier. The lake certainly was again dry in the 1840s, and heavy wool drays crossed it and stockmen's huts were even built in places normally covered by deep water. Russell suggested that in the nineteen-year cycles, every third cycle marked extreme weather. Thus a severe drought could be expected about every fifty-seven years. 'Surely', wrote Russell in 1877, 'we have here enough to justify a strong suspicion, to say no more, that we have waves of drought passing over the earth.' According to his theory the dry years of the 1840s would perhaps come again about the end of the century. His theory probably was erroneous but his prediction was correct.

Optimism about the climate was the normal mood in the 1870s and 1880s. That optimism was voiced lucidly by Henry Hayter, a celebrated statistician in a land where the archbishops of material progress were the official statisticians. Hayter could foresee no serious drought. In 1890 he reassured a science congress that climate would not check Australia's glorious future. Hayter could see no limit to the sheep and cattle which 'this great continent' – to use his own phrase – would ultimately support. And 'there will, I believe, be pasturage to maintain any increase in the numbers of livestock which is likely to take place during the existence of every person now living'. In short, the sheep and cattle would multiply and multiply even into the 1890s, without any serious setback. He did not live to see the grass dry up: he died on the eve of the great drought. His successor was left to record, in the fat year books which Hayter had founded, the calamitous effects of drought on Victoria.

We now know what the farmers and sheep-owners of eastern Australia could not know. They were experiencing the final phase of a climatic paradise. The half-century from 1840 to 1890 contained, by some definitions, only two general droughts, and both of these droughts were relatively short. One ran from 1857 to 1859, and the other ruled in 1888 and 1889. Henceforth droughts were to be frequent.

3

The first year of the drought was probably 1895. It was not yet called a drought – one year does not make a drought. By 1897 the long period of dry weather was being labelled as 'drought' in many districts where that word was not used lightly. The Great Drought had barely begun. Tens of thousands of small farmers suffered. In Victoria for three years the wheat belt produced virtually no wheat for export; and many Victorian bakehouses and confectioners were selling bread and cakes baked from Californian flour. Farmers slid deeply into debt. Blacksmiths and farriers, storekeepers and cordial makers in the small towns totted up with slate and pencil the increasing sums owed them, and they in turn owed increasing sums to banks, traders and agents in the city.

The Long Drought

In the interior the price of fodder soared. If a traveller decided in 1900 to drive his buggy five hundred miles across the plains on any track between Hughenden in north Queensland and the New Mallee in South Australia, he would have paid a small fortune along the way for chaff and hay for his horses. He would also have met, along the track, scores of people who told – if they were not too proud to tell – of the jobs, livestock, and savings they had lost in the drought.

Many old pastoralists, household names in their district, were fighting to survive. In the tropical ranges near Hughenden, Robert Christison watched the blue sky each day for a sign of a cloud. Even a cloud as large as a man's hand would have been welcome, offering the hope that more clouds would appear and that finally rain would fall.

Christison was in his sixties, an age when he hoped his pioneering ventures in Queensland would have been rewarded, but instead his livestock were dying in the warm mud of the waterholes or on hard, bare paddocks. As the grass disappeared, men were sent to cut the mulga scrub so that the leaves could be eaten by sheep and cattle: and Christison noticed how, at the sudden sound of an axe, the skinny sheep would break into a run in the hope that green leaves were awaiting them. In the whirlwinds of dust that sometimes brushed across the bare ground, the cattle became invisible from only five steps away. The dams were silted, and the mechanical pumps which lifted water from artesian bores were halted by the clogged dust. Many of the cattle and sheep were so weak they could no longer safely cover the long distances to the remaining points of water and fodder. Even when stock were sent in railway trucks to the meatworks near the coast, their price was pitiful because sellers were many and buyers were few.

Like many pastoralists Christison thought incessantly of rain – mostly the rainstorms and cloudbursts of long ago. Turning to the diaries he had kept for thirty-five years, he re-read them in the hope of finding patterns that might indicate when the drought would end. On humid nights he would sit inside his house, listening and listening for the

354

sound of drops of rain on the iron roof, and almost jumping with nervousness when the iron chanced to 'ping'. On some evenings the sky was black with clouds, and lightning was flickering on the horizon, and the air was so full of moisture that even the sugar and salt in the house were soggy; but in the morning he would arise and look outside to find not one puff of cloud floating in the blue sky.

Robert D. Barton, living out towards the Barwon River in north-west New South Wales, experienced drought from 1897 to 1902. He had brief relief when heavy rain fell on April Fool's Day 1899. As the drought ran on he skinned dead sheep until the bare plain 'was carpeted with skins spread on the ground'. In the long heat the ground cracked open, and several cracks were so deep that the horse wagon carrying the sheepskins sank to the axles. Five thousand of his sheep remained, and in the end he drove them east to the uplands of New England where rains were more regular. There he put up a tent, lived on bread and salt beef, and, with his dog for company, waited for news that the rains had fallen at home.

In many southern districts the roadways were congested with travelling stock, eating the grass on the wide fringes as they travelled slowly from nowhere to nowhere. But to reach those safer districts required risky expeditions. In 1899 drovers set out with 14,000 sheep on a short journey from Evesham station to Rockhampton, and 11,000 sheep died on the way. In the same year, 2500 fat sheep were driven only 45 miles in the Gilgandra district in New South Wales, and on the road 800 died of thirst. On dry stock routes many parched sheep refused to drink when they reached a dam, and pannikins of water had to be poured down their throats. Others drank too much and died.

The older pastoralists had spent a lifetime on the land and perhaps more than any other group of new Australians they had come to terms with it, but even they did not know the full range of its moods. In the 1880s they had spent huge sums in boring for water and in scooping out dams in the dry rim of the pastoral country. Their own experience suggested that they should prepare more for scarcity of water than for scarcity of grass. In this drought, however, millions of sheep died from starvation rather than thirst. The carcasses lay on hard earth, within sight of the gushing artesian bores which had been drilled with borrowed money. As many of the loans could not be repaid, scores of sheep stations passed into the hands of banks, pastoral companies and other mortgage-holders.

Overstocking was another sign of unfamiliarity with the new land. Too many cattle and sheep grazed in the years of expansion, and they imposed strain on the vegetation and topsoil. In the south-eastern quarter of Australia the food eaten annually by imported sheep, cattle, horses, rabbits and other herbaceous animals on the eve of the drought must have been many times the amount consumed by the native animals a century earlier. The country therefore would be slower in recovering from the drought. The drenching rains, when they came, would be less fruitful than if the land had been stocked cautiously.

In a large country no drought is universal. In every year between 1895 and 1903 a few districts had lush or passable seasons. There were even regions which, especially vulnerable to drought, escaped lightly. Between 1895 and 1903 the Gulf country of Queensland experienced only one miserable year. Most of the Gulf runs did not lose livestock, but they could rarely send cattle along the parched stock routes to the markets of the south. They were marooned, not crippled, by drought.

It is surprising to discover that the great drought was marked as much by cold weather as by hot. In Melbourne the drought years tended to be colder than average, though the Decembers tended to be hotter than normal. In many districts freak snaps of cold weather came during the drought. On 7 August 1899 the snow fell heavily in Melbourne, and at lunchtime schoolboys were throwing snowballs in the Fitzroy Gardens. In the first week of July 1900 many railway lines in New South Wales were blocked by falls of snow heavier than any previously recorded. A white blanket was spread westwards from the Upper Hunter to Condobolin. Telegraph lines collapsed, trains were halted by snow and slowly buried, and in the town of Bathurst many verandas and roofs collapsed under the weight of snow. A year later a heavy fall whitened virtually the length of a straight line drawn between Melbourne and Brisbane.

Dust storms preceded or followed snow storms. In south-eastern Australia the area of ground ploughed for wheat in 1900 was almost six times as large as that ploughed in 1866, and a vast extent of that tilled soil was no longer compacted by moisture and so it crumbled into powder and was blown away by the winds. Many fences were submerged by the drifting soil and stretches of railway were buried. On 12 November 1902 so much soil was blown from the interior that Melbourne was drenched with dust, and in the afternoon the sun was almost hidden by the dust in the air. In inland towns that afternoon the darkness of the dust storms was almost as intense as the blackest of nights, according to the Bureau of Meteorology. Lamps were lit in the houses, and along country roads on both sides of the Murray the falling fireballs emitted a strange light.

The grave year of the Federation Drought was probably 1902. Already the casualties were heavy. The number of sheep estimated to live in Australia had been almost halved in one decade, falling from 106 million in 1891 to 54 million in 1902. The cattle too had almost halved since 1894, declining from twelve to seven million, so that most working men virtually ceased to eat good beef. The rabbits too were decimated.

The losses of a long drought are not all recorded in statistics. Much of the loss is worry, disillusionment, and humiliation. Even when a drought is almost over, graziers have no sure way of knowing whether it has finally ended. A drought can die slowly, its dying watched almost disbelievingly by tens of thousands of families who are close to insolvency. Their tension is heightened by the knowledge that if a creditor presses them they can overnight be forced to leave a property, which, though now a liablility, could blossom into an asset after one day of rain.

On the northern plains of Victoria – now replacing South

Australia as the main wheat fields – Farmer Coote kept a diary. His neat ink entries show that the end of a long drought can be identified only in retrospect. On 5 March 1903 he noted that the overnight rain had been so heavy that his dam overflowed and sheets of water covered his paddocks, but a week later he was surprised to see – at eight in the morning – a fierce dust storm. Towards the end of that month he recorded another two dust storms driven from the outer lands by the northerly winds, and as he pickled the wheat seed in preparation for the next season's sowing the sky became black with dust. In April, while his draught horses were discing the paddocks, dust storms rolled past and stung his face and half-blinded him. In the first fortnight of April the dust blew on four different days, but sometimes the dust was milder and was prelude to a little rain. Later in the month heavy rains fell, and the big horse Bess was even bogged while pulling the plough and soon the new grass was sprouting everywhere.

That was not his diary's last reference to the red dust. On 1 July, with a high wind blowing, he rode a horse into the town of Quambatook. 'Dust flying for the greater part of the day', he wrote. He was worried, knowing that in winter a sand storm would endanger the green shoots of wheat and grass and sometimes smother them. But his drought in fact was over.

4

The drought which ran from 1895 to 1903 vividly marked a new phase in the climate of the south-eastern part of Australia. A climatic map of that vast block of land embracing Birdsville, Longreach, Rockhampton, Sydney, Melbourne and Adelaide shows the arid zone moving slowly towards the coast long after that drought was over. The arid zone encroached on the semi-arid zone, and the semi-arid zone invaded the sub-humid zone. From the late 1880s or the 1890s through to the end of the Second World War this most productive rural area of Australia was to experience, on average, relatively dry seasons. The evidence suggests that the fluctuations in climate were one of the vital causes of the long prosperity of the forty years to 1890 and of the leaner decades which followed.

Many times the mood and motivations in Australian history had been strongly influenced by climate. The first English settlement in Australia had been based on an unreal optimism about the climatic paradise at Botany Bay. Even after that paradise had vanished and the early estimates of climate had been falsified, a similar optimism began to illuminate the interior of the continent. A great inland sea was sought, and the lands near that imagined sea were assumed to be fertile. No sooner had the inland sea been replaced by parched land on the maps than a new optimism glazed attitudes to climate in the settled districts. That optimism, still strong in 1890, fostered the faith that Australia – in resources and population and economic power – could be a second United States. The fall of the banks and the unexpected drought in the 1890s ended that faith. The movement to federate the colonies into the Commonwealth of Australia was in part the result of that humbling. A people who had often floated in the blue sky of fantasy had come down to earth.

5

The drought marked a step in the slow discovery of our climate and resources, but another kind of discovery was even slower. The continent had to be discovered emotionally. It had to become a homeland and feel like home. The sense of overpowering space, the isolation, the warmth of summer, the garish light, the shiny-leafed trees, the birds and insects, the smell of air filled with dust, the strange silences, and the landscapes in all their oddness had to become familiar. Nearly every immigrant arrived with strong north European preferences in landscape, sunlight, colour, temperatures and vegetation – preferences which Australia could rarely meet, except perhaps in Tasmania and on the opposite coast. These preferences lived on through the songs and hymns the migrants carried here, the poems and paintings, the school lessons and sermons, and in the names they placed on the map. The preferences were subtly passed on to generations of Australian-born children, thus impeding their acclimatization. Waves of new immigrants came to bolster the European influences. The physical mastering of Australia was swift and often dramatic, but the emotional conquest was slow.

Nature, in the eyes of most Australians of 1900, remained an enemy. Most settlers tried to replace Australia with England, if the replacement was possible. W. M. Elliott selected hilly land in the forest of Gippsland in 1879 and like tens of thousands of pioneers he fought the forest. A third of a century later, almost blind, he recalled his life as a pioneer and wrote down his vision of the future:

> My task is nearly finished. Old age, with its attendant infirmities, press hard upon me. In a few short years I shall be gathered to my forefathers, and the place that knew me shall know me no more. Before I depart I have one ardent wish. It is granted. The mantle of the Seer envelopes me. I stand on the top of 'Kilynon', the whole district lies stretched out before me in one grand panorama. Not a vestige remains of the vast forest that once so stubbornly resisted our labours.

Not a vestige! Thousands of pioneers still hoped to plant England, its hedges and fruit trees and green and pleasant fields, to the exclusion of almost everything Australian.

A few young writers and painters made bold bridgeheads in an alien land. In the late 1880s, on the outskirts of Melbourne, a school of painters discovered the summer and gloried in the hot north winds, the white dry grass, the distant blue ranges and the strong light; but the summers they loved were those of the coolest corner of the continent. In the 1890s Henry Lawson wrote of the country far west of the dividing range but he warmed to the people more than to the terrain, heat and dust. In 1904 young Dorothea Mackellar wrote 'I love a sunburnt country' – a revolutionary statement – but her wide brown plains and her ragged mountain ranges were not in the outback but rather in the

360

fertile valley of the Hunter River, not far from Newcastle.

Most Australians did not love a sunburnt country. The governors still retreated in summer to the cool hill towns – to Sutton Forest and Mount Macedon and the Lofty Ranges and other colonial Simlas. On hot days the people did not sunbake on the beaches: they stayed beneath the verandas, shade trees and parasols. The Australian tropics were seen widely as a white man's grave, and medical opinion doubted whether white children born in Brisbane would have the stamina and physique and energy of those born in Melbourne. The night sky was probably more attractive than the blue sky to most Australians; and in the competition to design an Australian flag in 1901, more than half of the entries contained the stars of the Southern Cross. The stars were only a mildly nationalist symbol. They suggested the coolness of night, not the heat of day. Indeed the stars, more than the oceans, seemed a bridge linking Australians to their ancestral homeland.

Most Australians were still strangers in a new land. The land was only half won.

Acknowledgements

I am grateful to people who guided me to sources or who gave me information or corrected errors: to Dr Margaret Blackwood (of the Botany School) and Lloyd Robson, Graeme Davison, David Dunstan, Pat Grimshaw, Chris McGuffie, Noel McLachlan, Joy Parnaby, Alison Patrick, and Peter Yule, John Lack, Jackie Templeton (History School), Duncan Ironmonger (Economics), John Lovering (Geology), Frank Strahan (Archives), and the staff of the Baillieu Library and the Archives in the University of Melbourne; to Jim Main of Flinders University S.A.; and to Sir Lindesay Clark, Jean Gittins, S. E. K. Hulme, G. F. James, Mary Turner Shaw, Judah Waten and David Yencken of Melbourne.

I am also indebted to Mary Marazzita and Lynne Wrout for the typing, to Susie Boxshall of the University's educational technology section for drawing the maps, and to Robert Edwards of the Aboriginal Arts Board, Australia Council, for locating and lending photographs.

In listing below my main debts to written and published material, I have not listed the hundreds of different sources from which came small snippets of detail used in the narrative.

Abbreviations:
A.D.B.   Australian Dictionary of Biography (M.U.P.)
H.R.A.   Historical Records of Australia (Commonwealth Government)

362

Acknowledgements

H.S.   Historical Studies of Australia and New Zealand (Melbourne)

T.H.R.A. Papers and Proceedings of the Tasmanian Historical Research Association (Hobart)

Sources

1: The Europeans Come

NAVIGATORS: K. G. McIntyre, *The Secret Discovery of Australia* (London, 1977); Gunter Schilder, *Australia Unveiled* (Amsterdam, 1976); Andrew Sharp, *The Voyages of Abel Janszoon Tasman* (Oxford, 1968); visits to the Fremantle branch of the Western Australian Museum.

MACASSAR SHIPS: C. C. Macknight, *The Voyage to Maregé* (1976); In earlier books, *The Tyranny of Distance* (1966, pp. 82-8) and *Triumph of the Nomads* (1975, pp. 247-51) I discuss Macassarmen.

COOK'S VOYAGES: J. C. Beaglehole's *The Life of Captain James Cook* (London, 1974) and his edition of *The Journals of Captain James Cook* (Cambridge, 1955-67); G. M. Badger ed., *Captain Cook: Navigator and Scientist* (Canberra, 1970) esp. Badger's chapter on Cook as scientist; and Beaglehole's edition of *The Endeavour Journal of Joseph Banks 1768-1771* (Sydney, 1962).

WHY BOTANY BAY WAS CHOSEN: In *Tyranny of Distance* I had argued that the English sought a new place to which criminals could be transported and saw strategic value in the pines and flax of Norfolk Island. I also expanded K. M. Dallas's argument that Botany Bay would be a half-way house on potential trade routes from Europe but concluded on p. 26 that his argument was 'feasible' rather than documented at that stage. Since 1966 his argument has been so bolstered by new evidence – especially evidence found by the research of Dr Alan Frost of La Trobe University – that to me it is valid. The important evidence on Diego Garcia is in W. A. Spray, 'British Surveys in the Chagos Archipelago' etc. in *Mariner's Mirror*, vol. 56, January 1970. George Young's letter is in *Hist. Records N.Z.*, vol. 1, p. 72.

My view now is that Botany Bay was settled for four distinct reasons: the convict problem, the search for new naval supplies, the need for a half-way house on new trade routes, and not least the over-optimistic assumptions held about the climate and soil of Botany Bay.

CLIMATE OF EASTERN AUSTRALIA: In 1966 I missed completely the evidence on climate. I first outlined it briefly in 'Climate and Australia's History' in *Melbourne Historical Journal*, 1971, pp. 5-7. Further re-reading of Cook's and Joseph Banks' journals has convinced me that their

mistaken deductions about the climate and soil of Botany Bay were vital prerequisites for the English settlement in Australia.
GAOLS AND HULKS: John Howard, *The State of the Prisons* (Everyman, 1929) esp. pp. 252-5.

2: A Little Squadron Sails

FIRST FLEET: C. Bateson, *The Convict Ships 1787-1868* (Glasgow, 1959) esp. pp. 100-2; David Collins, *An Account of the English Colony in New South Wales* (Adelaide, 1971) esp. vol. 1, section 2, for call at Cape Town.
ABORIGINALS' REACTION: Sergt. James Scott, *Remarks on a Passage to Botany Bay 1787-1792* (Sydney, 1963) esp. p. 34; Private John Easty, *Memorandum of the Transactions of a Voyage from England to Botany Bay 1787-1793* (Sydney, 1965) esp. p. 88.
NORFOLK ISLAND: *H.R.A.* (1914) series 1, vol. 1, pp. 13, 20, 715; *Historical Records of New Zealand* (1908) vol. 1, esp. pp. 119, 215, 510-11, 684. The New Zealand volume has flax records which do not appear in Australian official publications. See also F. D. Bell and Fred. Young jun., *Reasons for Promoting the Cultivation of the New Zealand Flax* (Smith, Elder of London, 1842), esp. p. 4.
EARLY SYDNEY: Phillip on death penalty, *Historical Records of New Zealand* vol. I, p. 69; hanging of marines, Easty, p. 111; Sydney as commercial base, D. R. Hainsworth, *Builders and Adventurers* (1968); route to China, *Tyranny of Distance*, pp. 63, 75; road to west, *H.R.A.*, series 1, vol. 8, p. 314.

3: Colonizing with Thieves

CONVICTS AND THEIR WORK: I have relied much on Lloyd Robson, *The Convict Settlers of Australia* (1965). For an analysis of convicts – including sheep stealers – who came to Port Phillip in 1803, see Marjorie Tipping in *T.H.R.A.* 1975, vol. 22, pp. 49-76. Convicts who planted vines upside down, in the *Sydney Herald*, 2 January 1832, p. 2.
PRECURSOR OF POLICE STATE: The 'General Orders' in *New South Wales Pocket Almanack and Colonial Remembrancer 1806* (Sydney, 1966) pp. 37-51.
WOMEN CONVICTS: Beverley Kingston, *The World Moves Slowly: a Documentary History of Australian Women* (Sydney, 1977) esp. pp. 7-19.
RICH CONVICTS: Gwyneth Dow, *Samuel Terry: The Botany Bay Rothschild* (Sydney, 1974), and her article in *A.D.B.*, vol. 2; C. M. H. Clark, *A History of Australia* vol. 3, p. 191; John Ritchie, *The Evidence to the Bigge Reports* (1971) vol. 2, p. 242. The rise of Underwood in D. R. Hainsworth, *A.D.B.*, vol. 2, and his *Builders and Adventurers* (1968).
POLITICAL PRISONERS: George Rudé, *Protest and Punishment: the Story of the Social and Political Protesters Transported to Australia 1788-1868* (Oxford, 1978); Rudé in *T.H.R.A.*, vol. 17, 1970, pp. 111-128 and vol. 21, 1964, pp. 6-24; R. S. Neale's reference to three incendiaries hanged, *T.H.R.A.*, 1970, vol. 17, p. 70; R. M. Hartwell's note on tailors' strike of 1834 in *The Economic Development of Van Diemen's Land 1820-1850* (1954) p. 92.

4: The Quick March of the Sheep

EARLY SHEEP AND BREEDERS: H. B. Carter, *His Majesty's Spanish Flock* (Sydney, 1964); S. Macarthur Onslow ed., *Some Early Records of the Macarthurs of Camden* (Adelaide, 1973) esp. pp. 86-88, 94, for early shepherding.

SPREAD OF SQUATTERS: Joseph Hawdon, *The Journal of a Journey from New South Wales to Adelaide* (1952) describing trip of 1838; Marnie Bassett, *The Hentys* (Oxford, 1954) especially part 7 on Portland Bay; S. H. Roberts, *The Squatting Age in Australia 1835-1847* (1964); J. M. Powell, *The Public Lands of Australia Felix* (1970) with its insights into western Victoria; Lynnette J. Peel, *Rural Industry in the Port Phillip Region 1835-1880* (1974); Margaret Kiddle, *Men of Yesterday* (1961). Area of sheep-runs in R. V. Billis and A. S. Kenyon, *Pastoral Pioneers of Port Phillip* (1974, second edition).

SHEPHERDS: 'dirty and grey-bearded' comes from Judith Wright, *The Generations of Men* (1959) p. 36. Statistics of shepherds culled from the *Census of the Population of New South Wales on 2nd March 1846* (Sydney, 1846) esp. pp. 43, 48. William Westgarth, *Australia Felix* (Edinburgh, 1848) esp. 238 ff.

BOILING DOWN: Comment by Religious Tract Society in *Australia; Its Scenery, Natural History, and Resources* (London c. 1852-3) p. 147; K. Fry, 'Boiling Down in the 1840s' *Labour History*, November 1973; E. A. Beever, 'The Pre-Gold Boom in Australia 1843-51', *Australian Economic History Review*, March 1979, esp. pp. 4-5. For English soap and Russian tallow industries, see *Knight's Cyclopaedia of the Industry of All Nations, 1851* (London) pp. 1554, 1654.

5: White Ghosts Ride By

When I began lecturing on this topic to undergraduates about 1975, I could find no Australian anthropologist or prehistorian who had studied closely this theme. The evidence is tricky and calls for a greater knowledge of Aboriginal society than I possess. So this chapter is offered tentatively.

THE PUZZLE OF WHITE MEN: D. G. Brock, *To the Desert with Sturt* (Adelaide, 1975) pp. 134-5; M. F. Peron, *A Voyage of Discovery to the Southern Hemisphere* (London, 1809) p. 198; E. P. S. Sturt in T. F. Bride ed., *Letters from Victorian Pioneers* (1898) p. 248; Edgar Morrison, *Early Days in the Loddon Valley* (Yandoit, Vic., c. 1966, second edition) p. 62; lecture of 1854 by E. S. Parker, reprinted in E. Morrison, *Frontier Life in the Loddon Protectorate* (Yandoit, Vic., c. 1967) pp. 11, 25; George Grey, *Journals of Two Expeditions of Discovery* (London, 1841) vol. 1, pp. 301-3. For explanation of drought see Kirkland's 'Life in the Bush' in Hugh Anderson, *Flowers of the Field* (1969) p. 183.

PUZZLE OF LIVESTOCK: Brock, p. 136; Hawdon's *Journal of a Journey*, esp. pp. 24, 30, 34-35, 39-40; Ludwig Leichhardt, *Journal of an Overland Expedition in Australia* (London, 1847) p. 246.

Sources

PUZZLE OF EUROPEAN ARTICLES: Brock, 42, 43, Hawdon p. 29; T. L. Mitchell, *Three Expeditions into the Interior of Eastern Australia* (London, 1839) vol. 2, p. 288.

SHIPS: Mrs James Smith, *The Booandik Tribe of South Australian Aborigines* (Adelaide, 1880) pp. 24-5; Dick Roughsey, *Moon and Rainbow* (Sydney, 1971) p. 13.

6: War on the Grasslands

TASMANIA: J. Bonwick, *The Last of the Tasmanians* (London, 1870) esp. ch. 5; A. G. L. Shaw, intro, *Correspondence on . . . Military Operations* (*T.H.R.A.*, Hobart, 1971) inc. evidence on Ibbens, p. 55.

MAINLAND FIGHTING: 1830-40: P. Stanbury ed., *The Moving Frontier* (Sydney, 1977) p. 25; R. B. Walker, *Old New England*, p. 28; G. Jenkin, *Conquest of the Ngarrindjeri* (Adelaide, 1979) pp. 57-8, 63; *Letters from Victorian Pioneers* (1898) pp. 30-1 (Fighting Hills) and p. 121 (Old Balyang); W. K. Hancock, *Discovering Monaro* (Cambridge, 1972) p. 68. For attacks on livestock see Henry Reynolds in *Historical Studies*, no. 66, pp. 53.4.

POISON: P. L. Brown ed., *Clyde Company Papers*, vol. 4, p. 350; Jenkin, p. 63; M. Kiddle, *Men of Yesterday*, p. 128; C. D. Rowley, *The Destruction of Aboriginal Society* (Penguin, 1972) pp. 157-8.

TRIBAL WAR AND INVASION: Norman B. Tindale, *Aboriginal Tribes of Australia*, inc. pp. 217, 246; G. Blainey, *Triumph of the Nomads*, esp. pp. 108-111; W. Westgarth, *Australia Felix* (Edinburgh, 1848) p. 89.

DISEASES: I am grateful to Dr Earle Hackett of Adelaide for discussing the evidence on Aboriginal diseases. For diseases in the Americas see W. H. McNeill, *Plagues and Peoples* (New York, 1976) esp. ch. 5. The quotation is from *Memoirs of Simpson Newland* (Adelaide, 1926) pp. 88-9.

QUEENSLAND: L. E. Skinner, *Police of the Pastoral Frontier* (Brisbane, 1975); Stuart Rosewarne, *Aborigines in Colonial Queensland; an Analysis of the Aborigines' Response etc.* (M.A. thesis, Melbourne University, 1976).

MISSIONS, GUIDES: For Yuranigh see *A.D.B.*, vol. 1; for missions see Stanbury, esp. chapters 2 and 6.

ETHICS OF CONQUEST: J. Lort Stokes, *Discoveries in Australia* (London, 1846) vol. 1, p. 81, vol. 2, pp. 46, 319; Eyre cited in Sharman Stone ed., *Aborigines in White Australia* (1974) p. 66; George Grey, *Journals of Two Expeditions*, vol. 2, pp. 200-201.

7: West and South

WESTERN AUSTRALIA: J. Gentilli ed., *Western Landscapes* (Nedlands, 1979) esp. pp. 127, 207-09, 213-18, 357; R. T. Appleyard and Toby Manford, *The Beginning* (Nedlands, 1979) esp. pp. 50-2, 164-7; B. Chapman, *The Colonial Eye* (Art Gallery of W.A., 1979); F. K. Crowley, *Australia's Western Third* (London, 1960); For road to Toodyay see R. Erickson, *Old Toodyay and Newcastle* (Toodyay, 1974) p. 31.

SOUTH AUSTRALIA: The writings of Douglas Pike; biographies of Torrens, Angas, Kavel, Rowland Hill, and S.A.'s founders in *A.D.B.* vols.

1, 2, and English *Dictionary of National Biography*; J. Lyng, *Non-Britishers in Australia* (Melbourne, 1935) pp. 25-43. For Yankee Adelaide see *Letters from Victorian Pioneers* (1898) p. 238. For selecting of migrants see anon. (John Stephens) *The Land of Promise* (London, 1839) esp. 187 ff.

8: The Cities Rise: The Chains Break

RISE OF CITIES: Official census returns; J. W. McCarty, 'Australian Capital Cities in the Nineteenth Century' in *Australian Economic History Review*, vol. 10, 1970, esp. p. 119 where he reshapes the 1851 statistics; Tasmanian industries in R. M. Hartwell, *The Economic Development of Van Diemen's Land 1820-1850*, esp. pp. 144-161. My explanation of early urbanization is an enlargement of views in *The Tyranny of Distance* in 1966. RISE OF FREE INSTITUTIONS: A. C. V. Melbourne, *Early Constitutional Development in Australia* (St. Lucia, 1963); *Acts and Ordinances of the Governor and Council of New South Wales* (Sydney 1824-43); R. B. Walker, *The Newspaper Press in New South Wales, 1803-1920* (Sydney, 1976) esp. ch. 1-3; J. N. Molony, *An Architect of Freedom* (Canberra, 1973) esp. ch. 2, 3; D. K. Fieldhouse, *The Colonial Empires* (New York, 1966) esp. ch. 11. ELECTIONS: For Melbourne market election see 'Garryowen', *The Chronicles of Early Melbourne* (1888) vol. I, pp. 253-6. For Loddon election of 1851 see G. F. James ed., *A Homestead History* (1969, 3rd edn.) pp. 109-110. END OF CONVICT ERA: For last convict ships see C. Bateson, *The Convict Ships*, pp. 273, 325. For convict influence in Victoria see 1846 N.S.W. Census p. 38 and G. Serle *The Golden Age*, pp. 4-5, and for S.A. see Alex. Tolmer, *Reminiscences of an Adventurous and Chequered Career* (London, 1882) vol. 1, p. 150. For later convict influence in Tasmania, see H. Reynolds in *Historical Studies*, no. 53, 1969, p. 19 ff. For Groom and his career see D. Waterson in *A.D.B.* vol. 4 and *Commonwealth Parliamentary Debates*, 1901, esp. 21 May 1901.

9: Mysteries of a New Land

This is an important topic but because of its width and our slowness in studying the history of natural science it has not advanced far. Some evidence in this chapter has been scavenged over a long period of time; but I am conscious of great gaps in my knowlege and not even conscious of other gaps. NATURE A FREAK: G. Serle, *From Deserts the Prophets Come* (1973) pp. 14-15; Bernard Smith, *European Vision and the South Pacific 1768-1850* (Oxford paperback, 1960) which cites Field on p. 172; M. F. Peron, *A Voyage of Discovery*, pp. 304-06. THE SEAS EXPLORED: For the hazards of King Island see Bateson, p. 228 ff; R. H. Hooper, *The King Island Story* (Sydney, 1973) pp. 50-2; Garryowen, vol. 2, pp. 582-8; Victorian *Select Committee on Lighthouses*, December 1853, p. 15. For sailing directions on southern coast, see *Australia Directory* (London, 1876, 7th edn.) vol. 1; *Mercantile Marine Magazine* (London, 1854) vol. 1, pp. 104, 380; M. F. Maury, *The Physical*

Sources

Geography of the Sea (London, 1856 edn.) p. 292 for force of seas; George Neumayer's massive *Results of the Meteorological Observations Taken in the Colony of Victoria* etc. (Government Printer, 1864) esp. pp. 339-41; *The Tyranny of Distance*, esp. ch. 3, 8.

BIRDS AND ANIMALS: For gift to Scott see L. F. Fitzhardinge in *A.D.B.* vol. 1, p. 513. *The Australian Encyclopedia* (Sydney, 1977 edition) has valuable evidence on wildlife, esp. articles by A. H. Chisholm.

SKY: Harley Wood in *A Century of Progress* (Royal Society of N.S.W., late 1960s) ch. 13.

GEOLOGY: The economic implications of the geology of Sydney compared to Melbourne or Adelaide cry out in any detailed geological map of eastern Australia.

PLANTS: On eucalypt see *A Century of Progress*, esp. pp. 311, 334; James Griffin on Bosisto in *A.D.B.*, vol. 3; Roy A. Medvedev, *Let History Judge: the Origins and Consequences of Stalinism* (London, 1972) p. 523 n. On D-Day see G. Blainey, *Pharmacy 40,000 Years Ago* (Pharmaceutical Society of Victoria pamphlet, 1977). On early love of native plants see Onslow, *Some Early Records of the Macarthurs of Camden*, p. 312; Mary Fullerton, *Bark House Days* (M.U.P. paperback, 1965); and Morton Herman ed. *Annabella Boswell's Journal* (Sydney, 1965) p. 16.

HOT CLIMATES: See documents – especially appendix 1 by D. Gordon – in J. G. Steele's *Brisbane Town in Convict Days 1824-1842* (1975). For the possible influence of the maize diet on disease I am indebted to Dr Margaret Blackwood of the Botany Department at Melbourne University.

HATS AND VERANDAS: For the cabbage-tree hat, see Sidney Baker, *The Australian Language*, p. 259, and E. E. Morris, *A Dictionary of Austral-English*, pp. 75-6, and W. Fearn-Wannan, *Australian Folklore*, p. 113. For the early verandas, R. Campbell in *Western Towns and Buildings* (Nedlands, 1979) p. 104; exhibition of early W.A. paintings at Art Gallery of W.A., September 1979; J. M. Freeland, *Architecture in Australia: A History* (Penguin, 1972) esp. pp. 47-8. The strange view of the W.A. climate is in anon. *Geography of the Australasian Colonies* (Collins, U.K., probably 1880s) p. 93. Henry Lawson's first view of London in C. Roderick ed., *Henry Lawson: Autobiographical and Other Writings 1887-1922* (Sydney, 1972) p. 144.

BUSHFIRES: James Fenton, *Bush Life in Tasmania Fifty Years Ago* (Devonport, 1964) pp. 79-81; Margaret Kiddle, *Men of Yesterday*, pp. 181-3; Garryowen, vol. 1, pp. 442-5. For hot winds see C. Darwin, *The Voyage of the Beagle* (Everyman paperback, 1959) p. 425, and E. E. Morris, *Dictionary*, p. 204.

THE NATURALISTS: C. Darwin, *The Voyage of the Beagle*, esp. ch. 19; Philip Appleman ed., *Darwin* (Norton paperback, 1970) his wedge reference is on p. 84; A. J. Marshall, *Darwin and Huxley in Australia* (1970) esp. pp. 83, 125; T. E. Burns and J. R. Skemp ed., *Van Diemen's Land Correspondents* (Launceston, 1961) for letters by Gunn, esp. 22-3, 77, 92, 101-2; articles on Gunn and Hooker in *A.D.B.*, vols. 1 and 4.

369

10: Gold, Gold

PATTERNS OF DISCOVERY: Based on information collected for but only partly used in *The Rush That Never Ended* (Melbourne, 1963).

ROAD TO GOLDFIELDS: Report of Commissioners on 'Internal Communication of the Colony', Victoria, September 1854 – traffic density on pp. 71, 100, 103.

INFLATION: Computed from Commonwealth *Year Book*, 1919 (p. 1090), 1951 (p. 395), 1964 (p. 434), and W. H. Archer, *Statistical Register of Victoria* (1854) esp. pp. 404-06.

CHINESE: On opium and gambling see Rev. W. Young, 'Report on the Condition of the Chinese Population in Victoria', Victorian Parliament Papers, 1868, no. 56. On acupuncture see K. M. Bowden, *Goldrush Doctors at Ballaarat* (Mulgrave, 1977) ch. 10. *The Life of Quong Tart* (Sydney, 1911) esp. p. 5 for the red-headed savages.

11: That's Where the Dead Men Lie

EXPLORERS: This section is based mainly on the published journals of the explorers. See also Kathleen Fitzpatrick's preface to her *Australian Explorers: a Selection from their Writings* (London, 1958) and Bessie Threadgill, *South Australian Land Exploration 1856 to 1880* (Adelaide, 1922).

STEAM AND IRON IN OUTBACK: Darling steamers in Bobbie Hardie, *West of the Darling* (Brisbane, 1969) pp. 84-5. Artesian water in Hardie p. 180 and *Official Year-Book of N.S.W.*, 1905-06, p. 29. Wire fences in G. L. Buxton, *The Riverina 1861-1891* (1967) pp. 41, 246, and *The Australian Handbook*, 1881, p. xxiii, and *S. W. Silver and Co.'s Australian Grazier's Guide, no. II – Cattle* (London, 1881) p. 91 – said to be by Rolf Boldrewood. See also D. S. Macmillan, *Bowen Downs 1863-1963* (Sydney, 1963) p. 35 and Donald Macdonald, *Gum Boughs and Wattle Bloom* (London, 1887) pp. 13-15 for kangaroos.

OUTBACK TOWNS: See entries in *The Australian Handbook* (Gordon & Gotch) of 1880s and 1890s.

DROVERS: H. M. Barker, *Droving Days* (Melbourne, 1966) esp. ch. 6; E. S. Sorenson, *Life in the Australian Backblocks* (London, 1911) pp. 162-4, 177, 179.

BOAKE: A. G. Stephens ed., *Where the Dead Men Lie: and Other Poems* (Sydney, 1897) including Boake's letters.

12: Juggling the Squares and Rectangles

This chapter depends more on an attempt to reinterpret evidence than on the evidence itself, most of which is well known.

PORT PHILLIP SEPARATION: A. C. V. Melbourne, *Early Constitutional Development in Australia*, esp. p. 356; A. B. Keith ed., *Selected Speeches and Documents on British Colonial Policy 1763-1917* (London, 1933) vol. 1, pp. 199-200.

ISOLATION OF N. AND N.W.: Towns and their transport in *Australian Handbook*.

Sources

NORTH QUEENSLAND SEPARATION: G. C. Bolton, *A Thousand Miles Away* (Brisbane, 1963) esp. ch. 9; G. L. Buxton in F. K. Crowley ed., *A New History of Australia* (1974) pp. 201-2. The petitions of 1885 are in C. M. H. Clark, *Select Documents in Australian History 1851-1900* pp. 220-29.

13: The Rivals

CITIES GROW: F. J. B. Stilwell in I. H. Burnley ed., *Urbanization in Australia* (Cambridge, 1974) p. 39; T. A. Coghlan, *Seven Colonies of Australasia, 1897-8*, p. 60; Sean Glynn, *Urbanisation in Australian History, 1788-1900* (1975 edn.); W. A. Sinclair, *The Process of Economic Development in Australia* (1976).

MELBOURNE v SYDNEY: A. Deakin, *The Federal Story* (1944) pp. 14, 101; wool traffic in Annual Report of N.S.W. Railways, 1878, pp. 24-5.

BOOM: I am indebted to N. G. Butlin, A. R. Hall, E. A. Boehm, J. W. McCarty, G. Serle, Michael Cannon and their studies of the 1880s. On the timing of the downturn see Boehm, *Prosperity and Depression in Australia 1887-1897* (Oxford, 1971) esp. pp. 49-50. The value of Mt Morgan and B.H.P., compared to all banks, can be roughly calculated from evidence in A. R. Hall, *The Stock Exchange of Melbourne and the Victorian Economy 1852-1900* (Canberra, 1968) esp. pp. 147, 169-174.

SICK CITIES: T. A. Coghlan, *Wealth and Progress of New South Wales 1886-87*, pp. 172, 177; Proceedings of Victorian Institute of Engineers, vol. 4, pp. 137-43: W. A. Sinclair, *The Process*, p. 156.

14: Where Merchants are Princes

SECRET BALLOT: *The Diaries of Sarah Midgley and Richard Skilbeck* (1967) p. 21; E. S. E. Childers, *The Life and Correspondence of the Right Hon. Hugh C. Childers*, vol. 1, pp. 89-94; English *Annual Register*, 1872, pp. 61-74; Irish University Press Reprints of Parliament Papers, *Australia*, vol. 26, 1871-3; G. Serle, *The Golden Age*, pp. 208-10, 257.

PREMIERS IN 1880: Articles in the *A.D.B.*, those by A. W. Martin on Parkes and by G. Serle on Service being outstanding. For Parkes' 'far-away expression' see A. Deakin *The Federal Story* (1944) p. 25; for his ivory craft see *Knight's Cyclopedia of the Industry of all Nations, 1851*, p. 1075; for the 'tarpaulin' speech see Parkes, *The Federal Government of Australasia: Speeches* (Sydney, 1890) p. 63. McIlwraith's dignity in G. Parker, *Round the Compass in Australia* (London, 1892) pp. 235-6, and his money troubles in my *Gold and Paper* (1958) esp. pp. 207-08.

NEWSPAPERS: Censorship in Europe in *New Cambridge Modern History*, vol. 10, pp. 123-8; Sydney hunger for news in K. S. Inglis, *The Australian Colonists* (1974) p. 221; cheaper papers in Michael Cannon, *Australia in the Victorian Age*, vol. 3, pp. 122-4; information on old-style political reporters from June Yugovic; Syme's view of the press as educator in his *Representative Government in England* (1881) p. 122; C. E. Sayers, *David Syme* (1965); James Bryce, *Modern Democracies* (1921) vol. 2, p. 248.

371

15: Rich and Poor: The Economic Whirlpool

THE RICH: James Graham letter of 12 July 1839 (p. 25) in University of Melbourne Archives, which is the best collection of business history records in Australia. The priest in G. Serle, *The Rush to be Rich* (1971) p. 269.

THE ROAMERS: *Victoria and its Metropolis* (Melbourne, 1888) vol. 2, p. 745, where biographies of Usher and Williams occupy four inches of small print.

CHARITY HOUSES: N.S.W. expenditure (compared to clergy's salaries) is culled from *Statistical Register of N.S.W.*, 1864, pp. 6, 14. For the journalist in asylum, ch. 17 in *The Vagabond Papers*, ed. M. Cannon (1969). For Tasmanian charities see G. Blainey, *T.H.R.A.*, December 1968, pp. 85-6; Joan C. Brown, *Poverty is not a Crime* (Hobart, 1972) esp. ch. 3, 4.

PRIVATE CHARITY: For relief funds see J. H. Heaton, *Australian Dictionary of Dates and Men of the Time* (Sydney, 1879) part 2, p. 97; C. Roderick ed., *Henry Lawson: Letters* (Sydney, 1970) p. 248; Sidney Baker, *The Australian Language*, p. 107; M. Kiddle, *Men of Yesterday*, p. 298; J. O. Randell ed., *Adventures of a Pioneer* (1978) p. 222.

SELF HELP: For house-owning see G. Davison, *The Rise and Fall of Marvellous Melbourne* (1978) esp. p. 180-1; A. C. Gray, *Life Insurance in Australia* (1977) esp. 37, 44-5, 51, 60-1; W. I. Spratt, 'Lessons Learned' in *Australasian Insurance and Banking Record*, 1968, esp. pp. 132-4.

TAXATION: *Commonwealth Year Book*, vol. 1, 1908, pp. 670-685; Stephen Mills, *Taxation in Australia* (1925) esp. p. 66 for the politician of 1886; and various acts of parliament. Since 1945 millions of words have been written in theses, articles, and books on the early years of the Labor Party but oddly virtually nothing has yet been written on the rise of new taxes, without which Labor would be largely toothless.

16: Sharpening the Shears

SPENCE: W. G. Spence, *Australia's Awakening* (Sydney, 1909) inc. p. 51 for his career as 'tributer'; J. A. Graham, *Early Creswick* (1942); Vance Palmer, *National Portraits* (1940) p. 149 for Roberts' description; reminiscences of Harry H. Pearce in *Creswick Advertiser*, 1977-79, on unionism; 'Spence' in *A.D.B.*, vol. 6. For Spence's 'sheep stations', see *Australia's Awakening*, p. 92-3, and for his One Big Sunday School see his *History of the A.W.U.* (Sydney, 1961) p. 121.

SHEARERS' UNION: *Australia's Awakening*, esp. pp. 69-70, 81-2; W. G. Spence, *History of the A.W.U.* p. 9 for Mt Eba rules. J. A. Merritt, 'W. G. Spence and the 1890 Maritime Strike', *Historical Studies*, April 1973, p. 595. R. D. Barton, *Reminiscences of an Australian Pioneer* (Sydney, 1917) for union speaker near Moree; F. S. Piggin, 'New South Wales Pastoralists and the Strikes of 1890 and 1891', *Historical Studies*, September 1971; Humphrey McQueen, *A New Britannia* (Penguin, 1975 edn.) pp. 214-16; P. F. Donovan, 'Australia and the Great London Dock Strike: 1889' in *Labour History*, November 1972; T. A. Coghlan, *Labour and Industry in Australia* (1918) vol. 3, pp. 1591-1607 for maritime strike; J. A. La Nauze, *Alfred Deakin* (1965) pp. 131-2 for 'lay them low'.

SHEARING TALLIES AND MACHINES: Sorenson, *Life in the Australian Backblocks*, p. 242; J. A. Merritt, p. 595; 'Wolseley' in *A.D.B.*, vol. 6; 'Austin' in English *Dictionary of National Biography*, 1941-50; F. Wheelhouse, *Digging Stick to Rotary Hoe* (1966) ch. 8; G. L. Buxton, *The Riverina*, p. 264.

GEORGITES: Airlie Worrall, M.A. thesis on 'The Single Tax Movement in Eastern Australia', University of Melbourne Library; 'H. George and W. H. Gresham' in *A.D.B.* vol. 4; L. F. Crisp in *Labour History*, May 1979, pp. 32-4.

LABOR PARTY: The writings of Brian Fitzpatrick; John Rickard, *Class and Politics* (1976) esp. ch. 1; J. B. Hirst, *Adelaide and the Country 1870-1917* (1973) pp. 153-4; articles on 'C. J. Don' and 'Peter Brennan' in *A.D.B.*, vol. 4; D. J. Murphy et. al. ed., *Prelude to Power* (1970) pp. 85-6 and 236-8 (on Dawson); W. G. Spence, *Australia's Awakening*, pp. 597-8 for Labor's first platform; T. A. Coghlan, *Labour and Industry*, vol. 4, 1843-48.

17: The Veiled Maid of Adelaide

DISTINCTIVE S.A.: See John Hirst, *Adelaide and the Country*, p. 46, for fact that pastoral lands in S.A. could easily be resumed.

PREJUDICE IN NAMES: E. E. Morris, *Dictionary*, p. 413 for she-oak; S. Baker, *The Australian Language*, pp. 228-9 for Barker; 'Barker' in *A.D.B.*, vol. 3; *The Australian Encyclopaedia* (1926) vol. 2, p. 454.

WOMEN: W. Westgarth, *The Colony of Victoria* (1864) p. 398; 'An Act to Amend the Electoral Law', N.S.W., 1858, 22 Victoria, no. 20 for disenfranchised men; information on women's votes in Victorian municipalities from Dr Bernard Barrett, Victorian state historian; W. J. Gardiner, *Colonial Cap and Gown* (Christchurch, 1979) for women in universities; May Vivienne, p. 72; Patricia Grimshaw, *Women's Suffrage in New Zealand* (Auckland, 1972); Vida Goldstein in B. Kingston ed, *The World Moves Slowly* (1977) pp. 79-84; T. A. Coghlan, *Seven Colonies of Australasia* (1897-8) pp. 119-22 for divorce statistics.

MISS SPENCE: *Catherine Helen Spence: An Autobiography* (1910) esp. pp. 15, 45, 53 for public speaking.

18: Pistons of Prosperity

Illustrative quotations in this chapter come from: 'The noise' ... A. Sutherland, *A New Geography* (Melbourne, 1885) p. 61; the Albury railway banquet in anon. *The Union of the Railway Systems*, (Government Printer, Sydney, 1883) pp. 42-3, 80-2.

INVENTIONS: For Australia's role in the combine harvester, see A. G. Thompson in *Tools and Tillage*, 1977, vol. 2, p. 67 ff. For spectator sport and crowds see W. F. Mandle, 'Games People Played' in *Historical Studies* April 1973, p. 512 and also my 'History of Leisure in Australia: the Late-Colonial Era' in *Vic. Hist. Journal*, February 1978, p. 15. For the tempo of work see Sir Richard Tangye, *Notes on My Fourth Voyage to the Australian Colonies* (Birmingham, 1886) pp. 38, 40-1, 50.

19: The Rabbits are Coming
WEEDS: My evidence came in snippets from many sources. I gained much from hearing an address by Dr P. Michael of Sydney University at the botany section of the 1971 ANZAAS. The most accessible survey is J. H. Willis, 'Weeds' in *Australian Encyclopaedia* (1977) vol. 6.

EFFECT OF SHEEP: J. Robertson in *Letters from Victorian Pioneers* (1898) esp. pp. 33-5, but for a contrary view see p. 237. For Monaro see W. K. Hancock, *Discovering Monaro*, p. 65 and P. E. Strzelecki, *Physical Description* of N.S.W. and V.D.L. (1845) p. 239. J. M. Powell, *Environmental Management in Australia, 1788-1914* (1976) esp. pp. 30-2; H. J. Frith, *Wildlife Conservation* (1973) esp. pp. 307 (tree-rat), p. 104, 272 (kangaroos) and 228 (squatter pigeon).

RABBITS: Eric C. Rolls, *They All Ran Wild* (1969), an outstanding book; Royal Commission 'Into Schemes for Extermination of Rabbits' (Sydney, 1890) esp. pp. 63-4, 66, 109; jam recipe in *The Victorian Settlers' Guide* (Government Printer, 1905) p. 75; C. E. W. Bean, *On the Wool Track* (1945 paperback) p. 71; Commonwealth *Year Book* 1909, pp. 340-1 for exports. The Cobar man was George Frew in 'Royal Commission on Western Lands', N.S.W., 1900. For the Austins see Kiddle, *Men of Yesterday*, p. 279, P. L. Brown in *A.D.B.*, vol. 1, and 'Glastonbury' in *Encyclopaedia Britannica*, 1910-11.

20: The Banks Crash
BANKS: S. J. Butlin, *Australia and New Zealand Bank* (1961) esp. ch. 11, 12; R. F. Holder, *Bank of New South Wales: A History* (1970) vol. 1, esp. ch. 25, 26; anon., *A Century of Banking* (C.B.C. of Sydney, 1934) ch. 10; my *Gold and Paper* (National Bank, 1958) ch. 10-12; E. A. Boehm, *Prosperity and Depression in Australia 1887- 1897*, esp. ch. 10; and files of *Australasian Insurance and Banking Record*, Melbourne, 1888-93. For banker Burgess see P. Bolger, *Hobart Town* (1973) pp. 195-6 and *A.D.B.* vol. 3. My comparison with the other bank crashes of 19th century is based partly on M. Friedman and A. J. Schwartz, *A Monetary History of the United States* (1963), and on a variety of European economic histories.

PENANCE: J. Watsford, *Glorious Gospel Triumphs* (London, 1900) p. 292; Goe in M. Clark ed., *Sources of Australian History*, pp. 416-17; G. Davison, *Rise and Fall of Marvellous Melbourne*, p. 249.

21: Retreat from Paradise
MELBOURNE'S SLUMP: Orange peel in J. Grant and G. Serle, *The Melbourne Scene* (1957) p. 211; empty offices in E. M. Clowes, *On The Wallaby Through Victoria* (1911) p. 128 and evidence of W. Zeal in Parliamentary Standing Committee on Flinders Street Railway Station, 1899, p. 51; population movements calculated from statistical registers and year-books.

Sources

PARAGUAY: I relied heavily on Gavin Souter, *A Peculiar People: the Australians in Paraguay* (1968). Also see B. Ovenden in *Mary Gilmore: A Tribute* (Sydney, 1965) pp. 34-7.

LABOUR COLONIES: T. A. Coghlan, *Labour and Industry* esp. vol. 4, pp. 1987-91, 2084-5; L. J. Blake, 'Village Settlements' *Victorian Historical Magazine*, November 1966; Report from Select Committee on 'Leongatha Labour Colony' (Melbourne, 1900) esp. pp. 163-5 for Wallace.

REVIVAL: E. A. Boehm, *Prosperity and Depression*, pp. 68, 109-112; *Western Australian Year Book for 1902-04*; *The Rush That Never Ended*, esp. ch. 21.

22: The Long Drought

WEATHER PROPHETS: D. W. Meinig, *On the Margins of the Good Earth* (Chicago, 1962) esp. pp. 59-60; J. E. Brown, the S.A. forester, in *A.D.B.*, vol. 3; *Papers Relating to Forest Conservancy*, Victorian Parliamentary Papers, 1874, esp. pp. 11, 24-5; H. C. Russell, *Climate of New South Wales* (1877) esp. p. 182 and pp. 29-33 for Lake George; H. H. Hayter, *Report* of the Australasian Association for Advancement of Science (Sydney, 1890) pp. 578-9; J. C. Foley, *Droughts in Australia: A Review* (Commonwealth Bureau of Meteorology, 1957) Bulletin 43; H. B. Wall, *Manual of Physical Geography of Australia* (1883) pp. 113-114.

THE LONG DROUGHT: M. M. Bennett, *Christison of Lammermoor* (London, late 1920s) ch. 25, 26. E. S. Sorenson, *Life in the Australian Backblocks* (1911) on droving losses; R. D. Barton, *Reminiscences* (1918) ch. 21; unpublished diaries of C. W. Coote, Mallee farmer, in Univ. of Melb. Archives; H. A. Hunt et. al., *The Climate and Weather of Australia* (1913) p. 84 for dust storms; R. L. Heathcote, *Back of Bourke* (1965) pp. 148, 153-7, 165.

PATTERNS: C. H. B. Priestley et. al., *Report of a Committee on Climatic Change* (Australian Acad. Sci., 1976). The report is tentative on some facets of the change in weather from 1880s but correspondence with Dr Priestley confirms that the implications of the report for historians are profound. A version of this chapter appeared in the *National Times* in 1977.

A LAND HALF WON: W. M. Elliott's reminiscences in *The Land of the Lyre Bird* (Shire of Korumburra, 1966) p. 197; Heidelberg school's attitude to summer in R. H. Croll ed., *Smike to Bulldog* (1946) pp. 14, 21-2, 124; preface by A. Matzenik in *The Poems of Dorothea Mackellar* (1971); G. Blainey, 'Climate and Australia's History', *Melbourne Historical Journal*, 1971, pp. 8-9.

Index

ence on growth of towns and
ports, 120-2; continuity of
output during gold-rushes,
168. *See also* sheep
Worker (Qld), 339
working hours, 272, 297-9

Yarralumla, 53

Yass, 53
Yilgarn, 169
York, 101
Young, Admiral Sir George, 17
Yuranigh, 94

Zeehan, 260